Of Heart and Mind

Social Policy Essays
in Honor of Sar A. Levitan

Garth Mangum
University of Utah

Stephen Mangum
Ohio State University

Editors

1996

W.E. Upjohn Institute for Employment Research
Kalamazoo, Michigan

331.12042
031

Library of Congress Cataloging-in-Publication Data

Of heart and mind : social policy essays in honor of Sar A. Levitan /
 Garth Mangum and Stephen Mangum, editors.
      p. cm.
   Includes bibliographical references and index.
   ISBN 0–88099–171–2 (paper : alk. paper). — ISBN 0–88099–172–0 (cloth : alk.
   paper.)
   1. Labor policy—United States. 2. Full employment policies—
United States. 3. Levitan, Sar A.   I. Levitan, Sar A.
II. Mangum, Garth L.   III. Mangum, Stephen L.
HD8072.5.036   1996
331.12 ' 042 ' 0973—dc20   96–41343
                                                                                  CIP

Copyright © 1996
W. E. Upjohn Institute for Employment Research
300 S. Westnedge Avenue
Kalamazoo, Michigan 49007–4686

Cover design by J. R. Underhill
Index prepared by Shirley Kessel.
Printed in the United States of America.

Foreword

As individuals who have had the dual honor of claiming Sar Levitan as friend and serving the working men and women of America as Secretaries of Labor and Commerce, we commend the editors and publishers of this appropriate volume. Each of those Levitan friendships preceded by many years our cabinet roles, Wirtz and Dunlop beginning with Korean Wage Stabilization and Kreps, Shultz, and Marshall from service together on the National Council on Employment Policy from the mid-1960s, Dunlop sharing the latter connection and Wirtz being the original target of the council's advice.

Each of us was therefore fully aware of Levitan's perceptiveness. We long admired his objectivity, sometimes mixed with a touch of irascibility. We were impressed, though occasionally momentarily irritated, that friendship was never allowed to taint that objectivity. That objectivity could remain unsullied from even a whisper of special treatment; he insisted upon being foundation-supported and resisted any offer of public funding. Levitan shared the devotion to the well-being of American workers, which is the Department of Labor's *raison d'etre*, as well as the economic development role of the Department of Commerce. He was a strong advocate of DOL and Commerce programs, but he was an equally strong critic when he felt that performance was less than it might be.

We learned that he was not only our friend but that his friendship network extended throughout our entire departments, as well as in departments concerned with education, health, and human services. It was rare for information in which he had an interest to be beyond his reach. And if that information could be used to improve programs' performance, one could be assured that it would appear in a Levitan publication or congressional testimony where his contacts were also legion—always fair but always forthright, whether positive or negative. That forthrightness was occasionally irritating to those closest to program operation and responsible for the *status quo*, but it was of great value to a cabinet officer often challenged to obtain objective reporting and appraisal from within one's own organization. The fact that, though long-time friends of each other as well as Levitan, we served in administrations of both parties and were never treated differently by him is adequate testimony that no punches were ever pulled nor kudos given for partisan purposes.

The world was better for Sar Levitan having been in it and suffers to the same degree from his absence. We commend his life as an example to anyone who would become a productive and selfless public servant, whether from inside or outside the governmental establishment. We trust that this book will serve as a reminder to old friends and an inspiration to those who come anew to devote hearts and minds to the world of social policy.

Willard Wirtz, *Secretary of Labor, Kennedy and Johnson Administrations*

George Shultz, *Secretary of Labor and Treasury, Nixon Administration, Secretary of State, Reagan Administration*

John Dunlop, *Secretary of Labor, Ford Administration*

Juanita Kreps, *Secretary of Commerce, Carter Administration*

Ray Marshall, *Secretary of Labor, Carter Administration*

Preface

A Festschrift usually honors a living scholar toward the end of an outstanding career. But what to do for one who refuses during his lifetime? We urged Sar Levitan to do an autobiography of his life and times. We offered to write it for him or do a biography if he would tape record his memoirs. We suggested an endowed professorship or trust in his name. But he was intent on leaving nothing behind with his name on it, though he could hardly bury his extensive bibliography. Despite his protests, we intended to do a biography after his death, but the unanticipated death of his wife almost immediately after removed a vital source of information. Having just decided to abandon the project, we were rejuvenated when at the January 1995 meetings of the American Economic Association and the Industrial Relations Research Association Trevor Bain proposed to Allan Hunt of the W.E. Upjohn Institute for Employment Research and then to us a Festschrift in Levitan's honor.

We sent out an invitation letter to approximately 100 of Levitan's closest friends inviting their participation. Nearly all replied, all with enthusiasm for the project through many had commitments which precluded their participation. Still, far more wanted to submit papers in Sar's honor than we had space for. Painful choices were made, we hope without seriously alienating anyone.

At any rate, we offer here a Festschrist in honor of a unique human being who dedicated his prodigious scholarship to the improvement of public policies on behalf of direct betterment of the economic and social conditions of the less fortunate of our nation's people. The contributions of the few represent the profound respect and gratitude of the many for the inspiring role Sar Levitan played in the lives of all of us.

Authors

Avner Ahituv is a NICHD Postdoctoral Fellow at the Population Research Center of NORC and the University of Chicago. He holds a Ph.D. in economics from the University of Chicago and has taught at Tel Aviv University. His current research focuses on fertility and economic development and the school-to-work transition. His only Levitan connection is the constant flow of anecdotes from his major professor, Marta Tienda.

Trevor Bain is Professor of Management and Director of the Human Resource Institute at the Manderson Graduate School of Business, University of Alabama, and an active arbitrator in labor-management relations. He is the author of an earlier Upjohn Institute volume, *Banking the Furnace: Restructuring of the Steel Industry in Eight Countries*. Trevor interacted with Sar, beginning in 1968, through the Labor Department's Manpower Administration research and institutional grants program

Stephen E. Baldwin is a Senior Economist with KRA Corporation, a research and consulting firm in Silver Springs, MD. He was an economist and policy analyst in the executive and legislative branches of the federal government from 1971 to 1995, concentrating on labor markets, worker training, and education policy. His intellectual understanding of these issues and his stock of epigrams were both enriched by a professional friendship with Sar Levitan that began in 1980.

Burt Barnow was Director of the Labor Department's Office of Policy Evaluation and Research during the mid-1980s, where he was responsible for partial funding of and oversight of relations with the National Council on Employment Policy and worked with Levitan in that regard. He is now Principal Research Scientist of the Institute for Policy Studies at Johns Hopkins University, where he specializes in evaluation of employment and training programs.

Vernon M. Briggs, Jr. is Professor of Labor Economics at the School of Industrial and Labor Relations at Cornell University. He is the author of numerous books and articles over the years on a variety of labor market issues, but in recent years has concentrated especially on immigration-related problems. After service from 1968 as an associate member of the National Manpower Policy Task Force overseen by Sar Levitan, he served with Levitan as a member of the National Council on Employment Policy from 1977 to 1987 and as its chairman during 1985-87.

Susan P. Curnan, is Associate Professor of Human Services Management and Director of the Center for Human Resources at the Heller Graduate School of Brandeis University, where she chairs a Masters of Management degree program in Children, Youth and Family Services. Sar Levitan was a strong advocate and support for her commitment to combining theory and practice and valuing "different ways of knowing" when developing youth policies and programs.

Audrey Freedman is an economist and management consultant. Author, radio and television commentator and frequent speaker at industry association and corporate retreats, Ms. Freedman advises business executives and government statistical agencies on the economy, productivity, and related business issues. Her friendship with Sar Levitan goes back to the mid-1960s when she directed a number of Labor Department programs experimenting with assisted geographical mobility and continued through her membership on the National Council on Employment Policy in the 1980s.

Neal Fogg is Research Associate at the Northeastern University Center for Labor Market Studies and co-author with Andrew Sum of many of the products of that Center. His Levitan connection is also intergenerational through Andy Sum's loyalties.

Eli Ginzberg is a long-time Professor of Economics at Columbia University, where he has been Director of the Eisenhower Center for the Conservation of Human Resources since its establishment in 1948. He served as a consultant to the federal government during all of the presidencies from Franklin D. Roosevelt to Ronald Reagan. He served Levitan as professor, mentor and advocate in a friendship extending from Sar's graduate school days until his death.

Robert Goldfarb is Professor of Economics at George Washington University. His research has focused on wage determination and wage regulation. He is also interested in the problem of drawing believable inferences from empirical literatures in economics. Sar Levitan was a valued colleague from the time Goldfarb joined the George Washington University faculty more than two decades ago.

William Grinker is a consultant on public policy and management and a member of the City Planning Commission of New York City. He was founder and first president of the Manpower Demonstration Research Corporation and later Commissioner of New York City's Human Resources Administration. He first worked with Sar Levitan as Senior Program Officer of the Ford Foundation in the 1970s and thereafter sought guidance from him on issues of employment, training, and welfare policy.

James Heckman is Henry Schultz Distinguished Service Professor of Economics and Public Policy at the University of Chicago. He has become, in recent years, a major protagonist in debates over both the methodology and results of evaluations of employment and training programs. In that capacity, he and Sar Levitan carried on a long friendly debate in which they found more upon which to agree than disagree.

Clifford Johnson is Director of Programs and Policy at the Children's Defense Fund in Washington, D.C. He served as research assistant under Sar Levitan at the George Washington University Center for social Policy Studies from 1981 to 1984 and co-authored numerous books and articles with Levitan, including an earlier Upjohn Institute volume, *Second Thoughts on Work*.

Miriam Johnson, as manager of a San Francisco office of the California State Employment Service, designed and conducted during the 1960s what was probably the nation's first job search training workshop for disadvantaged workers. After retirement and two decades as a consultant, evaluator, and author, at 77 years of age, she is back at that same San Francisco office as a volunteer conducting job search workshops. Her friendship with Levitan was formed during her evaluation assignments.

Christopher King is Associate Director of the Center for Study of Human Resources in the Lyndon Baines Johnson School of Public Affairs at the University of Texas. He had been introduced to Levitan's writings by Charles Killingsworth and Vernon Briggs during his graduate studies at Michigan State University, but had the opportunity to work closely with Sar during a 1976-80 period of service with the office of the Secretary of Labor. He remembers "at times feeling the sting of his sharp but witty tongue" and at other times "receiving heartfelt encouragement to keep fighting the good fight for the less fortunate."

Irene Lurie is Associate Professor of Public Administration and Policy in the Rockefeller College at the State University of New York at Albany. She was co-director of the ten-state JOBS Implementation Study performed by the Rockefeller Institute of Government. Her friendship with Sar Levitan emerged during her service with the Council of Economic Advisers, the President's Committee on Income Maintenance, and at the Brookings Institution during the 1980s.

Garth Mangum is Max McGraw Professor of Economics and Management at the University of Utah and Secretary-Treasurer of the National Council on Employment Policy. Author of over fifty books and monographs and numerous articles on labor market issues, he served in the Kennedy and Johnson administrations and has continued as an adviser to federal, state, local, and foreign governments. He and Sar Levitan were close friends and collaborators for over thirty years.

Stephen Mangum is Associate Professor of Management and Human Resources and Associate Dean of the Fisher College of Business at Ohio State University and is author of substantial works on military, employer-sponsored, and publicly supported skill training programs. Levitan was his "Uncle Sar" during his youth and professor and mentor during his graduate school days. One of the monographs he co-authored with Sar was the latter's final published work.

Alan Melchior is Deputy Director and Senior Research Associate at the Center for Human Resources at Brandeis University. He is author of a number of papers and practitioner guides on youth employment issues and is currently involved in national evaluations of school-based community service programs and in research into the uses of telecommunications in urban community-building.

Colletta Moser is Professor of Agricultural Economics at Michigan State University, where her work focuses on economic development, especially in Michigan. She has numerous publications in labor relations and, among other courses at MSU, teaches a course on women and work. Her friendship with Sar Levitan began when she was a Ph.D candidate in economics at the University of Wisconsin. During the 1970s, Sar advised her as she directed the Rural Manpower Research Consortium under a USDOL grant to MSU.

Markley Roberts, who retired in April 1996, was Assistant Director of the AFL-CIO Economic Research Department and Chairman of the Bureau of Labor Statistics Labor Research Advisory Committee on Employment and Unemployment Statistics. Sar Levitan was his boss at the Wage Stabilization Board in 1951, and they remained lifelong friends.

David W. Stevens is Executive Director of the Jacob France Center in the Merrick School of Business at the University of Baltimore. He was a charter member of the National Manpower Policy Task Force Associates in 1968, and was fortunate to have regular opportunities to interact with Sar Levitan for the next twenty-five years.

Andrew M. Sum is Professor of Economics and Director of the Center for Labor Market Studies at Northeastern University, where he is author and co-author of numerous studies on the labor market problems of youth and young adults. His friendship with Sar Levitan dates to his late 1970s authorship of a background research report for the National Commission on Employment and

Unemployment Statistics. The two subsequently co-authored two books related to training activities under the Comprehensive Employment and Training Act, and Sar was responsible for Andy's subsequent service on the Board of Directors of the National Council on Employment Policy.

Marta Tienda is Ralph Lewis Professor of Sociology and Department Chair at the University of Chicago and Research Associate of the Population Research Center of NORC and the University of Chicago, where she has written widely about Hispanic issues. She describes as one of the great thrills of her career, while still an assistant professor, being invited by Sar Levitan to become a member of the National Council on Employment Policy and "learn about policy writ big with the most experienced and thoughtful analysts."

Alan Zuckerman is currently the Executive Director of the National Youth Employment Coalition. He has worked for the governors of New Jersey and Pennsylvania, the OICs of America, Temple and New York Universities, and the U.S. Department of Labor developing, managing, and supporting job training programs for youth and adults. It was in the latter assignment that he had continuous interaction with Sar Levitan.

CONTENTS

Of Heart and Mind

Social Policy Essays
in Honor of Sar A. Levitan

CHAPTER **1**

Introduction

Stephen Mangum

I carry numerous reflections on Sar A. Levitan, two of which I share here. My earliest memories of Sar are from the mid-1960s when I was about ten years old. I loved to visit the National Geographic Society exhibits with my brother, who was two years younger than I. Following our visit, we would walk to our father's and Sar's 17th Street Upjohn Institute office to catch a ride home at day's end. Frequently, Dad would be on the telephone. Sar would gather the two of us up and take us to the corner People's Drugstore for an ice cream cone while we waited out the telephone call. That is a small indicator of the reasons he was considered a generous uncle to all four Mangum children.

I returned as a graduate student in the fall of 1981, and enrolled in Sar Levitan's seminar on human resource policy. It was for me a pleasurable yet frequently frustrating experience. I was exposed to a method of analysis very different from that which characterized most of my graduate training in economics. Sar immersed me in an analysis of social problems. He continually asked, "what are the facts?" This was inevitably followed by the question, "what are the social institutions for resolving these problems, and what do you know about these institutions?" I could never know enough about those institutions! No matter how diligently I looked, no matter how deeply I investigated, the kind but stern professor was suspicious. The message was: "your search is good, but never be satisfied. There is no substitute for a deep understanding of institutions and how they operate."

"Are the institutions working?" he would ask. My answers would frustrate him for they were "too narrow." He would tell me to "think with both your mind and your heart." He would then teach me to broaden my perspective, to remember that problems need solution, and that problems and their solutions are not one dimensional. I marveled at his ability to identify public policy options and to translate these principles into proposed legislation and administrative action.

The underlying assumptions of the class were made obvious at the outset. My notes from that first class session and those that followed reflect what I have subsequently read multiple times in his writings. That day, he said:

> While federal social welfare programs during the last two generations have achieved impressive gains, their most glaring deficiency lies in the nation's failure to couple income transfers to meet basic needs with opportunities for work and self advancement. Its destructive impact is visible everywhere: in the deprivation of the working poor, the lack of work incentives for welfare recipients, the hopelessness of the underclass, and in the denial of equal opportunity. To expand opportunity is difficult, challenging, and costly. But, if the ideal of an equitable society is to be realized, there can be no alternative.

This volume pays tribute to Sar A. Levitan through a collection of essays authored by just a sample of the many who were influenced by him in person and through the written word. The volume opens with an overview of Sar's life and accomplishments. Written by Garth Mangum, who knew Sar better than perhaps any one other than Sar's wife Brita and their longtime friends Seymour and Ethel Brandwein, the life described is a remarkable one. Affectionately titled "The Secular Rabbi," the chapter chronicles a life centered on public policy and built on a unwavering belief that humankind is basically and inherently good, and that all can rise to accomplishment and prosperity given adequate opportunity and reasonable incentive. This philosophy was the foundation to Sar's interest in social policy. It guided his activities and his accomplishments. While he would have undoubtedly expressed embarrassment at a tribute being written for one self-labeled "first and foremost a writer of footnotes," all who knew Sar will find themselves nodding in agreement and in remembrance as they read this essay. The biography is enhanced by the memories of close friends verbalized in a memorial service held shortly following his death and included in this volume to personalize the responses.

Of the many possible ways to organize the scholarly contributions to this volume, one feels most appropriate. The ordering reflects the method of analysis that Sar taught: identifying problems through examination of facts, developing a thorough understanding of institutions, assessing institutions and policies, evaluating policy options. While some of the contributions do not conveniently fit this categorization scheme, the scheme works overall.

The first two essays enumerate social problems, reflecting Sar's proverbial first question: "what are the facts?" Andrew Sum, Cliff Johnson, and Neal Fogg contend that the most severe and persistent labor market problem currently facing the nation is a sharp two-decade decline in the real weekly and annual earnings of America's young adults. Reviewing the statistical evidence, the authors argue that no demographic group has been more adversely affected by the recent transformation of the U.S. wage structure than have young men, particularly those with limited schooling. The authors expand their scope to examine the impact of earnings trends on young families, documenting that these—particularly young families with a female head of household and/or a household head lacking a high school diploma—have fared much worse in income growth terms over the past twenty years than have other families. They find in this set of facts much of the explanation for out-of-wedlock births, the rise of the single-parent family, the pervasiveness of child poverty, and the decline of many of the treasured values of the family itself.

After exploring other dimensions of the problem, including impacts of health insurance, pension coverage, and training access, the authors present policy options constituting a wide-ranging mosaic for continued social policy discussion. Sum, Johnson, and Fogg cite the advantages of high rates of job growth in improving the prospects of young adults. They argue that strong labor markets disproportionately increase the in-school employment opportunities of high school students, and that this work experience has favorable short- and long-term impacts on post-high school employment and earnings.

It is on this issue that Marta Tienda and Avner Ahituv contribute to the volume. Specifically, they examine the extent to which adolescent employment interacts with and sometimes precipitates early school withdrawal among white, black, and Hispanic male youth. Their empirical work finds the probability of school retention encouraged by modest hours of after-school work, but thereafter withdrawal rising with the number of weekly hours worked, accompanied by even higher withdrawal rates among youth who do not work at all. Both of the withdrawal effects are found to be more pronounced for disadvantaged than for nondisadvantaged youth. The challenge to the school-to-work movement and to advocates of work-based learning is obvious.

A second group of essays, seven in number, reflect the Levitan charge to deepen understanding of relevant institutions, programs and policies. Eli Ginzberg was Sar Levitan's professor and mentor during and after graduate work at Columbia University and thereafter an admired friend. If for no other reason than this, it is appropriate to include his thoughts in this volume. Adding to this Ginzberg's long and extensive impact on U.S. social policy from the Second World War forward, it is an honor to have him contribute. In his essay, Eli Ginzberg offers a retrospective visit and appraisal of the first two decades of federal training policy, the MDTA and CETA years. Every participant and observer perceives a set of events from his own vantagepoint. Others might stress different influences, but Ginzberg's key role is undoubted. His reflections, laced with personal anecdotes, offer an implicit challenge to those concerned with "improving the operations of the U.S. labor market as the nation comes to the end of the twentieth century." Levitan's challenge to us would probably be little different. The Manpower Development and Training Act was clearly the grandfather of current workforce development policy for the economically and culturally disadvantaged, and its CETA and JTPA descendents have changed remarkably little in basic substance—for better and for worse.

David Stevens' essay on American vocational education is set in the context of current proposals to consolidate federal investment in employment and training. Stevens reviews the history of vocational education in the United States and the evidence of its actual performance. He argues that documentation of labor market impacts has been futile at the national level, but not at the state and local level. Stevens then identifies factors that influence vocational education's "performance management challenge" and discusses the relationship between this challenge and the current drive for consolidation legislation. Stevens foresees a possible revolution in program accountability systems through expanded access to wage record data, pointing to a Maryland database effort as exemplary. Employment and training advocates who at this critical juncture find themselves lacking trustworthy evidence of their program's worth should join him in that pursuit.

The next in the collection of essays is Miriam Johnson's paper on the public employment service. Johnson, describing the agency as "besieged, underfunded, expected to accomplish the undoable," explains the inconsistencies inherent in its mandated mission. With the benefit of over forty years of association with the employment service and from a variety of vantage points, she examines the agency's functioning by comparing the specific tasks performed by staff and the environment in which those tasks are accomplished in two time periods, four decades apart. Her perspective is that the job service has become increasingly insignificant in the labor exchange arena, concluding that survival of the agency hinges on discovering different and better ways to serve, despite lessening resources. Its labor market information role is still essential, but the administration of unemployment insurance has been automated into labor market meaninglessness. She identifies increased use of technology and increased reliance on self-help as likely trends of the future, discussing the one-stop center within this context. What she sees is an employment service "turned inside out"—"providing the public with all of the information and knowledge that it has heretofore guarded unto itself." Even then, its survival is in question.

Audrey Freedman created the label, "contingent work." In her contribution to this volume, Freedman reviews the forces behind the rising incidence of contingent work arrangements and what such arrangements require of individual workers. She then focuses her discussion on the temporary help supply industry and the roles that firms in this industry are increasingly playing in today's fluid labor markets. Addressing issues of comprehensive job information, worker credentials, employment continuity, and security, Freedman argues that the temporary help industry is becoming a leading labor market intermediary, characterized by flexibility and market responsiveness. Adding specifics to the claim, she reviews temporary help industry accomplishments in the areas of employee screening and testing, the provision of training, and ancillary personnel services including temporary services as a "work-test" through which approximately a third of temporary workers are hired into permanent positions. These specifics then support a possibility that she raises in conclusion: that the temporary help industry be viewed as a parallel employment service, one that views employers as the true clients needing and being willing to pay for services found nowhere else in today's labor markets. Her advocacy of privatizing labor market services may be unsettling to those trained to perceive those services as a public responsibility. But Johnson's public sector lament followed by Freedman's positivism are an invitation to rethink the need and possibilities.

The effects of the minimum wage was an issue about which Sar Levitan felt strongly and wrote frequently. This led him to adopt an advocacy role on the issue. Consequently, it is appropriate that this topic be addressed in this volume. In their essay, Steve Baldwin and Bob Goldfarb discuss the impact of minimum wage legislation in the context of controversy surrounding recent empirical studies, particularly work by David Card and Alan Krueger. Following review of critiques of these studies, Baldwin and Goldfarb structure their paper as a conversation between two policy-interested colleagues of institutional and neoclassical bias, respectively. In so doing, they identify key differences in individual viewpoints. They find agreement that employment effects are an incomplete basis upon which to judge minimum wage efficacy. They then explore their disagreements as to what other dimensions for judgement should be considered relevant to the broad issue of minimum wage impact. Goldfarb focuses on the income distribution aspects of the minimum wage, while Baldwin voices "labor standard" and "work incentive" rationales for minimum wage laws. Starting at opposite ends of the economic spectrum, they argue each other toward the center, with Baldwin valuing primarily the announcement effect of the social minimum wage while Goldfarb confesses the conclusion that the minimum wage does not do much (though some) harm.

Sar believed that a publicly funded job creation program was an essential element of a comprehensive human resource development system. In his words, "society's work is never done, and there is no shortage of useful work that job creation programs could supply. A jobs program can offer ample work opportunities to fill needs currently unmet" while drawing on "the skills of underutilized workers." William Grinker contributes to the volume by reviewing the record on public sector job creation, with particular attention to the Works Progress Administration (WPA) of the Depression years and the Public Service Employment (PSE) component of CETA during the 1970s. Grinker also provides a brief discussion of Western European experience. He sees little likelihood of reintroduction of public service job creation, except possibly in the case of long-term welfare recipients. However, Grinker questions the effectiveness of job creation in that setting. He perceives a history of success when the targets of public service employment have been people of strong past work experience temporarily deprived of outlets for their abilities and willingness to work. He does not believe the historical record supports the likelihood of success when the target is the hard-to-employ. In concluding, he reiterates the Levitan refrain of public sector job creation's past successes, reminding us of characteristics critical to future success in this arena, but expressing profound pessimism concerning its viability in the current political context. But even if it were politically salable, he seems to be saying that much more experimentation would be necessary to prove PSE viability for such populations as former welfare recipients before advocating that as a general policy.

Vernon Briggs' essay explores the intersection of immigration policy within broad national economic and social policies. Approaching immigration policy as an evolutionary process affected by historical circumstances, he argues that it has overwhelmingly reflected political rather than economic goals; that current policy is inconsistent with emerging economic trends; and that immigration's impacts are undermining human resource development policy effectiveness.

Briggs identifies the Immigration Act of 1965 as a turning point in U.S. immigration policy. He characterizes this Act as replacing a system premised on ethnic discrimination with one premised on nepotism. He argues that in this Act the opportunity of tying immigration policy to labor market reality was lost and that subsequent legislative efforts have dramatically increased immigration at the very time that many other nations have become more restrictive in their policies. He also finds the declining supply characteristics of immigrants to be increasingly inconsistent with the demand characteristics of the national economy. At a time when immigration provides one-third of labor force growth, it does so by deepening the competition faced by those least able to compete while making only limited contributions to meeting labor market need. As with all economic policies, there are winners and losers. While employers, consumers, and immigrants may gain, Briggs' sympathies are clearly with those who, absent immigration, might have been in short supply and rewarded for their scarcity. The essay ends with a plea for reform, asking that immigration policy be made accountable for its economic as well as its social and political consequences.

The third group of essays deal with the assessment and evaluation of employment- and training-oriented policy options. Sar Levitan wrote extensively on federal employment and training programs, beginning with the Area Redevelopment Act. His book evaluating the Job Training Partnership Act (JTPA), *A Second Chance: Training for Jobs* written with Frank Gallo, is perhaps the most widely cited work on this program. It is appropriate that this memorial volume include a piece on JTPA and lessons for the future of employment and training programs. This is ably accomplished by Burt Barnow and Chris King.

Barnow and King provide a review and evaluation of the significant changes to JTPA currently being debated on and around Capitol Hill. Particular attention is given to issues of vouchers, block grants, and performance management. Based on past experience, the authors question the utility of vouchers for economically disadvantaged populations, doubt whether significant cost savings can be gained by block granting, and evaluate the current JTPA performance management system as superior to the reform proposals being advanced. While current programs have not been able to demonstrate sufficiently positive outcomes to defend themselves against growing criticisms, the proposed cures, these two authors predict, will be worse than the disease.

Evaluations of JTPA and other related programs have generally found few significant earnings gains for disadvantaged, out-of-school youth (the Job Corps being a notable but expensive exception). This is the departure point for the essay by Susan Curnan, Alan Melchoir, and Alan Zuckerman. Drawing on a wealth of programmatic experience, they address what works best for whom in at-risk youth programs and propose key characteristics of effective at-risk youth programs. They admit the past ineffectiveness of JTPA youth programs which have typically provided about one week of rehabilitation for each year these youth have spent in dysfunctional circumstances. But they view favorably recent efforts to move youth programs from pursuit of immediate employment to an employability development focus. Grouping characteristics of effective programs around the principles of (a) integrating understanding of adolescent development into youth program design, (b) connecting work and learning, (c) providing for longer-term and potentially discontinuous sequencing of services, and (d) promoting quality through decentralization, their recommendations would surely receive endorsement from he whom this volume honors.

Irene Lurie and Collette Moser honor Levitan's three decades of emphasizing "the symbiotic relationship between poverty reduction, welfare reform, and employment." Their paper is set in the current context of forced welfare reform, as the nation contemplates imposing AFDC time limits, terminating statutory welfare entitlement, and block granting poverty program to state government. Drawing lessons from a ten-state implementation study of the JOBS program with detailed analysis of Michigan, they cast the welfare reform movement as motivated by changing values as to women's roles, frustration with the ineffectiveness of remedial education and training programs, and the political gain of "standing tough," in addition to the immediacy of budget reduction efforts. In Levitan style, the authors close by offering a forecast of where the legislative and programmatic debate will lead. They are not sanguine. The ten-state study found jobs for low-education, low-skill women to be plentiful—but also low paid. Only the continuation of child care and health care at public expense and some form of income supplementation such as the Earned Income Tax Credit could make such employment viable for single mothers. And there would be neither budgetary savings nor political gain in that.

Evaluation and critique being Levitan's livelihood, it is natural that he would enter, in his own way, into the debate over alternative approaches for evaluating social programs. Authoring a book on program evaluation with Greg Wurzberg earlier, Sar returned to the subject in a monograph written during the last years of his life. That monograph was influenced by a series of conversations that Sar had with Jim Heckman. Heckman summarizes the results of evaluations of the outcomes of government-sponsored skill training programs, finding youth programs to have had negative results and those for adults positive but far below the rate of return common to private investments in human capital. His conclusions would probably not have startled Sar, knowing Heckman's predilectons, and he would have objected to only part of them. Heckman would abandon most short-term remedial programs for youth and concentrate on earlier and longer-term preparation. He would also abandon most remedial training programs for adults, preferring to subsidize and supplement their low earnings power until they left the workforce. Levitan would not have been surprised at nor would he have objected to the recommendation that tax incentives be relied upon to encourage private employers to take over most of the skill-training burden. Levitan's objection would have been to that as the exclusive reliance. He had not lost confidence in the efficacy of public services.

Concern for the integrity of economic data was a fundamental characteristic of Levitan's career and his legacy. Even in this area of great interest to him, Sar was more comfortable in supporting than in starring roles. Seldom would he allow circumstances to bring him from behind the scenes to the forefront. One starring role, however, was his service as chairman of the Carter administration-appointed National Commission on Employment and Unemployment Statistics. In his essay, Markley Roberts, who understudied his boss, AFL-CIO Research Director Rudy Oswald, as member of the Commission, reflects on the resultant changes in the nation's labor statistics program. He finds several Levitan Commission recommendations to have been adopted in the January 1994 redesign of the Current Population Survey and in periodic Bureau of Labor Statistics publications such as the recent "A Profile of the Working Poor." Roberts finds little progress on other recommendations, such as addressing the "untapped potential of UI data for labor market analysis." In that, his reflections undergird David Stevens' earlier advocacy of use of the data for program evaluation purposes. In closing, Roberts laments that current budget cutting efforts will further harm the health of the labor statistics programs in which this nation once led the world and now appears to be lagging behind.

It was Trevor Bain who originally suggested a volume of essays honoring Sar A. Levitan and written from among Sar's many colleagues, students, and associates. It is therefore fitting that this volume conclude with an essay by him. Bain's paper explores nonunion arbitration, assessing the applicability of this traditional union grievance procedure to the nonunion setting. The burgeoning use of alternative dispute resolution (ADR) mechanisms outside the employment sphere is noted, motivated by a desire to reduce costly court litigation and settlements. In that setting, arbitration is the least commonly used alternative—negotiation, mediation and fact-finding being more common. But in the nonunion employment sector, ADR bumps up against the absence of any employee representation support structure or any neutral substitute for it. Bain finds understandably significant employer-initiated interest in arbitration, but less obvious payoff to the employee. He identifies eight critical issues to be addressed if arbitration procedures are to be adapted to the nonunionized private employment sector. Concluding this volume with a paper related to grievance arbitration also allows us to end at the beginning by reminding us of where Sar's career began, with a master's thesis on the American Federation of Teachers followed by a Korean-era wage stabilization assignment in the unionized sector and years as a Legislative Reference Service collective bargaining expert before making his mark as a preeminent anti-poverty scholar and even then keeping his hand in as an arbitrator. Thus, this work may come full circle. But even his collective bargaining involvement was but an element of Sar Levitan's life-long commitment to the reduction of poverty through policy-buttressed self-reliance. All those who contributed to this volume appear to share that dedication.

A bibliography of his lifetime writings completes the volume as a fitting tribute to the footnote scribbler extraordinaire, Sar A. Levitan.

CHAPTER 2

Secular Rabbi
The Life and Times of Sar A. Levitan

Garth Mangum

Trust the always self-directed Sar Levitan to even choose his own name. Born September 14, 1914 in Siauliai, Lithuania to Rabbi Osher Nissan Halevi and Yocheved Rappaport Levitan, he was the youngest of four brothers: Joseph, Nathan, Meyer and, himself, Abraham. But the patriarch Abraham had been called in the Book of Genesis the Prince of God, prince being Sar in Hebrew. Therefore, the young Hebrew scholar, after arriving in the United States in his late teens, decided to call himself Sar Abraham Levitan, soon reduced to Sar A.

Family Background

Sar's father was a third generation rabbi, half-brother of two other rabbis and nephew of another. Blossom (Bluma) Kuselewitz Neuschatz, one of Sar's three living cousins and one of the two who are the only living persons who knew Sar's family in Lithuania, remembers "Der Onkel," as she and her siblings and even her parents in his absence called him, as "a handsome man with small features, a fine, light complexion, and a flowing bifurcated beard." But, she adds, "he was very short-tempered, intolerant and tight-fisted man and a strict constructionist in his interpretation of Halacha (Jewish religious law and tradition); a difficult man as father and husband." One of Sar's other cousins, David M. Levitan, adds that his father, Rabbi Solomon L. Levitan joined Sar's father as teaching colleagues about 1922-23 when the latter was dean of a Yeshiva in Shavel (now Shavly), the city in which the family lived throughout Sar's childhood and early teens. David, his father, and brother lived with Sar's family until they obtained their own quarters. Typical of such extended families, the term "cousins" does not imply that the fathers were brothers. David's father was the son of Sar's father's older half-brother, though there was less than ten years differences in their ages. The two men served *pro bono* as rabbis in their respective communities, their wives operating handicraft businesses to help support their families.

"Tante Yocheved," daughter of a founder of one of the early, pre-Israel Palestine settlements, was, on the other hand, according to Blossom, "a saint. While it was almost impossible to get close to her—she was so quiet and reticent—she was nevertheless sharp-witted and demonstrated an ironic sense of humor in few words. Nothing escaped her. She was a short, round woman with a pretty face (Sar resembled her in appearance), very low-voiced, great tolerance, long-suffering and very wise. When she spoke, which was infrequent, her voice was so low that one had to listen closely to hear. But what she said was always on the point, diplomatic and pacifying. I never heard her complain or gossip. She suffered for many years with an unnamed illness and died as quietly and as unobtrusively as she had lived."

Blossom, who was only a year older than Abraham, does not remember the older brother, Joseph, who emigrated to South Africa when she was a child. "The next brother, Nathan, was the tallest, handsomest, and the most outgoing of the brothers. Meyer was short, intense and good-natured but not good-looking. Abraham, the youngest, was short for his age. We called him Avrom'ke, the diminutive form of Abraham. He was a shy child, and we all considered him a mathematical genius because he could instantly add and subtract, multiply and divide any numbers thrown at him."

She remembers no pogroms motivating the family's exodus from Lithuania, but her family emigrated and settled in the Bronx during 1927 with Sar's family following in 1930 and settling two miles away. There Blossom's father became rabbi of a small Bronx congregation and teacher at a Yeshiva in Brooklyn. "Der Onkel secured several positions as Mashgiach (Rabbinical inspector of Koshrus) with several well known Kosher food producers." David Levitan also notes that, though his father served as rabbi of a community in the United States, Sar's father never did.

Blossom completes the family history by recounting that Nathan married a gentile who changed her name from Mary to Miriam and claimed to be a familyless orphan in order to keep that secret from her father-in-law, though Nathan's mother knew and helped keep the secret. Nathan, a chemist, died of cancer in his late forties. According to Blossom, Sar subsequently supported the daughter of Nathan and Miriam through medical school. Meyer, who married a Holocaust survivor, specialized in food chemistry, became an expert in cheese production, and worked as a quality control inspector in California where he also died relatively young from cancer.

Sar often said in later life that his family had expected him to continue the rabbinical tradition, but Blossom has no memory of that and doubts that expectation would have focused on the youngest son, even if it had existed. Of the teenage Sar she says:

> While seemingly shy, he was given to little tricks, challenging his older siblings and cousins. While low man in the pecking order, he was actually observing and digesting all that he saw and heard and storing it in his heart and head. I suspect that he had an almost photographic memory which, to us, was phenomenal and mysterious. He came in for much teasing but he took it all good-naturedly while he continued doing what he wanted to do. I realize now that this was a characteristic of his that persisted all through his life. In the family, on the whole, he was underestimated because he was self-abnegating and did not promote himself and his many achievements.

Education

Arriving in the Bronx at age 16, the soon to be self-named Sar attended Yeshiva during the mornings and spent the afternoons and evenings studying English and secular topics taught in a Catholic high school after its sessions. In 1933, three years after arriving in the United States without any knowledge of English, he graduated from Morris High School.

His best friend during that stage of his life, Philip Gordis, remembers visiting in the Levitan household. Philip's brother Robert Gordis was then making a name for himself as a conservative rabbi. When introduced to Philip and told of the relationship, Rabbi Levitan responded, "If he is so devout, why does he desecrate the holy name?" referring to the fact that a conservative could read the Lord's name directly from the scriptures rather than substitute a synonym as did the orthodox.

After completing his high school studies, Sar continued on to City College of New York. A list of courses taken extending from June 1934 to June 1937 reveals a broad liberal arts curriculum with no apparent emphasis. During this period, according to Blossom Neuschatz, Sar served, along with herself and her future husband, as Hebrew teachers, helping to organize and being active in the Hebrew Teachers' Union. Blossom recalls that she and others considered themselves to be Marxists, while one of their number fought in Spain and was listed as "missing in action." However, though Sar read the radical press and was in general sympathy with their antifascist activities, he never took part in them. Philip Gordis also remembers that while he and others of Sar's friends of the late thirties considered themselves radicals and Marxists, Sar seemed amused at their protestations. Blossom's assessment is that "Sar was never politically 'left.' He was progressive, politically aware, humanist, liberal, basically a very decent human being, interested in and working hard to further his own career, but always aware of the struggle of people in the world around him."

Sar once recounted that he had intended to study philosophy but that an uncle had warned him, "who would ever hire a Jewish philosopher?" Blossom reflects that was more likely her paternal uncle rather than Sar's, Chanan Saks, eleven years older, handsome, and articulate, and very influential in Sar's life, who was at the time studying labor and economics at Columbia. At any rate, Sar enrolled in the Graduate School of Political Science at Columbia University in September 1937, completing a Masters in Economics in 1939. His thesis, "The American Federation of Teachers: A Study of a Union for Professionals," ranged across the importance of teachers in society, the problems they faced in gaining adequate recognition, salary, and security, the need for extension and equalization of educational opportunity for all children, and the need for teachers to organize themselves effectively to accomplish those objectives. Tracing the history of teachers union organizing efforts, he stressed the need for affiliation with rather than aloofness of "professionals" from the broader labor movement. Moving directly into a doctoral program, he thereafter continued taking classes from Paul F. Brissenden, Leo Wolman and Eli Ginzberg of labor economics fame, among others, until interrupted by the outbreak of war.

Military Service

Eli Ginzberg, who joined the Columbia faculty in 1939, was to become particularly influential in Sar's subsequent life. Sar had become a citizen of the United States on October 14, 1940 at age 26. He was described on his certificate of citizenship as being white, of dark complexion, having brown eyes and black hair, standing 5 feet 6 1/2 inches tall and weighing 140 lbs. Drafted into the U.S. army in the spring of 1942, Sar soon found his way into Officer Candidate School and came out with an administrative designation, including a stint as assistant personnel officer of a training center at Grinnell College in Iowa. Meantime, Eli Ginzberg had become personnel consultant to the Commanding General of the Army Service Forces. As Eli tells the story, "Sar had succeeded in getting himself commissioned but was looking for a meaningful job, not easy for a lieutenant to find on his own. I got him an assignment in the Transportation Corps in the Port of New York where he spent the war carrying out a number of constructive assignments," all of them undoubtedly more attractive than what the army was then expecting of most other newly commissioned second lieutenants.

Assigned to the Port of Embarkation in Brooklyn, not far from his home in the Bronx, Sar served out the war as Chief of the Statistical Branch of the Control and Planning Division. Philip Kaplan, who served under Captain Levitan as a civilian statistician remembers that their responsibilities "consisted principally in preparing a top secret monthly summary of activities at the Port for distribution to higher authority." He also remembers that "Sar was not a military type. The office operated in a manner that left no doubt who was in charge but without any outward sign of authority." (Hyman Minsky, who was later to pursue a distinguished career as a Washington University economist, was an enlisted man among the usual complement of about a dozen military and civilian personnel.) Kaplan also remembers that Sar reported to a Major Flicks of the regular army. Flicks had little love for nonregular officers who moved up the ranks much too quickly for his taste and even less love for statistics, so Sar was not his favorite person.

Relieved from active duty in February 1946 and discharged as a captain on May 1, 1946, Sar remained in the active reserve until 1961, attaining the rank of lieutenant colonel, then moving to inactive status until final retirement on September 14, 1974.

Marriage

Though he does not remember just when it occurred, Sar's longtime friend Philip Gordis was present at what Sar would likely have designated as the most important event in his life. A group of old friends had the habit of having dinner together occasionally. One evening, he recalls, a beautiful blond daughter of Danish immigrants was present. Her name was Brita Ann Buchard Kohle. He remembers Brita and Sar as being immediately attracted to each other, conversing together throughout that entire evening. Gordis does not remember who brought or invited her, but has the impression that she was a singer with Dean Dixon, an African-American musician who became popular in England after having a struggle getting a start in New York. Blossom Neuschatz remembers that the group was enamored of Dixon but doesn't remember Brita being involved with him. Seymour and Ethel Brandwein, close friends of the Levitan's throughout their Washington years, remember no mention of Dixon but do remember Brita recalling with some pride spending a year during her youth with a theatrical touring company playing in Blossom Time. However, she also reminisced that she found the touring so wearing that she decided to leave the theater after that year. Of her subsequent employment nothing is known, though her social security benefit record shows substantial years of contributions.

There exists in the Levitans' files a 19 October 1945 certificate of annulment of the marriage of Brita Anna Kohle and Otto Kohle, justified by the "fraudulent representation of the defendant" and awarding $8 per week for the support of an infant son, Gary. The Brandwein's recall Brita having recounted how her first husband failed to warn her that he was a victim of Huntington's Chorea, a disease which is passed on to male descendants. Her outrage upon learning of that fact after the birth of their son led her to seek annulment of the marriage. Huntington's is a progressive and incurable disease of the central nervous system which includes progressive brain deterioration and loss of control of bodily movements. Whether there were signs at birth that Gary would suffer throughout his life and finally die of the disease is not known. The Levitans were never prone to share their personal tragedies, though they participated for years in a support group of Huntington's disease families and, at their death, left a substantial bequest to the Huntington's disease research program at Johns Hopkins University. Gary suffered throughout his life from the rigors of the disease until dying from it in about 1967 or 1968, barely into his twenties. Sar and Brita were never to have children of their own.

There is also in the files a Certificate of Marriage of Sol (sic) Levitan and Brita A. Kohle dated October 15, 1946, certified by the Brooklyn Deputy City Clerk who performed the marriage and witnessed by Valia Hirsch and Philip Gordis. According to Gordis, Rabbi Levitan did not know for some time of his youngest son's marriage, was at first told that his new daughter-in-law was Jewish, but finally learned the bitter truth via "the family grapevine." Blossom Neuschatz doubts that the father would have been that unaware, but has the impression that father and son were not close after the death of Sar's mother.

Launching a Career

Leaving active military duty in February 1946, Sar was employed as a statistician with the Veterans Administration from that month until his marriage in October. Simultaneously, he began work on his dissertation, which would be completed and published in 1950 as *Ingrade Wage-Rate Progression in War and Peace: A Problem in Wage Administration Techniques.* As recounted by Sar years later, that topic did not impress his father. Rabbi Levitan who, according to Sar, had published such learned papers as one debating whether or not an orthodox Jew could open the refrigerator door on the sabbath knowing that the action would switch on the light, thought Sar's topic choice to be of limited significance. "In-Grade Wage Rate Progression? That's a dissertation?"

Eli Ginzberg remembers another instance related to Sar's completion of graduation requirements. Sar, for whom English was already a second language, wanted to substitute Hebrew for French as the other language required for the Ph.D. Upon approving the substitution, the question arose about who on the faculty was qualified to assess his facility. Finally Eli offered and the faculty accepted Eli's own distinguished rabbi father as the judge who attested to the completing student's impeccable Hebrew.

But receipt of the doctorate did not come until 1949. Meantime, in the fall of 1946 with ABD (all but dissertation) in hand, the newly formed family of three were off to Sampson, New York where Sar had been hired to teach economics on that campus of the Associated Colleges of Upper New York. There he served as chairman of an eight-person economics department and dean of business administration at a munificent $5100 salary. After two and one-half years, that institution was taken over by the State University of New York, opening the opportunity for Sar to transfer to Champlain College in Plattsburg, New York, where he remained from 1949 into 1951. His final salary in the New York system was $6200.

Wage Stabilization Board

Perhaps it was his expertise in internal wage administration attested by his doctoral dissertation which, despite his active reserve status, saved him from further military service in the Korean "police action." At any rate, within a month of the outbreak of U.S. involvement in Korea, Sar Levitan's name was back on the federal payroll as director of the National Case Division of the Office of Case Analysis of the Wage Stabilization Board, along with special assignments as a technical expert on internal wage administration problems. Involved as members or staff of the WSB were most of the academic labor economics fraternity who had served the War Labor Board during the Second World War, with the addition of younger men such as himself who had been in military service during the earlier conflict. John Dunlop,

Nathan Feinsinger, and Benjamin Aaron were public members of the Board to whom he reported. Morris Horowitz, later of Northeastern University, was his immediate superior. He directly supervised Ethel Weiss, who later married Seymour Brandwein, another Wage Stabilization staff member. The Brandweins remained lifelong friends of the Levitans and administrators of both their wills upon their deaths. Other WSB colleagues were Curtis Aller, Beatrice Burgoon, Frank Kleiler, Mollie Orshansky and Al Weiss, all of whom were to serve later in the U.S. Department of Labor, as well as some of them in other government, union and university positions. Lifetime friendships were established which would be important to Levitan's later role as policy kibitzer. Sar described his Wage Stabilization assignment on a later application for federal employment:

> The Office of Case Analysis was responsible for the analysis of all wage and compensation adjustment petitions under the general policies of the WSB. As Director of the National Case Analysis Division, I was responsible for the technical adequacy and conformance to policy of the analyses of all cases involving large scale enterprises covering more than one region of the Board, and novel and precedent establishing issues. As top level staff, I participated in recommending policies and issues in existing policies for the submission to the Board itself. I had full responsibility for organizing the staff of the division [averaging 60 Grades GS-3 to GS-14], the final selection of personnel and management of the staff and direction of all of its activities.

Seymour Brandwein adds:

> His initial position, with a staff of 60, was to direct analyses of petitions for approval of wage changes involving large firms in more than one region and all cases involving major new policy or precedent. In September 1952, he was named a public member of the Board's Review and Appeals Committee, a tripartite body which was delegated authority to decide certain types of cases, make recommendations to the Board on others, and to hear and make recommendations to the Board on all appeals from decisions by regional boards and special industry commissions and panels.

Legislative Reference Service

By the time of his appointment to the Review and Appeals Committee, it was apparent that the Korean conflict was of limited duration, and it was time for Levitan to be looking for the next step of his career. General and President of Columbia University Dwight D. Eisenhower was campaigning for president, in part with the promise that "If elected, I will go to Korea...." Sar and Brita had resolved to stay in Washington, but no immediate permanent employment appeared when the Wage Stabilization Board went out of business in mid-1953. Sar sought consulting work for some months without success before taking a temporary six-month appointment in January 1954 as an analyst with the Legislative Reference Service (LRS) of the Library of Congress. He then moved on to work for two months for the Social Security Administration on a study of compensation systems for veterans. In August 1954, he accepted an economic analyst's position with the Puerto Rico Planning Board, but after six months in San Juan the Legislative Reference Service contacted him to offer a regular position as a specialist in labor economics and industrial development.

Levitan was to remain with the Legislative Reference Service until 1961, preparing upon request from individual members of Congress and congressional committees reports analyzing pending legislation or precedent to the preparation of legislative proposals. Increasingly, that included special assignments with the Senate Committee on Labor and Public Welfare, the Senate Committee on Banking and Currency, and the Joint Economic Committee, as well as the Hoover Commission on reorganization of the federal government. Not forgetting his academic background, he availed himself of the opportunity to spread his reputation beyond government by publishing results of his studies in scholarly and public policy journals. His yearning to teach was also partially fulfilled by adjunct lecturing at Johns Hopkins and American Universities.

One high point of his LRS assignments was service from October 1959 to March 1960 as research director of the Senate Special Committee on Unemployment Problems, chaired by Senator Eugene McCarthy and including among its members Senators Joseph Clark, Winston Prouty, and Jennings Randolph, the first two of whom would become architects and supporters of the Manpower Development and Training Act and the latter of public works and area development legislation during the 1960s. That was a transition, both for Levitan and the Senate and senators. Now it was recognized that unemployment had been creeping upward since the close of the Korean conflict. The watchword was John Dunlop's declaration before the committee that the problem was now class unemployment in contrast to the mass unemployment of the Great Depression.

But before moving wholeheartedly into the emerging antipoverty concern, there was to be one more assignment in the collective bargaining realm in 1960-61 as assistant director of the Presidential Railroad Commission, appointed by President Eisenhower to determine the need for firemen on diesel locomotives and other railroad labor issues. It was probably more than coincidence that John Dunlop was also a member of that commission.

The first blood in what was to become characterized later as a war on poverty and structural unemployment was drawn by Senator Paul Douglas, former University of Chicago Economics professor and World War II soldier, in pursuit of legislation to aid depressed areas, particularly the coal mining areas of southern Illinois. Completing the Presidential Railroad Commission assignment in 1961, Levitan moved back to his future by assisting Senator Douglas with the culmination of his depressed areas legislation. How Sar became involved with Douglas is not known. It may have been an accident of the LRS assignment, though the likelihood of their attraction to each other is obvious. At any rate, immediately following Levitan's Unemployment Committee involvement, Douglas sent him to Germany in early 1960 to study that country's area development experience. As a matter of fact, the area development legislation was old business. Douglas, looking to his downstate Carbondale and adjacent Illinois coal country constituency, had agitated from the late 1950s for federal aid to depressed areas. The Douglas bill had passed the Senate twice and the House once during the 1950s, only to be vetoed by President Eisenhower. All it needed was an endorsing president, so the Area Redevelopment Act (ARA) was S.1 in the new Congress and was signed by President Kennedy on May 1,1961. The ARA experience was to point the direction of the rest of Levitan's career, not as a triumph but because it was such a disappointment to him.

To attract votes, Congress had defined depressed areas in such a fashion that one-third of the nation's 3,100 counties were so designated under the new legislation. The $389 million appropriated the first year followed by $455 million the following year seemed like big money in those years, but did not go far in the attempt to get at least one project into every congressional district. Sar served briefly as a consultant to the director of the new Area Redevelopment Administration, then sought and received a grant from the Ford Foundation to study and evaluate the results of this first program of the Kennedy New Frontier. That grant, which he took to George Washington University for administration, began what he later described as his personal Ford Foundation welfare program which would last the rest of his life.

The resulting *Federal Aid to Depressed Areas* (1964) was also a pattern-setter, both for Levitan and for review of federal programs. Data would not have been available for a formal cost-benefit study, even had that been his predilection. Instead, his evaluation was a narrative process of describing the problems leading to legislative concern, tracing the legislative path, following the passage through to administration, and comparing the potential of the new machinery to the realities of the problems. Awaiting results, measuring them, and then comparing benefits to costs was a lengthy process Sar knew from his LRS experience that Congress would not stand still for. Some assessment must be available before the next election. Better to identify legislative misconceptions and emerging administrative problems before their inevitable negative results threatened potentially productive programs.

A familiar Levitan technique emerging during the depressed areas study was early circulation among program administrators of drafts of what he intended to say about them and their programs. This was followed by informal, and often hotly contested, conferences. There, errors of fact could be identified and perceptions tested against those most knowledgeable and most concerned and under pressure to be persuasive. Levitan later reminisced about his first such encounter, reviewing a draft of his book with ARA staff:

> I thought I had written a sympathetic account, while calling the shots as I had seen them. I had come to realize that the tools of ARA, which I had helped design, were a very weak reed for helping depressed areas. Well, I anticipated a nice discussion at the Cosmos Club where I had set up the meeting, after which we

would part happily ever after. Were they mad at me! One of the most stinging attacks came from a fellow who had told me earlier that he had not had time to read the material. After another six-hour session the comments cooled down somewhat.

But the reader is not surprised. What comes through the pages of *Federal Aid to Depressed Areas* is sincere concern for the residents of depressed areas, a strong commitment to the essentiality of the legislation, but totally honesty in recognizing limitations in both structure and application, reassessing the experience in pursuit of improvement, let the chips fall where they may. It is not surprising that the program administrators did not perceive the book as supportive. The conclusions of that first social policy study also set a pattern which would become identified with Levitan. He was forthright in his criticisms. The focus of the new program was to fund infrastructure and promise to train the workforce to attract employers from prosperous to depressed areas. But not only had the money been spread "too thin" so that few of the projects were of meaningful size, but more than half of the designated areas were already growing in population while others were too isolated to be viable. That did not mean abandon the effort, however. The Levitan prescription was to do more but do it better and more selectively. Not every depressed community could or should be saved:

> Many resource-based depressed communities are located in isolated areas where new economic activity can be introduced only at prohibitive costs. Other depressed areas, particularly rural, have never developed an adequate economic base and the social capital invested in such areas is normally insignificant. . . . A depressed areas program can be effective only when the number of depressed areas is reduced to manageable proportions and only areas with a potential for development at a reasonable cost are made eligible to participate in the program.

For greater potency, according to Levitan, preferential tax treatment should be given to companies that move to depressed areas. Only then would "blue chip companies" be persuaded to move. At the same time, he thought the only solution to unemployment in many depressed areas was to "equip the unemployed with skills which would be marketable in other areas."("Early Supporter Now Doubts ARA Value," *The Washington Post*, 3 November 1963, p.2) Obviously, *Federal Aid to*

Depressed Areas was not likely to be favorably quoted in either congressional or administration circles.

Center for Social Policy Studies

But Levitan had found his niche. By the time the depressed areas study was completed and the George Washington University grant expired at the end of 1963, the Manpower Development and Training Act (MDTA) had been enacted (1962) and numerous alternative youth programs and other initiatives were under discussion. But a more secure base was needed. George Washington University had provided office space and administrative responsibility for the depressed areas grant but had not incorporated the activity into its structure, nor had the initial Ford grant provided for any staff. Now Levitan sought not only a base but company.

Moving to the Washington, D.C. office of the W.E.Upjohn Institute for Employment Research at the beginning of 1964, Levitan broadened his activities to include congressional testimony, presentations at a variety of conferences, and Upjohn Institute publications on vocational education legislation, the new Youth Employment Act (which he could not know would soon be subsumed into the emerging Economic Opportunity Act), the need for adult retraining, reduction of work time to reduce unemployment, and increasing the minimum wage to combat poverty, along with continued advocacy of expanded but improved and concentrated area development efforts. Then, after a lapse of one and one-half years, he returned to the Ford Foundation for a grant to study the administration and impact of the Economic Opportunity Act of 1964 to be administered through the Upjohn Institute, reestablishing a relationship with the Foundation which would continue until his death. A Foundation staffer later recalled of Levitan's application that he was challenged for having no outline of his intended antipoverty assessment. He remembered Levitan responding, "If you give me the grant, I will give you a book with a table of contents and an index too!"

Welcomed among Sar's more informal LRS services had been his role as personnel matchmaker. His professorial instincts included looking out for career opportunities for friends and acquaintances as well as students. His recommendations had come to be trusted by congressional staff recruiting to meet the needs of their principals. That matchmaker role would expand as his acquaintance broadened from the legislative to the executive branch. As one example, at the Presidential Railroad Commission he had taken under his wing Garth Mangum, a 35-year-old former teaching assistant of Commission member John Dunlop, brought aboard for the summer of 1961 and continued as a consultant on that and other Dunlop involvements operating from his Utah base. When, in the spring of 1963 Senator Joseph Clark, now chairman of the Senate Subcommittee on Employment and Manpower, was searching for an economist to serve as research director of an investigation into emerging manpower issues, Levitan introduced Mangum for the job. The congressional position led to related assignments within the administration, but when in 1966 his protegee began yearning for a more academic environment, Levitan was there to supply it. He served as middleman, negotiating for Mangum a parallel Ford Foundation grant at the Upjohn Institute to evaluate the 1962 MDTA, amendments to which had been part of Mangum's 1963-64 Clark Committee responsibilities.

Levitan and Mangum initially took their new Ford grants to the former's Upjohn Institute base for a pleasant and productive year. But the transition proved difficult from Levitan's previous staff position to the new role as independently funded tenants, and both yearned for teaching opportunities. Therefore, when their Ford grants came up for renewal in March1967, they sought and received Foundation cooperation and the assistance of program officer Marvin Feldman in moving to the George Washington University. There they were given academic status as research professors of economics, authorized to launch the Center for Manpower Policy Studies in their own off-campus facilities and to teach in those facilities their own annual seminar in manpower policy. The new grant also allowed for the hiring of clerical staff. The greatest reward of the Upjohn Institute attachment was that they acquired there two personal secretaries, Iris Steele for Levitan and Audrey Barber for Mangum. Both women had long experience and wide contacts on the Washington scene; both were devoted to their bosses and jobs; and both remained with those bosses until retirement, Barber for Mangum under other auspices.

At the end of 1968, Mangum was offered and accepted an endowed chair at the University of Utah. Levitan became the sole director of the Center, changing its name in the early 1970s to the Center for Social Policy Studies, as the "manpower" term had come under attack for its sexist connotations.

Meantime, the Ford Foundation relationship had changed from one of periodic reapplications to an assumption of continuity requiring only the submission of research and publication plans for a subsequent two or three years. Those plans, which extended over the entire range of economic development, workforce development, employment, family, welfare, and poverty issues and included labor force statistics, labor law, collective bargaining, military manpower and critiques of evaluation methodology were never questioned. Especially memorable were Levitan's *The Great Society's Poor Law*, an assessment of the Economic Opportunity Act, and *The Promise of Greatness,* an evaluative review of the entire Johnson administration's Great Society and its aftermath. A total of fifty major books were eventually to carry his name and be the base for literally hundreds of articles, interviews, addresses, and congressional testimony. By the end of the eighties, he had become convinced that few of the people he wanted to reach had the time to read books. He therefore began to concentrate upon the policy monographs which he described as "shorties." (A bibliography is included in this volume.)

His productivity and the policy relevance of his work had come to be undoubted. There was in Levitan's files a negative confidential evaluation by a Ford Foundation staffer which someone had apparently leaked to him. It complained that Levitan's methodology was not sufficiently rigorous and that he tended to pull his punches to protect advocated programs and favored agencies. But apparently the report found no favor among the Foundation's decision makers. The frequent federal agency resentment of the supposedly favorable evaluations was already legend, and besides, Foundation officers were already finding Levitan to be a valuable consultant and advisor in their own internal activities.

The Center also became a productive apprenticeship program as well as a source of policy critique and recommendation. At first working alone and then with peers, Levitan soon learned to productively use research assistants, but he never publicly relegated them to that status.

They were coauthors. Usually drawn from among students in his GWU seminars but sometimes from recommendations of others, they were employed at comfortable salaries but given to understand that their positions were temporary. They would be expected to move on when their skills were honed. They became his legs, hustling among agencies in person or by telephone to gather data and interview program operators at all levels, as well as drawing upon libraries and among reports and issuances for published data. They were also to draft their descriptions and conclusions and then accept with good grace drastic revisions, also delivered with good humor. Then, after two or three years, there would be recommendations to government agencies, public interest groups, and research organizations known to be searching for newly minted journeypersons—a head start on a social policy career. What once had been an informal Levitan placement function had become a semiformal apprenticeship system. Only a few of these Levitan protegees can be listed here as examples: Robert Taggart, formerly director of the Office of Youth Programs in the Carter Department of Labor and now president of the Research and Training Institute; Richard Belous, vice-president and chief economist, National Planning Association; Clifford Johnson, director of programs and policy, Children's Defense Fund; Joyce Zickler, assistant director, Research and Statistics, Federal Reserve Board; Isaac Shapiro, formerly special assistant in the Office of the Secretary of Labor and now vice-president of the Center for Budget and Policy Priorities; and Gregory Wurzburg, principal administrator, Organization for Economic Cooperation and Development in Paris. That career development activity was but a part of Levitan's continuing role of aggressive placement broker, at the request of either seeker or provider of human resources. Not only assistants but other students and acquaintances whom he knew to be competent were beneficiaries of the Levitan personnel service.

National Council on Employment Policy

Upon the entry door of the Center for Social Policy Studies (and its manpower predecessor) over the years at various addresses was to appear another sign identifying the home of the National Council on

Employment Policy. Senator Clark's Employment and Manpower Sub-committee in a 1964 report entitled *The Nation's Manpower Revolution* had recommended coordinating the emerging programs and functions through a cabinet-level President's Committee on Manpower, and the senator had recommended his research director, Mangum, as its executive director to implement the concept. Though the title had perhaps been overdone to attract political attention, the concept of a "manpower revolution" had been the result of no minor conceptualization. As the fertility of the soil had been the source of wealth for the agrarian age and capital investment for the industrial one, manpower, or as it would be more accurately described a decade later, human resources, was conceived to be the key resource of the emerging postindustrial society. Senator Clark, like Eli Ginzberg who was a trusted advisor, had served in a personnel capacity during the Second World War and was wedded to a notion of "staffing freedom." Others, such as John Dunlop of Harvard and Willard Wirtz of Northwestern University, had arrived at similar concepts from War Labor Board experience, or like Frederick Harbison of Princeton from a vantage-point of international economic development. In retrospect, a continuity had been perceived among the education provisions of the World War II GI Bill, the Employment Act of 1946, and the National Defense Education Act of 1958. The Manpower Development and Training Act of 1962 was to be the charter for workforce development in general, as well as the specifics of retraining displaced workers as it sought to do in 1962, or as a weapon in the war on poverty as it became after 1964. The Vocational Education Act of 1963 was to broaden that activity from its restricted agriculture, trade and industry, and homemaking niches to the full range of nonbaccalaureate occupational preparation.

Within that vision, the President's Committee on Manpower was to be the means of coordination within the federal government concerning issues as diverse as meeting military manpower needs, mounting the scientific manpower capability to get a man on the moon during the decade without stifling other scientific development, rejuvenating depressed areas, and ending rural and central city poverty. Largely from the advocacy of Professor Frederick Harbison, a National Manpower Policy Task Force had been instituted as an adjunct to the President's Committee on Manpower as a device to bring the counsel of academic experts into the perceived and emerging manpower policy process. Chaired by Harbison, its original membership included two future Secretaries of Labor, George Shultz and John Dunlop, along with other academics of similar stature such as Charles Myers of MIT and Charles Killingsworth of Michigan State University. The Task Force met regularly, usually quarterly, to discuss and formulate policy recommendations to Secretary of Labor Willard Wirtz, a long-time colleague whom many of the members served and advised individually in other capacities. Wirtz found the concept attractive, but the infrequency of the meetings and the inevitabilities of struggle for group consensus led him to once respond, "its reassuring to have you recommend what we have already decided upon in house and have begun to implement."

Levitan was not an initial member, but the Task Force enters his biography because of his subsequent involvement. The President's Committee on Manpower was soon swallowed up in the emerging anti-poverty effort. All other departments and activities atrophied as it became primarily a means of coordination among the Departments of Labor and Health, Education and Welfare and the Office of Economic Opportunity in the administration of the Economic Opportunity Act and MDTA. Then as soon as Labor won primacy in the administration of the war on poverty, the President's Committee on Manpower was abandoned and with it the Task Force.

But that was not the end of the story. Shortly after the launching of the GWU Center for Manpower Policy Studies, Howard Rosen, who was responsible for MDTA-funded research within the Labor Department, approached Levitan and Mangum with the request that they reconvene the Task Force to advise him on research priorities. To those members retained such as Shultz, Dunlop and Eli Ginzberg were added a younger tier among whom were future Secretary of Labor Ray Marshall and future Secretary of Commerce Juanita Kreps. With Mangum's departure, Levitan became permanent vice-chairman, providing continuity among rotating chairmen (there were always women members but, as it happened, never a chairwoman).

With the abolition of the manpower terminology, the Task Force became the National Council on Employment Policy at the same time the Center became the Center for Social Policy Studies. Confusion was generated as numerous name changes followed replacement of the MDTA by the Comprehensive Employment and Training Act (CETA). in 1972. The Labor Department's Manpower Administration became

the Employment and Training Administration, and the advisory com-
mittee to those acts was renamed by Congress from the National Com-
mission on Manpower Policy to become the National Commission on
Employment Policy. Eli Ginzberg chaired the National Commission on
Employment Policy while a member of the National Council on
Employment Policy, the Labor Department financed both, and the Ford
Foundation added to the funding of the National Council activities
along with its support of the host Center for Social Policy Studies.

Advice was given and received on research priorities, and assistance
was provided in preparing the annual Manpower Report of the President required by MDTA. But in the main, the National Council on
Employment Policy (NCEP) became a vehicle for exploring emerging
labor market-related issues, both in Council meetings and in broader
conferences sponsored by the Council, and through the sponsorship of
research and publication of policy papers. Council membership,
changing over the years with aging and changing of status, would
include most of those making major contributions to employment and
training policy during the 1970s and into the 1980s. Housing the
National Council at the Center for Social Policy Studies also brought a
new position of executive director, a position filled at Levitan's choice,
usually from among his graduate students. Since the logistics of meetings and even drafting reports concerning Council conclusions did not
require full time and attention, the executive directors then became
Levitan co-authors.

The Reagan administration was the cause of the Council's demise.
The Council's Labor Department sponsors chose to retire, and the new
departmental administration was not sympathetic to the Council's
activist positions and saw no reason to fund a "viper in its own bosom."
The Ford Foundation was not willing to pick up the whole load of the
Council budget, impacted as the Foundation was by cries of distress
from other social activists losing governmental funding, though their
commitment to Levitan and his Center for Social Policy Studies did not
diminish. In fact, funds for research staff were expanded to partially
make up for the loss of the executive directors' contributions to Center
productivity.

Levitan did not give up easily on the Council, however. He thought a
respected academic voice in favor of employment and training programs to be even more important in the hostile environment. After

arguing unsuccessfully with the Ford Foundation, he solicited in vain alternative funding sources. Finally, when the funds were exhausted by the mid-1980s, he accepted the cessation of meetings. But he appealed to the final meeting to delegate a smaller group consisting of himself, Robert Taggart, Marion Pines, and Garth Mangum to serve as residual watchdogs while he kept up annual reports to the District of Columbia and Internal Revenue Service to maintain the organization's legal charter and not-for-profit status. Once, about 1990, he sought and obtained funding for a study which he could have pursued through his Center but instead took the grant in the name of the Council, prevailing upon Pines and Mangum to join in the research and the publication of *A Proper Inheritance: Investing in the Self-Sufficiency of Poor Families* under Council imprimatur in an attempt to restore its visibility. He also used that occasion to persuade Mangum, Pines, Taggart, Gordon Berlin, Mitchell Sviridoff, Andrew Sum, and Linda Harris to constitute a new Board of Directors for his Council, but without further funding he was unable to restore life to it.

That occasion laid the foundation for a resurrection which was only accomplished in Levitan's death. Despite the protests of Mangum, to whom he revealed his intent, the wills of Sar and Brita Levitan were modified to leave the single largest legacy of their estate (an amount that turned out to be larger than anyone ever imagined, for reasons discussed below) to the NCEP. (It was Mangum's view that the funds should be used to establish a Levitan Chair at George Washington or some other university or a Sar and Brita Levitan Trust Fund dedicated to good purposes, but Levitan refused to leave anything behind with his name on it.) The 1990 Board were surprised upon learning of the will, having forgotten the occasion of the aborted resurrection. But they took revenge for having been left with the unexpected responsibility by funding the creation of a Sar Levitan Center for Social Policy Studies at Johns Hopkins University as the primary vehicle for carrying on Levitan's life work.

Extracurricular Activities

In addition to the Center's research and publications and those of the NCEP, the breadth and depth of Levitan's one-man role on the Washington labor scene is exhausting. Sharing a special affinity for congressional staff, he and Mangum began early in their Center's life to hold seminars on Capitol Hill, both to instruct congressional staff and to offer them a forum for interchange among themselves and with practitioners who would have to administer their programs. Those continued into the mid-80s under Levitan's solo leadership. But it was not only staff contact.

Levitan kept up a personal relationship with key senators and members of congress interested in employment and training and welfare legislation. Among those, he had a close affinity for liberal Republicans, figuring that the usually Democratic majority had its own extensive staff and the help of departmental staff during Democratic administrations and of advocacy and public interest groups at all times. He became an almost professional witness before congressional hearings, as his bibliography indicates. Lunch at the George Washington University Faculty Club until his mobility became limited and thereafter in a restaurant near his office where a table was always reserved was devoted to keeping up a wide range of contacts with policy makers and their staffs. Rarely was a conference held on employment, training, welfare or antipoverty matters in the Washington, D.C. environs without an invitation to Levitan, who almost always attended, participating vigorously in discussion if not invited to speak formally. His media contacts were legion because he was always available for interview by telephone or in person and could be depended upon for a quotable quote, generally an acerbic one.

A vigorous defender of public programs in his chosen field, he never pulled his punches in criticism of the manner in which they were conducted. In addition to his own program and policy evaluations, he urged the General Accounting Office to enter the program evaluation field and took pleasure in advising and encouraging them once they had done so. Of what he saw as more esoteric "numerologist" evaluators he was less enamored. He wanted a sophisticated institutional sense of the possible in public administration and an awareness that the

best of evaluation methodology could provide no more than an approximation of reality. Numbers were essential but they had to be tempered
with judgement.

Though reluctant to be gone long because of the situation at home,
to be explored later, he journeyed to New York for Ford Foundation
meetings and occasionally accepted invitations to speak to academic or
practitioner groups around the country. He never let that appear to constitute field work, however. His research domain was Washington government offices. He kept over his desk a Peanuts cart′ ⁄n with one of its
characters declaring that "If you have seen one field, you have seen
them all." Upon an appearance at the University of Utah, Mangum took
him on a dirt road high on one of his beloved mountains to overlook
the valley and lake, only to have Levitan exit briefly from the car to
comment, "If you've seen one mountain, you've seen them all."

In addition to his one semester per year seminar at George Washington, usually attended by part-time students already employed in the
agencies he frequented, Levitan established a continuing relationship
with Cornell University, both visiting the Ithaca campus frequently and
conducting regular seminars in his office for students in Cornell's
Semester in Washington program. He joined the faculty of a Harvard-
sponsored three-week seminar for European academics in Salzburg,
Austria. He made one pilgrimage to Israel, where his Hebrew
impressed all hearers. And when Mangum and his colleagues at the
University of Utah launched a weekend, external degree program held
in federal offices around the country to offer Human Resource Management master's degrees to employment and training program practitioners, Levitan taught in all of those along the eastern seaboard.
Whether in the congressional hearing room, around the conference
table, or in the classroom, he was, as he put it, "first and foremost a
writer of footnotes," but close behind it, a teacher.

National Commission on Employment
and Unemployment Statistics

After leaving the Area Redevelopment Administration (ARA), Levitan religiously refused any consulting assignments or research con-

tracts with federal agencies, avoiding even the appearance of accepting rewards from those he evaluated. However, he found great satisfaction in his one federal post after leaving ARA. Long-time friend and coauthor, Labor Secretary Ray Marshall prompted President Jimmy Carter to appoint Levitan in March 1978 as chairman of the National Commission on Employment and Unemployment Statistics. The assignment was to review the adequacy of the nation's labor force data, considering the mammoth changes the American economy had undergone since the data system had last undergone a similar review by a comparable committee headed by Berkeley's Robert Aaron Gordon during the 1960s. Supported by a coterie of special studies, the Commission's report, *Counting the Labor Force*, issued on Labor Day 1979 has guided over the intervening years a variety of significant changes in the ways in which the nation counts and tracks its workforce, with other recommendations still under debate as enumerated by participant Markley Roberts later in this volume.

The Last Liberal?

With the advent of the Reagan administration, the Washington, D.C. intellectual environment began to change as it had not under Nixon and Ford. Throughout the 1960-80 era, social policy had been essentially bipartisan, with activist Republicans differing from their Democratic colleagues only in degree, and conservative Democrats as numerous as their Republican counterparts and allied with them in a decided minority. The same was true of their staffs, whereas cabinet members of either party tended to be academic experts devoted to their disciplines more than political parties and generally like-minded. "Think Tanks" were predominately liberal with even the Nixon era somewhat right of center American Enterprise Institute not all that far away ideologically from the only slightly left of center Brookings Institution and Urban Institute. Civil servants were overwhelmingly advocates of the programs they administered. Enjoying playing the "crusty curmudgeon," Levitan was more likely to generate the arguments he enjoyed by criticizing programs he believed in, arguing for their improvement because hardly anyone argued for their elimination.

Levitan was a consummate classical liberal who truly believed that all people could rise to prosperity if given adequate opportunity, as contrasted with the American version of the colonial British "white man's burden" concept that "the poor are a different breed from us but it is our humanitarian duty to carry them." Part of his crusty curmudgeon act was to address women's groups as "you broads," but that was only for effect. He harbored no prejudice, but was a little disturbed at appearing too politically correct. However, his intellectual convictions would not allow him to depart far from the liberal conviction that a faulty institutional construct was primarily to blame for human misconduct. For instance, he was reluctant to join with Garth and Stephen Mangum in a monograph entitled *The Economics of Rectitude: Necessary but Not Sufficient* until there was added to the primary message that poverty could be overcome only if social deviancy was abandoned the corollary message that society could expect rectitude only if it restructured the reward system to assure that such conduct did in fact return the promised rewards, hence the subtitle. He did not want to be accused of blaming the victims, but once convinced, was forthright in preaching the message of right conduct.

As the political climate shifted during the 1980s, conservative think tanks such as the Heritage Foundation rose to prominence, and some former liberals migrated to neoconservatism, Levitan began to speak of himself as the "last liberal in Washington." That was not true, as his continued relationships demonstrated, but their ranks were certainly thinned, and the press seemed to believe it as they intensified their pursuit of him for quotes in defense of liberalism. However, liberal convictions did not narrow his range of affections, as note his close friendship with Charles Murray, whose *Losing Ground* blamed welfare programs for poverty and whose coauthored *Bell Curve* claimed evidence that the economically disadvantaged were characterized by intellectual deficiencies. He could argue vigorously without animosity and demanded of his friends only intellectual integrity and aggressive pursuit of their convictions.

The Home Front

The Levitans lived briefly at 318 Livingston Terrace in Southeast Washington and then settled in for a long stay at 1717 Harvard Street in the Northwest. Sar had given up driving during his Bronx youth after he wrecked a car while distracted by his own meditations. However, Brita drove for shopping, visits to friends and relatives, and sight-seeing.

Sar had cousins resident in nearby cities and others who came down from New York on business and kept in contact. There were also many friends of both from the earlier years and, for some years, they kept up a fairly active but quiet social life. However, as time passed, Brita became more reclusive. Gary's persistent illness, consequent to Huntington's Disease, was probably a cause, but his death in the late 1960s did not stop that trend. According to Sar's cousin, David Levitan, "Brita suffered from a disease which caused extreme dryness of the skin, and she got relief only from spending many hours daily in the bathtub." She was heard to say that she had no living relatives and no friends of her own who had emerged from other origins than Sar's work. Sar and Brita continued to take long walks together in the evenings, but went out less and less.

That reclusiveness had an economic payoff, however. Brita began playing the stock market vicariously and then in earnest. Sar's Ford Foundation-authorized salary had been set at the federal GS-18 level. He refused any honoraria which had federal origins as implying a possible conflict of interest. But an occasional honorarium from other sources, along with a minor amount of labor arbitration added to household income. That was more than adequate to their modest circumstances and tastes and allowed a surplus for saving and investment. Under Brita's care, the surplus income multiplied into a modest fortune, left by joint bequest to the George Washington University Home Care and Student Scholarship Programs, the City College Alumni Association, the Johns Hopkins Baltimore Huntington's Disease Project, the United Jewish Appeal of Greater Washington, the United Way of the Capitol Area, the Center on Budget and Policy Priorities, and the National Council on Employment Policy.

As Brita ceased driving and the Harvard Street neighborhood deteriorated, they moved closer in to the St. George Apartments at 21st and N, NW, just a few blocks from George Washington University and Sar's various offices over the years. There they were to spend the rest of their lives. Sar worked six days a week, keeping the Christian rather than the Jewish sabbath as a matter of convenience rather than belief. Evenings and Sundays both were almost always at home except for evening walks and occasional eating out in neighborhood restaurants.

Though Sar appeared delicate, his health was generally excellent, as his long hours and regular attendance at work attested. However, he was persistently plagued with a skin cancer problem which almost took his life in 1968. He remembered having had x-ray treatments for a skin condition when he was seven or eight years old, his hair falling out temporarily as a result. Then a lesion appeared on his scalp in 1956 which was diagnosed as cancer and more x-ray treatments followed over the next two years. Another occurrence in 1959 resulted in further x-ray treatments and a 1960 eruption was surgically excised and covered with a skin graft taken from his leg. A further recurrence in 1964 resulted in several excisions, closures and grafting with further excisions of lesions as well as electrodessication in 1966 and 1967. However, as little as possible was said about the condition, and even his closest friends now have to reconstruct this sequence from medical records.

An eruption in early 1968 was too serious and too extensive to keep hidden, however, and he was referred to the University of Wisconsin Medical Center where he was to spend the months of February through April of that year. The entire scalp was removed from the middle of his forehead back and from ear to ear. The skull was exposed and in two places penetrated to remove cancerous growth. Extensive grafting then resulted in the full flowing wig which he thereafter described as his "goldilocks." Released on 27 April 1968, he returned home, minimizing the experience and manifesting more pride in having been written up in a medical journal than in any of his own publications.

But that was a temporary interruption involving no permanent change in schedule or productivity. Medical records show frequent returns to Wisconsin over the next five years as protrusions of bone would penetrate the grafted scalp and have to be chiseled away. There is a gap in the medical record from 1973 to a final recorded visit for further chiseling in October 1978, but all of this was done with as much secrecy as possible. As age advanced, there were minor surrenders, though Sar continued to walk to work until the year before his death shortly before his 80th birthday. But as walking became difficult, the rigorous schedule did not change. There was merely more shuffle in the walk to lunch or to a taxi to be hurried around town to conferences or to GWU faculty meetings.

It was Brita's health that would first make a substantial difference. In the 1980s, Brita's eyesight began to fail. When she was no longer able to read comfortably, Sar arranged for books on tape from the Library of Congress and, through Metropolitan Washington Ear, for a radio device through which the daily newspapers and other matter were read to the blind. When she no longer felt comfortable out of the apartment, the walks and restaurant meals ceased. When she could no longer manage their portfolio, their accumulation was switched from stocks to bonds. When Brita could no longer see to do housework, Sar, now in his late seventies, dropped back to five days a week at the office and left promptly at five to shop and prepare the evening meal. No servants were hired, but the apartment manager and staff looked in on Brita during the day and were always on call.

The Final Chapter

But then cancer reappeared in 1993 at age 78, this time not in the head but in the prostate with the malignant cells spreading to other parts of the body. At first nothing was said to anyone, but by the late summer of 1993 the terminal nature had become apparent and it was necessary to start making plans for the end which might still be months away. Typically, there were five concerns: How was Brita to be cared for? How should existing projects be completed? What other projects could be undertaken and completed in the time remaining? What should be the future of the Center? What should be said to the Ford Foundation in fairness concerning the completion of the current grant which would end in mid-1994 and the desirability of beginning another round which inevitably someone else would have to complete?

There were no laments. There were jokes about Dr. Kervorkian, but in reality only stoic acceptance of the inevitable. Research assistants were recommended for other employment. A departing secretary was replaced by one knowing of her uncertain but short tenure. Wills were rewritten with old friends Seymour and Ethel Brandwein as administrators and charged to see to Brita's well-being thereafter. The Ford Foundation was informed and unspent funds returned. All studies underway were completed and published but one which was not far advanced. Others already planned with various coauthors but not begun were shelved. *The Displaced vs. The Disadvantaged: A Necessary Dichotomy?,* a May 1994 monograph coauthored by Stephen Mangum, turned out to be the last publication in a forty-five year stream of more than fifty books, over seventy shorter monographs, and literally hundreds of published articles and government reports.

When the daily trip to work became too painful, work was continued at home with the secretary going and coming with missives and manuscripts and coauthors telephoning or visiting for consultation. When, in May 1994, caring for himself became a greater burden than caring for Brita, his energy level became too depleted to get around, and a high level of pain-killer became necessary, Sar was off uncomplainingly to a hospice where staff affection was evident and visitors frequent. Those visits included a dignified ceremonious farewell visit from Secretary of Labor Robert Reich to celebrate long, faithful, but often critical service to that department and its assigned interests.

Then life ended quietly on 24 May 1994 with his wife of 47 years, to everyone's surprise, following after a brief illness on 25 July 1994. She had developed a bloodclot in her leg, was hospitalized for it to be neutralized, but just before being discharged simply collapsed and died, claimed by a clogged vascular system which her heart could no longer master. Her departure caused a memorialist to remark, "In life they were not separated, by death they are not divided."

In late May an invitation went out to a several hundred-name mailing list to whom Sar had regularly sent his publications:

> You are invited to join the colleagues of Sar A. Levitan in remembering the contributions, wit and wisdom which made him such a unique and durable institution shaping our nation's social policy. Sar died on May 24. He requested that there be no memorials and testimonials. He wanted to be remembered for his work. We will

be gathered together on Wednesday, June 8, 1994 from 3:00 to 5:00 p.m. at 2175 Rayburn House Office Building. Some of Sar's closest associates will help us recall the epochs of his long and distinguished career. Honoring his wishes, we will try to emphasize what Sar brought to us, rather than what we have lost.

Some 200 of Levitan's closest associates gathered on the day designated. A transcript of that proceeding seems an appropriate ending for this biographical essay, before turning to the papers prepared in his honor by a selected few of his scholar-friends.

Remembering Sar Levitan

Garth Mangum
University of Utah

Born in Lithuania in 1914, emigrating to the Bronx in 1930, educated at City College and Columbia, expected by his family to be the fifth or sixth generation Rabbi, preferring to study philosophy but asked by a family friend, "Who would ever hire a Jewish philosopher?", accepting second best by studying economics under some of the greats, including Eli Ginzberg, serving four years in the U.S. Army during the Second World War and finishing in the reserves afterward as a Lt. Colonel, completing a Ph.D. in Economics at Columbia in 1949—His Talmudic scholar father exclaiming, "In-Grade Wage Rate Progression in Peace and War? That's a dissertation?", serving on the staff of the Korean War Wage Stabilization Board, followed by several years as collective bargaining expert for the Congressional Legislative Reference Service, assigned to staff the McCarthy (Eugene, that is!) Special Committee on Unemployment in 1959, serving as Deputy Director of the Eisenhower Presidential Railroad Commission in 1960 and 1961, assisting Senator Paul Douglas in the design and passage of the Area Redevelopment Act during the same period, and thereafter enjoying 32 years of what he called the Ford Foundation's personal welfare program as evaluator, critic and promoter of social policies on behalf of the poor and downtrodden at the George Washington University Center for Social Policy Studies, Chairman of the National Commission on Employment and Unemployment Statistics, author of over

50 books and hundreds of articles (his bibliography goes on for 36 pages), constant testifier before Congressional Committees, confidante of Congressional staff, enlightener of journalists, teacher of many, husband of Brita and unselfish benefactor of everyone of us in this room and hundreds more—that is the unique human being we meet to memorialize this afternoon.

He opposed the notion of such a gathering, but he was wrong. We are not met here today for his sake but for our sakes—to draw lessons from his life and thereby to hope to make our lives better and our service more fullsome.

Realizing that everyone of you would like to speak in his memory and have choice Levitan anecdotes to impart, the committee of his office mates of 30 years duration have asked a few to represent us all. For no better reason than seniority, they have honored me by asking me to conduct this memorial service. In the following order we would like these people to reflect from their own personal experiences as well as representing different times and aspects of Sar's career: Ray Marshall, Gordon Berlin, Marion Pines, Jon Weintraub, Isaac Shapiro, Cliff Johnson, and Andy Sum.

Ray Marshall
LBJ School
University of Texas

Thank you Garth. I thought when I was contacted in Texas and learned of this event that I was sure that Sar would register his disapproval but that he would appreciate it just the same. Therefore, I thought it was a good thing to do and I'm glad that I got the chance to participate in it. It's hard to talk adequately about Sar because he had such a breadth of knowledge and understanding. The first word that comes to mind is scholar because he loved to study facts. He loved analysis and believed that if you are going to be in the policy world you needed to pay a lot of attention to gathering the facts and doing the analysis and that you needed to be broader than any particular discipline. That was one of the things that first attracted me to Sar. He let the problems define the method rather than the method define the problem. He made extremely important contributions to policy understanding in a broad range of areas. He believed in evaluations, learning by experience and experimentation. I think one of the important lessons that he tried to teach everyone was never assume that what you are doing will work automatically because if everything you tried to do worked it probably was not worth doing. You just experiment and learn as you go along. He thought that you learned just as much from your mistakes as by your successes. He said you rarely know why you succeed. It might just be luck—I think that he said that particularly in respect to me. You almost always know why you mess up and you know that you can learn a lot from that if you pay attention to it.

Another term that comes to mind is intellectual integrity. Sar always called it the way he saw it. He was not timid about speaking up even when he knew that everybody else in the room disagreed with him. I have seen him do that many times and I always respected that. After he came to his conclusions on the basis of his analysis he called it like he saw it.

The next word that comes to mind is that he was a democrat with both a large and a small D. He had a strong belief in democratic institutions, in the ability of informed opinion to get things done. He particularly believed in the ability of the federal government to do things, which caused him to be at odds increasingly with a lot of the so-called "New Democrats" who, as Sar once said, were always trying to beat the Republicans to their conclusions. He wouldn't have any of it.

He believed that there was a role for competition in politics as in other things and that the federal government could in fact do a great deal to improve the lives of people. And the reason he thought that is because it is true. He could see it in his own life as can most of us who have come down pretty much the same path that Sar came down. Think of all the things that the federal government did that we could never get the states to do. For all of those people who believe in states' rights and want to turn everything over to the states, Sar believed that there is a role for the states but it had to be under the guidance of federal policy. This was particularly true of those things that were important to the whole nation. Someone has called him the last of the New Deal Democrats. I am not sure of that. I think that there are still a lot of New Deal Democrats around if you mean by that those who believe the federal government can do a lot to improve the human condition, can look out for the interests of all of the people in the country, and especially the least advantaged who would not have been looked out for if it had not been for the federal government. Being a Democrat with faith in demo-cratic institutions was a strong part of his character.

Sar also was communicative. He probably was one of the best com-municators I have ever known. He communicated in all kinds of media. He wrote great volumes with great clarity. You never came away from any of his writings not knowing at least what he thought. He was also a good oral communicator. He was witty. He was a wordsmith. He had the best ability I've known of to name things, to give titles to things and also to capture a few words that said it so well that when you heard it you realized that was exactly the way it was.

Now I understand that his family wanted him to be a Rabbi, and in some ways he was a Rabbi. He was a teacher and realized that his syn-agogue was the world and therefore tried to communicate to improve the conditions of people in the United States, particularly workers and the people who needed the most help.

The last word that comes to my mind when I think of Sar is "friend." I don't think I ever spent an unpleasant moment in Sar Levitan's com-pany. I don't ever remember him saying anything unpleasant to me, even when he was taking me to task, usually for some sin of omission. He was never really after me for sins of commission but was always talking about things I ought to be doing that I didn't do and always try-ing in a friendly way. I always found it a lot of fun to be with him. He never gave up on me; that's the way he looked at it. I felt a little dis-tance from him as I suppose most of you did. But when he felt I needed some attention he gave me the attention. I always appreciated that. I'm going to miss him but I will always remember him. The fact that he communicated so well in writing means that he will always be with all of us. Thank you.

Gordon Berlin
Manpower Development Research Corporation

I have been asked to speak about Sar's relationship with the Ford Foundation. No institution or individual had a longer standing relation-ship with the Ford Foundation. That relationship spanned some three decades. It was extraordinary both for its longevity and its productivity. And also, I think, for the influence Sar had on the personal and professional lives of the individual Ford Foundation program officers who worked with him over those years. It was a period which saw the Foundation undergo several major changes in priorities, grant-making styles, and personnel. It was also a period in which the country underwent remarkable change—from the Great Society, the Civil Rights Movement, and the baby-boom to the New Federalism, the tax revolt, and the baby-bust. The country changed and the Foundation changed, but not Sar. His message always seemed timeless.

The Ford Foundation's first grant to Sar was at the forefront of an emerging interest in poverty and its alleviation. Victor Fuchs was the program officer responsible for making this first grant; it was to evaluate the Area Redevelopment Act. As many of you know, Sar worked for Senator Douglas on the drafting of the Area Redevelopment Act; yet the evaluation he completed was quite critical of the way the Act was implemented. That was the beginning of a trend for Sar in which he could be at the same time the strongest and most vociferous critic of social programs and their staunchest supporter. He took the implementers of the Area Redevelopment Act to task in a number of ways, expressing tremendous disappointment at the lost opportunity reflected in its early shortcomings, but also counseled keeping the faith and urging program managers to see that the program lived up to its promise. This was to be the central message of the many books that followed. "Keep the faith"—in government's ability to deliver on its promises, and in people's ability to use those programs to improve their condition.

After this first grant Victor Fuchs left the Foundation. Paul Ylvisaker was at the Foundation by then and just beginning the Grey Areas Program—the predecessor to what would become the community development and community organization movements and many of the Office of Economic Opportunity programs that comprised the Great Society. Because the Foundation wanted an independent view of these and other new social programs, Ylvisaker continued to provide support for Sar's evaluation work. After Ylvisaker moved on, the Foundation reorganized, creating the Office of National Affairs which was led by Mike Sviridoff. The new office focused on community development, and it continued to support Sar. As Mike said to me when I talked to him this morning, "Sar was a resource, another arm, that everybody at the Foundation drew upon in one form or another." Under Mike Sviridoff's leadership, such luminaries as Stan Brezenoff, Basil Whiting, and Bob Schrank, were, as Sar called it, his benefactors. Lou Winnick, Susan Berresford, and Bill Grinker all had dealings with Sar at some point during this period.

In the mid-80s, the Foundation's leadership changed. Frank Thomas and Susan Berresford began a restructuring of its programs and personnel. A new Urban Poverty program was formed under Bernie McDonald and then Bob Curvin's direction. The new program was designed to better integrate the Foundation's U.S. and developing country work. I joined the Foundation as this restructuring was getting underway. It was clear from the outset that Sar's work would be an integral part of the Foundation's new future.

I discovered my role in Sar's ongoing relationship with the Foundation at a going-away party for Bob Schrank. Sar approached me, introduced himself, and said with a twinkle in his eye, "I understand that you are my new benefactor." As I reflect upon the Foundation's and my subsequent personal relationship with Sar, I think he saw his mission as helping us to make a difference in the world and, at least in my case, keeping me from embarrassing myself. He did a reasonably good job of both. He worried with me about youth unemployment and deepening poverty, and read and commented on virtually everything that I sent him for review. He was a terrific editor.

Sar had an uncanny way of seeing the future. Every two years he had to write a proposal to the Foundation telling us what he would work on over the next two years. More than once we argued about the importance of something on the list. "No," I would say, "that is not going to be the next big policy concern." "Trust me," Sar would say. Time usually proved Sar right. Remarkably, Sar took this list seriously. If something else came along that Sar wanted to do, he would just add it to the list rather than drop a study he'd promised.

My most recent experience with Sar's prescience happened about two years ago when we were both writing about homelessness. Having recently worked in New York City government, I thought I had a somewhat unique perspective to bring to the problem. I asked Sar to review an article I was writing, he agreed, and mentioned that he had just finished up a piece on the same subject. Since Sar seldom left the six-square block area between his home and office, and at the time not a lot was published about the problem, I didn't anticipate much overlap between the two pieces. Two days later my article came back full of substantive and editorial suggestions, and attached was a copy of Sar's article. It was a first-rate piece of work, had covered much of the ground I had hoped to cover, and it was already published and thus much more timely than mine. That was Sar, always ready to read and edit anything I had written, always ready to give me advice and counsel, and already having written a definitive piece on the subject of the moment long before the rest of us.

I know, as all of you do, that Sar's helpfulness had very little to do with the fact that I was his benefactor. In fact, he gave that same kind of time and attention to virtually everyone who called him. He was a tremendous resource to reporters and many, many others.

Sar Levitan took a very strong personal interest in the people that he touched and worked with. Having met my future wife he would always ask me before I was married how my "pillow mate" was doing, and after my marriage, he continued to ask about her and to send us those funny little notes with a cartoon character complaining about being the last liberal. After my son was born, the first words from Sar in any conversation were to ask how my son was doing. He even asked about my family first when I visited him several weeks ago at the Hospice.

Sar worried about my career as well. When I left the Ford Foundation to join Ford alumnae Stan Brezenoff and Bill Grinker in New York City government, Sar and I continued to speak every Saturday morning. He worried incessantly about whether I would survive untarnished the political quagmire of that city's human resources department. And more recently, when the Clinton administration began its search for people, Sar urged repeatedly that I not try to get a job in Washington, arguing that the Clinton people would spend most of their time being constrained by the budget, prescient yet again.

For all of us who worked with him while we were with the Ford Foundation, Sar was a very special person. Throughout our post-Ford careers we stayed in touch with him, sought his advice and counsel, and leaned on him. Several years ago, having just left New York City government as first deputy mayor and before taking the job as president of the Port Authority of New York and New Jersey, Stan Brezenoff was helping the Commonwealth Fund rethink its agenda. He called Sar. Similarly, when Mike Sviridoff was completing an article on community development for the Public Interest last year, he asked Sar to review it, just as he relied on Sar when he was the head of the Foundation's National Affairs division and wanted Sar's advice in setting the division's agenda. And I know that Susan Berresford continued to call on Sar throughout her tenure as vice-president for Programs whenever the foundation was considering a change in direction.

In the month before his death, Sar called all of his former benefactor's to announce that he was going off of welfare!! He said now that the President wanted to "end welfare as we know it," he felt it was his responsibility to be the first one off of welfare, and so he had decided to stop accepting grants from the Foundation. I naively asked if that meant he might consider retiring, and doing something different, since he would no longer be able to mix work and welfare. "No," he said, "I have several pieces in various stages of completion, and I intend to try working without welfare. Isn't that what the president has in mind?"

He also spoke to me quite a bit about being Jewish. It had a special meaning for him, not so much in a religious sense, but in a secular sense. As Eli Ginzberg mentioned to me, when Sar was completing his doctoral dissertation in economics at Columbia, he had to be fluent in a foreign language, and convinced the school to let him use Hebrew. Everybody at Columbia was at a loss as to how to test whether or not Sar had the necessary competency. So Eli pressed his own father, a Talmudic scholar, into service. He spent an hour or two with Sar and reported he was as good as anyone he had ever spoken with in Hebrew. Howard Rosen, Sar's federal benefactor for many years tells a similar story: They went to Israel together and they were asked to say a few words to assembled manpower experts, Howard looked on dumbfounded when Sar stood up and gave a 30-minute speech in Hebrew.

In conclusion, I want to echo what Ray said, Sar had a tremendous amount of integrity and he was not afraid to be a critic. In that regard, he set a unique example because he did it without a lot of animosity. That is an unusual quality. I want to close in the way that Sar often concluded a meeting with me: "Keep the Faith," and in Hebrew, "LeChaim ZeleAvodah!"—to Life and to Work!

Marion Pines
Institute for Policy Studies
The Johns Hopkins University

In thinking about how to remember Sar today, I decided that the best way is to think back to some of his writings that influenced me the most. I'd like to share some of those quotes with you. As others have said, what we often remember about Sar is his rigorous mind. He had a way of cutting through the floss and getting right to the guts of an issue. In the most recent piece he wrote, coauthored with Steve Mangum, speaking of the current rhetoric about "one-stop shopping," Sar said, "What is most important to the concept of the one-stop shop is not the one stop, but what is on the counter at the shop." I remember when JTPA came in to replace CETA and all income supports for people who were in training were eliminated and we all were desperately trying to figure out what to do, Sar said, "That's simple. Let them eat training."

We all remember his absolute disdain for any kind of pomposity. I came across something last night that I want to share with you. He wrote a letter to the editor of the *Journal of Human Resources* at the University of Wisconsin: "As a contributor to the initial issue of your learned journal and as a cash subscriber ever since, I have watched with consternation your journal's progressive dedication to obscurity. When I reached the second article of the current issue, I decided enough was enough. A drop of 0.04363 percent of the paid circulation of the journal might not be statistically significant, but I wouldn't be surprised if other subscribers share my frustration with your propensity to confuse if not torture the English language. And then he went on to suggest that one of the favorite devices of those teaching Greek was to have the Greek on one side of the page and the English on the other. He suggested that the journal adopt that practice. He finished with the admonition, "If you ever decide to begin publishing in English again, please inform me that I might resubscribe."

Someone mentioned already his somewhat unorthodox approach to evaluation. He said, "The selection of priorities and the rejection of existing programs must remain largely a matter of value judgement and gut feeling, all models for computer-generated data notwithstanding." Well, obviously, that did not make him overpopular with the newest generation of evaluators who were much more orthodox in their approach. He was aware of that but he enjoyed irritating people who he thought took themselves and their pet methods too seriously.

In a letter that Sar wrote to Garth, he said, "I am making slow progress on the random assignment project. As I may have mentioned, when I told Taggart about my plans to embark on this project, he warned me I was taking on an 800 lb. gorilla. He was right. However, he assured me that I was not about to be nominated as the most popular evaluator in the business and therefore I had little to lose."

Despite his acknowledged ability to intimidate others, I remember his comment when someone said he had written eight books that year. I said, "Nonsense, it is impossible for anyone to write eight books in one year." He responded, "Its not difficult. You just change the chapter headings."

But the one time that I found Sar faced with a challenge beyond his reach was when he ran into an audit problem with a federal grant to the National Council for Employment Policy. He could solve any economic policy problem in the world but he was completely thrown by this $12,000 audit finding. He called me in absolute panic. I sent to him two people from my Baltimore City Prime Sponsor office who were magicians at making audit problems go away. I never knew how they did it but I never had an audit problem they couldn't handle. After they had handled Sar's problem, he wrote them a letter saying, "We mailed six boxes to the auditors as scheduled. Upon comparing your reply and our draft notes, the difference between professional communication and amateur reaction was only too clear. As an inveterate pencil pusher, I tried hard to find something to change in your draft but couldn't even find a misplaced comma. The record should show that the Baltimore Manpower Consortium came once more to the rescue of another employment and training organization." We were happy to have solved that less than major problem.

As much as he enjoyed the life of the mind, Sar was very, very committed to the practitioners in the field around the country. He was everybody's favorite speaker, everbody's favorite keynoter. He loved to take on the role of challenging them and pushing them onward to new thinking. He kept encouraging us to professionalize our activities. At his continued urging, we finally did about ten years ago and he honored the organization by becoming its first paid member. He was a practitioner of research but understood and appreciated the challenges faced by practitioners of service delivery.

Several have referred to the fact that Sar was kind of a storehouse of information. He was my own personal *Book of Knowledge*. If I ran too late in preparing a speech. I could always call Sar because I always figured that he had the information needed in his head or at his fingertips. He would say, "You can find that in the census tapes," but I would say, "I don't have to. You know it already." Mike Sviridoff told me of a time when he had a last minute call from the McNeil-Lehrer television show about 4:30 in the afternoon when they go on the air at six. He didn't want to embarrass himself, so he called Sar and asked what he had written on the subject. Sar immediately faxed him five pages of the most important pertinent data and made an expert of him. That was part of his role. Above all, as everyone has said, he was a warm, loving friend. I found something that Garth wrote him in 1990. It is very apropos today. Garth said to him, "It is time for you to do what should be a fascinating and meaningful life story. No one I know has a stronger and more consistent commitment to serving humanity. You represent a people, a tradition, a time, an ideology and a methodology which should be recorded and examined, as well as an individual unique story." Garth even suggested to him a title, "The Secular Rabbi: The Life and Times of Sar Levitan." You can imagine Sar's response: "The title is enticing, the invitation is flattering, but I doubt if anyone would be interested." And then he compared himself to Eli Ginzberg and said, "I suddenly realized that I had never advised even one president, much less nine, and therefore I concluded that an audience that might be interested in the life of Sar Levitan is nonexistent." That is one time that Sar was wrong.

Jon Weintraub
House Committee on Education and Labor

I've asked Isaac Shapiro to join me because we were involved in presenting Sar with the Secretary of Labor's Lifetime Achievement Award. There were some of us on the outside that pushed and some on the inside that pushed to get this done. It is appropriate having this memorial service in this room because Sar is really the intellect and the conscience of this committee. Although there are other pictures on the wall, Sar, like Carl Perkins, is a spirit which will always be in this room. His shadow will always be here. Sar, as Marion intimated, was really the adviser to many presidents through their staffs. His intellect drove policy for all of them. As he was presented with this lifetime achievement award, Secretary Reich just casually mentioned that, although labor secretaries come and go with each administration, Sar will always be the permanent labor secretary.

Isaac Shapiro
Office of the Secretary
U.S. Department of Labor

When Labor Secretary Reich said this to Sar, his immediate response was, "I accept." Here is what the award said: "In recognition of your numerous contributions to the Department of Labor over several decades, you have set the highest standards in your dedication to work, the American worker, and the fight against poverty. Your scholarship, wisdom, wit and kindness have inspired us all." Robert Reich, Secretary of Labor.

In response Sar had prepared the following:

> My scribblings over the years have aimed to combine right and rationality to improve social welfare. This award, from those who share this goal, is gratifying recognition of these labors. I would gladly trade it for an indexed increase in the minimum wage to reduce hardship, a network of community learning centers to skill our youth, or a few thousand public service jobs to move people from welfare to work. But since these are not on offer, I am honored to accept this award. If right and rationality continue to be recognized, these critical education, employment and earnings policies may eventually come to pass to realize this nation's "promise of greatness."

As you can see, Sar remained feisty to the very end and a guiding light to all of us.

Cliff Johnson
The Children's Defense Fund

I will always think of Sar as a teacher and mentor. I had worked here in the House for a member of the Education and Labor Committee for several years and thought it best that I leave and try to get a master's degree. Most of the graduate courses at GW were pretty uninteresting but it was very hard not to pay attention in Sar's courses. He had a way of challenging students that put us in two different categories: You were either brain dead or you were engaged. There was no way to be in the middle. Even with the most apathetic of students, he managed to draw out and challenge us. He pushed arguments to the point of absurdity so that we had to fight back.

Sar had that instinct to be engaged intellectually in the battle and to stimulate others to do the same. By the time I was in his course, I assume he had taught the course a million times before, but the material and the approach was always fresh. He brought to it to life and gave it energy that made it seem new.

I think Sar's first love was teaching. Had GW not had a mandatory retirement policy, I suspect Sar would have been teaching this past semester. (It is an indictment of retirement policies now mercifully expunged.) His commitment to teaching was a reminder to me of how much Sar really cared about people. There were very few personal effects in his office but there would be many plaques and photos from past or recent students such as the picture of a class from Cornell which he taught in his office as they studied in an external program in the nation's capital. There would be mementos thanking him for his wit and wisdom and guidance. It told me that it made an enormous difference to him that he was a teacher. It was in his way fulfilling his calling, even if not as a Rabbi. He fulfilled that in many other ways.

Barbara Dunn was telling me last night about a doctoral program that Sar was involved in for many years before I came to know him. He would take many of the brightest under his wing and work with them, afterward feeding them into government agencies, foundations and advocacy organizations in a way that enriched the human resources available to the social welfare community. I know that a lot of you in this room came up that ladder.

I think the luckiest ones, at least from my perspective, were those apprentices who actually got to work directly with and for Sar as research assistants. The numbers are not great—perhaps not more than a dozen or two over the years. If you saw his 30 or 40 books on the book shelf, you would see that most of them carry the name of one or more coauthors. Some appear more often than others depending upon their length of tenure. Yet there was an apprenticeship behind each of those books. There were tremendous opportunities for each of us who were able to work with Sar in that capacity, of rolling up our sleeves and working through an area of inquiry and being paid for the privilege.

I think that there was nothing that Sar loved more than to get a draft of a chapter from one of his apprentices, to read it and mark it up. He would be truly absorbed in the act of editing and commenting upon the text. He would tear it to shreds. When he was finished, you would come into his office, at first with trepidation and later with a sense of anticipation and excitement at the challenge that lay ahead. He would tell you all of the things that you had done wrong, all the ways in which you had missed the point. In the end you would have some wonderful battles with him, the chance to argue and fight and be part of that intellectual process leading to conclusion and recommendation.

Over time it was impossible not to recognize the caring and time Sar invested in that process. There was no way of thinking of it as just Sar's wanting to publish another book or finish another chapter or to get to the end of another work day. Rather, it was a deep and serious responsibility that he assumed to teach and nurture and contribute to the regeneration of young people who would think critically about things and take nothing for granted and who would care about those things which mattered most. Then in the end what was remarkable to me was that he was always ready to share the credit, whether you were a 24-year-old still wet behind the ears or whether you were further on in your career and widely published in your own right. While others in academia might be tempted to exploit young research assistants, it was never a matter of question with Sar. He was enormously generous in using his offices and his caring and nurturing ways as a wonderful path of career development.

When Sar received his award from the Department of Labor last month, I had the chance to tell him what an extraordinary impact he had on his students and research associates. I told him that I believe his greatest legacy lies not in the dozens of books he wrote over the years but in the countless students and young researchers who he taught to think critically, write clearly, and argue effectively. I reminded him that the seeds he planted would bear fruit for decades to come. And while he did not reply, I believe with all my heart that he understood what I was telling him and knew the importance of all of his good work as a teacher and mentor over the years.

I think for all of us he will be the teacher of our lifetime. The best we can do is to use that learning and instruction as he would have done for the betterment of mankind.

Andrew Sum
Center for Labor Market Studies
Northeastern University

The only thing worse than being second to last speaker is to be the last speaker. I will try to make my remarks relatively brief and resist the temptation to give a lecture. I was asked to comment on Sar's work of the last few years. I felt honored, having known Sar since he came to Northeastern University in the mid-1970s to give a series of lectures on human resource development. Then I had the opportunity to get professionally involved with him when he took over the chairmanship of the National Commission on Employment and Unemployment Statistics, and I had the opportunity to draft a few of the reports of the commission.

I want to share a rule of work in Sar's personal life and secondly a rule of work in Sar's professional writing and then conclude with fifteen seconds of our role in carrying on Sar's life work.

I think it is fair to say that his commitment to work as an element of his personal life was the essence of what he truly tried to share with us in his writings over the years. Reflecting back on Sar's writings, I took a look at Sar and Cliff's 1982 book, *Second Thoughts on Work*. There at the beginning of the book is this quote: "Life grants nothing to us mortals without hard work." Yet Sar's hard work was both a pleasure to him and a source of joy and being delighted in the work of others. He was known to say to Barbara and Bob that Labor Day was the day to honor labor by working. He said, "If the day is productive, reward the staff by letting them go home at 4:30." I have a feeling that as September 3rd of this year rolls around, I am going to open the mail and, sure enough, there is going to be one last publication from Sar dated Labor Day 1994.

Sar's professional work over the last three decades was devoted to three sets of issues: preparation for work, public policy to provide job opportunities to the unemployed and a guarantee of adequate pay to all of those who have the opportunity to obtain work. Again, in *Second Thoughts on Work*, Sar and Cliff noted, and I think it sums up much of Sar's work, "As we continue to rely upon work as the mainstay of our lives and our economy, we must also continue to search for vehicles by which we can offer that role and its many benefits to all of society's members."

If you look at Sar's work over the last few years, the monographs that he thought it was important for him to produce, this case about the need for jobs is made more evident than ever before. In *Spending to Save*, Sar persisted in making the case for a conscious public jobs strategy. As Sar used to say to me, "I told Thomas Jefferson, 'Tom, we need a public service jobs strategy.'" Sar also noted in his book on welfare reform the clear need that to succeed in the JOBS program we had to have a comprehensive job creation strategy for welfare recipients. Sar also recognized work's necessity if we were going to make a difference in the lives of young people. In his monograph, *You've Got To Learn To Earn*, Sar said that we've not only got to assure that there are jobs at the end of the line, but we've got to be sure that the young people have the education and training necessary to boost their earnings and allow them to achieve the American dream. And in his last monograph with Stephen Mangum, *Displaced vs. the Disadvantaged* on page 46, there's Sar again: "If we are going to do well for the disadvantaged and the displaced and guarantee them a place again in the American dream, we need an expanding economy to make that effective displaced worker policy a reality." And there again on that page is one last time Sar saying, "While also it will be helpful to have a standby public service jobs strategy."

I think one ought to read Sar's work as I've been told the great Rabbi said in the Torah, "One does not study to know but to learn." There is always much to be learned in reading Sar's monographs if for no other reason than to challenge your own perceptions and beliefs about what we have thought was good for American employment and training policy. Let's all start with that and add the belief that public policy is not only to promote job opportunities but to add adequate compensation. His monograph on *Working but Poor* for Johns Hopkins, his work on the minimum wage, his previous works on employment and earnings adequacy, his works on labor market hardship were all devoted to the goal of guaranteeing that earnings and income standards for all Americans in the workforce were at least sufficient to guarantee everyone an adequate standard of living.

I think all of us gathered here today can best honor Sar's lifelong work by continuing that search for those appropriate public policy vehicles to achieve the goals of full employment and earnings adequacy. Part of that search will require faith in the ability of government to do good. As Gordon Berlin said in Sar's obituary in the New York Times, and Ray Marshall noted here today, that message was essential to Sar's beliefs throughout his life: that while government could make blunders, it was in the power of government to do the good that we all wanted for ourselves. But we all note that by itself is not enough. We don't need logicians or philosophers to tell us that necessary does not imply sufficient. For James 2:20 tells us that "Wilt thou know, o vain man, that faith without works is dead." but later on James tells us "through works was faith made perfect."

Let us continue. It behooves us to go on to update Sar's work on *Working but Poor*. But let's all work for the day when that particular series can be abolished and look forward to the day when we can change that title to *Poor No More*. No greater legacy I believe can we leave behind in the memory of Sar Levitan.

Garth Mangum

We have a letter from Sar's last living professor, Eli Ginzberg, who could not be with us today:

> My friendship with Sar goes back to 1939 when he enrolled in my course at Columbia, "Economics and Group Behavior." He soon made all of us aware of his presence because his sharp comments revealed a broad and deep knowledge of events and people. Sar was enrolled in the PhD program in Economics and faced the

requirement to demonstrate competence in two foreign languages. Since he was still in the process of fully mastering English, he explored the possibility of substituting Hebrew for French as his second language. When the Chairman of the Economics Department, Roswell McCrea, asked my advice, I encouraged him to allow the substitution. McCrea then raised a second question. Who would examine Sar? I volunteered my father who reported after examining him that Sar had demonstrated good mastery of Hebrew.

Sar and I stayed in touch and early in World War II he sought my help. I had joined the Commanding General of the Army Service Forces with consulting responsibility for personnel. Sar had succeeded in becoming commissioned but was looking for a meaningful job, not easy for a lieutenant to find on his own. I got him an assignment in the Transportation Corps in the Port of New York where he spent the war carrying out a number of constructive assignments.

I recall a meeting at Princeton with Fred Harbison in the lead, the other participants being John Dunlop, Charlie Myers and myself, exploring what might be done to establish outside the federal government a point of strength in the development of manpower policy. I was pleased beyond words to hear my colleagues conclude forthwith that Sar was the logical, in fact the only person, to lead such an effort.

Two concluding observations that tie together Sar and my relations over a span of 55 years. Several years ago, out of the blue, Sar made a totally unexpected contribution to the Eisenhower Center with a brief note saying that it represented a small effort on his part to pay his indebtedness to Columbia. About a year following arrived another generous check, this time without a note.

Sar and I always exchanged books, but the one book that I authored that he really responded to was my autobiography—*The Eye of Illusion*. I heard from many, most recently Bob Taggart, that his last conversation with Sar was about my book. I believe I know what Sar especially liked about that book. Europe had helped to shape Sar and it had also helped to shape me via my father and my sophomore year at Heidelberg. Europe was our bond that tied us closely together,

Never had I a more dedicated and productive student. The world is better because Sar lived. All of us must be grateful for a friendship with a man such as Sar.

Garth Mangum

Now will you pardon me for adding a few of my own memories of Sar?

Though I had read his collective bargaining writings from the Legislative Reference Service while in graduate school, I first met Sar Levitan in his capacity as assistant director of the Presidential Railroad Commission in the summer of 1961. While teaching at the Brigham Young University, I had been brought on the Commission staff for that summer by John Dunlop. As a 35-year-old ex-coal miner-steel worker-construction worker with a newly-minted Harvard Ph.D., I was no impressive young scholar, but Sar chose to take me under his wing anyway. When Senator Joe Clark was seeking someone to staff a series of hearings which he wanted to call *The Nation's Manpower Revolution*, Sar recommended me and I came to Washington on a one- year leave that extended for seven rich years.

When after moving from the congressional assignment through two Johnson administration assignments, I yearned for return to a more academic setting, it was Sar who recommended me to the Ford Foundation such that he and I set up together at George Washington University the Center for Manpower Policy Studies, initially, he to evaluate the impact of the Economic Opportunity Act and me the Manpower Development and Training Act. When after three years together I opted to raise my kids in the Utah mountains and deserts, instead of justifiably rejecting me as the ungrateful pup I was, he continued to provide me with a Washington base and opportunities to work with him on various projects from that time to this.

That story could be repeated in differing detail by nearly everyone in this room.

Sar's philosophy and convictions can be no better rendered than by his own response to the presentation of the lifetime service award by Secretary of Labor Robert Reich that we have already heard.

Because he kept his private life so private, I suspect few of you are fully aware of his devotion and commitment to his wife, Brita. Six days a week he slaved at scribbling more footnotes, as he always put it. But nights and Sundays belonged wholeheartedly to "Snub" as he called her for reasons unknown to me. His snide rejection of "field work" was in part related to his reluctance to be away from her. When blindness reduced her mobility, he limited his workdays and work hours to assume homemaking responsibilities and cheer her darkening hours.

But one bit of field work my wife and I will never forget—the triumph of this refugee from Lithuanian pogroms as he stood with us at Berchtesgarten once in the 1970s and remembered the previous 40 years.

I happen to be convinced that at least a preponderance of evidence testifies to the continuance of life beyond the grave. I never could get Sar to express an opinion, though I pointed out that the odds were on that side. We believers will never know if we turn out to be wrong, whereas an unbeliever will never know if he turns out to be right. But one of my favorites from literature is Stephen Vincent Benet's story of Old Doc Mellhorn.

This old country doctor had died, passed through some pearly gates and sat down to confab with Hippocrates and other medical greats, but soon found it boring. He wandered around and stumbled upon a faint trail leading downhill and came to another realm. There he had a great time running a burn clinic and even setting a fractured tail. But soon, because of his ministrations, Hell wasn't hellish any more and the proprietor kicked him out. This time, however, he found himself in an intermediate setting where there were just enough colds and stomach aches to keep an old doctor busy without seriously inconveniencing his patients.

I could easily imagine Sar watching today's proceeding with facetious and self-deprecating asides. But I think it more likely that he would be too busy kibitzing the remaking of social policy in some not quite perfect afterlife.

But whatever he is doing will reflect a life of generosity to innumerable friends, devotion to a wife and commitment to a life's work of making the world a little bit better for the poor and downtrodden among his fellow human beings.

Bon voyage, Sar Levitan, a name he once told me meant "Prince of Levi"—and I sincerely believe it. Thank you all for being here to join in his memory. Let us all remember that the best way to remember Sar is to go about doing good.

With that, farewell until we meet again in good causes.

CHAPTER 3

Young Workers, Young Families, and Child Poverty

Andrew Sum
Clifford Johnson
Neal Fogg

The nation's young adults face a diverse array of labor market problems. For example, during March 1994, nearly 29 percent of the nation's 18-29-year-olds in the adjusted civilian labor force were either unemployed, employed part-time for economic reasons, wanted a job but were not actively looking for work, or worked but were unable to earn enough to exceed the poverty threshold for their household size. The incidence of these labor market problems ranged from a low of 9.6 percent among those young adults completing 17 or more years of schooling to a high of 54 percent for those young adults lacking a high school diploma or GED.

In response to an array of research studies documenting the difficulties experienced by young people with no formal education beyond high school as they seek to enter the labor market, the U.S. Congress in 1994 enacted modest new school-to-work legislation (School-to-Work Opportunities Act of 1994) designed to encourage states to experiment with comprehensive approaches for improving labor market prospects for some high school graduates. Two years earlier, a comprehensive set of amendments to the federal Job Training Partnership Act (JTPA) also was approved, at least in part to respond to continuing concerns about the labor market problems of young Americans. Yet current policy debates continue to overlook and fail to respond in any meaningful way to the most severe and persistent labor market problem facing the nation's young adults—the sharp declines in their real (inflation-adjusted) weekly and annual earnings over the past two decades. These deteriorating earnings represent the greatest single threat to their future economic prospects, their ability to marry and form stable families, and their capacity to financially support their children. These earnings declines in many cases have persisted for more than two decades and, despite renewed job growth among young adults in 1993 and 1994, continue unabated. Current congressional proposals to consolidate federal job training programs and provide block grant monies to states offer no serious response to these profoundly disturbing trends, and current major reductions in federal funding for those JTPA training programs focused on economically disadvantaged youth may even exacerbate them. Pending welfare reforms completely ignore the problems of families arising from inadequate earnings among young adults and are largely rooted in the baseless premise that personal lack of motivation to work is the central economic issue for parents now receiving welfare benefits.

It is essential that the nation refocus its energies on the crucial economic challenges that lie ahead: bolstering the real earnings potential of young workers, providing a stronger economic foundation for young families, and reducing the growing incidence of child poverty and the enormous associated costs that it imposes on American society. Without future interventions to assist young dropouts and high school graduates on a scale far surpassing those currently in place, the patterns of falling earnings for young workers and rising poverty among young parents and their children will continue to erode the very foundations of the nation and undermine our future productivity and prosperity for generations to come.

Declining Weekly and Annual Earnings of Young Workers

During the past two decades, the real weekly earnings of many subgroups of workers have been stagnant or declining. Young workers (those under 25) have been most adversely affected by these developments. The inflation-adjusted median weekly earnings of males younger than 25 who were employed full-time fell by 31 percent over the 1973-94 period, while those of young women dropped by 14 percent (table 1). [1]

While older males (ages 25 and over) also experienced real weekly earnings declines during this period, the relative size of their wage declines was considerably smaller than among young men. During the late 1960s, the median weekly earnings of full-time employed young men were equal to nearly three-fourths of those of older men, allowing them to assume critical adult responsibilities at a relatively early age, to marry, and to provide adequate economic support for their families and children. By 1994, however, the median weekly earnings of these full-time employed young men had fallen to only one-half the size of those of older men.

Table 1. Median Real Weekly Earnings of 16-24-Year-Olds Employed Full-Time, by Gender, Selected years, 1973 to 1994 (in Constant 1993 Dollars)

Year	Men	Women
1973	$417	$315
1979	$388	$299
1982	$349	$293
1989	$316	$286
1994	$286	$271
Percent change:		
1973-1979	–7%	–5%
1979-1989	–19%	–4%
1989-1994	–9%	–5%
1973-1994	–31%	–14%

SOURCE: U.S. Bureau of Labor Statistics, findings from the Current Population Survey, Nominal weekly earnings have been converted into their constant 1993 dollars by the authors using the CPI-U-X1 index for the entire country.

While employed young men under 25 years of age experienced the most severe deterioration in their real weekly earnings position over the past two decades, other young males also suffered a steep decline in their real weekly earnings. For example, among men in the 25-34 age group, median real weekly earnings (in constant 1993 dollars) plummeted by 21 percent between 1974 and 1994 while full-time employed males ages 35-44 incurred an 8 percent drop in their real weekly earnings (table 2).

Table 2. Trends in the Median Real Weekly Earnings of Full-Time Male Wage and Salary Workers, 1974 to 1994, by Age Group (in Constant 1993 CPI-UXI Dollars)

Age group	(A) 1974	(B) 1994	(C) Absolute change	(D) Percent change
All	$568	$509	$–59	–10.4
Under 25	407	286	–121	–29.8
25-34	590	467	–123	–20.9
35-44	654	601	–53	–8.1
45-54	630	654	+24	+3.8
55-64	571	88	+17	+3.0

SOURCES: Bradshaw and Stinson 1975; U.S. Department of Labor 1995a.
NOTE: Data for 1974 are for May of that year, while the 1994 data are annual averages. Prior to 1979, the weekly earnings data from the CPS were only collected once per year.

In contrast, older men (45-64) actually earned slightly higher real weekly earnings in 1994 than they did twenty years earlier. The age structure of male earnings has changed markedly over the past two decades, with the size of the age-related differentials in weekly earnings widening considerably. In the early 1970s, employed men in the 25-34 age group obtained median weekly earnings that were only 6 percent below those of males in the 45-54 age group; by 1994 the differential was nearly 30 percent.

The sharp decline in the real weekly earnings of young men has contributed in a substantial manner to the severe drop in the *real annual earnings* of young adult men, particularly those without any post-secondary schooling; i.e., the so-called "Forgotten Half" (Commission on Work, Family, and Citizenship 1988). Mean annual earnings of the nation's young male adults (ages 20-29) in constant 1993 dollars peaked in 1973 at just under $20,800. After falling moderately through the late 1970s, the mean annual earnings of young men declined considerably in the recessionary and highly inflationary environment of 1980-82, improved by nearly 11 percent during the boom years of the mid- to late-1980s, and then fell again sharply in the early 1990s. By 1993, the mean annual earnings of young adult males had declined to $15,175, a 27 percent reduction from their peak 1973 level (table 3). The magnitude of this real earnings decline clearly constitutes a prolonged "silent depression" (See Peterson 1994). The mean level of real annual earnings of young men in 1993 was actually below that of 1959. No other demographic group has been so adversely affected by the transformation of the U.S. wage structure.

Table 3. Mean Real Annual Earnings of 20-29-Year-Old Males, Selected Years, 1967-93 (Constant 1993 CPI-UX1 Dollars)

Years	Mean earnings
1967	$18,875
1973	20,796
1979	20,033
1982	16,486
1989	18.244
1993	15,175
Percent change 1967-73	+10.2
Percent change 1973-93	-27.0

NOTE: Earnings estimates in this table include those young men with no paid employment during the year.

These trends stand in sharp contrast to those evidenced in the 1960s and the early 1970s when the nation's young adult men experienced sustained gains in their real annual earnings. Between 1959 and 1973, the mean real annual earnings of 20-24-year-old and 25-29-year-old men increased by 24 percent and 35 percent, respectively. These earnings gains were enjoyed by both black and white men and by young men in each major educational attainment subgroup, including high school dropouts. The rising affluence of young men allowed them to marry at high rates before they reached their mid-20s and to increasingly support their families and children at income levels well above the poverty line. Real incomes of young families (head under 30 years of age) rose sharply over this period, and poverty rates of young families, especially those with dependent children, fell sharply.

The year 1973 was a watershed year for both the national economy and the nation's young adult men. The mean level of real annual earnings obtained by young men that year remains the post-World War II high, and, as noted above, their average annual earnings have declined considerably since then. A diverse array of economic, social, and technological forces has been at work to produce these steep declines in young men's annual earnings, particularly among men with no formal schooling beyond high school. The nation's tolerance of higher aggregate unemployment rates, a reduction in year-round, full-time job opportunities for young men, shifts in the industrial structure of employment away from higher paying jobs in goods-producing sectors, and reduced earnings prospects for young men within most major industries have contributed to the deterioration in their real earnings position over the past twenty years.

The degree of deterioration in the economic fortunes of young men has varied considerably by their formal schooling backgrounds, with those with limited schooling being most adversely affected. Among those young male adults (20-29) with some employment during the year, median real annual earnings declined from $21,124 in 1973 to $14,589 in 1993, a drop of nearly 31 percent. (table 4).

The relative size of these median earnings declines was quite substantial for males in each major race-ethnic group, including white, non-Hispanics. Those men with more limited schooling, however, were characterized by the largest absolute and relative earnings losses, with employed high school dropouts experiencing a 42 percent drop and high school graduates with no post-secondary schooling a 36 percent decline in their median annual earnings. College graduates were not isolated from these developments; however, the relative size of their annual earnings losses was considerably smaller. As widely noted in the labor and education literature, the relative earnings advantages of young, male four-year college graduates improved markedly over the past two decades; however, none of this gain was attributable to a rise in their real earnings position. During 1993, the median real annual earnings of employed male four-year college graduates ($24,000) was actually only several hundred dollars above that earned by high school graduates twenty years earlier. Young male high school *graduates* in

1993 had median annual earnings that were several thousand dollars *below* those earned by comparable age male high school *dropouts* two decades earlier. Young men needed several more years of formal schooling to maintain the earnings power that existed for them in the early 1970s. As Sar Levitan would have noted, "longer" not necessarily "higher" education became more essential for labor market success among young adults. Nearly all of our national initiatives to address this problem have been aimed at keeping young men in school for longer periods of time.

Table 4. Median Real Annual Earnings of Employed 20-29-Year-Old Civilian Males by Race/Ethnic Origin and Educational Attainment, 1973 and 1993 (in Constant 1993 CPI-UX1 Dollars)

Group	(A) 1973	(B) 1993	(C) Absolute change	(D) Percent change
All	$21,124	$14,589	–6,535	–30.9
White, non-Hispanic	$21,678	$15,500	–6,178	–28.5
Black, non-Hispanic	$15,919	$11,800	–4,119	–25.9
Hispanic	$18,295	$11,500	–6,795	–37.1
Student	$4,898	$4,900	+2	0.0
Less than 12 years	$17,352	$10,000	–7,352	–42.4
12 years	$23,573	$15,031	–8,542	–36.2
13-15 years	$21,430	$18,000	–3,430	–16.0
16 years	$27,069	$24,000	–3,069	–11.3
17 or more years	$31,227	$28,200	–3,027	–9.7

The deterioration in the real annual earnings position of young men has been exacerbated by increased difficulties in obtaining any paid employment. Since the late 1960s, there has been a secular rise in the share of young men (20-29 years old) who report no paid employment whatsoever during the year. During 1967, only 4 percent of young men, including college students, reported no paid employment. By the end of the 1970s (a cyclical peak year), this ratio had risen to 6.5 percent. During the deep recession of 1981-82, the share of young men with no paid employment rose above 10 percent, then fell throughout the remainder of the 1980s as the economy generated a substantial number of net new jobs, and aggregate unemployment rates declined steadily. During the slow growth years of the 1990s, however, young men experienced greater difficulties in finding employment, and the share with no reported earnings rose above 10 percent in 1993, nearly double the rate prevailing in 1973.

The rise in the nonemployment rate of young adult men between 1973 and 1993 occurred in each major race-ethnic and educational attainment subgroup. This problem, however, became most intense among young black men and among those males lacking a high school diploma or GED certificate. During 1993, nearly two of every nine young Black men and one of every six high school dropouts reported no paid employment whatsoever. Given the importance of cumulative work experience in influencing earnings in later adult years, these findings do not bode well for their future labor market prospects. Work experience is both a source of annual earnings and an investment in one's human capital.

The rise in the share of young men with no paid employment during the year has been accompanied by a declining share of young men reporting full-time, year-round employment; i.e., 50 or more weeks of paid employment for an average of 35 or more hours per week. The fraction of young adult men employed year round, full time fell from 57 percent in 1973 to 52 percent in 1993. The decline was particularly steep among young black men (from 52 to 40 percent) and among both high school dropouts and high school graduates with no post-secondary schooling. Males with one to four years of college actually improved their ability to obtain year-round, full-time jobs over this time period..

The severe deterioration in the real annual earnings position of young men has reduced their ability to form independent households and to marry. Over the past twenty years, the fraction of 20-29-year-old men who remain living at home with their parents or other family relatives has increased from 32 percent to 43 percent, and the marriage rate of young men—those married and living with their spouses—has declined considerably from 58 percent in early 1974 to under 34 percent in 1993. These social trends have been driven in part by the relative decline in the earnings of young males.

One of the more widely used measures of the adequacy of workers' earnings is their ability to earn enough to lift a family of four above the poverty line. In 1993, the average weighted poverty threshold for a four-person family was $14,763. Findings in table 4 reveal that the fraction of young civilian males who were able to achieve this minimum earnings threshold in 1993 was slightly under 45 percent, representing a substantial drop from the 63 percent share who were able to do so in 1973. (table 5). Again, the declines in this minimum earnings adequacy measure were quite large among whites, blacks, and Hispanics. During 1993, only one-third of young black and Hispanic males had succeeded in obtaining an annual earnings level above the four-person poverty line.

Table 5. Percent of 20-29-Year-Old Civilian Males with Annual Earnings above the Four-Person Poverty Line, by Race/Ethnic Origin and Educational Attainment, 1973 and 1993

| | (A) | (B) | (C) Absolute |
Group	1973	1993	change
All	62.6	44.7	–17.9
White, non-Hispanic	64.9	49.7	–15.3
Black, non-Hispanic	49.2	32.9	–16.3
Hispanic	57.2	32.5	–24.7
Student	10.0	11.1	1.1
Less than 12 years	55.7	24.9	–30.8
12 years	75.1	50.4	–24.7
13-15 years	65.4	56.3	–9.1
16 years	76.7	68.6	–8.1
17 or more years	77.5	75.2	–2.3

All educational attainment subgroups with the exception of college students experienced a decline in their ability to obtain an annual earnings level above the four-person poverty line between 1973 and 1993.

Again, the declines in minimum earnings adequacy were considerably larger among those young men who had completed twelve or fewer years of schooling. The steep deterioration in the earnings capacity of young men with no post-secondary schooling has contributed in a substantive way to the decline in their marriage rates. Using a form of shift share analysis, we have estimated that the shifts in the distribution of dropouts and high school graduates across real earnings categories between 1973 and 1993 can account for 30 to 40 percent of the decline in their marriage rates over this time period. Unfortunately, the drop in their marriage rates was not accompanied by an equally large decline in their parenting rates; thus, a rapidly growing fraction of young families with dependent children now consist of single-mother and single-father families, whose poverty rates are considerably above those of married-couple families.

While the mean and median real annual earnings of young men were declining markedly over the past two decades, the earnings distribution for employed young men has become substantially more unequal (table 6). The share of total earnings from wages, salaries, and self-employment income received by employed men in the top quintile (fifth) of the earnings distribution has risen from 39.7 percent in 1973 to 43.5 percent in 1993, a relative increase of 10 percent. The top decile (tenth) alone increased their share of total earnings from 21 percent to 27 percent. Thus, all of the gain in the top quintile's share accrued to those earners in the top half of this quintile.

Table 6. Earnings Shares of Employed 20-29-Year-Old Civilian Males by Quintile of the Earnings Distribution, 1973 and 1993 (in percent)

Quintile	(A) 1973	(B) 1993	(C) Absolute change	(D) Percent change
Bottom	3.6	2.9	−0.7	−19
Second lowest	11.8	9.9	−1.9	−16
Middle	16.8	17.0	0.2	1
Second highest	28.1	26.7	−1.4	−5
Highest	39.7	43.5	3.8	10

This growing earnings inequality among young men reflects sharp growth in the size of the earnings differentials between the best-educated males and their less-educated counterparts. Formal education is sorting the winners and losers in U.S. labor markets more strongly than before. However, even within most educational attainment subgroups, earnings inequality also widened; this was particularly true for high school dropouts and for those high school graduates lacking any post-secondary schooling, but was not true of those completing four or more years of college.

The steep annual earnings declines of young men over the past two decades have been accompanied by fairly sizable reductions in their access to key employee benefits, including health insurance coverage and pension coverage.[2] Young adult males (20-29) are the most poorly insured age/gender group in the United States, and their health insurance coverage has declined over time (table 7)

Table 7. Percent of 20-29-Year-Old Civilian Males with Some Form of Health Insurance and Employer-Financed Health Insurance by Race/Ethnic Origin and Educational Attainment, 1979 and 1993

	(A)	(B)	(C) Absolute change	(D) Percent change
Any Health Insurance	**1979**	**1993**		
All	79.4%	66.7%	−12.7	−16
White, non-Hispanic	82.0%	73.4%	−8.7	−11
Black, non-Hispanic	68.4%	58.1%	−10.4	−15
Hispanic	68.0%	43.1%	−24.9	−37
Other, non-Hispanic	67.7%	64.3%	−3.4	−5
Student	66.5%	74.2%	7.7	12
Less than 12 years	69.6%	42.4%	−27.2	−39
12 years	82.0%	64.3%	−17.7	−22
13-15 years	81.2%	70.1%	−11.0	−14
16 years	89.2%	81.7%	−7.5	−8
17 or more years	92.6%	91.4%	−1.2	−1
Employer-financed health insurance				
All	56.1	38.6	−17.5	−31%

During 1979, just under 80 percent of the nation's young adult men (ages 20-29) were covered by some form of health insurance coverage at work, at school, through the plan of their spouse or another family member, through a self-purchased plan, or through Medicaid. By 1993, their incidence of health insurance coverage of any type had declined to 67 percent. These declines in coverage occurred among young men in every major race/ethnic group and in all educational attainment subgroups. The relative and absolute size of these declines were most severe among Hispanics, high school dropouts, and high school graduates lacking any post-secondary schooling. During 1993, health insurance coverage rates for young adult men ranged from lows of 42 percent for those lacking a high school diploma to a high of 91 percent for those men having completed one or more years of college beyond the bachelor's degree.

Expectations that young adults will generally enjoy relatively good health have diminished concern for this phenomenon. During 1992, however, one of every six young men (20-29) who reported no employment during the year cited "illness or disability" reasons for not working.[3] Among high school dropouts and graduates with no post-secondary schooling, nearly 30 percent cited health-related reasons for their inability to secure any employment during that year. Substantial growth in the SSI disability caseloads among young adults also provides evidence of growing health-related labor market problems (including substance abuse) that do not bode well for the future labor force participation of such men.

The same trends mark access to pensions which has also plummeted for young men since the late 1970s. During 1979, only 37 percent of young men (20-29) were covered by a pension plan at their work site; however, by 1993, their pension coverage rate had dropped to 23 percent. With the exception of students, pension plan coverage has fallen for males in each educational attainment subgroup, with high school dropouts and those completing only twelve years of school experiencing the most severe declines in coverage. During 1993, pension plan coverage rates ranged from 9 percent for high school dropouts to a high of 43 percent for males completing one or more years of schooling beyond the bachelor's degree. In a recent address to the nation's newspaper writers, President Clinton commented on the existence of a growing economic divide in the United States and claimed that formal education was its "fault line." This finding appears to be particularly true of the widening economic inequalities among the nation's young men in the mid-1990s.

The Influence of the Changing Industrial Structure of Jobs

A number of potential explanations of the declines in the average earnings of young men have been advanced by labor market analysts and sociologists (see Johnson and Sum 1987; Kasarda 1985; Sum and Fogg 1991). Most supply-side explanations (with the exception of increased immigration) have little validity, particularly in explaining earnings declines during the past decade, since the absolute number of young male adults has been declining, the formal educational attainment of young men has improved, and a higher fraction of 20-29-year-olds in recent years were in their mid- to late-20s relative to the situation in 1973. Slightly higher mean ages should imply a greater number of years of potential work experience and higher expected earnings.

Among the demand-side explanations for the declining annual earnings of young men has been the shift in the industrial structure of job opportunities, especially the loss of jobs in key goods-producing industries and the increased movement of young men into the retail trade and selected private service industries (business services, personal and entertainment services) with their attendant lower wage levels. The reduction in the relative share of job opportunities for young men in key manufacturing, mining, transportation, communications, and utilities industries—combined with important changes in the occupational staffing patterns of these industries and hiring policies of employers—have had the effect of decreasing the number of skilled and semiskilled blue collar jobs for young men, especially those with no post-secondary schooling.

Comparisons of the industrial structure of the jobs held by employed young men in 1973 and 1993 clearly reveal a shift in employment away from most goods-producing industries (especially durable manufacturing) and the relatively high-wage transportation, utilities, and wholesale trade sectors toward retail trade and the nonprofessional service industries (table 8). In 1973, nearly 30 percent of employed young males held jobs in the nation's manufacturing industries; however, by 1993, their share of jobs in this sector had declined to 19 percent, with major losses occurring in the more heavily unionized durable goods-manufacturing industries (primary metals, fabricated metals, automobile production). Employment shares also declined in mining, construction, transportation, public utilities, and wholesale trade. Retail trade and nonprofessional service industries became major employers of young men, with their combined share rising from 22 percent in 1973 to just under 38 percent in 1993. Retail trade industries became the dominant employer of young men by 1993, with eating and drinking establishments and convenience stores absorbing a substantial number of young men within this sector.

Table 8. Distribution of Employed 20-29-Year-Old Civilian Males by Major Industry, 1973 and 1993

Major industry group	(A) 1973	(B) 1993	(C) Absolute change
Farming, forestry, fishing, mining	4.8%	4.9%	0.1
Construction	11.9%	10.2%	−1.7
Durable manufacturing	19.1%	10.9%	−8.1
Nondurable manufacturing	10.1%	7.7%	−2.4
Transportation, communication, & utilities	7.7%	6.6%	−1.1
Wholesale trade	4.8%	4.1%	−0.8
Retail trade	15.1%	23.5%	8.5
Finance, insurance, real estate	3.8%	3.7%	-0.1
Professional services	10.6%	11.2%	0.6
Other services	7.2%	14.0%	6.8
Public administration	4.8%	3.1%	−1.7

Given the prevailing interindustry wage structure in 1973, these sectoral employment shifts by themselves would have been expected to generate modest earnings declines for young men over the past two decades. During 1973, the mean annual earnings of employed men in durable manufacturing industries were 9 percent above the average for all employed young men, and those employed in transportation/communications and wholesale trade earned annual wages 14 to 16 percent above the average (table 9).

Table 9. Mean Real Annual Earnings of Employed 20-29-Year-Old Civilian Males, by Major Industry Group, 1973 and 1993

Major industry group	(A) 1973	(B) 1993	(C) Absolute change	(D) Relative change
Farming, forestry, fishing, mining	$16,808	$12,642	–4,165	–25%
Construction	$21,800	$17,231	–4,569	–21%
Durable manufacturing	$24,022	$19,925	–4,097	–17%
Nondurable manufacturing	$22,713	$19,667	–3,045	–13%
Transportation, communication, & utilities	$25,423	$20,898	–4,525	–18%
Wholesale trade	$24,961	$19,237	–5,725	–23%
Retail trade	$18,896	$12,690	–6,206	–33%
Finance, insurance, real estate	$26,105	$25,361	–743	–3%
Professional services	$20,330	$17,158	–3,173	–16%
Other services	$17,405	$14,541	–2,864	–16%
Public administration	$26,330	$25,925	–405	–2%

Retail trade and other service industries, which rapidly expanded their shares of employed men, were characterized by mean annual earnings levels 14 to 21 percent below the average in 1973. Thus, the observed interindustry employment shifts would have been expected to exert some downward pressure on young men's earnings in the absence of sustained productivity gains in these sectors.

A careful review of the annual earnings data by major industry for 1973 and 1993 reveals that young men also experienced substantial earnings declines within most of these eleven industrial sectors. Excluding the finance/insurance and public administration sectors, which together employed only 7 percent of young males in 1993, the estimated relative sizes of these annual earnings declines ranged from 13 percent in nondurable manufacturing to 33 percent in retail trade.

A modified form of shift-share analysis can be used to illustrate the contribution of each of the above two factors (interindustry shifts in employment *and* declining real earnings within industries) to the observed decline in the mean annual earnings of employed young men between 1973 and 1993. If the interindustry distribution of jobs in 1993 had been identical to that of 1973 but real earnings within each major sector remained at their 1993 levels, then the mean annual earnings of young men during that year would have been $17,971 rather than the $16,916 actually observed in 1993. The interindustry shifts in employment would have been expected to reduce real 1993 annual earnings by $1,055, or only 21 percent of the actual observed decline. The overwhelming share (82 percent) of the earnings decline of young adult men was attributable to steep earnings reductions within most industrial sectors.

Earnings declines within sectors are due in part to shifts in employment toward industries in lower-paying segments of each sector (e.g., the greater movement away from employment in steel, metals manufacturing, machinery, and auto-related industries in the durable manufacturing sector and the shift toward eating and drinking establishments within retail trade). In 1973, the number of 20-29-year-old men employed in metals, machinery, and auto-related manufacturing industries was 1.92 million, nearly six times as many as were employed in eating and drinking establishments. By 1993, there were nearly twice as many men in eating and drinking firms (1.36 million) as in all of the above manufacturing industries. Part of the earnings decline, however, is due to the fact that many employers were able to reduce entry-level wages for jobs occupied by young men, especially those outside of the traditional college labor market.

Within certain key segments of the retail trade sector, such as eating and drinking establishments, food stores, grocery stores, and variety stores, the failure of real wages to rise is attributable to the decline in labor productivity in these industries over the 1973-92 period (see U.S. Department of Labor 1995c). The sizable earnings declines for young men within manufacturing, however, cannot be explained by productivity factors. Output per hour of labor in the nation's manufacturing industries is estimated to have increased by more than 40 percent between 1979 and 1993.[4] These large productivity gains, however, were not shared by most manufacturing workers, especially blue-collar production workers whose real hourly earnings actually declined over this period (see Sum and Goicoechea 1991). Productivity gains, thus, seem to be necessary but not sufficient for boosting the real earnings of young males in the current U.S. economy.

Training Experiences of Young Adults

The sizes of the annual earnings differences between male college and high school graduates and between high school graduates and dropouts tend to widen considerably as they move through their adult years. Among the possible explanations for the increasing size of the gaps between the age-earnings profiles of workers by years of formal schooling are the impacts of greater training investments (both formal and informal and both on-the-job and off-site) in better-educated workers. A number of recent longitudinal and cross-sectional studies of the training experiences of young adults reveal that the likelihood of young workers receiving training from their employers tends to vary significantly by both their years of education and their literacy proficiencies (see Veum 1993).

Findings of the January 1991 CPS survey on the training experiences of U.S. workers can be used to provide insights on this set of issues. The survey captured information on the receipt of training by employed workers (16+) since they were hired for their current job. Findings for employed young adults (20-29, both sexes combined) reveal that nearly three of every eight had received some training to improve their skills since being hired (table 10). However, the incidence of their receipt of such training varied widely by years of schooling completed, ranging from a low of 18 percent for those young adults lacking a high school diploma to a high of 53 percent for those completing 16 or more years of schooling. The personal economic payoffs from training to improve skills in the form of higher weekly earnings to dropouts and high school graduates appeared to be quite sizable at the time of the survey (see Eck 1993).

Table 10. Training Experiences of Employed 20-29 -Year-Olds, (Men and Women) by Educational Attainment: U.S., 1991 (N = 21.2 Million)

Training status	(A) All	(B) Less than 12 years	(C) 12 years	(D) 13-15 years	(E) 16 or more years
Received some training to improve skills since being hired	36.6	17.9	30.2	40.2	52.9
Percent of training in a formal company training program	36.7	25.4	31.7	35.4	45.4
Percent of training in informal on- the-job training	42.0	62.1	48.6	44.1	29.3
Received some training to improve skills in a formal company program	13.4	4.5	9.6	14.2	24.0

SOURCE: January 1991 CPS survey, Job Training Supplement, tabulations by Center for Labor Market Studies, Northeastern University.

Among those young adults obtaining some training to upgrade their skills, the types of training received also varied markedly by years of schooling completed. Four-year college graduates were much more likely than their less-educated counterparts to obtain formal training from their employers, while school dropouts and high school graduates were more likely to receive informal on-the-job training. When the receipt of any type of training and the incidence of formal training are taken jointly into consideration, the gaps in formal training among schooling groups widen considerably. Fewer than 5 percent of young high school dropouts had received any formal training from their employers since starting their current jobs versus 10 percent of high school graduates and 24 percent of four-year college graduates. Formal company training has been found to have the most consistent and largest economic payoffs to workers while informal on-the-job training has much more moderate and less-persistent earnings effects (see Lynch 1994). The training investments of the nation's employers, thus, likely have a considerable influence on the expected lifetime earnings of workers and contribute in an important way to the rising earnings differentials between the best- and least-educated workers in American society.

Trends in the Economic Well-Being of Young Families and Their Children

The state of affluence among families in the United States has often been represented by the real income level of the average American family, and the median income is most often used to portray the average. Following a more than doubling in its real value between 1949 and 1973, the median real income of U.S. families has been basically stagnant over the past two decades. While real family incomes continue to rise during periods of sustained economic growth and fall during recessions, the long-term secular trend over the past two decades has yielded just a 3 percent rise. Given the steep declines in the real earnings of many young male adults and the continued growth in the share of single-parent families among young families, one would expect that young families (those headed by a person under 30 years of age) would have faced greater difficulties than their older counterparts in maintaining their real incomes over the past twenty years. Such unfortunately was clearly the case. Between 1973 and 1992, the median real income of the nation's young families declined by 20 percent, while families with a householder between 30 and 64 years of age experienced a moderate increase (4 percent) in their living standard over this time period. The nation's elderly families (those with a householder 65 and over) fared the best over the past twenty years, experiencing a 34 percent rate of growth in their median income at a time when their numbers were rising rapidly.

Families with one or more own children (under 18 years of age) present in the home have experienced real income losses over the past two decades, while families without children boosted their median real incomes by just under 14 percent. These differences were particularly pronounced among the nation's young families. Young families with one or more own children in the home were characterized by a one-third drop in their median real income, while young families without children boosted their real income by 4 percent over the 1973-92 period. By 1992, the median income of young families without children ($35,000) was nearly twice as high as that of families with children. The latter group of young families contained a growing share of single-parent families (including a growing number of single-father families) and were more likely than childless families to be headed by young adults with no post-secondary schooling. Their deteriorating economic position was thus influenced by a combination of demographic forces and the changing structure of earnings for young adults with more limited formal schooling.

Trends in the real income position of the nation's young families varied widely by type of family and the educational attainment of the householder. Young married couple families came closest to maintaining their purchasing power over the 1973-92 period; however, married couple families with children fared considerably worse than their counterparts who remained childless (−10 percent versus +5 percent). By having the wife participate more frequently and intensively in the labor market and by postponing childbearing, young, childless married couple families were able to moderately improve their real income position over the past few decades. Young male- and female-headed families with no spouse present incurred substantial declines (−21 percent and −24 percent) in their median real incomes over the same time period. The absence of a second earner to cushion the income declines from the reduced earnings power of the head was largely responsible for this set of findings. By 1992, young female-headed families had a median income of less than $8,000, only one-fourth the size of the median income of young married couple families. The frequent absence of any child support income for young single-parent families kept their incomes quite low. Fewer than one of six single never-married mothers under the age of 25 reported to have received any child support income during 1992.

Changes in the economic fate of young families have been strongly associated with the educational attainment of the householder. Young families headed by an individual lacking a high school diploma experienced a 47 percent decline in their median real incomes over the past two decades, while those headed by a high school graduate fared only marginally better (−37 percent). In sharp contrast, those young families headed by a four-year college graduate improved their real income position by 14 percent, a result entirely due to the increased annual earnings of the wives in such families.

Given the steep decline in the average real incomes of young families and growing income inequality among such families, one would expect poverty problems to have intensified, particularly among those young families with children. Progress in reducing overall family poverty problems on a sustained basis came to an end in 1973. The poverty rate for all families in the United States was 11.7 percent in 1992, three full percentage points or one-third higher than in 1973. All of the rise in the overall family poverty rate was attributable to families with children. During 1992, slightly more than 17 percent of all such families were poor, a near two-thirds rise from their poverty rate of 1973. Young families with children experienced the largest absolute and relative rise in poverty, with their poverty rate more than doubling to 35 percent by 1992. All of the important gains achieved in reducing poverty problems among the nation's young families with children between 1959 and 1973 were completely eliminated by 1992.

The nation's children have been most profoundly affected by these family income and poverty developments. Between 1973 and 1992, the poverty rate among all children (under 18) living in families rose from 13 percent to just under 21 percent, substantially surpassing the poverty rate of adults. Children had become the most poverty prone group in American society. Children residing in young primary families were most severely impacted by these developments, with the poverty rate of these children more than doubling over the past two decades. By 1992, slightly more than 42 percent of the children in the nation's young families were poor.

Poverty rates among children in young families rose in each family subgroup, including married couple families as well as single-parent families and among whites as well as among Asians, blacks, and Hispanics. In fact, poverty rates among children in young married couple families rose more rapidly in relative terms, nearly tripling over this time period, and the poverty rate among white, non-Hispanic children more than doubled, rising to nearly 30 percent by 1992. Despite their lower relative increases in poverty rates over this period, children in young black and Hispanic families remained highly poverty prone in 1992. During that year, seven of every ten black children and a slight majority of Hispanic children (52 percent) in young families were living in poverty conditions. Given the adverse influence of poverty living conditions on many aspects of child development, these trends are likely to have severe adverse consequences for the nation's economic and social future.

The Growth of Young Subfamilies

All of the above analyses of the real incomes and poverty status of young families have been based on the experiences of primary families, i.e., those young families that occupy their own separate living quarters. Over the past two decades, however, there has been a growing number of young families with children who either remain in the home of their parents or other relatives (related subfamilies) or share the household living quarters of others to whom they are not related (unrelated subfamilies). Since the early 1980s, the U.S. Census Bureau has made a more concerted effort to explicitly identify the number of such subfamilies in the CPS household survey. The number of such subfamilies headed by a person under 30 years of age is quite considerable (nearly 1.9 million in March 1994), and nearly 90 percent of these young subfamilies have one or more own children under 18 living with them.

Between 1983 and 1993, the estimated number of young subfamilies with children increased from 1.54 million to 1.69 million while the number of primary young families with children was actually declining as a consequence of a reduced number of young adults and declining marriage rates. During 1983, these young subfamilies with dependent children accounted for just under 19 percent of the total number of young primary families and subfamilies with a child. By 1993, however, these young subfamilies, most of whom are headed by a single parent, accounted for nearly 22 percent of all young families and subfamilies with children.

Given the high fraction of young related subfamilies that consist of single-parent families and the limited schooling and work experience of the subfamily householders, many of these subfamilies with children have very low incomes and would be classified as poor if they did not live with their parents or other relatives with higher money incomes. While the poverty status of unrelated subfamilies is determined solely on the money income of the subfamily, the poverty status of these related subfamilies and their children is based on the combined money income of all related members of the family household. During March 1993, there were 2.33 million children living in young subfamilies. Using existing Census Bureau procedures for classifying their poverty status, somewhat more than 845,000 of these children, or 36 percent, were residing in poor families. If the poverty status of these children had been based solely on the money incomes of the subfamilies to which they belonged, then 1.67 million or 72 percent of them would have been classified as poor. Combining the findings for children in young primary families with those in all young subfamilies, nearly *48 percent* of all children in the nation's young families and subfamilies would have been classified as poor in early 1993.

Children raised in poor families face a number of critical developmental problems, including malnutrition, poor health care, limited cognitive skills, inadequate housing, and more limited exposure to high-quality preschool educational services, that often have long-term consequences for their educational attainment, intellectual development, parenting behavior, and criminal justice experiences.[5] Given the increasing importance of human capital investments for the labor market success of adult workers and the economic growth of the nation, the existence of these extraordinarily high rates of child poverty among young families and subfamilies does not bode well for the nation's social or economic future.

Policy Options for Strengthening Young Worker Earnings and Family Incomes

The deterioration in the economic fortunes of many young workers and families over the past two decades has been quite severe and pervasive, especially among those young adults who did not graduate from college. Given the multiple sources and causes of these declines in real earnings and incomes, there is no single economic strategy or public policy intervention that by itself will ensure the future economic well-being of young workers and their families. Concerted and coordinated actions, both private and public, now are needed to address these problems. Forthcoming demographic developments, including a sustained rise in the number of 18-24-year-olds as we move through the end of the 1990s decade, will create new labor supply pressures and may exacerbate the problem of declining real earnings for many young adults. Yet initiatives on a variety of fronts, including macro-level labor market developments, innovative school programs, employer practices, and public policy interventions at the national, state, and local level, could contribute to a substantive improvement in the future economic fortunes of young adults and families.

First, high rates of job growth and the attainment of full employment conditions in the nation's labor markets (an overall unemployment rate ranging from 4 percent to 5 percent) would facilitate a steady expansion of employment opportunities for young male adults and provide increased access to year-round, full-time jobs, especially for those males with no post-secondary schooling and African-American males. A strong labor market also disproportionately increases in-school employment opportunities for high school students. Early work experience has favorable short- and long-term impacts on the post-high school employment and earnings experiences of high school graduates, particularly those not enrolling in four-year colleges and universities.

Second, continuing efforts must be made by state and local educational agencies to increase high school graduation rates and improve the basic academic proficiencies of all high school students, especially those from economically disadvantaged families and from race-ethnic minority groups. Findings from the National Longitudinal Survey of Youth (NLSY) on the adult poverty experiences of poor adolescents reveal that those youth who completed more years of formal schooling and obtained stronger basic skill proficiencies were far more successful in avoiding poverty problems in their mid- to late-20s. Similar strong relationships between schooling/basic skills and adult poverty status also prevailed among those adolescents who lived in families with incomes above the official poverty line. State and local school improvement initiatives, reinforced by federal investments targeted on disadvantaged children, can make an important difference in this area.

Third, there is a critical need for expanding formal training activities for young adults at the workplace, both in the private sector and in government agencies. Research has revealed that apprenticeship training and formal training from employers has consistently generated large economic payoffs for workers. Unfortunately, members of the nation's "Forgotten Half" are considerably less likely than college graduates to receive formal training from their employers, and few (under 3 percent) participate in a formal apprenticeship training program within the first six years following high school graduation. Under the newly enacted School-to-Work Opportunities Act of 1994, state and local education agencies, including community colleges, should work closely with employers and labor unions to expand formal training and apprenticeship opportunities for young adults. Financial incentives for both students and employers to participate in such programs should be provided, including the ability of students to use Pell grants to purchase certified formal training from private sector employers, the use of state UI trust funds to encourage industrywide formal training activities and new apprenticeship programs, and the use of federal workforce development funds by states to expand formal company training opportunities for entry-level workers with no post-secondary schooling.

Fourth, young workers need to obtain jobs in a more diversified set of industries and firms, including larger employers in goods-producing industries, professional service industries, and government agencies. Sustained efforts should be made by high school training programs, postsecondary education and training programs, the Job Service, and JTPA Private Industry Councils to work with private sector firms and government agencies to reduce the high concentration of young adults employed in retail trade and nonprofessional service industries.

Fifth, high schools, community colleges, and local training agencies should be encouraged to work closely with private sector employers in retail trade and private service industries (which are expected to account for 70 percent of the net increase in employment over the next ten years) to restructure existing jobs so that entry-level workers can become more productive and stable, thereby allowing them to earn higher hourly wages and obtain key employee benefits, including health insurance.

Sixth, efforts to strengthen the real income position of young families must focus upon increasing the real earnings potential of the family householders, both men and women. Many of the above policy recommendations would assist in achieving this objective; however, other actions could help complement these policies. The expanded Earned Income Tax Credits (EITC) for low income families with children enacted in 1993 should be maintained by the Congress. Many young families with children would benefit from these larger tax credits. Expanded health insurance coverage for low-income families with children and increased child care assistance for parents in low-wage jobs would boost their financial stability and strengthen economic incentives to work. The federal and state governments also should experiment with wage subsidies for welfare recipients to increase incentives to work and to boost their disposable incomes from paid employment. Early findings from the Canadian Self-Sufficiency Project, which was designed to supplement earnings from employment for former public assistance recipients, suggest that such programs can boost both employment rates and net incomes ("Canadian Research Focuses on Many Employment/Unemployment Aspects" 1995). Such efforts, if combined with steady increases in the minimum wage to offset erosion in its real value due to inflation, could reduce reliance upon welfare and poverty among young working families.

Seventh, national, state, and local governments should provide greater economic incentives for young adults to form married-couple families through joint investments in their human capital. Additional earned income tax credits at the state level for low-income married-couple families, expanded access to health insurance coverage for young workers and their children, and priority status in housing allowance and home buyer assistance programs all deserve consideration by policy makers. Family investment plans that outline the responsibilities and obligations of young family heads and their spouses for the receipt of such assistance could be developed at the local level through family investment centers that contained representatives of key local and state employment and training, health, housing, and social service agencies (see Levitan, Pines, and Mangum 1989).

Finally, the federal and state governments must expand the awarding and enforcement of child support orders for all absent fathers and mothers, especially among the young and unwed. Single, never-married mothers under the age of 30 are the least likely to receive any formal child care support from absent fathers.[6] These are the same families that are most likely to be poor, and they experience the most severe poverty income deficits. Efforts to improve the earnings capacity and parenting responsibilities of young absent fathers also should be promoted. The higher the annual earnings of young absent fathers, the more likely they are to pay child support on a regular basis and the higher will be their average level of child support payments. Fathers who have strong ties with their children and visit them frequently also are significantly more likely to pay child support. Unfortunately, few existing employment and training programs are designed to simultaneously improve young fathers' employability and earnings capacity, as well as their daily relationships with their children.

The economic plight of young workers and young families has intensified over two decades, and the powerful forces driving their real earnings and incomes downward will not be reversed easily or quickly. Yet the nation must turn its attention to this essential task. If serious responses are not developed and sustained over time, there is little hope of reversing the increases in out-of-wedlock childbearing and child poverty that now place the well-being of future generations of Americans in grave jeopardy.

NOTES

1. The more conservative CPI-UXI index of the U.S. Bureau of Labor Statistics rather than the CPI-U index was used to convert the nominal weekly earnings for young men and women into their constant 1993 dollar equivalents. Use of the CPI-U index would have increased the estimated size of the weekly earnings declines between 1973 and 1994 by a little more than 6 percent.

2. For an earlier review of trends in health insurance coverage among all young adults through the late 1980s, see Sum and Fogg (1991a).

3. For evidence on these issues, see Sum, Heliotis, and Fogg (1993).

4. For a review of labor productivity trends of the nation over the past twenty years, see U.S. Department of Labor (1995b).

5. For a comprehensive review of the long-term personal and social consequences of childhood poverty, see Sherman (1994).

6. For a review of national evidence on this issue for young absent fathers in the mid-1980s, see Sum and Ostrower (1994).

References

Bradshaw, Thomas F., and John F. Stinson. 1975. "Trends in Weekly Earnings: An Analysis," *Monthly Labor Review* (August).

"Canadian Research Focuses on Many Employment/Unemployment Aspects," *Workforce Journal* (Spring, 1995): 21-32.

Commission on Work, Family, and Citizenship. 1988. *The Forgotten Half: Pathways to Success for America's Youth and Young Families.* Washington, DC: W.T. Grant Foundation.

Eck, Alan. 1993, "Job-Related Education and Training: Their Impact on Earnings," *Monthly Labor Review* (October): 21-38.

Johnson, Clifford, and Andrew Sum. 1987. *Declining Earnings of Young Men: Their Relation to Poverty, Teen Pregnancy, and Family Formation.* Washington, DC: Children's Defense Fund.

Kasarda, John. 1985. "Urban Change and Minority Opportunities." In *The New Urban Reality,* Paul Peterson, ed. Washington, DC: Brookings Institution, pp. 33-67.

Levitan, Sar A., Marion Pines, and Garth Mangum. 1989. "A Proper Inheritance: Investing in the Self-Sufficiency of Poor Families." Center for Social Policy Studies, George Washington University.

Lynch, Lisa M. 1994. "Payoffs to Alternative Training Strategies at Work." In *Working Under Different Rules*, Richard B. Freeman, ed. New York: Russell Sage Foundation.

Peterson, Wallace. 1994. *The Silent Depression: The Fate of the American Dream.* New York: Norton.

Sherman, Arloc. 1994. *Wasting America's Future.* Boston: Beacon Press.

Sum, Andrew M., and W. Neal Fogg. 1991a. "The Adolescent Poor and the Transition to Early Adulthood." In *Adolescence and Poverty: Challenge for the 1990s*, Peter Edelman and Joyce Ladner, eds. Washington, DC: Center for National Policy Press, pp. 37-109.

_____. "Labor Market Turbulence and the Labor Market Experience of Young Adults." In *Turbulence in the American Workplace*, Peter B. Doeringer, ed. New York: Oxford University Press.

Sum, Andrew M., and Julio Goicoechea. 1991. *Broken Promises: Rising Labor Productivity in Manufacturing and the Decline in the Real Earnings of Production Workers, 1979-89.* Boston: Center for Labor Market Studies, Northeastern University.

Sum, Andrew M., Joanna Heliotis, and Neal Fogg. 1993. *Health Insurance Coverage Rates, the Incidence of Health Problems, and the Labor Market*

Status of Young African American Men in the U.S. Boston: Center for Labor Market Studies, Northeastern University, December.

Sum, Andrew M., and Jay Ostrower. 1994. "Fathers, Child Support and Welfare Reform: The Missing Link." Report prepared for the Pioneer Institute, Boston.

U.S. Department of Labor, Bureau of Labor Statistics. 1995a. *Employment and Earnings* (January).

_____. 1995b. *Multifactor Productivity Trends, 1993.* Washington, D.C., February.

_____. 1995c. *Productivity by Industry, 1993.* Washington, D.C., February.

Veum, Jonathan R. 1993. "Training Among Young Adults: Who, What Kind, and for How Long?" *Monthly Labor Review* (August): 27-32.

CHAPTER 4

Ethnic Differences in School Departure

Does Youth Employment Promote
or Undermine Educational Attainment?

Marta Tienda
Avner Ahituv

Labor demand shifts away from unskilled, blue-collar production jobs in favor of more-educated workers with adequate problem-solving skills have increased the returns to formal schooling and decreased market opportunities for youth. Twenty years ago a high school diploma could ensure youth of a job that paid a family wage, and many dropouts were able to secure some type of low-wage job. In the current economic environment, employment opportunities for youth with low education levels are very limited. Real wages and employment rates have fallen steeply for young, uneducated men, but most especially for disadvantaged and minority youth. Joblessness among minority youth who did not complete high school exceeded 70 percent in 1993 (U.S. DOL 1994c).

Unfortunately, several demonstrations designed to improve the labor market prospects of disadvantaged youth have yielded discouraging results, particularly when compared to the adult outcomes (U.S. GAO 1991, 1993; U.S. DOL 1994a, 1994b). For example, the Supported Work Demonstration produced positive program impacts on adult earnings beyond the period of subsidized employment, but *negative* effects on youth post-program earnings (U.S. DOL 1994c). Similarly, the Summer Training and Education Program (STEP), which included remedial education, life skills, and sex education, as well as traditional summer employment, achieved short-term improvements in the test scores of participants, but no long-term impacts on their rates of school completion, employment or teen pregnancy (Walker and Vilella-Velez

1992). Programs offering close mentoring, role models, and genuine opportunities to exercise and develop personal responsibility have yielded greater successes, but these programs are the exception rather than the rule.

The generally dismal results of youth demonstration programs have rekindled policy interest in dropout prevention programs and school-based work programs that strengthen ties between schools and employers. This idea has long policy antecedents. Adolescent employment has been advocated since 1974, when the President's Science Advisory Committee recommended that high school students acquire work experience to improve their labor market opportunities and to secure a modest degree of autonomy during adolescence. Acquisition of valuable work experience would appear to be especially important for urban minority youth, whose employability and wage prospects have declined precipitously (Kasarda 1995).

Policy proposals to strengthen the transition from school to work by enhancing job opportunities for teenagers who are enrolled in school presume that youth employment does not undermine scholastic achievement (U.S. GAO 1991). Two stylized facts support this idea. One is that employment is pervasive among high school youth: virtually all youth hold at least one job while enrolled in school (Levitan and Gallo 1991a; Ahituv et al. 1994). Conceivably, employment can improve scholastic outcomes if time allocated to work decreases unproductive leisure activities while improving the efficiency of time spent on scholastic tasks (Tienda, Schoenhals, and Schneider 1995; Levitan and Gallo 1991a). Second, there is consensus that early work experience is associated with positive short-term labor market outcomes, as measured by employment and wages at age 25 (Hotz et al. 1995).

Nevertheless, there remains much uncertainty about the educational consequences of adolescent employment, because most studies of the school-to-work transition either ignore employment during periods of school enrollment, or disregard educational outcomes (see reviews in Ahituv et al. 1994; Hotz et al. 1995; Tienda, Schoenhals, and Schneider 1995). Furthermore, there is no compelling evidence that adolescent employment has lasting effects on adult labor force outcomes. Although several studies have concluded that youth employment does not undermine scholastic achievement *provided that time*

allocated to market activities remains well under 20 weekly hours
(Levitan and Gallo 1991a; Tienda, Schoenhals, and Schneider 1995),
there is less certainty about the school disincentive effects of employment for minority youth whose home environments frequently lack
support for academic pursuits.

The high rates of premature school withdrawal among youth aged
16 to 24 (ranging from 8 to 29 percent in 1992 according to the
National Center for Education Statistics) suggest the testable and pol-
icy-relevant hypothesis that the educational consequences of youth
employment are not negligible, as previously claimed. Accordingly, we
examine patterns of school departure among white, black, and Hispanic male youth to determine whether, and under what conditions,
adolescent employment may precipitate early school withdrawal. We
are particularly interested in the effects of adolescent employment on
school continuation and withdrawal decisions. Specifically, we evaluate the influence of average weekly hours worked on the odds of
remaining in school at specific ages for minority and nonminority
youth.

The following section frames our empirical analysis by summariz-
ing some recent trends in youth labor market prospects and describing
the data analyzed. This is followed by a description of the variation in
school attendance and employment patterns of white, black and Hispanic youth, along with empirical estimates of the schooling consequences of adolescent employment. Results show that the odds of
leaving school at ages 17, 18, and 19 increase as the number of weekly
hours spent at work rises, but that youth who did *not work at all* also
were at higher risk of withdrawing from school at each age. The final
section discusses the policy implications of these findings in light of
recent changes in youth employment opportunities, lessons about what
interventions enhance labor market options of disadvantaged youth,
and selected proposals to strengthen the links between school and
work.

Data and Variables

We analyze the National Longitudinal Survey of Youth (NLSY), a
national probability sample of 12,686 individuals aged 14 to 21 as of

January 1, 1979 who were interviewed annually for over a decade. The original cohort also included oversamples of black, Hispanic, and economically disadvantaged white youth, and an oversample of military enrollees. This analysis focuses on the civilian sample, excluding the oversamples of disadvantaged white youth, but including the over-samples of black and Hispanic youth.[1] Because the retrospective information on school and labor force histories was less complete than the prospective data, we further restrict the sample to men aged 13 to 16 in 1978 to reduce left censoring of schooling careers. Our final sample of 2,553 young men includes 1,253 whites, 793 blacks, and 507 Hispanics.[2]

Most variables presented below are self-explanatory, but our primary dependent variable—school enrollment—and key independent variable—work activity—warrant further elaboration. We define school enrollment status using monthly data, and consider students to have withdrawn from school if they were not enrolled for six months in a calendar year.[3] Measures of work activity are derived from a prospective employment history based on weekly time units. The NLSY contains several indicators of time at work, including hours worked last week; average hours worked in the main job last year; and total hours worked last year in all jobs (calculated by NLSY). Respondents were also queried about the number of weeks spent at work in each year.

We hypothesize that two aspects of youth employment activity may influence school continuation decisions, namely the intensity and the duration of time spent at work. Therefore, we compute two indicators of adolescent employment: percent of time (in weeks) worked during high school and average weekly hours worked by grade level and by specific ages. Average weekly hours was computed by dividing annual hours by annual weeks worked.[4]

A vast literature has established that family background, notably parental education, family income and fathers' occupational status, is the most significant factor influencing the educational outcomes of youth. Summarily stated, well-educated parents have the knowledge, financial resources, and values conducive to positive school performance. For parsimony in presenting the tabular results, we use mothers' educational attainment as the key indicator of family background to designate advantaged and disadvantaged youth. Although both household income and parental education are important predictors of a child's educational attainment, there is no obvious way to combine these socioeconomic indicators. Use of mothers education provides a clear measure of educational disadvantage, which is central to our substantive concern. The multivariate analyses include two additional measures of family background: family income and headship structure.[5]

Results

Table 1 summarizes race and ethnic differences in educational and employment experiences of young men according to mothers' education (our proxy for disadvantage). As expected, youth from advantaged backgrounds were more likely to graduate from high school by age 18 than their age counterparts whose mothers did not complete secondary school. Among advantaged youth, whites were more likely to graduate than minorities. However, among disadvantaged youth, blacks were more likely to graduate than either white or Hispanic youth. This generalization obtains through age 20, whether or not GED recipients are included among high school graduates. By age 20 we find that 68 percent of disadvantaged black youth completed secondary school or received a GED, compared to 62 percent of disadvantaged white youth, and only 60 percent of disadvantaged Hispanic youth. This result reflects the dramatic educational progress of disadvantaged blacks since 1960 (Mare 1995). White youth, who are less likely to be disadvantaged than blacks, are significantly more likely to graduate than minority youth. A comparison of rows 1 and 2 provides strong evidence of age-grade delay for minority youth.

About 7 percent of Hispanic youth graduate from high school between the ages of 18 and 20, compared with only 3 percent of white youth. Age-grade delay for blacks is even more striking, but larger shares of blacks compared to Hispanics eventually graduate.

As expected, youth from relatively advantaged backgrounds were more likely to attend college than their disadvantaged race and ethnic counterparts. Moreover, white sons of more educated mothers had higher rates of college attendance than their minority counterparts, but Hispanics were more likely to attend college than black sons of high school graduates. Among disadvantaged youth, blacks and Hispanics were more likely to attend college than their white counterparts. This finding has been documented elsewhere (Hauser and Phang 1993; Stevenson et al. 1993), but no satisfactory explanation has been provided. These race and ethnic differentials in college attendance of disadvantaged youth may result from advantages associated with affirmative action and preferential admission of promising minority students.

Table 1. Educational and Early Work Experiences of Minority and Nonminority Youth by Mother's High School Graduation Status (Means or Percents)

	White		Black		Hispanic	
	Mom HS+	Mom <HS	Mom HS+	Mom <HS	Mom HS+	Mom <HS
H.S. grads, age 18	79.6	49.7	65.4	50.5	60.2	41.1
H.S. grads, age 20[a]	81.1	53.0	69.6	60.3	66.2	48.8
GED, age 20	6.1	8.7	9.5	7.6	10.0	10.8
Attended college, age 20	45.2	10.3	32.9	14.7	38.5	14.2
Ever worked during H.S.	73.9	71.7	65.6	65.2	68.1	68.8
Time (weeks) worked before age 18, H.S. grad[c]	37.1	34.8	22.1	24.2	33.2	27.5
Time (weeks) worked before age 18, H.S. dropout[c]	28.5	28.4	23.4	22.6	27.2	24.2
[N][b]	[896]	[302]	[350]	[370]	[133]	[326]

a. Excludes GED

b. N's computed for age 18

c. These variables were constructed from weeks worked using the work history file.

Table 1 also shows that variation in youth employment by mother's education and group membership was less pronounced than differences in educational attainment. By age 18, nearly three-in-four white youth had ever worked while enrolled in high school, compared to 65 percent of black and 68 percent of Hispanic youth. From these data it is not obvious whether adolescent employment is associated with persistence in secondary school, because there is no systematic relationship between the share of time worked during high school, disadvantaged status, and youths' graduation status. For white and to a lesser extent Hispanic youth, graduates worked more weeks by age 18 than their counterparts who dropped out of high school, but for black youth there were only trivial differences in weeks worked by age 18 between those who graduated from high school and those who did not.

Of course, it is impossible to establish any causal relationship from the cross-sectional tabulations because total number of weeks worked do not indicate the weekly intensity of work effort. Table 2, which summarizes mean hours worked during 9th, 10th, and 11th grades for minority and nonminority youth according to eventual graduation status provides some insight into this matter.

Table 2. Labor Market Activity During High School: Average Hours Worked during High School According to Mother's Education

| | Student graduation status | | | | | |
| | White | | Black | | Hispanic | |
Student grade by mother's education	Grad[a]	Never grad	Grad	Never grad	Grad	Never grad
Mother<HS						
9th graders	3.4	12.3	6.7	9.1	6.1	6.6
	(9.3)	(18.0)	(13.1)	(15.4)	(13.2)	(15.2)
10th graders	10.8	13.9	12.5	18.4	15.3	17.8
	(13.4)	(17.2)	(15.9)	(16.3)	(17.8)	(18.4)
11th graders	18.7	19.1	16.0	20.3	20.7	22.2
	(15.1)	(16.1)	(14.8)	(15.2)	(16.7)	(18.3)
Mother HS +						
9th graders	2.2	4.3	2.6	5.0	3.4	7.8
	(7.9)	(11.3)	(9.0)	(11.1)	(10.1)	(17.1)
10th graders	11.7	13.7	10.0	11.6	13.6	10.8
	(14.1)	(17.1)	(15.1)	(14.5)	(15.6)	(14.7)
11th graders	20.3	22.8	17.0	17.9	20.8	32.8
	(13.7)	(14.6)	(15.2)	(16.8)	(15.0)	(19.1)

a. Excludes GED recipients.

First, with only one exception (Hispanics whose mothers were high school graduates), dropouts averaged more weekly work hours prior to

12th grade than their socioeconomic counterparts who finished high school. This result differs from table 1, which shows that dropouts work fewer weeks than graduates and points to the significance of work intensity as a mechanism precipitating premature school withdrawal. This supports the view that working too many hours has deleterious educational consequences (Levitan and Gallo 1991a; Tienda et al. 1995). Second, the pattern of excessive work commitment that we hypothesize eventuates in premature school withdrawal begins early in the high school career. For example, the average hours disadvantaged white dropouts worked during 9th grade far exceeded those of their race counterparts who did eventually graduate (12.3 vs. 3.4). Similar patterns obtain for black and Hispanic youth, although the differentials for blacks arise among 10th graders, and for Hispanics they are less pronounced. Third, race and ethnic differences in the association between high school graduation status, work effort and grade progression are more pronounced among disadvantaged compared to advantaged youth. From these tabulations we draw two inferences. One is that the "detrimental" work level may be less than 20 weekly hours. Another is that the 11th grade may be a particularly vulnerable point in an adolescent's school career, because it represents the first real choice between school and work for students who are not age-grade delayed.

These descriptive results are consistent with our hypothesis that adolescent employment can lower educational achievement by accelerating the odds of school withdrawal. However, it is impossible to ascertain from the tabular results whether educational consequences of adolescent employment differ by race and Hispanic origin because the observed group differences may simply reflect underlying socioeconomic inequities between minority and nonminority groups. Therefore, we turn to our multivariate analysis to examine this hypothesis further.

Multivariate Analyses

Our approach to school departure considers four sets of factors known to influence these decisions: (1) *family background,* notably household income, parental education, and family headship (i.e., whether raised by one or two and parents);[6] (2) *scholastic aptitude*, depicted by respondents' (age-adjusted) AFQT score at the time of the first interview;[7] (3) *ascribed traits* (race and national origin; birthplace, and age cohort) that are correlated with school and employment out-comes;[8] and (4) *work behavior*, average weekly hours during the previous year. The dependent variable is coded 1 if respondents did not withdraw from school at specific ages (i = 16, 17, 18 and 19) and 0 otherwise.

Our empirical model represents a reduced form specification of factors influencing the decision to persist or withdraw from school at specific ages. All variables included in the analysis are presumed to be predetermined and exogenous to the choices made at any point in the life cycle. We estimated two models of school continuation for specific ages—one which included all youth, and another which was restricted to youth who were enrolled in school the previous year. The latter essentially focuses on recent dropouts.[9] That empirical estimates were qualitatively similar inspires confidence in the robustness of our estimates. Therefore table 3 presents the results of the final probit models predicting school persistence at specific ages. In the interest of parsimony, we restrict our discussion to variables of central interest, namely minority group status and work activity.

The main effects on school persistence of minority group membership and work effort are of great substantive interest. Although the tabular results showed that black youth were less likely to graduate from high school than their white counterparts, these differences largely reflect differences in socioeconomic background (family income, parental education, and AFQT scores. In fact, given their background characteristics, black youth are less likely to withdraw from school between ages 16 to 19 than statistically comparable whites. Similarly, Hispanic youth are no more likely to withdraw from school at ages 16 and 17 than white youth who share their individual and family characteristics. Rather, Hispanics are more likely to persist in school at ages 18 and 19 than statistically similar white youth (see also Hauser and Phang 1993).

These findings corroborate those of other studies showing that race and ethnic differentials in dropout status largely reflect variation in family socioeconomic background (Hauser and Phang 1993, among others). In other words, group differences in socioeconomic composition are responsible for average differences in dropout rates of minority and nonminority youth. Nevertheless, the *higher* school persistence rates of minority youth relative to statistically equivalent whites beg for

Table 3. Probit Estimates of School Persistence at Specific Ages[a]
(Asymptotic standard errors)

Variables	Age 16	Age 17	Age 18	Age 19
Hispanic	.237	-.115	.231**	.330**
	(.177)	(.111)	(.085)	(.094)
Black	.577**	.494**	.349**	.384**
	(.162)	(.104)	(.072)	(.081)
Foreign born	-.120	-.016	.153	.230
	(.232)	(.162)	(.123)	(.134)
Age 14 in 1978	.033	-.192*	.019	.024
	(.124)	(.097)	(.079)	(.086)
Age 15 in 1978	b	-.057	-.010	-.103
		(.114)	(.080)	(.087)
Age 16 in 1978	b	b	.096	.024
			(.079)	(.088)
AFQT test score	.025**	.019**	.011**	.019**
	(.004)	(.002)	(.002)	(.002)
Missing AFQT test scores	-.340	-.058	.153	.936**
	(.321)	(.237)	(.184)	(.225)
Family income in 1979 ($ in 1000)	.021*	.012**	.014**	.013**
	(.008)	(.005)	(.003)	(.003)
Missing family income information	.116	.222	.343**	.251**
	(.195)	(.124)	(.086)	(.093)
Highest grade completed by respondent's mother	.042	.006	.038**	.042**
	(.023)	(.014)	(.011)	(.012)
Missing information about mother's education	.251	.026	.239	.245
	(.291)	(.197)	(.151)	(.178)
In female headed household at age 14	-.126	-.205*	-.047	.077
	(.151)	(.095)	(.071)	(.080)
Average weekly hours worked last year	-.025	-.022**	-.011**	-.022**
	(.020)	(.005)	(.002)	(.003)
Did not work last year	.032	-.504**	-.162	-.476**
	(.626)	(.188)	(.091)	(.106)
Constant	-.668	.291	-.992**	- 1.799**
	(.689)	(.273)	(.169)	(.194)
[N]	[1184]	[1850]	[2407]	[2155]

a. Conditioned on school enrollment during previous years.
b. Not included in the model.
*Significant at 10 percent level.
**Significant at 5 percent level.

an explanation of the race and ethnic differentials in school continuation because they have implications for the design of employment and training policy that builds on the human capital potential of disadvantaged youth.

Our major interest is in the effects of youth employment on school continuation decisions. We consider two measures of work effort: no work activity and average weekly hours worked during the previous year.[10] Two striking results emerge. First, youth who have no attachment to the labor market are significantly more likely to withdraw from school at ages 17 through 19. This finding provides some support for current policy initiatives that recommend employment as a way of strengthening the connection between school and work, and particularly for disadvantaged youth. However, a second result tempers this conclusion. The strong negative effects for ages 17, 18 and 19 of average weekly hours indicates that excessive commitment to work during adolescence increases the likelihood of premature withdrawal and also lowers the odds of continued education beyond secondary school. Both results have important implications for the design of school-to-work transition programs that have gained popularity in the current administration.

Because the tabular results imply race and ethnic differences in both graduation rates and employment activity, we estimated age-specific probit models predicting persistence in school that included interactions between minority status and weekly hours. This was done to ascertain whether the employment effects on school continuation decisions differed among Hispanic, black and white youth. Virtually all interaction effects were statistically insignificant, therefore we reject the hypothesis that youth employment effects on school withdrawal differ among demographic groups.

The probit coefficients do not lend themselves to direct comparisons across groups from differing backgrounds. Therefore, we estimated the elasticities of school persistence implied by the average hours coefficients. These calculations are reported in table 4 by age, minority group membership and mother's education status. Each entry indicates the percent change in the probability of remaining in school that is associated with a percentage change in the average weekly hours worked in the previous year.

Three noteworthy lessons emerge. First, school continuation decisions of disadvantaged youth are more sensitive to the variation in hours worked than are decisions of nondisadvantaged youth. For example, each percent increase in weekly hours lowers the probability of school continuation by 5.6 percent for 17-year-olds whose mothers had not completed secondary school compared to 3.4 percent for 17-year-olds whose mothers were high school graduates. This generalization obtains for all race and ethnic groups, although the magnitudes of the elasticities differ along race and ethnic lines, which points to a second major lesson. School continuation decisions of disadvantaged Hispanic youth are more sensitive to changes in hours spent at work relative to white or black youth. However, black school continuation decisions are less sensitive to changes in labor supply than those of whites, irrespective of class background.

Table 4. Estimated Elasticities of Average Weekly Hours on School Persistence

	Age			
	16	**17**	**18**	**19**
Mother graduate from HS				
All	-.001	-.034	-.139	-.661
Hispanic	0	-.038	-.172	-.846
Black	-.002	-.032	-.112	-.543
White	-.002	-.033	-.145	-.682
Mother less than HS				
All	-.009	-.056	-.180	-1.403
Hispanic	-.015	-.081	-.193	-1.441
Black	-.002	-.041	-.152	-1.300
White	-.009	-.050	-.202	-1.508

Third, the disincentive effects of adolescent employment on school continuation are quite large for age 19, which represents the transition from secondary to post-secondary schooling for kids who are not age-grade delayed.[11] Our results imply that the work effort of 18-year-olds lowers the probability of continuing to college by 66 percent for youth whose mothers graduated from high school, and by 140 percent for those whose mothers were dropouts. Given the rising returns to schooling during the past fifteen years, these results portend substantial race and ethnic income inequality for young workers in the future unless employment and training policy can increase incentives of youth to complete high school, and encourage larger shares of minority youth to pursue postsecondary training.

Conclusions and Policy Implications

The Clinton administration, under the direction of Labor Secretary Robert Reich, has acknowledged the plight of disadvantaged youth, particularly those needing a second chance to acquire work-relevant skills. Calls for youth apprenticeship programs and new partnerships between labor and education leaders explicitly recognize that the United States lacks a system to facilitate the transition from school to work for noncollege-bound youth. Growing employment and wage differentials between high school graduates and dropouts, and between college- and noncollege-educated youth increase the urgency of improving high school graduation rates as a strategy to *prevent* economic hardship among adults. Yet dropout rates remain alarmingly high. The National Center for Education Statistics reported dropout rates of 8 percent for white, 14 percent for black, and 29 percent for Hispanic youth in 1992.

A popular proposal to lower dropout rates entails a revival of work programs that allow youth to acquire work experience as they complete their formal schooling. The presumption, of course, is that job experience is valuable in socializing youth to the world of work, and that employment helps youth envision connections between academic subjects and the skill requirements of jobs. Our findings showing deleterious effects of work intensity on decisions to persist in school lead us to question conventional wisdom about the educational consequences of youth employment.

Of course, spending large amounts of time in low-wage work while enrolled in school does not mean that a well-designed school-to-work program that integrates school-based and work-based learning will not be productive. In fact, our results showing that youth who do not work at all are at extremely high risk of dropping out of school warrant special consideration. These youth pose the greatest challenges for employment and training policy, and *should* be the target of school-based work programs that provide strong and clear links between academic subjects and concrete work activities. A well-conceived academy program should incorporate industry-specific training in basic curricula, and should include job guarantees for satisfactory performance. To be successful, these programs must begin well *before* the legal age for youth to withdraw from school, and hopefully can be enhanced with mentoring activities during early adolescence.

This raises a second policy issue, namely, the legal age to withdraw from school. The future labor market has little room for high school dropouts, at a time when graduates are facing income insecurity. Given recent wage trends for skilled and unskilled workers, it seems reasonable to raise the legal limit to withdraw from school from age 16 to age 18. This change would make the greatest difference for Hispanics, who currently experience the highest rates of school withdrawal. A corollary of this proposition is that enrolled youth should be legally prohibited from working above 15 hours weekly, which is the level several studies deem inconsequential for scholastic outcomes.

A third policy implication of our results concerns the meaning of race and ethnic differences in the educational consequences of adolescent employment. We do not believe group-specific programs are warranted. However, our results showing different elasticities for Hispanic and disadvantaged youth indicate that program emphases should be tailored accordingly. Specifically, for Hispanic youth, employment and training programs would be maximally effective by focusing on school retention and school-based learning. Our results clearly show that youth whose parents have very low levels of education are at extremely high risk of premature school withdrawal. Therefore, the special needs of disadvantaged youth, including provision of remedial skills and work experiences that are tightly linked to school-based learning, should be a priority for future youth employment training programs.

The most concrete recommendation that encompasses all three policy issues derives from Sar Levitan's writings, which appropriately complain that the current training system is ill-equipped to prepare noncollege-bound youth for the workforce of the twenty-first century (Levitan and Gallo 1991a, 1991b). In several of his last papers, many co-authored with Frank Gallo, Levitan proposed "tech-prep" as the best solution to prepare noncollege-bound youth to pursue technical occupations (see Levitan, Mangum, and Mangum 1993; Levitan and Gallo 1993). Their conception of tech-prep is that training will begin during the last two years of high school (with no major loss if students switch preferences) and continue for an additional two years in a community or technical college. To be successful with "hard-to-reach" disadvantaged youth, tech-prep programs must include incentives for successful completion of the program (i.e., nontrivial wage increases and guaranteed jobs, which requires strong ties between schools and businesses). The U.S. Department of Labor (1994c) has identified several successful programs that embody these principles. What is lacking is the political will to bring them to fruition.

NOTES

This research was supported by a grant from the Russell Sage Foundation and institutional support was provided by the Population Research Center of the University of Chicago. We are indebted to Paulette Kamenecka for able research assistance.

1. This decision was based on extensive diagnostic analyses that revealed significant differences between the white random and nonrandom samples, but relatively minor differences between the Hispanic and black oversamples (see Ahituv et al. 1994). Descriptive statistics are appropriately weighted to approximate population parameters, thus the decision to include the minority oversamples does not distort statistical inferences.

2. These samples represent the full-risk set at the beginning of the panel, i.e., in 1979. Sample sizes vary for specific analyses owing to differential attrition and randomly missing date. We have conducted extensive sensitivity tests to ensure the randomness of the missing data and include appropriate controls in all instances where missing data were not ignorable.

3. We experimented with various definitions of school enrollment, both more and less restrictive, and obtained similar results.

4. We conducted sensitivity tests to determine whether our findings varied according to the measure of work effort used. Our results are quite robust, as they are similar for all measures of work effort.

5. We opted to use mother's educational attainment rather than that of fathers because there was less missing data for this indicator, partly because of the share of families with an absent father. When mother's education was missing, we substituted father's education. Owing to assortive mating, results are substantively similar using either measure.

6. Because each of these variables had high levels of missing data due to nonresponse, we constructed companion variables to flag missing data. This strategy has the twin advantages of avoiding unnecessary loss of sample observations and monitoring the selectivity of nonresponses.

7. The Armed Forces Qualification Test, or AFQT, is the sum of the scores on four of the 10 subtests in the ASVAB: the Work Knowledge, Paragraph Comprehension, Arithmetic Reasoning and Mathematics Knowledge subtests. The military interprets the AFQT score as a measure of general trainability, and uses the scores to screen out individuals who are likely to have a low probability of successfully completing military training. Labor economists have used the AFQT as an indicator of general ability, arguing that it performs like an aptitude test.

8. Respondent's age in 1978 (or age cohort) serves as a control for left-hand censoring of the school and work histories.

9. We conducted sensitivity tests using alternative definitions of school withdrawal, namely nonenrolled for six and twelve months, and obtained similar results. We also compared estimates of models conditioned on being enrolled in the previous year and unrestricted by prior enrollment status to determine if re-enrollment patterns influenced our results. Conclusions were fundamentally unchanged because of the low incidence of re-enrollment.

10. Our measure includes summer employment, but the vast majority of job spells occurred during the academic year. It is very difficult to separate summer and academic year employment because most work episodes cross boundaries. Furthermore, NLSY lacks precise information about the timing of school withdrawal, which makes this distinction less critical analytically.

11. Because many youth are still enrolled in high school at age 19, our estimates for this age confound late graduation with college entry. They are, therefore, conservative.

References

Ahituv, Avner, Marta Tienda, Lixin Xu, and V. Joseph Hotz. 1994. "Initial Labor Market Experiences of Black, Hispanic and White Men." Population Research Center Discussion Paper 94-5, University of Chicago.

Hauser, Robert M., and Hanam Samuel Phang. 1993. "Trends in High School Dropout Among White, Black, and Hispanic youth, 1973-1989." Paper presented at the 1993 Annual Meeting of the Population Association of America.

Hotz, V. Josep, and Marta Tienda. 1995. "Education and Employment in a Diverse Society: Generating Inequality through the School-to-Work Transition." In *American Diversity: A Demographic Challenge for the Twenty-First Century*, Nancy Denton and Stuart Tolnay, eds. Albany, NY: SUNY Press.

Hotz, V. Joseph, Lixin Xu, Marta Tienda, and Avner Ahituv. 1995. "Work Experience in the Transition from School to Work for Young Men in the U.S.: An Analysis of the 1980s." Unpublished paper, NORC and the University of Chicago.

Kasarda, John D. 1995. "Industrial Restructuring and the Changing Location of Jobs." In *State of the Union*, Volume 1. New York: Russell Sage Foundation.

Levitan, Sar A., and Frank Gallo. 1991a. "Preparing Americans for Work," *Looking Ahead* 13, 1/2: 18-25.

_____. 1991b. "Wanted: Federal Public Service Program." *Challenge* (May-June): 32-40.

_____. 1993. "Education Reform: Federal Initiatives and National Mandates, 1963-1993." Occasional paper 1993-3, Center for Social Policy Studies, George Washington University, November.

Levitan, Sar A., Garth L. Mangum, and Stephen L. Mangum. 1993. "A Training Agenda for the 1990s," *Workforce* (Spring): 8-16.

Mangum, Garth, and Stephen Mangum. 1995. "Toward a Workforce Development Reality Check." In *The Harassed Staffer's Reality Check*, Baltimore: Johns Hopkins University Press.

Mare, Robert D. 1995. "Changes in Educational Attainment and School Enrollment." In *State of the Union: America in the 1990's*, Reynolds Farley, ed. New York: Russell Sage, pp. 155-213.

Stevenson, David, Jeffrey Link, Barbara Schneider, and Kathryn Schiller. 1993. "Early School Leavers." Paper presented at the 1993 Annual Meeting of the American Sociological Association.

Tienda, Marta, Mark Schoenhals, and Barbara Schneider. 1995. "Educational Consequences of Adolescent Employment." Paper presented at the 1995 Annual Meeting of the Population Association of America.

U. S. General Accounting Office (U.S. GAO). 1991. *Transition from School to Work: Linking Education and Worksite Training*. Report to Congressional Requesters.

U. S. General Accounting Office. 1993. *Transition from School to Work: H.R. 2884 Addresses Components of Comprehensive Strategy*. Presented to the Committee on Education and Labor, U.S. House of Representatives.

U.S. Department of Education. 1994. *Mini Digest of Education Statistics*. National Center for Education Statistics.

U.S. Department of Labor (U.S. DOL). 1994a. "The Role of Job Training in Expanding Employment Opportunities and Increasing the Earnings of the Disadvantaged." Unpublished paper, Office of the Chief Economist, July.

_____. 1994b. "Background Paper on JTPA Programs for the Disadvantaged." Unpublished paper, Office of the Chief Economist, July.

_____. 1994c. "Future Directions for Job Training." Unpublished paper, Office of the Chief Economist, November.

Walker, Gary, and Frances Vilella-Velez. 1992. *Anatomy of a Demonstration*. Philadelphia: Public/Private Ventures.

CHAPTER 5

MDTA and CETA
A Personal Revisit

Eli Ginzberg

In the mid-1990s there are a great many concerns about the continuing ineffective functioning of the U.S. labor market as evidenced by the growing difficulties of high school dropouts and pro-forma graduates in gaining access to regular jobs that pay initially or prospectively a reasonable wage and provide the holder a basis for future job security and income. Other problems include the continuing large differentials in the employment experiences of the white majority and selected groups of minorities, particularly blacks and Hispanics, the growing numbers of long-term corporate white-collar and blue-collar employees in their forties and fifties who are dismissed as a result of the continuing downsizing of business firms, and the continuing geographic mismatch between concentrations of large numbers of the urban and rural poor and areas of employment expansion often located in the outlying regions of metropolitan areas.

This list could be expanded to include the vulnerability of workers who are computer-illiterate in an era when computerization has become the dominant technology. Attention could also be directed to the intensified competition in selected locations between the large number of native-born marginal workers in search of jobs and incomes and the continuing large-scale inflow of immigrants from abroad who are seeking opportunities to work and improve their prospects in this country. Cognizance must also be taken of the large numbers of persons on welfare who, under appropriate conditions of access to job training, child care and health benefits, could be encouraged to work and support themselves and their dependents and of the sizable numbers of disabled persons who can work only to the extent that employers and the community at large lower the physical and other barriers that currently interfere with their getting and holding a job.

This restricted list of large groups who continue to face major hurdles in gaining entrance into the labor market and becoming self-sufficient through work may provide a useful introduction to the selected insights and assessments that will be offered about the two decades when active federal manpower policy, as represented by MDTA and CETA (1962-1981), was enacted and implemented. There may be a number of useful lessons to be extracted from this earlier experience, the beginnings of which date back a third of a century. Further, since I had the privilege of serving as the chair of the National Commission for Employment Policy and its predecessors from 1962 to 1981, I will call attention to selected aspects of the first two decades of federal manpower policy that will be of interest and of value to those who continue to be concerned with improving the operations of the U.S. labor market as the nation comes to the end of the twentieth century.

Reflections on MDTA

An analysis of the MDTA experience raises questions as to the source of the political momentum that led to this potentially significant enlargement of the capacity of the federal government to improve the operations of the labor market. There was no strong constituency in either the Democratic or Republican parties that had lobbied long and hard for federal action such as in the case of medical care for the elderly. Neither did the newly elected president, John F. Kennedy, nor his advisors focus much attention on manpower issues as a way of "getting the economy moving again," their primary campaign slogan in 1960. For the most part they looked to macro demand expansion to revive the sluggish economy; improving the match between the unemployed and the labor needs and demands of employers was not an issue high on this agenda. Rather, the growing unemployment of even skilled workers due to automation became the focus of general concern.

It is worth noting that President Kennedy, in his meeting on September 16, 1962 with the newly appointed members of the National Manpower Advisory Committee (NMAC), singled out the victims of technological change as one of the three categories of workers who could benefit the most from the new statute. The other two were poorly educated, unskilled youth and those older persons who had lost their jobs and would not be likely to find another without a period of retraining. While waiting to see the President, the members of the NMAC heard a gloss from Vice-President Johnson who explained that he had successfully lobbied the southern conservative senators to support MDTA on the ground that it would help many poor southern blacks become self-supporting, with the promise that the administration would not publicize the goal.

The scale and scope of the MDTA and the goals that it was intended to achieve are reflected in an early session that I had with Secretary of Labor Arthur Goldberg after he indicated his intention to appoint me as the chair of the NMAC. I explored at some length with the Secretary whether the final version of the bill might link a job creation measure with new training opportunities. The Secretary informed me that he favored such a linkage and had in fact explored it with the White House staff. He had been told, however, that MDTA would be solely a training measure or there would be no act.

It is my recollection that Senator Joseph Clark and Representative Elmer Holland, both from Pennsylvania which was going through wrenching industrial change at the time, took the lead on the Democratic side to push for MDTA, and that they were able to elicit considerable support from several Republicans who were friendly to a "structural" approach to remedy the shortfalls in the U.S. labor market and had little interest in macro-demand stimulation. In any case we know that MDTA had strong bipartisan support throughout the 1960s, much of which carried over to CETA in the 1970s until the waning days of the Carter administration.

It should be pointed out that a manpower program that first came into being because of the nation's growing concern with the adverse effects of automation on skilled workers shifted focus over time to the severely disadvantaged members of the nation's workforce. MDTA had been in operation for less than one year when the research staff of the U.S. Department of Labor became aware of the strikingly low level of education, training, and skill of many of the MDTA applicants. They had initially shared the general assumption that rising unemployment was largely a by-product of the advances in automation, and for that reason they had concentrated the training programs on persons with at least three years of labor market experience.

The enabling legislation had specified that the ten members of the NMAC were to consist of representatives of employers and labor with additional representatives from the public at large. Secretary of Labor Willard Wirtz, who had succeeded Arthur Goldberg when he was appointed to the Supreme Court, told of an informal agreement between the U.S. Chamber of Commerce and the AFL-CIO to assign three seats to each, but that he persuaded them to settle for two each. Clearly, the Congress recognized that the new legislation, to be effective, had to have the support, or at least avoid the opposition, of either or both of the two critical parties whose actions and reactions had such a pervasive influence on labor market activities.

One of the two employer representatives on the NMAC who had the responsibility of exploring relations with the business community was far advanced in gaining the support of the Advertising Council to inform the business community and the country at large about the new training program when Secretary Wirtz put an end to this effort by explaining that he could not personally deal with still one more special interest group. I failed to understand then, or now, how a federal training initiative could go forward without the active involvement and input of at least a significant sector of the business community.

Some of the labor representatives on the NMAC were skeptical of involvement by the federal government in the training of skilled workers, since that was a critical responsibility of the craft unions. The AFL-CIO supported the passage of MDTA but played a relatively restrained role until late in the 1960s, when the issue of providing public service employment (PSE) opportunities was placed on the national agenda. At that point I recall that a principal advisor to George Meany and his staff made a special trip to my summer house on Martha's Vineyard to offer a trade: strong labor support for the expansion of MDTA for NMAC support of PSE. I explained to the emissary that while I favored PSE, I could not give him any firm assurance that the Committee would agree—although I anticipated that the majority would do so, as in fact it did. I will indulge myself to point out that in the 76 advisory meetings that I chaired over the nineteen-year span, only one issue was ever put to a vote. My preference was to send summary reviews of our meetings to the Secretaries of Labor and HEW, to whom we initially reported, and later to the President and the presiding officers of the Senate and the House of Representatives, distilling the "essence" of our discussions and recommendations. Voting, in my view, would harden differences instead of expanding the areas of agreement among the members of the advisory committee. To the best of my recollection, no member ever challenged any of my summaries. With the advantage of hindsight, I might be more inclined today to let at least selected issues come to a vote as one way of sharpening and clarifying the views of the members.

In the middle 1960s, the MDTA youth component was expanded and the antipoverty Economic Opportunity Act added the Neighborhood Youth Corps and the Job Corps. The vocational educational lobby in the Congress had strongly supported MDTA when the legislation was first discussed and played a key role in its later extension. The fact that some large corporations, including leaders in aerospace, were willing to bid on Job Corps contracts added another important interest group that favored the expansion of MDTA and other federal training efforts. A third new "constituency" consisted of the community-based organizations that found an opportunity to organize training programs in their local areas and occasionally over a broader area. Some years later an astute observer of MDTA concluded that the individuals who profited the most from the new training structure were selected minority members who got an early start on the management ladder and then moved into more responsible positions as training programs expanded.

The summer of 1965 saw the outbreak of widespread disturbances in many urban areas, including Los Angeles, where black youth and adults had become exasperated by the gaps between the promise of America and the reality they faced. A quick trip to the area highlighted for me the difficulties of any quick and easy solutions since the secondary school system was seriously malfunctioning and the absence of public transportation between the inner city where the minority poor lived and the expanding jobs in the outer regions of the metropolitan areas could not be easily resolved, not even with liberal federal transportation subsidies.

President Johnson, in responding to the rioting of 1965, appointed a "secret" task force chaired by George Shultz, which consisted of key black leaders and white representatives from business, law, and academe, on which I was invited to serve in my capacity as chair of the

NMAC. It was to take an in-depth look, at least on a demonstration basis, to assure that all children growing up in an urban ghetto could enjoy the developmental and educational opportunities that they needed to qualify as future workers and family heads.The group took its assignment seriously, and after extensive field visits to a number of urban ghettos it concluded that adequate schooling from prekindergarten to the end of high school could be provided only if schools could be detached from the existing bureaucratic structures and placed under the supervision of a major university's school of education.

The reason that we were a "secret" task force reflected the President's concern that, with the escalation of the war in Vietnam, Congress might not agree to fund new manpower and social welfare demonstrations; in such an event, the President didn't want to be embarrassed. We had reached a semifinal stage in our deliberations with a prospective recommendation of a demonstration budget of about $13-14 billion a year. At that point the President's assistant, Joseph Califano, came to our meeting and confiscated all copies of our draft report.

Determined to do something to improve the employment and income prospects for blacks and other poor persons and recognizing that new large-scale funding from the Congress would not be forthcoming, the President assumed the leadership, working with Henry Ford II and other business leaders of the National Alliance of Business to elicit their help in expanding employment opportunities for the hitherto excluded. (In the process the Department of Labor was sidetracked.) With the labor market booming in the late 1960s, many industrialists made a serious effort to respond to the President's request, and large numbers of blacks, of both sexes, were hired. Unfortunately, when the downturn in the cycle occurred in the early 1970s, a significant proportion of the last hired were the first fired.

For most of the 1960s the U.S. Department of Labor struggled to deal with the many thousand training contracts that it had negotiated in different sectors of the country, a reflection of the fact that 90 percent of the funding for MDTA came from the federal government. But with the passage of time it became increasingly clear that the operation of MDTA had to be decentralized to the states and the cities—and the issue of public service employment for the hard-to-employ had to be faced. After President Nixon's election and assumption of office in early 1969, the Department of Labor and the interested committees of the Congress set about drafting a reform bill which included a limited appropriation for public service jobs. The members of the NMAC were at Camp David to explore the changes that would follow the new legislation when a telephone call announced that the President had vetoed the bill on the ground that he wanted no part in reestablishing leaf-raking jobs reminiscent of the New Deal era.

Faced with a looser labor market in 1970-1971 and an acceleration in the release of soldiers who had fought in Vietnam, the President was willing to accept a substitute legislative reform package that included 200,000 PSE jobs. The NMAC had put the issue of PSE and full employment on its agenda as early as 1965, but after an exploratory discussion had let the issue lie, having concluded that the time was not ripe for pressing ahead on that point. True, there were a few senators who wanted to move ahead with such a proposal, but it was clear to the NMAC that with the escalation of the war in Vietnam, the increasing unease of the Congress about the budgetary outlook, and the war-fueled expansion that was occurring in the job market, the time was not opportune for making a push for a full-employment policy.

It may be useful to recall that the "federal deficit" issue, which has dominated the Washington scene during the last fifteen years, resulted from actions taken in 1964 in which Congress adopted a counter-cyclical spending and tax policy so that when the economy was slack the government would lower taxes and spend more and when the economy approached full utilization the reverse measures—tax increases and moderation of spending—would be followed. I thought at the time that it would be easier for Congress to learn the first lesson and forget the second—which would result in a long-term loss, not a gain in macro-policy.

President Nixon's willingness to reverse his opposition to PSE was not only a reflection of the pluses and minuses of dealing with the Democrats who controlled the Congress, but also reflected the continuing evolution of the role of manpower policy on the national scene. MDTA was seen as a vehicle for speeding the employment of Vietnam veterans, opening a new area of opportunity for manpower policy. Since the rate at which soldiers were sent home from Vietnam was relatively modest and would continue over many months and even years, the availability of 200,000 PSE jobs to be used as needed to speed their reentry into the domestic labor force seemed appropriate. And there were many in the Congress who looked with favor on the rapprochement between Republicans and Democrats who, until the President's veto, had worked closely together on manpower legislation.

By the time that MDTA approached its tenth and final year it had been pulled and pushed to respond to a great number of different "at-risk" persons for whom opportunity for training and later for a public service job held out some reasonable prospect of benefit. These included:

- Skilled workers who had lost their jobs because of automation

- Large numbers of poorly educated, poorly skilled adults who sought training from MDTA

- Young people, especially in low-income urban areas, who needed to earn some money during their summer vacations

- Young people who had dropped out of school before attaining a high school diploma and who could profit from the kind of new residential environment provided by the Job Corps where they could catch up on their education, obtain some basic skills, and be in a stronger position to make their way in the world of work

- The more disadvantaged members of the labor force who in addition to the drawbacks of limited education and skills also belonged to families trapped in poverty

- Older persons who might be helped to get a job or improve their earning capabilities if a modest number of training slots were reserved for them

- Prisoners, either current or recently released from the criminal justice system

- Returning Vietnam veterans

This list does not pretend to exhaust the many groups of disadvantaged persons identified as potential beneficiaries of the various types of training opportunities made available under MDTA.

The Advent of CETA

With so many potential applicants for training slots, with MDTA relying primarily on vocational education and the employment service as the principal service deliverers, and with almost half of the budget spent on stipends, the tension between funding and the length and quality of the training that could be provided was with some exceptions very great. The inadequate basic educational skills of so many of the trainees only exacerbated the situation since the available funding was grossly inadequate to bring many of them up to an acceptable educational level and at the same time provide them with even modest skill training. The average MDTA enrollee had only 22 weeks in a training program, much too brief a period to make them competitive even for an entrance-level job. Even worse, the failure to decategorize and decentralize the MDTA program further reduced its potential effectiveness. Fortunately, the Nixon administration and the Congress were able to agree on the passage of the Comprehensive Employment and Training Act of 1973 (CETA). The new legislation decategorized by bringing together all elements of both MDTA and the Economic Opportunity Act which had launched the antipoverty effort (leaving only Job Corps free-standing) and decentralized by funneling most of the federal funds to prime sponsors—that is, local planning agencies dominated by local and county officials who were given broad discretion in the selection of service deliverers.

The new CETA structure had been in place for only a relatively short period of time when the country experienced the most serious depression since the 1930-33 debacle. The Democratic leaders of the Congress were not satisfied with the antidepression recommendations forwarded by President Ford and decided to take the lead in designing policies and programs that would be more responsive. The subsequent transformation of CETA can only be understood in the light of previous approaches.

Shortly after Nixon defeated McGovern in the election of 1972 he made public his intention to streamline the federal government by consolidating a number of cabinet departments. Haldeman was initially scheduled to meet with the senior officials of the Department of Labor, who invited me to be present, but with Watergate preempting more of

his time and energy, Ehrlichman came in his place. I have no clear recollection of what the details of his message were, but I think it per-
tained to the proposed merger of Labor and Commerce, together with
plans for substantial cutbacks in programming and in staff. It was a
most unpleasant presentation, since the speaker elicited no questions
and tolerated no discussion. As an outsider listening in, I did not
assume, as did many of the others in attendance, that all of the White
House plans were misconceived and could lead only to trouble, but I
was chilled by the arrogance of the speaker and concluded that with
persons like him in senior staff roles at the White House, policies and
programs were unlikely to be strengthened.

I was reminded of a comment that my long-term friend and colleague Arthur F. Burns made to me on a walk to his home after dinner
at the White House Mess during which we had avoided all serious subjects. Burns had been serving at the time as Counsellor to the President. He said that he was unable to put his finger on just what disturbed
him about the President's senior staff, but it was quite unlike anything
he had ever experienced. Nothing seemed to be straightforward—
either in speech or in written communications. And there was little or
no feedback. Burns said he had made up his mind to leave and to do so
very shortly. Watching Ehrlichman in action at the Department of
Labor reminded me of Burns' disquietude and determination to leave
the administration. I too, from this single exposure, felt squeamish.

But in fairness, I must report on several more positive experiences
with the Nixon administration. With the passage of CETA, the advisory
committee structure underwent a significant change. The new legislation provided that the National Commission for Manpower Policy
report to the President and Congress. William Kohlberg, the new Assistant Secretary of Labor, asked me whether I would be willing to
assume the chair of the new Commission but pointed out that I would
have to obtain "political clearance" from the White House. This was
the only time in my nineteen years of service as chairman that I had to
obtain such clearance. The White House official with whom I talked
was a reasonable and relaxed interviewer who did not press me very
hard after I explained to him that as a New Yorker I had never enrolled
in either party; that I had worked closely with President Eisenhower;
and that I had worked constructively with key members of Congress of

both parties. I have no way of knowing whether and how thoroughly he checked me out, but my clearance came through expeditiously.

At one point near the end of the first or at the beginning of Nixon's second administration the insiders got nervous that the administration planned to cut back radically on its request for new manpower funding. Sar Levitan got in touch with me and suggested that we jointly set up an appointment with George Shultz, who was serving at the time as Secretary of the Treasury but who continued to be interested in the manpower domain and at the same time was viewed as one of the President's intimate advisors. Sar and I had no difficulty in arranging an early meeting with George, who provided us with ample time to set out our concerns and pinpoint the kinds of help that we thought the program required. Subsequent to our visit the ominous rumors about the forthcoming emasculation of the manpower programs ceased.

The third "interaction" between the NMAC and then-President Nixon occurred when the Department sponsored a luncheon celebrating the tenth anniversary of MDTA. The President was invited to speak, but he could not accept, sending instead a warm letter of appreciation to the members of the NMAC and to me commending us for our helpful participation in the shaping and reshaping of the program.

These observations enable us to pick up the main threads. There were a number of hearings and subsequent amendments to CETA, so that it could respond more successfully to the serious recession of 1974-5. I was asked to testify at these hearings—as I had attended most congressional hearings during the two decades when various committees were reviewing issues that had been and continued to be of concern to what was now called the National Commission for Manpower Policy. The main purpose of CETA had been to focus increasingly on the more disadvantaged members of the labor force who required assistance to enable them to get and hold a job. But early on the rumor circulated that the key members of the Congress, especially the Democratic leaders, were looking to CETA as a major solution to the growing unemployment brought on by the worsening recession.

In my testimony I tried very hard to be sympathetic to the proposals for expanding CETA to serve more effectively as an antirecession measure without undermining the increasing emphasis that the Congress had been placing on directing manpower efforts primarily to the more, if not the most, disadvantaged. I accepted the idea that a spell of a week's unemployment be made the basis for qualifying for a CETA job but that this brief period of unemployment be linked to family income, making eligibility for a CETA job depend on low family income even if the spell of unemployment was brief. I pointed out that with ever increasing numbers of women from middle and upper income homes entering the labor force, many for the first time, many CETA jobs would otherwise go to families that were not in need of federal assistance.

As was my usual experience, the senators and representatives who showed up at the many hearings at which I testified were almost without exception interested, polite, and occasionally probing. But this time I drew a blank. My arguments, no matter how formulated, failed to elicit any favorable response. I assume that the Democratic leadership wanted to go to the country and claim credit for having passed new legislation that would address the worsening recession and permit all unemployed Americans, not just the poor, to profit from their actions.

Shortly after Ford replaced Nixon in the White House, Arthur Burns, at the time the chair of the Federal Reserve Board, invited me as a luncheon guest of honor to meet the senior economic officials of the new administration. There were about eight around the table. Early on, the conversation focused on what America most needed—an inexpensive auto. I listened attentively but could make little or no sense of the consensus that was early arrived at that such a car would assure the long-term success and expansion of the American economy. Fortunately, there was one dissenter in the group—the President's economic assistant who came from Michigan, who knew much about the automobile industry and could make little or no sense out of this suggestion either. Later on, when I had an opportunity to reflect on what had happened, I decided that such ramblings were a form of relaxation for officials who were forced most of the day to work very hard on very difficult issues.

In the course of my ongoing visits and talks with Arthur Burns I noted his increasing concern with the fact that nobody in Washington apparently had any idea about how to respond to the worsening recession other than to spend more money, an approach that did not appeal to him. If truth be told, it did not particularly appeal to me either, since I had never gotten over my childhood encounter with high inflation in Germany in 1922. At this point I offered Burns a deal. I would do my best to moderate the manpower spending proposals put forward by the National Commission for Manpower Policy if he in turn would recommend that the federal government become the employer of last resort. The discussions continued for the better part of a year and Burns finally accepted the challenge in a speech at the University of Georgia in Augusta, adding a special twist—these government jobs should be paid at 10 percent below the minimum wage!

Burns' Georgia address was largely ignored by the press but at a manpower conference some months later George Meany launched an all-out attack on Burns for recommending a federal wage 10 percent below the minimum wage even if the proposal carried with it the promise of a job for everybody who wanted to work. Senator Hubert Humphrey alone remarked that he welcomed the support of Arthur Burns for the idea that the federal government had an obligation to help every unemployed person get a job if the private demand for workers fell short.

For the first time, except for the initial reception at the White House, members of the manpower advisory committees were asked to meet with President Ford for an exchange of information and views. During the first half of the meeting the President was an active participant in the two-way discussion, but after that he appeared to tire, lose interest, or both, to the dismay of his staff and of the advisory committee members.

Many were surprised when Governor Carter—a largely unknown name outside of the South—captured the Democratic nomination for the Presidency in mid-year 1976, but no one was more surprised than I when, several weeks later, I received a phone call from Jody Powell from Georgia asking whether I would prepare a memorandum for the Governor on work and welfare. I explained that I had taken great care since my initial appointment as chair in 1962 not to become involved in partisan politics; that I had been reappointed by President Ford; and I could not possibly become involved in the presidential campaign. Powell replied that I had misunderstood the Governor's request. On the assumption that he won the election, he would like to move forward expeditiously with new reform legislation, and the paper that he was asking me to prepare was related to his postelection planning. In the face of this reassurance, I told him that I felt free to develop such a paper and would be pleased to do so if he could once more reassure me that it would not be used in any way in the current campaign. With renewed reassurance in hand I prepared a 35-page memorandum with suggestions as to the best ways of using employment and training policies to reduce the large numbers of long-term clients on welfare, emphasizing that all such clients of working age without major disabilities should use these programs to improve their employability and become self-supporting, at least in part. I recall specifically that I emphasized the legitimacy of the federal government's requirement that recipients undertake appropriate training and/or PSE jobs to receive welfare support.

The end of this story is simple: Jody Powell kept his word. I suspect that some parts of my analysis and recommendations were helpful to the new President as he tackled the difficult subject with no greater success than his predecessors and successors. While my paper had oversimplified a very complicated subject, at least it did not point to an easy political solution.

President-elect Carter designated Ray Marshall of the University of Texas as his Secretary of Labor, and the two of us had dinner early on with Seymour Wolfbein of the Department who was a mutual friend. We reviewed a large number of issues that Marshall would soon confront. On the trip back to town, Marshall told me of the President's tremendous enthusiasm for the PSE program and that in fact Marshall had to persuade him not to request funding for more than the 750,000 jobs proposed, since it seemed to him that neither the federal government nor the prime sponsors would be able to expand more rapidly. It is worth noting that Carter was the only one of the six presidents from Kennedy to Reagan who was enthusiastic about using manpower policy as the major stimulus for an economy that was operating at less than full capacity.

Nevertheless, one of the more confusing and discouraging episodes in the area of manpower legislation was the bungled manner in which the Humphrey-Hawkins Full Employment and Balanced Growth bill was handled. In an increasingly difficult environment of inflation, stagflation, and federal deficits and with no real constituency in favor of such a far-reaching proposal, the horrendous difficulties of implementation were left for a later time. Because of the decision of the Congress to pay tribute to a distinguished colleague who had been stricken with a fatal disease, an innocuous piece of legislation was finally passed (1978), but it remained a tribute, not a challenge to new national action.

I arranged early on in the Carter administration to have a meeting with Dr. Charles Schultze, the Chair of the Council of Economic Advisors to President Carter, to see how the National Commission for Manpower Policy could be helpful to an administration that was clearly so partial to employment and training programs as a cyclical stimulus. I recognized after leaving Schultze's office that presidents and their economic advisors did not always read the economy from the same perspective. Schultze did his best to mask his skepticism about the president's enthusiasm for manpower programs as a tool for macroeconomic stimulus. In any case Schultze conveyed to me that he did not believe there was much scope for cooperation between the Council of Economic Advisors and our Commission.

Since our Commission reported to both the President and the Congress after each quarterly meeting, I was pleasantly surprised to find that not once, but repeatedly, the copy that I forwarded to the President was returned to me with marginal notes both substantive and stylistic. While I and my fellow committee members were clearly pleased with this evidence of presidential interest and concern, I for one wondered whether such careful readings and notations were warranted, given the extraordinary demands on the time and energy of the President. My concern was heightened as I observed the difficulties that Carter was having in assuming a leadership role and in developing relations with both the Congress and with the media, two centers of influence with which every successful president had to cooperate.

In early 1979 the President recognized that his administration was facing growing difficulties with inflation and other important issues, domestic and foreign. This led him to take counsel with a diverse group of advisors in meetings at Camp David preparatory to reorganizing the leadership of many Cabinet departments. I was invited to one of these Camp David retreats to which the top command of the nation's trade unions were present, together with selected leaders of the Senate and the House and a sprinkling of others including a few prominent industrialists, making altogether about 35 to 40 persons.

Almost everyone present endorsed increased spending on manpower programs. My turn came near the end, and I took a different approach, emphasizing that the President faced certain defeat in a reelection bid if inflation was not brought under control, since further inflationary pressures would make it more difficult to prevent a downward spiral in the economy and the labor market. I urged the President to freeze his requests for additional federal spending on the manpower front but to avoid cutbacks in training for inner-city minority youth who had to be protected, no matter how severe inflationary pressures had become.

Even while I was pressing these points, I saw that several of the White House aides who were sitting on the outer rim looked at me as a traitor. After all, who would have expected the chair of the NCMP to advise the President to spend less, not more? The news of my "treachery" reached the Washington insiders before I got back to town in the late afternoon. But it seemed to me at the time—and since—that the President was entitled to hear what his advisors recommended, not what their constituents desired. I was in the fortunate position of not having a constituency!

About six months later the President invited several of us who had been at Camp David to a luncheon at the White House to hear from him directly how he had moved to strengthen his administration. I had the good fortune to draw Mrs. Carter as my luncheon partner so I was able to hear not only the President's account, which was not all that clear, and Mrs. Carter's footnotes, which impressed me greatly. She clearly had a highly developed political sense and an ability to cut through verbiage and get quickly to the central points. It was a long and pleasant luncheon, but I came away almost certain that the President's reelection was doomed, even if he were to rely increasingly on his talented wife.

To return to the main theme—the last years of CETA boasted an annual appropriation of around $12 billion or 50 times the initial appropriation for MDTA (in real dollars). With the passage of every year the media was able to identify new stories of program malfunctioning, incompetence, lack of effectiveness, outright chicanery, and fraud. It appeared to me at the time, and on later reflection, that while each negative story probably was grounded in fact the overall impression building up in the public's mind that CETA was a failure was wrong. Most of the federal funds were spent on the poor, and after the 1976 amendments on those who were the most disadvantaged. It was true, however, that the program failed to achieve its proposed objective of shifting the unemployed and underemployed poor into regular jobs.

There were success stories of young men who went through a well-structured automotive mechanics course lasting eight or nine months who were then placed in regular jobs paying considerably above minimum wage and who were able with the skills they had acquired not only to hold a job but even to advance. The most spectacular example of what a year's focused training could do was found among health aides and unskilled workers who at the end of their course became "licensed practical nurses" at a wage approximately double of what they had earned earlier and with further career and income mobility still before them. The young men who attended the residential Job Corps and completed the training cycle also appeared to be on their way to more education, greater skills, and better job prospects.

But after singling out these favorable outcomes for some who had been previously only marginally attached to the labor force and could now find a good opening, most of the CETA money went to education, training, and PSE work which improved the current earnings of these marginal persons but did not translate into real long-term gains for them in the labor market. Most of the applicants were too severely handicapped at the time that they applied, and there were too many of them to support a sufficiently long period of remedial education and training to change their long-term prospects.

Because many members of Congress, both Democrats and Republicans, realized that CETA funding made it possible for the districts that they represented to do something positive for the many different groups of disadvantaged persons who lived in the area—even if the federal programs could not lead most of the recipients into a regular job—they continued to vote for new and larger appropriations. But when I appeared before the Senate Budget Committee in 1979 and underwent critical questioning by "liberal" Democrats, I realized that CETA was likely to be in serious trouble in the years ahead, particularly if the next Republican candidate for the presidency adopted a critical stance towards the program, which in fact Reagan did. Had it not been for some astute maneuvering by the leadership of the National Alliance of Business, which had the interest and support of many liberally inclined leaders of the employer community, Reagan in his first year would have liquidated the program completely rather than accepting a large-scale reduction in the previous rate of spending for the new JTPA program.

Reprise

This review of my role as chair of the successive advisory committees between 1962 and 1981 gives me the opportunity to revisit and reappraise MDTA and CETA as follows:

- Federal manpower policy as exemplified initially by MDTA and reinforced by related efforts of the Great Society program of 1964-67 represented in the first instance ad hoc efforts of members of Congress concerned with assisting various groups that faced above average difficulties in the labor market. There was no broad constituency, intellectual or political, to expand the role of the federal government to make it a significant third party—in addition to employers and trade unions—to improve the functioning of the U.S. labor market.

- Mainline macroeconomists who advised the successive presidents and held key positions in policy formulation had little if any interest in manpower policy early in the 1960s or late in the 1970s. They were preoccupied with budgetary and fiscal instruments that could affect the level of total employment. The lack of interest among mainline economists in manpower policy resulted in inadequate evaluations of the ongoing programs and only sporadic attempts to strengthen them.

- With the single exception of Jimmy Carter, none of the six presidents from Kennedy to Reagan had any interest in using manpower policy as a major instrument for effecting desirable changes in the economy. Accordingly, most of the public, which understood little about the potential and limitations of manpower policy, failed to become actively involved.

- The fact that for the better part of a decade the federal government sought to oversee, if not directly run, employment and training programs throughout the fifty states and in all of the nation's larger cities almost guaranteed poor performance. Although CETA led to the decategorization and decentralization of manpower programs, difficulties remained in creating a strong infrastructure, given the bureaucratic history of vocational education, the weaknesses of most employment services, and the preference of most employers to keep their distance from governmental efforts to reshape the labor market. The countervailing forces were community leaders, new federal dollars, and a growing body of knowledge and experience about how to restructure and improve employment and training programs.

In sum, this personal revisit to MDTA and CETA was a lesson for me about the relative flexibility in the use of new federal dollars in the 1960s and 1970s on behalf of disadvantaged persons, despite little prior planning and limited attention to organization, administration, and evaluation. Manpower funding in the 1960s and 1970s reflected a particular phase in the development of American democracy where efforts at improvement have often exceeded accomplishments. But in the long run, a society that is willing to make efforts on behalf of the weak and vulnerable is surely to be preferred to a society that is focused on maintaining the status quo.

CHAPTER **6**

Vocational Education Accountability in a "Block-Grant-to-States" World
Historical Perspective

David W. Stevens

Performance measurement in U.S. vocational education will be affected by pending congressional action to consolidate federal investments in vocational education and employment and training. This chapter explores the accountability antecedents of the Job Training Consolidation Act of 1995 (S. 143) and Consolidated and Reformed Education, Employment, and Rehabilitation Systems (CAREERS) Act (H.R. 1617). Conferees will soon attempt to reconcile these into a mutually satisfactory compromise that the President can be expected to sign.

National assembly of reliable training-related placement information is futile in today's context of educational choice, occupational complexity, and fragile employee-employer bonding. A new generation of labor market outcome measurement initiatives is needed. These investments should favor data collection and accessibility refinements that will support the difficult choices among stakeholders that the consolidation legislation and appropriations levels will compel.

Federal Legislation

The historical record should be reviewed before attempting to predict the effect of the consolidation legislation on performance measurement (Giodarno and Praeger 1977; Cuban 1982). The dawn of the twentieth century found the American Federation of Labor, the National Association of Manufacturers, and the National Society for the Promotion of Industrial Education promoting federal funding for vocational education to sustain economic progress through a more relevant curriculum. A Commission on National Aid to Vocational Education was appointed by Congress in 1914. The Commission's recommendations led to the landmark Smith-Hughes Act of 1917, which authorized federal investment in a limited number of occupational clusters. States were required to match the federal commitment. The Federal Bureau of Vocational Education and Federal Board for Vocational Education established to carry out Smith-Hughes are the precursors of today's Office of Vocational and Adult Education in the U.S. Department of Education and federal, state, and local advisory boards with diverse membership.

World War I, the Depression, World War II, and Sputnik are defining events that molded vocational education in the United States during the forty-six years that elapsed between Smith- Hughes and passage of the Vocational Education Act of 1963. The wars and Sputnik heightened awareness of the Nation's uneven capacity to satisfy industrial skill requirements in a timely and sustained manner. The Depression fostered cooperative education alliances as a substitute for the purchase of expensive equipment and revealed vocational education's vulnerability when asked to serve displaced adult workers and to carry on in a world of limited employment opportunity.

The Vocational Education Act of 1963 drew back from categorical funding of particular occupational skill clusters and stated an expectation that federal funds should flow to vocational programs serving disadvantaged students. Planning and evaluation activities were introduced to manage the new block grant approach. Neither served as an effective control mechanism.

Subsequent amendments of the 1963 Act in 1968 and 1976, the Carl D. Perkins Vocational Education Act of 1984, and the Vocational Education and Applied Technology Act of 1990 each specified categorical opportunities that were intended to offer the carrot needed to realign state vocational education programs. The 1990 Perkins Amendments encouraged the integration of academic and vocational curricula and promoted combinations of high school and postsecondary courses as tech-prep programs. The CAREERS Act and Job Training Consolidation Act, passed in September and October 1995 by the U.S. House of Representatives and U.S. Senate, respectively, would devolve these management decisions to the states.

The Evolution of Performance Expectations

Outcome expectations for vocational education in the United States have been documented (Evans and Violas 1983; U.S. Congress, Office of Technology Assessment 1994). Stakeholders often have inconsistent views of what vocational education ought to be and do. Evans and Violas assert that:

> Prior to 1963, it was clearly understood that trade and industrial education produced employees, agricultural education produced entrepreneurs, and home economics education produced homemakers. Now it seems to be assumed by nonvocational educators that all should produce employees. (p. 35)

> Prior to 1968, the only substantial national data on vocational education were on enrollments in subject matter areas...No one knew how many people were completing programs or how much time they spent in class...It would appear that both defenders and critics were reasonably happy to make assumptions about outcomes based on logic or exhortations, rather than to test outcomes with data. (p. 36)

Today's consolidation dialogue reveals the same basic outcome expectations that preceded successful passage of the Smith-Hughes Act in 1917.

1. certification of student competencies (on behalf of employers),

2. qualification to earn a "living wage" (on behalf of students),

3. gender advocacy,

4. acculturation of workers, and

5. sustained funding for each stakeholder's own desired portfolio of vocational education activities.

Smith-Hughes was highly prescriptive with regard to process and the use of federal funds, but contained no explicit outcome expectations. The Vocational Education Act of 1963, which was far less prescriptive about the use of federal funds, advised states that their vocational offerings would be assessed with respect to current and projected manpower needs and job opportunities. Congressional intent was also expressed for these funds to be concentrated on vocational education programs serving the disadvantaged. This shift from "what to offer and how to do so" to "who to serve toward what end" has persisted through the Carl D. Perkins Vocational Education and Applied Technology Act of 1990.

The 1963 Vocational Education Act offered the vocational education community an opportunity to use federal funds to respond to the social and economic challenges of the times with few strings attached. An avalanche of complementary federal employment and training legislation and funds cascaded to the states at the same time (Levitan and Mangum 1967; Levitan and Taggart 1971; Pines et al 1995). These included youth-oriented amendments in 1963 to the Manpower Development and Training Act of 1962, both in-school and out-of-school components of the Neighborhood Youth Corps, Job Corps authorizations in the Economic Opportunity Act of 1964, and introduction of an Apprenticeship Outreach Program in 1968. Both long-standing and new community-based organizations appeared to carry out these aggressive federal initiatives. Many traditional vocational educators watched from the sidelines.

A consensus soon emerged that vocational educators had not responded to the 1963 Act's carrot. So, in 1967 an Advisory Council on Vocational Education was appointed. Many of the Council's recommendations became law in the 1968 Vocational Education Amendments. Now, for the first time in the United States, enrollment figures became a factor in the allocation of federal funds to the states. Cooperative education was endorsed, and states were told that federal funds should only be used to prepare students for employment or be of significant assistance in making an informed and meaningful occupational choice. Subsequent 1976 amendments added sex equity as a federal vocational education priority and introduced the now familiar training-related placement criterion as a performance review factor.

Looking back, it is now easy to cast the tumultuous '60s in terms of a growing tension between the traditional instrumental role of vocational education as one source of energy to power the engine of economic growth and the emerging view that vocational education should be seen as a key to unlock the gate to individual opportunity (Lewis 1990; Benavot 1983). Perceptive observers cast the dialogue in these terms while the legislative battles were still being fought.

> The "solution" often advocated in recent years has been to equip the school leaver with a specific skill for the job market. The rationale has been twofold: (1) early school leavers are not academically inclined and are more likely to remain in school if provided specific occupational training; and (2) the school leaver must have something to sell in the job market and that requires skill training, limited as it may be. The alternative arguments appear more persuasive: (1) the high school youth's exposure to alternative occupational choices has usually been too limited for a valid and lasting vocational decision; (2) distaste for "academic" subjects is more an argument against existing teaching methods than an argument for elimination of "academic" content; (3) specific occupational training, as a substitute for broader education, drastically limits the options available both at the time of entry into the labor market and later in life; and (4) good vocational education is expensive and the failure of vocational high schools to provide it is notorious. (Levitan and Mangum 1967, pp. 33-34)

The Comprehensive Employment and Training Act of 1973 (CETA) created a strong federal-local tie that was out of sync with vocational education's federal-state governance. This represented yet another challenge to the exclusivity of public vocational education. Little evidence of voluntary cooperation between the two networks in the next few years led to 1976 amendments of the Vocational Education Act and 1978 amendments to the CETA mandating cooperation and earmarking funds for this purpose (Stevens 1979).

The Comprehensive Employment and Training Act also authorized a Summer Program for Economically Disadvantaged Youth, which was followed by the Youth Employment and Demonstration Projects Act in 1977. These, in turn, were consolidated as Title IV in the 1978 amendments. The Youth Employment and Training Program component of

Title IV became a work experience program, although a much broader range of services was allowed.

The Carl D. Perkins Vocational Education Act of 1984 advanced federal expectations about state and local accountability. States were directed to develop measures of program effectiveness, including identification of the competencies that would be used to assure that vocational students satisfy the hiring requirements of employers.

> By 1990, Congress had concluded that prior calls for change had not spurred significant improvements in the quality of vocational education. Influenced by experiences with outcome based accountability in other federal education and training programs, Congress amended the Perkins Act to require states, within 1 year, to develop and implement statewide systems of "core standards and measures" that defined the student outcomes expected in local programs. (U.S. Congress, Office of Technology Assessment 1994, p. 5)

Two important conclusions about this federal mandate, each by acknowledged experts in vocational education accountability, quickly deflate any expectation that federal authorities were finally prepared to hold states' feet to the fire. Hoachlander and Levesque, who have provided technical assistance to, and documented the responses of, the states in developing statewide systems of core standards and measures, warn that

> It is essential to understand that the primary purpose of these performance monitoring systems is local and state program improvement: helping local and state educators respond more effectively to the needs of students and the marketplace. To this end, the systems must reflect the diversity that characterizes vocational education by adapting to local and state needs and circumstances. (Hoachlander and Levesque 1993, p. 81)

In other words, do not expect the statewide systems to be amenable to straightforward aggregation at the national level. This warning was echoed by John Wirt, the former director of the U.S. Department of Education's second National Assessment of Vocational Education that was completed in 1989.

> The 1990 legislation marks a significant turning point in federal accountability by explicitly tying the process of state and local

review to standards based on outcomes...The requirement for standards is also significant as much for what it does not require as for what it does. First, Congress did not authorize the Secretary of Education to issue national standards and measures.... Second,... the standards are not intended to certify or credential individuals.... Third, Congress chose not to link the vocational education performance standards to federal funding or any other incentives or sanctions. (U.S. Congress, Office of Technology Assessment 1994, p. 5)

Three decades of federal attempts to create bundles of performance incentives to promote the formation of teams of advocates for student opportunity and economic prosperity have fostered limited and unstable state and local alliances. This pattern is expected to continue in a "block-grant-to-states" context because vocational education reforms pass through three distinct stages: (1) program design; (2) execution; and (3) consequence.

The expectations of diverse and changing parties have affected the design of vocational education programs since the turn of the century, particularly as federal legislation and funds have influenced these expectations. These designs have often been transformed into action by educators who had a limited, or no, role in the design phase. A weak link between the execution and consequence stages lessens the incentive for those who execute to remain faithful to the original design. This decoupling also restricts the timely flow of reliable information through a feedback loop to guide redesign adjustments.

Substantial state and local management energy has been absorbed in complying with federal reporting requirements, and with devising ways to do what you want to do without federal sanction. This has drawn resources away from routine state and local management diagnostics. Despite this federal investment in data collection, compelling documentation of a causal link between vocational education's enhancement of occupational competencies and a student's subsequent access to challenging and rewarding jobs remains an elusive goal.

Measurement of Labor Market Outcomes

Fifty years ago, at the end of World War II, vocational education in the United States was defined by categorical occupational concentrations, a public high school home, separate white male and female student populations, parity of federal and state/local funding, and a fragile but stable consensus that satisfaction of employer skill requirements was the basic objective. Few competitors provided skill training opportunities outside the workplace. Organized labor maintained pervasive control over apprenticeship ports-of-entry into the internal labor markets of major manufacturers who offered stable employment, relatively high wages, and retirement benefits.

While vocational education's actual performance had been controversial since the turn of the century, long before Smith-Hughes, no serious attempt was made to back up these doubts with reliable evidence. Recurring debates about continued federal funding for agriculture and home economics programs did not rely upon performance data. The growth of career counseling coincident with passage of the G.I. Bill focused more on the projection of occupational opportunities than on vocational education's success in responding to these projected needs.

Nearly two decades elapsed after the end of World War II before vocational education's accomplishment of mission became a data-based issue. Among the most important reasons for this ascendancy of interest in performance measurement are: (1) the National Defense Education Act of 1958 had opened the door to federal funding of postsecondary vocational education for the first time, which in turn triggered new requests for information about the relative payoffs on federal investments in high school and postsecondary programs; (2) cost-benefit analysis was in vogue; and (3) the revolutionary turn of attention away from categorical occupational clusters and toward categorical student populations was accompanied by a heated debate about the anticipated consequences of this change, which created a new demand for performance information.

Strong cross-currents swirl through the vocational education evaluation literature. Vocational educators question the motives and methods of outsiders (Evans and Violas 1983). Outsiders have challenged each other for many years (Grasso and Shea 1979; Gustman and Steinmeier 1980; Meyer 1982; Kane and Rouse 1995a; Grubb 1995). Insiders equivocate (U.S. Department of Education 1994b).

Few published results have been actionable in the sense that an identifiable agent might be expected to take a predictable, and different, action affecting vocational education based on the reported finding (Stevens 1994b). Consider Grasso and Shea's 1979 results that were the basic labor-market outcomes foundation for the first modern-era national evaluation of vocational education in the U.S.

> With respect to wages and earnings, findings (based largely on the NLS) differed by sex. Among males, enrollment in an occupational program during high school was on average unrelated to rate of pay and to annual earnings. (It should be noted, however, that analysis by speciality area, such as welding and automobile repair, was not possible.) (Grasso and Shea 1979, p. 183)

Who could be expected to take what action based on this finding? We now treat reported findings of this type as quaint reminders of how humble were our analytical origins, and how meager were the actionable implications of such findings. Fortunately, recent exemplary exceptions are available (Stern et al. 1994).

Three national assessments of vocational education since 1980 have now attempted to find and report evidence of vocational education's net impact on the subsequent labor market success of former vocational education students (National Institute of Education 1981; U.S. Department of Education 1989; and U.S. Department of Education 1994a). None of the three national inquiries succeeded in uncovering what the authors considered to be reliable evidence of net impact. Each time the failure to come forth with compelling evidence of vocational education's net impact on labor market access and achievement has been blamed on data—wrong unit(s) of analysis and time coverage, failure to document pertinent student and institutional attributes, and unknown or insufficient quality of information. Should we conclude after fifteen years and three attempts that documentation of labor market impact is a futile exercise? Yes at the national level; but no at the state and local level. The remainder of the chapter explains this answer.

The "all the eggs in one basket" phenomenon. Sar Levitan offered the following measured counsel regarding this issue, which masks the passionate disdain that he harbored for the victory of form over substance: "Both sides of the qualitative- quantitative debate would seem to be well advised to employ multiple approaches to evaluation" (Levitan 1992, p. 43). This sage advice flowed from exasperation with the tilt toward federal funding of evaluations featuring costly experimental designs at the expense of complementary research designs.

The relevance of theory. A decade ago I described how four theories of labor market institutions and behavior—human capital, signaling, job competition, and segmented labor market—would each assign a different role to vocational education. The outcomes estimation process must logically start by embracing a theory (Stevens 1983). No one has come forward with a more succinct statement of this point than Heim and Perl (1974).

> It is important to remember that analyses of this sort are going to omit some dimensions of input and measure others only in broad aggregate. These difficulties should not be a basis for rejecting the conclusions of these analyses. In evaluating an analysis, two critical questions should be asked: are the dimensions of input omitted from the analysis systematically and significantly related to those included and are the variables sufficiently disaggregated for policy purposes? (p.4)

This general alarm was soon brought front and center for evaluators of investments in vocational education.

> While within-firm studies of worker performance can potentially provide valuable evidence on the question of whether individuals with more education (or more of some other characteristics) are more productive, they suffer from a serious statistical flaw. . . . If firms prefer more-educated applicants, less-educated applicants who are hired are likely to have "compensating virtues" known to the hirer but often not to the researcher. (Brown 1982, p. 178 and 180)

Progress has been slow and limited.

> The empirical evidence, from the production function literature, on the connections between the measurable characteristics of the learning process in schools and student achievement can best be characterized as being decisively unidentifiable. (Summers and Johnson 1993, p. 1)

The interplay of high school curriculum, participation in postsecondary education, and concurrent and subsequent employment, add to the severity of the challenge (Stern and Ritzen 1991; Bishop 1995).

> High school background variables are related differently to earnings and wages across. . . . (1) former students who did not attend any postsecondary institution, (2) chose postsecondary technical education, or (3) chose higher education]; and postsecondary characteristics effects differ for the two groups that attended some form of postsecondary education. . . . Results are not consistent with the hypothesis that postsecondary technical education students would fare better in the labor market than higher education students if the higher education students would have pursued postsecondary technical education nor with the hypothesis that individuals who did not pursue any form of postsecondary education would fare better in a labor market where no one had pursued postsecondary education. (Hollenbeck 1992, p.29)

> An elegant theory has been developed that attempts to explain how the quantity of training is determined and who pays for and benefits from it. However, the absence of data on the key theoretical constructs of the theory—general training, specific training, informal training, and productivity growth—means that the only predictions of the theory that have been tested relate to the effects of formal training and tenure on wage growth and turnover. Definitive tests of the OJT theory have not been forthcoming because the large number of unobservables means that any given phenomena has many alternative explanations. (Bishop 1991, p. 1)

The unit of analysis. The most recent available study (Kane and Rouse 1995b) adds to the already long list of evaluations that have relied upon the National Longitudinal Survey of the High School Class of 1972 (e.g., Grubb 1993; Kane and Rouse 1995a), the National Longitudinal Survey of Youth (e.g., Kane and Rouse 1993), or the High School & Beyond data (e.g., Farkas, Hotchkiss and Stromsdorfer 1989; Haggstrom, Blaschke and Shavelson 1991).

None of this research was designed to produce actionable results as that term was defined earlier, so the authors are not faulted here. But the federal, state and local authorities who manage the Nation's vocational education system want reliable evidence of outcomes defined at a level they can do something about.

Progress in responding to the need for actionable insights has emerged largely independent of the academic community; see (Pfeiffer 1990; Seppanen 1990). Stakeholders want straightforward answers to basic questions.

Average versus "other" outcomes. The research community has aimed its sophisticated statistical weapons at the detection of statistically significant differences in measured outcomes, such as post-program earnings, between populations whose members have or have not been exposed to a particular vocational education experience. The presentation of a standard error statistic is intended to alert readers to the likelihood that an observed difference is "real'." Apologies are often tendered for the absence of any test of the estimate's sensitivity to a different: (1) specification of the model; (2) population of students; (3) comparison group; or (4) labor market. While each of these considerations is important for some purposes, they all miss the point that vocational education's constituents usually want to know whether a particular vocational program is exemplary or deficient, however either of these terms is defined. I am aware of only one study of school effectiveness that concentrated explicitly on outliers (Klitgaard and Hall 1973).

The supply- versus demand-side imbalance. A student's exposure to vocational education pales in comparison to other factors that determine labor market opportunity and reward (Stevens, forthcoming). Substantial progress has been made in refining the number and quality of supply-side variables that are available to researchers. The design and execution of surveys, investment in longitudinal coverage, and access to transcript data have dramatically extended the range and power of supply-side information. Progress on demand-side data elements has been much slower, despite the fact that equal or greater importance is given to such information by experts (Bureau of Labor Statistics 1994).

The "available data" magnet. The story of federal investments in longitudinal data sets covering education and labor force participation has not been written, but it should be. Howard Rosen's pivotal role in choreographing the tiny federal carrot that attracted current academic luminaries and provided their students with the National Longitudinal Survey database irrevocably changed the course of labor market research. That's the good news.

The bad news is that expediency has been a basic ingredient in the recipe for subsequent federal investments in data collection and maintenance (Levitan and Gallo 1989). Extraordinary breakthroughs have been followed by compromises. The difficulty of creating and then sustaining a new research database cannot be overstated. The best available research talent often gravitates to already available data sets that in most cases were created for some long forgotten historical purpose. These scholars have exhibited extraordinary creativity in advancing our knowledge base, but there is a conspicuous absence of consensus on any major conclusion about vocational education's impact on a former student's subsequent labor market success. No currently available database was designed to answer this question.

The post-program outcomes fallacy. Most of today's vocational education students, high school and postsecondary alike, have previous and/or concurrent work experience. The contribution(s) of this accumulation of human capital to post-program employment status and earnings should not be erroneously attributed to the vocational education exposure (Stevens forthcoming).

Many former students, particularly community college students, maintain a previous employment affiliation when they leave school with or without a credential. It is incorrect to refer to this employment affiliation as a placement. This error is particularly misleading if the so-called placement is defined as "training related," since the causal flow may be from employment affiliation to vocational curriculum, not from curriculum to affiliation.

A single point-in-time snapshot of post-program employment status offers no information about previous and/or intervening events. The complexity of the education/work portfolios of former students today far exceeds the capacity of simplistic pre-post snapshots to capture the net impact of an isolated exposure to vocational education.

Training relatedness: measurement challenges. A case has been made for the practical futility and distortion of mission that the training relatedness metric introduces in vocational education performance measurement (Stevens 1994b). Supporters of the measure simply assert that the payoff on investments in expensive facilities, equipment, and instructional expertise must be recorded in the form of immediate use of the new competencies students have acquired. The National Assessment of Vocational Education's 1994 *Final Report to Congress* asserts that "the strongest, most consistent finding throughout the literature is that improved earnings do accrue in situations where vocational training is directly related to job tasks" (U.S. Department of Education 1994b, p. 137). But, on the next page, the *Report* warns that "the sensitivity of the research findings to the methodology employed is a question that has not been explored in the literature, but may affect results" (p. 138).

Consider the following scenarios: (1) A high school student completes a cooperative education program, which combines classroom instruction and complementary work experience and on-the-job training; (2) A community college student completes a self-selected module of three courses that were chosen to enhance the student's candidacy for promotion in a business affiliation held before, during, and following enrollment; (3) A college graduate acquires a vocational certificate at a community college and then accepts a new job; (4) A tech-prep graduate enrolls in a four-year college and holds a part-time job unrelated to the tech-prep curriculum. What cause-and-effect relationship can, and should, be attributed to vocational education's contribution to the observed employment status? This is the real world. No obvious decisions about the allocation of vocational education dollars flow from the National Assessment's conclusion that "improved earnings do accrue in situations where vocational training is directly related to job tasks."

The definitional precision of occupations is crumbling. Employers seek and achieve discretionary authority to reassign employees to new responsibilities. A snapshot of current assignment is a weak measure of training relatedness. This demand-side perspective has a mirror image on the supply side. The definitional precision of vocational exposure is rapidly deteriorating. The integration of academic and vocational curricula blurs the historical distinction between the two (U.S. General Accounting Office 1995a). Encouragement of creative bundling of courses by students, diverse cooperative education programs, and multiple forms of tech-prep sequences increase the difficulty of describing vocational exposure in a way that can be aligned with workplace application (U.S. General Accounting Office 1995b).

This outcomes measurement challenge has been a major impetus behind current efforts to design competency certification systems that will provide employers with a more accurate understanding of each student's actual achievements (U.S. Department of Labor 1995). The old program-level labels are obsolete, and the vocational designation itself may not be far behind.

The eight bullet-items above describe the performance measurement challenge that will face the nation's vocational education community after congressional action on the pending consolidation legislation. Effective state and local management decisions will require improved documentation of the link between vocational education services offered, student competency gains achieved, and subsequent labor market access and reward. Uneven, but aggressive, advances are already underway across the United States. These are state-level initiatives. There is no common denominator. This is why practical measurement of national impact is futile at this time. The action will, and should, be at the state and local level. Promising examples of state and local measurement of labor market outcomes on behalf of the vocational education community are provided in the next section.

From "Beyond the Horizon" to Routine Accessibility

Six years ago, Levitan and Gallo wrote that meeting the policy challenges of the 1990s amid rapidly changing economic and social conditions and increasing international competition will require renewed dedication to the quality of workforce statistics. (Levitan and Gallo 1989, p. 34)

One source of workforce data that was beyond the horizon in 1989 has recently ascended into the full glare of advocate endorsement and adversarial attack. This new dawn promises to revolutionize accountability systems in vocational education and other complementary employment and training programs. The recently passed CAREERS Act and Job Training Consolidation Act encourage states to use this data source for accountability purposes. This data source is the quarterly report of employee earnings that is submitted to a State Employment Security Agency by, or on behalf of, each employer who is required to comply with the state's unemployment compensation law.

The Job Training Reform Amendments of 1992 required the Bureau of Labor Statistics, in cooperation with the states, to submit a report to

Congress describing how a national wage record database containing information on the quarterly earnings, establishment, industry affiliation, and geographic location of employment for all individuals for whom such information is collected by the states will be established and maintained. That report was completed, cleared through Secretary Reich's office, and sent to the Office of Management and Budget in March 1995, where it remains pending congressional actions that may affect the recommendations that are sent forward.

Meanwhile, the Employment and Training Administration in the U.S. Department of Labor has two initiatives underway that have kept the ball rolling. One of seven state consortia funded through an America's Labor Market Information System (ALMIS) initiative is titled "Research on the Enhancement and Use of the Unemployment Insurance (UI) Wage Record Database as a Labor Market Information Tool." Maryland's Department of Labor, Licensing and Regulation is the lead state agency for this consortium, which includes six other funded states, two universities, and seven other affiliated states. More recently, the Unemployment Insurance Service's Information Technology Support Center (ITSC) has begun the pilot phase of a project to create and maintain a national wage record distributed database capability. This is one of two national databases recommended in the Bureau of Labor Statistics report that has been at the Office of Management and Budget for six months. The second database recommended by the Bureau of Labor Statistics is a wage record database that it would maintain exclusively for research purposes. The vocational education community will be a major beneficiary of the ALMIS and ITSC initiatives (Stevens 1994a, 1994b, and forthcoming), and would realize indirect benefits from the Bureau of Labor Statistics research database.

Sar Levitan recognized the latent value of wage records use.

> Social security and unemployment insurance data can potentially provide significant information on the long- and short-term labor market experiences of individuals. Computer advances have generated new opportunities, but statutory restrictions have frustrated the use of [these] data. (Levitan and Gallo 1989, p. 33)

Bill Spring recently concurred.

> Massachusetts and a number of other states are attempting to organize the information on the quality of education and training

and on placement.... Most of that information can be acquired by matching the social security numbers of graduates with those of new hires reported quarterly through the unemployment insurance payroll system, with individual privacy protected. This information is reported regularly but lies fallow, never analyzed and disseminated. (Pines et al. 1995, pp. 65-66)

The Joint Commission on Accountability Reporting (JCAR) has endorsed the use of wage records for accountability purposes, but cautions that not all states and education systems are prepared to act on this recommendation immediately (Joint Commission on Accountability Reporting 1995, pp. 5-6). This is another reason why a national roll-up of state data is not feasible at this time.

This author and Princeton University professor Cecilia Rouse are collaborating in the assembly and analysis of a new longitudinal database of confidential records that will contain the "universe" of student records for: (1) the Baltimore City Public Schools; (2) at least seven of Maryland's seventeen public community colleges, which enroll more than 90 percent of the system's students; (3) all University of Maryland System students; and (4) the 1985-1994 decade of Maryland wage records and related employer data elements. Steps (1), (3) and (4) have been completed. Step (2) is underway. Data-sharing agreements with each of the community colleges have been signed. One school has submitted its data. The word "universe" must be qualified because only records containing a student's actual social security number can be used. Coverage and accuracy are important concerns.

Research using the consolidated database described in the previous paragraph will advance our understanding of the interplay of high school, community college, university, labor market, and personal characteristics. School administrators and institutional research personnel are active participants in this ongoing investigation. At this time there is no survey complement to the database, but one is planned. Exclusive reliance on administrative records allows obvious cost savings.

This progress has been possible because Maryland's Assistant Secretary for Employment and Training in 1989, Chuck Middlebrooks, had the foresight and fortitude to enter into a pioneering data sharing agreement with the author. Together, between 1989 and 1995, a team of Maryland Department of Economic and Employment Development managers, staff members of the Governor's Workforce Development Board, and the author and colleagues in the Jacob France Center at the University of Baltimore, have demonstrated how administrative records drawn from multiple public agencies can be archived and then accessed by authorized researchers for specified purposes.

Respect for and assurance of the confidentiality of archived records is of paramount importance. It is easy to provide such guarantees in a research environment. Only a small team of professional colleagues are granted access. Each person signs an oath indicating their awareness of and willingness to abide by legal stipulations regarding the handling of the administrative records. It is more difficult to sustain this level of confidence when education authorities seek actionable information, such as how the completers of a particular vocational class in a designated school have fared in the local economy. The identities of individual former students and of any employer can not be revealed. This limits the uses that can be made of consolidated databases of administrative records.

The availability of a national distributed database capability will pose new challenges. The intent is to overcome the historical ceiling on the value of wage records that is inherent in not knowing the status of anyone who does not appear in the home state's own wage records. State Employment Security Agency administrators and the Unemployment Insurance Service's executive team are properly worried about the integrity of their records. New technologies, such as fingerprint identification, are now available to control access to databases in a cost effective manner; if your fingerprint is not in the access authorization file, then access will not be granted, and every authorized access can be documented so subsequent misuse of data can be traced back to its origin.

Speculation about the Future

Many layers of protective insulation have been peeled away from high school vocational education since the 1950s. Today's vocational systems lie exposed to numerous political and economic forces. Emerging cognitive theories of learning deemphasize the relevance of traditional contextual settings for skill acquisition (U.S. Congress,

Office of Technology Assessment 1994). This is a direct threat to vocational curricula. The renewed popularity of cooperative education relationships serves as both an opportunity and a threat, depending upon
what balance is struck between classroom and worksite learning and
whether employers can be retained in high school alliances or gravitate
to community college competitors. There will be an inevitable shake-
out of early tech-prep relationships. Some will prosper, but others will
self-destruct.

The connection between the forces described in the previous paragraph and wage record databases is that vocational education's supporters and opponents both want a straightforward answer to the
question: "How are we/they doing?"

There will be room at the table for the successful components of
vocational education. This success has to be demonstrated using a unit
of analysis that is actionable. The data have to be of sufficient quality
to withstand the inevitable attacks. The analytical approaches that are
adopted have to clearly identify the exemplary and deficient performers, so resources can be reassigned from the latter to the former; a clear
definition of average performance will be of little value.

The state-level labor market outcome measurement initiatives that
are underway across the country are establishing a solid foundation for
responding to the accountability features of the pending consolidation
legislation. The federal government would be wise to nurture, learn
from, and promote these initiatives. Such advocacy should be given a
higher priority than the design and introduction of any new uniform
national reporting requirements that will inevitably result in the collection of performance information that cannot withstand the scrutiny of
objective experts using quality and actionability criteria to assess the
data. This pessimistic conclusion could be negated by a serious congressional investment in assuring the necessary quality and actionability of accessible national performance measures.

References

Benavot, Aaron. 1983. "The Rise and Decline of Vocational Education," *Sociology of Education* 56 (April): 63-76.

Bishop, John H. 1991. "A Program of Research on the Role of Employer Training in Ameliorating Skill Shortages and Enhancing Productivity and Competitiveness." Center for Advanced Human Resource Studies, Cornell University.

_____. 1995. "Expertise and Excellence." Working Paper 95-13, Ithaca, Center for Advanced Human Resource Studies, Cornell University.

Brown, Charles. 1982. "Estimating the Determinants of Employee Performance," *Journal of Human Resources* 17, 2: 178-194.

Bureau of Labor Statistics. 1994. *National Wage Record Database Design Project Report*. U.S. Department of Labor, draft dated September 15.

Cuban, Larry. 1982. "Enduring Resiliency: Enacting and Implementing Federal Vocational Education Legislation." In *Work, Youth and Schooling: Historical Perspectives on Vocationalism in American Education*, Harvey Kantor and David Tyack, eds. Palo Alto, CA: Stanford University Press.

Evans, Rupert N., and Paul Violas. 1983. "History of Changes in Outcomes Expected of Vocational Education." In *Selected Evidence Supporting or Rejecting Eighteen Outcomes for Vocational Education*, Floyd L. McKinney and Patricia Fornash, eds. Columbus, OH: National Center for Research in Vocational Education, Ohio State University.

Farkas, G., L. Hotchkiss, and E.W. Stromsdorfer. 1989. "Vocational Training, Supply Constraints, and Individual Economic Outcomes," *Economics of Education Review* 8, 1: 17-30.

Giodarno, A., and R. Praeger. 1977. *A History of Federal Vocational Education Legislation in the Twentieth Century*. Washington, DC: Library of Congress.

Grasso, John T., and John R. Shea. 1979. "Effects of Vocational Education Programs: Research Findings and Issues." Planning Papers for the Vocational Education Study, Vocational Education Study Publication No. 1, National Institute of Education.

Grubb, W.N. 1993. "The Varied Economic Returns to Postsecondary Education: New Evidence from the Class of 1972," *Journal of Human Resources* 28, 2: 365-382.

_____. 1995. "Response to Comment," *Journal of Human Resources* 30, 1: 222-228.

Gustman, Alan L., and Thomas L. Steinmeier. 1980. "Labor Markets and Evaluations of Vocational Training Programs in the Public High Schools—

Toward a Framework for Analysis." Working Paper No. 478, National Bureau of Economic Research.

Haggstrom, G.W., T.J. Blaschke, and R.J. Shavelson. 1991. *After High School, Then What? A Look at the Postsecondary Sorting-Out Process for American Youth.* Santa Monica, CA: Rand Corporation.

Heim, J., and L. Perl. 1974. "The Educational Production Function: Implications for Educational Manpower Policy." Institute of Public Employment Monograph No. 4, New York State School of Industrial and Labor Relations, Cornell University.

Hoachlander, E.G., and K.A. Levesque. 1993. "Improving National Data for Vocational Education: Strengthening a Multiform System." National Center for Research in Vocational Education, University of California at Berkeley.

Hollenbeck, K. 1992. "Postsecondary Education as Triage: Returns to Academic and Technical Programs." Staff Working Paper 92-10, Upjohn Institute for Employment Research.

Joint Commission on Accountability Reporting. 1995. "Handbook for Accountability Reporting." Draft dated May 8.

Kane, T.J., and C.E. Rouse. 1993. "Labor Market Returns to Two- and Four-Year Colleges: Is a Credit a Credit and Do Degrees Matter?" Faculty Research Working Paper No. 93-38, Kennedy School of Government, Harvard University.

_____. 1995a. "Comment on W. Norton Grubb, The Varied Economic Returns to Post-secondary Education: New Evidence from the Class of 1972," *Journal of Human Resources* 30, 1: 205-221.

_____. 1995b. "Labor-Market Returns to Two- and Four-Year College," *American Economic Review* 85, 3: 600-614.

Klitgaard, R.E., and G.R. Hall. 1973. "A Statistical Search for Unusually Effective Schools." Report No. R-1210-CC/RC, RAND Corporation.

Levitan, S. 1992. "Evaluation Industry Impacts Policy," *Workforce* (Fall): 34-45.

_____. and F. Gallo. 1989. "Workforce Statistics: Do We Know What We Think We Know—and What Should We Know?" U.S. Congress, Joint Economic Committee, December 26.

Levitan, S., and G.L. Mangum. 1967. "Making Sense of Federal Manpower Policy." Policy Papers in Human Resources and Industrial Relations No. 2, Ann Arbor/Detroit, Institute of Labor and Industrial Relations, University of Michigan/Wayne State University.

Levitan, S., and R. Taggart III. 1971. *Social Experimentation and Manpower Policy: The Rhetoric and the Reality.* Baltimore, MD: Johns Hopkins University Press.

Lewis, T. 1990. "Toward a New Paradigm for Vocational Education Research," *Journal of Vocational Education Research* 15, 2: 1-30.

Meyer, Robert H. 1982. "An Economic Analysis of High School Education." In T*he Federal Role in Vocational Education.*Washington, DC: National Commission for Employment Policy.

National Institute of Education. 1981. "The Vocational Education Study: The Final Report." Vocational Education Study Publication No. 8, U.S. Department of Education.

Pfeiffer, J.J. 1990. "Annual Report." Florida Department of Education, Florida Education and Training Placement Information Program.

Pines, M., G. Mangum, S. Mangum, and B. Spring. 1995. *The Harassed Staffer's Guide to Employment and Training Policy.* Baltimore, MD: Johns Hopkins University, Institute for Policy Studies, Sar Levitan Center for Social Policy Studies, June.

Seppanen, L. 1990. *Vocational Education Outcomes in Washington Community Colleges.* Olympia, WA: State Board for Community College Education.

Stern, D., and J.M.M. Ritzen, eds. 1991. *Market Failure in Training? New Economic Analysis and Evidence on Training of Adult Employees.* New York: Springer-Verlag.

Stern, D., N. Finkelstein, J.R. Stone III, J. Latting, and C. Dornsife. 1994. R*esearch on School-to-Work Transition Programs in the United States.* Berkeley, CA: National Center for Research in Vocational Education, University of California at Berkeley.

Stevens, D.W. 1979. "The Coordination of Vocational Education Programs With CETA." Information Series No. 151, National Center for Research in Vocational Education, Ohio State University.

_____. 1983. "Outcomes for Vocational Education: Economic Perspectives." In *Selected Evidence Supporting or Rejecting Eighteen Outcomes for Vocational Education*, F.L. McKinney and P Fornash, eds. Columbus, OH: National Center for Research in Vocational Education, Ohio State University.

_____. 1994a. "The School-to-Work Transition of High School and Community College Vocational Program Completers: 1990-1992." EQW Working Paper No. 27, National Center on the Educational Quality of the Workforce, University of Pennsylvania, November.

_____. 1994b. "Performance Measurement Revisited," *Journal of Vocational Education Research* 9, 3: 65-82.

_____. (forthcoming). *New Perspectives on Documenting Employment and Earnings Outcomes in Vocational Education.* Berkeley, CA: National Center for Research in Vocational Education, University of California at Berkeley.

Summers, A.A., and A.W. Johnson. 1993. *What Do We Know About How Schools Affect the Labor Market Performance of Their Students?* Philadelphia, PA: National Center on the Educational Quality of the Workforce, University of Pennsylvania.

U.S. Congress, Office of Technology Assessment.1994. "Testing and Assessment in Vocational Education." OTA-BP-SET-123, March.

U.S. Department of Education. 1989. *Final Report*, Volume I: *Summary of Findings and Recommendations*. Washington, DC: National Assessment of Vocational Education.

_____. 1994a. *Final Report to Congress*, Volume I: Summary and Recommendations. Washington, DC: Office of Educational Research and Improvement, Office of Research, National Assessment of Vocational Education.

_____. 1994b. *Final Report to Congress*, Volume II: *Participation in and Quality of Vocational Education*. Washington, DC: National Assessment of Vocational Education.

U.S. Department of Labor. 1995. "Skills, Standards and Entry-Level Work: Elements of a Strategy for Youth Employability Development."

U.S. General Accounting Office. 1995a. "Vocational Education: Changes at High School Level After Amendments to Perkins Act." GAO/HEHS-95-144.

_____. 1995b. "Adult Education: Measuring Program Results Has Been Challenging." GAO/HEHS-95-153.

CHAPTER 7

Employment Service Revisited

Miriam Johnson

Since 1933, when the Wagner Peyser Act established the public employment service as a state/federal partnership, the state agencies, under the Department of Labor, have operated as the primary public labor exchange mechanism. These agencies have also administered the unemployment insurance (UI) program established by the Social Security Act in 1935, charged not only with making the payments but also with administering a work test to insure that those claiming benefits were, indeed, involuntarily unemployed and actively seeking work. For a fair amount of the ensuing sixty years, these agencies have been besieged, underfunded, and expected to accomplish the undoable. Except for the war years and periods of manpower shortages, the employment service has never succeeded in playing a significant role in labor exchange. A basic condition, without regard to agency competency, is that public policy always insisted, and rightly so, that *all* job seekers who have a legal right to work would be registered as applicants, thus providing a virtually unlimited supply of workers in the most common occupations On the demand side, however, there has never been an effective public policy, in this free labor market, that requires employers to place their job openings with the public agency, thus severely limiting access to the demand for workers. The employment service has historically reflected all of the imbalances in the market place and all of the discriminatory tendencies in the social fabric, including the gap between skills demanded and skills available.

Now, in this season of the Republican "revolution" marked by the general undoing of the Roosevelt era social gains, the continued existence of this agency is again in question. Whatever the outcome of the current debates in Congress, it is a foregone conclusion that the basic operating budget of Job Services will be further reduced. Only unemployment insurance out of the Social Security Act gains seems to have avoided attack.

After a number of years in the labor movement, I began an employment service career in 1953 when I signed on as a temporary hourly worker at the Ferry Building in San Francisco, paying or refusing to pay unemployment insurance benefits to long lines of the unemployed. Since then, I have been almost continuously involved with, have worked for, researched, criticized, written about, deplored, and cheered this much-attacked, often abused, sometimes inept, but still essential labor market arm of government. Forty-two years has seen enormous changes in the atmosphere, the culture, the environment, and the policies in which the public employment service functions. Through all of the permutations, through all of the reorganizations, new mandates, changing labor market conditions, technological changes, and perhaps most important of all, changes in public consciousness, an immutable core has persisted, with more or less emphasis: Daily, unemployed workers have come through the doors seeking work and/or UI benefits. Daily, employers have sought help from the agency to find workers for their jobs, and daily, the agency has sought to bring the two together—worker and job.

It is not my intention to undertake a comprehensive history of those forty-three years, but rather to supply a few snapshots in time. My main focus is the position where I started—the delivery point at the counter in a local office. In my view, it is the only significant way to look at a service—the way the consumer user experiences it. After an interim as a researcher and evaluator following retirement from the California employment service, I returned to the front-line counter six years ago working part time for the San Francisco office, running job search workshops for professionals, for youth, for new immigrants, and for welfare clients. More recently, because of budget cuts, I no longer get paid, but I continue to work a few hours a week on a volunteer basis, calling employers to verify the disposition of their job orders. My perceptions are, indeed, fresh.

In 1972, I published a rather angry, critical book about the employment service called *Counter Point,* in which I used the counter as a metaphor for the alienation, distance, and even hostility between the public in front and the staff behind the counter. It was my contention then that both sides suffered. Both were caught in an essentially inhuman and unsatisfying process, each attempting to accomplish goals that were most often beyond fulfillment. I described, in some detail, what specific tasks each staff member performed. In this article, I will also focus on the same critical point: the delivery of services at the counter in one office—San Francisco—in one state—California—at two points in time—1953 and 1995.

When I described the San Francisco local office in the 1972 book it could have been any office in the United States. The oversight and control exercised by the Department of Labor on the state agencies and they, in turn, on the local offices was extreme. In fact, I highlighted that sameness by sketching a picture of the employment service office in Barrow, Alaska, the northernmost point of the United States, where I had gone on a research and evaluation assignment. Despite being well above the Arctic circle, with a mainly Eskimo population of 4,000, its counter, its forms, its layout, its gray metal desks, its signs on the wall, and the process of taking applications and job orders were exact duplications of a New York or San Francisco office. That would no longer be the case in 1995. To describe the San Francisco office is now to describe that office only. I cannot be surmised that the offices in the rest of the country, indeed, even in California, are the same. Though still governed by common mandates, the local office managers and the regional offices appear to exert considerably more control than I had ever seen before. However, that control is very proscribed. It cannot transcend the limitations of budgets and staffing or the constraints inherent in funding sources.

But before comparing the San Francisco office in the mid-1950s and the mid-1990s, it will be useful to offer a statewide perspective.

Statewide Perspective

Computerization has made a substantial difference. After many years of experimentation and partial installation, all of Job Service and unemployment insurance activities went on-line in California in 1991. This finally spelled the end of banks of files, desperate searches for the missing claim, the application card misfiled, and the inadequacy of hand record keeping. In the unemployment insurance system, the change to computers is almost totally positive for staff, for supervision, and most important, for the convenience of the unemployed claimant. Before, claimants would have to wait at least two weeks to discover if the new claim was valid or what the monetary determination would be. If, as often happened, the wrong social security number had been given either to the interviewer or to the former employer resulting in no monetary award, indignant claimants would assault the counter, outraged. It would take another two weeks to straighten it all out. Now, a person filing a new claim can know immediately exactly what the monetary award will be and what if any problems are connected with the claim. Continued claims are filed almost completely by mail on a two-week basis, and if eligible are paid by mail. Interviews to determine eligibility are conducted almost entirely by telephone. It is projected that by 1997, even new claims will be filed by telephone and continued claims will be filed by a touch tone system in the entire state. The Director of Operations estimates that the completed computerization of the unemployment insurance program will reduce staffing requirements by at least one-third. Though it is true that the ability of the agency to fulfill its role of administering a work test seems weakened by the computer, that role had actually never been fully realized. Current planning may strengthen it again.

It cannot be said, however, that the unqualified success of computerization in the unemployment insurance program is duplicated in the Job Match program. The following comparison of activities is instructive:

California activities	1978	1994	Percent +/–
Active applications	1,479,159	1,041,640	–30
Openings received	725,518	456,452	– 38
Placements	451,724	259,352	-38
Population (est)	23,000,000	32,000,000	+72

On the face of it, the conclusion is clear: In the past fifteen or so years, the employment service in California has registered 30 percent fewer people looking for work, received 38 percent fewer job listings from employers, and filled 38 percent fewer job openings. All of this occurred while the population of California increased by 72 percent. The introduction of computerized Job Match has given no indication that the downward trend has been reversed. The agency continues to lose its share of labor market exchanges and public use.

Though state, area, and local officials are keenly aware of these trends and are engaged in intensive planning for the future, they explain these developments as follows:

- State computerization provided a more accurate count of transactions and people than the previous hand count had been and must therefore be viewed as less than comparable.

- In the past, applicants and job orders often were listed in more than one office, thus inflating the count. State computerization eliminated that possibility.

- A marked increase in the percentage of registrants from minority groups has made placements more difficult because of low skills and language barriers. (Though the population of California increased by 25 percent in a ten-year period, the Asian/Pacific Islander population increased by 118 percent and Hispanics increased by 69.2 percent. Minorities made up 42.8 percent of the population in 1990.)

- Though the employment service national staffing had, for years, been frozen at 30,000, 1982 budget cuts reduced that by nearly 25 percent to 23,000. California had to absorb its share of the cut while its population was increasing. The falling ratio of staff to population has reduced staff effectiveness, as has the elimination of the specialized domestic desks.

- With greater emphasis on automation, a higher ratio of the reduced staff has been shifted to Sacramento away from the local offices.

- A change in the Department of Labor's method of measuring services to Veterans and placements, eliminating the short range casual labor jobs from the count, changed the focus of the local offices and significantly reduced the placement statistics.

• The explosion of twice as many temporary help agencies in the past ten years and the doubling of the number of temp workers in the past five years has changed the job market completely to the detriment of the employment services.

• In late 1969, the California legislature passed a bill transforming the employment service into the Human Resources Department (HRD), resulting in a near-abandonment of the labor exchange role and the commitment of all of its resources to the "disadvantaged." Cited as an example of the result was a local office with 105 employees who placed three individuals in a month. The impact on agency market share of that passing phase which ended in 1972, has continued in one form or another ever since. Each new permutation of the job training programs passed by Congress that calls for training and placing the most difficult-to-place clients has thrust the public employment service into the center of the delivery system.

• The inherent imbalance between supply and demand, in numbers and skills, is reflected more starkly as the skill demands get higher and higher.

• The applicant pool is deteriorating. There are now in the active applicant file more welfare clients, more homeless, more drug addicts, more with arrest and conviction records, more mentally unstable, more school drop-outs, more mentally unstable individuals with a multiplicity of problems, and more minorities with language problems in the active application file than ever before.

Whether or not these facts provide adequate explanation, two developments are undeniable:

1. The staff available to serve the general public has declined drastically. California Job Service currently has approximately 2,400 individuals on the payroll. However, only 1,400 are funded by basic Wagner Peyser Title lll funds, compared to 2,000 positions in 1962. The remaining 1,000 or so work under reimbursable contracts for targeted programs, which did not exist at the earlier date and are not available for service to the general public.

2. Though the employment service has always been heavily involved in serving the low-skill, low-pay job market, the years of sin-

gular focus on the most difficult-to-place clients, together with the gross loss of such jobs in the economy, are certainly major contributors to the decline.

The 1994 printout provided interesting information about the active applicant file. The proportion of minorities among those applying for work at California Job Service offices has increased from 47.4 percent in 1979 to 56.7 percent in 1994, but the proportion of blacks has slipped from 17.1 percent to 12.5 percent with the difference made up by Hispanics and Asians with far less industrial experience and the added challenge of language facility. The printout also provides some information about client economic status. Only about 5 percent of registered active clients declared themselves as economically disadvantaged, with a smaller percentage stating that they were on welfare. However, when the state office ran the social security numbers of Department of Social Service welfare clients against the employment service registered clients, it was discovered that closer to 20 percent of the applicant file were receiving welfare and failing to give that information to the interviewer. Perhaps they feared that it would militate against referral to a job.

The foregoing offers some insight into the continuous erosion or, at best, stagnation in employment service usage. Computerization of the Job Service functions has not been an unqualified success, and it has not succeeded in reversing the downward trend. The Job Service job-matching functions, especially those involved with serving hard-to-place clients, demand intensive one-on-one relationships, a very different ball of wax from unemployment insurance administration. All of the national criteria for evaluations were, for years, based on the assumption that a placement could be counted only if the agency had the opening listed, selected a qualified client, negotiated with the employers, referred the person, and the person was hired and actually working on the job. Every element had to be true to earn a validating placement count. Giving labor market information, conducting Job Search workshops to facilitate a self-help search for work—all of the rest was well and good, and has since been counted as "entered employment." But despite that, the bottom line payoff measurement has traditionally been placements.

There is a widespread notion that the downward spiral is solely attributable to the decade between 1962 and 1973 when national policy shifted from the placement numbers count to emphasis on the minorities and the disadvantaged. That period did, indeed, see a huge increase in staffing and an equally huge decline in labor exchange transactions. In 1973, the Department of Labor sought to reverse the trend and recommitted the state agencies to labor exchange and the placement count while retaining some commitment to difficult-to-place clients.

In truth, the problem of decline and stagnation has a much longer history that predates the policy shift. As early as 1958, then Secretary of Labor James Mitchell noted that there had been a steady decline in the activities of the employment service. Between 1952 and 1962, nonagricultural placements nationally dropped 11 percent, while nonagricultural employment was increasing by 13 percent. In 1958, a Department of Labor evaluation declared that the employment service nationally had been through "eleven years of stalemate, if not progressive decline." The report concluded that the employment service had fewer placements in 1958 than it had in 1947 despite an increase of 21 percent in nonagricultural employment in the same period. The historical perspective throws light on the essential problems.

The soul searching, the inherent dichotomy between serving the employers with the most qualified applicants and serving the least prepared segments of the workforce, has apparently reached something of a resolution, at least in the California agency, judging from the current planning. About the future—more later.

The San Francisco Office—1950s

The description that follows is from memory—mine and others still available, supplemented by my earlier writings. Statistical data are long consigned to dusty basements and are irretrievable without enormous effort. The impressions, however, are vivid though precision may be faulty, and memory tends to accordion events.

The office of the fifties was intensely concerned with its labor exchange role, and the size, functions, and appearance of the staff reflected this. My particular office was one of four in San Francisco, which were separated by occupations. One office dealt primarily with white-collar occupations. A second office handled only industrial and casual labor jobs. Service jobs were the province of the third office. A special office for maritime workers also existed. In time, the industrial and service offices were combined, and the maritime office was eliminated. Most of the offices handled both employment and unemployment insurance. (In the history of the agency, there were countless occasions when these two functions were co-located and then separated again.) In my office, which at that time was the white-collar one, there was one black interviewer among about fifty Caucasians. His job was assessing overpayments on the unemployment insurance side of the office. This one African-American was unusually personable and competent. However, he was a recent addition, and when there were severe budget cuts in 1953, all of the hourly workers like myself were laid off, as were a few in the permanent classification. "Last hired, first fired" was the rule, and Percy, who was permanent, was laid off, much to the distress of the Manager. Three months later, with some budgetary relief, an attempt was made to hire him back, but he had already gone to work in a better job. So began and ended racial integration in staffing for many years to come. However, most of the very large clerical staff were Asian women.

Many of the professional interviewers were assigned occupational desks. The reception point at the counter was always a bottleneck, and long lines were commonplace. Completion interviewers, generally working at the counter, corrected the self-completed work applications and assigned occupational codes from the Dictionary of Occupational Titles. Clerical applicants were referred to one of the three clerical desks. When employers called in their job openings, their calls were often referred to the appropriate occupational desk. The same interviewers who took the order attempted to fill it from the boxes of application files at their desks. At various times, the occupational desks in our office included an Engineering desk, presided over by Margaret, who knew all there was to know about that market in the city; a Social Worker desk; two sales desks; a general professional desk, and others. Each of these specialists had intimate knowledge of their clientele. They were often on a first name relationship with the personnel directors of major companies in those occupations. In the industrial and service office, there were special desks for restaurant workers, domestics, garment workers, machinists, casual labor, and for general blue-collar and service occupations. Our office regularly scheduled typing tests, the results of which were entered on the application card. The testing room had only manual typewriters, and many clients objected because electric typewriters were coming into play. On the other hand, when the office installed some electric typewriters, there were complaints because some had never used one.

A six-point program was developed as early as 1946, but was still the objective in 1954. The six points were as follows: *Placement*—To provide an effective placement service for all persons seeking work and provide all employers with workers; *Employment Counseling*—To provide a vocational counseling service to assist job seekers in making valid occupational choices: *Services to Special Applicant Groups*—To provide special assistance and counseling to veterans, youth, older workers, and the handicapped, with the goal of placing these workers in satisfactory jobs: *Management Services*—To assist employers and labor unions in the use of tools and techniques to reduce labor turnover. This would include job analysis and the development of proficiency and aptitude testing for more effective selection, assignment and transfer of workers: *Labor Market Information*—To provide accurate and timely information on the workings of the labor market for the use of government, job seekers, employers, training authorities, and others; *Community Participation*—To cooperate with community organizations designed to increase economic opportunity and raise levels of employment.

Even the writing of the period sounds quaint, wonderfully naive, and hopeful. Then, and to this day, confidentiality of information was promised and firmly observed, especially in regard to the employer's job order. No job seeker was ever permitted to see an order. The agency hugged its knowledge firmly to its own breast.

To fulfill the six-point program, our office had a number of employment counselors who had undergone one week of employment service training in counseling, case work management, and interpreting the General Aptitude Test Batteries. These three-hour tests were given at regular intervals in the office. The GATB was a major tool for the counselors.

Various members of the staff were designated as specialists for youth and for older workers. These were assignments to already-overburdened interviewers who spent very little time with their specialty. The one full-time specialist assignment was for handicapped workers.

The interviewer was a very serious man whose desk was surrounded with books pertaining to various handicaps. Clients with visible physical disabilities were often seen at his desk. He represented the Department in all the city committees dealing with handicapped workers and was regarded by the handicapped community as an important resource.

The office also designated one or more individuals as employer relations representatives. The job of marketing the services to employers required that these interviewers spend considerable time out of the office visiting employers to solicit jobs. Interviewers also maintained an employer card file in the office that showed the names of the personnel people in companies, their hiring practices, average pay, range of occupations, and other data that helped them plan their employer visits, and also were useful when trying to develop a job for a likely applicant.

Unemployment insurance was paid weekly—in person and in cash. Interviewers would approve the certification, which the claimant then took next door to the cashier's office for payment. Inevitably, the San Francisco office was robbed, and for over a year, there was silence. Then one morning our newspapers carried a front page story stating that a man was suing Greyhound Bus because a considerable sum of money was stolen from a locker. When asked where he had gotten so much cash, he indignantly declared that it was *his* money, that he had gotten it from the unemployment office, and what is more, that he had done all the work himself. The staff squealed with delight at this kind of "chutzpah." I don't recall how his suit came out, but he did go to San Quentin.

The offices of the 1950s were primarily labor exchange offices, with occupational desks and with knowledgeable interviewers intimately involved with both clients and employers. On the face of it, this should have been ideal, with enough staff to perform the broker function. But there was another side, a dark and seldom discussed side, to the seemingly halcyon picture.

I remember noticing small pencil marks on the applications, and I soon understood that they were secret codes that designated a minority—mostly black—and that meant "don't refer except to Negro jobs." True, the agency had an official "no discrimination" policy, but the rationalizations were endless. "We don't want to lose the employer's business." "I don't want to embarrass the client." She would never get hired." "It would be a waste of his time and money to send him on the job." The agency was, without a doubt, a helpful conduit for maintaining the discriminatory status quo. There were, understandably, not many African-Americans who came to the employment service for any but traditional jobs. The treatment at the counter was discouraging, cursory, and just short of rude. When the employment service managed to get an African-American woman hired in a major utility company, it was kept quiet, though some staff rejoiced. In 1962, I was appointed to act as State Minorities Specialist in the Central Office—the first time the job was to be full time. I remember thinking then that my most pressing task was to stop the interviewers' fingers as they rummaged through the applicant file box—to stop them from automatically bypassing a suspected nonwhite applicant and actually to make that referral, whatever the consequences.

Whenever I now hear assertions about how nothing has changed, my mind flickers back to a meeting I held in Sacramento with about thirty all-white, all-male officials from IBM at an elegant restaurant. The purpose was to explore with them the possibilities of opening some occupations to the training and hiring of "Negroes." Since I was representing the State of California, my presentation was low key and accommodating. As we reviewed various occupations, I suggested repair and maintenance of the IBM typewriters in the offices. Gingerly, the gentlemen present explained to me, patiently and politely, that the suggestion was out of the question because these "Negro men would be working around the desks of white women in the office. . . ." The rest left to my imagination. Swallowing hard, but still trying to be accommodating, I expressed wonder at the objection since "Negro" janitors were always seen working around the desks of white women towards the end of the day in all of the offices, and no one seemed offended. Somewhat shamefacedly, a few of those present granted that they were, perhaps, stuck in a prejudiced mode and needed to rethink their options. IBM, the employment service, and indeed, the world has changed mightily since then. Maybe it had little choice.

The San Francisco Office—1995

Comparing the local office of the 1950s to that of the 1990s offers a microcosmic glimpse into the amazing social, institutional, and technological changes that have reshaped this country in the past forty years and how these changes are reflected in the Job Service local office. The current staff of 63 is approximately one-third white, one-fourth black and one-fifth each of Hispanic and Asian. Of the ten supervisors, four are white, and two each Black, Asian and Hispanic. Eighteen of the 29 professional staff are in the Permanent Intermittent (PI) category. Because of the seasonal nature of employment and unemployment, Civil Service rules allow the Employment Development Department (EDD) to hire and train people in this PI category. Though their hourly pay and fringe benefits are the same as those of permanent employees, they are subject to immediate layoff, depending on budget. At this moment (which may not be true tomorrow), all 18 PIs are working on a 70 percent basis, or about 24 hours a week. This equates with 10.8 full-time people or, in bureaucratic terminology, personnel equivalents. Hence, the basic, permanent core staff of the San Francisco EDD office consists of 53.8 personnel equivalents. Out of this number, 16 are either in management, supervision, clerical, or technical services. Only 29 permanent professionals plus the equivalent of about 10 PIs, or a total of roughly 39 personnel equivalents are actually available to provide direct services to the public. But listing their assignments demonstrates how few are really available to the job or UI applicant who is not a member of some program target group.

Intensive Service Program (ISP)

Mandated by state government but funded by both state funds and Wagner Peyser discretionary funds, this program targets those who have been out of work for a total of 15 weeks during the past 26 weeks; receive public assistance; are referred by agencies providing employment-related services; or are persons with a disability. The eight permanent full-time professional staff assigned to ISP are called case managers. They provide individualized case work for a limit of 60 days. Services include job referrals, referrals to training, desk coaching, testing, job search training workshops, and referrals to other agencies. Priority is given to AFDC clients who are enrolled in the Greater Avenues for Independence (GAIN) program, California's version of the Job Opportunities—Basic Skills (JOBS) program. At a minimum, 25 percent of the case load are to consist of welfare clients. Directives call for each case manager to handle a minimum of 35 cases, and each is expected to produce favorable outcomes at the rate of approximately 9 a month or 110 a year. A favorable outcome would be employment at a 30-day follow-up, or inclusion in an authorized training program.

Staff has acknowledged that case loads at this point are considerably less than 35 each. Clients are referred from other internal services, from community-based organizations, and from other sources, and there has apparently been a limited flow of referrals. A good number of the ISP staff is relatively new to this particular assignment. Nevertheless, in the third quarter of 1995, these eight people recorded 36 placements and registered 168 new clients. This is an average of four placements per months for each case manager. As with other programs, this staff is prohibited from serving any clients other than their own, by definition, difficult-to-place cases.

Veterans Program

Another eight permanent professionals work only with veterans to insure that they, with special emphasis on Viet Nam and disabled veterans, receive all the services to which they are legally entitled. EDD is required by law to reserve for veterans all job openings for 24 hours, after which the job, if unfilled, is opened to the active applicant file. In addition, staff work with local veterans organizations and committees to promote employer interest in hiring veterans and visit hospitals and military bases to give employment information and advice to those about to be discharged. Of the eight individuals in this program, one is permanently assigned off-site, and four spend four to six hours a week in outreach activities. In the third quarter of 1995, the seven on-site staff registered 225 veterans and placed 79 on jobs—an average of nearly five placements a month each.

Job Agents

State mandated and funded, the Job Agent program is directed towards the most difficult clientele— those who lack job skills, have language barriers, disabilities, limited education or poor work habits and attitudes, or who face legal problems. They may also have problems of housing, lack of transportation and child care. Operating on a caseload basis, the Job Agents provide vocational counseling, referrals to remedial education, job training, job referral, extended postemployment follow-up, and referrals to other agencies as needed by the client. The three job agents in the San Francisco office registered 51 new clients and made 29 placements during the third quarter of 1995, a placement average of about three per month each.

"Experience Unlimited" Job Clubs

This is a self-help statewide program targeted especially for the professional, managerial, and technical workers who assist each other in the search for work. It is a no-fee, EDD-sponsored service that, in San Francisco, provides space, equipment, computers, telephones, workshop rooms, a library and typewriters. As a self-help group, it demands a certain level of volunteer work from all members. It also requires that all members participate in job search workshops such as resume writing, interviewing, and other job-related issues, conducted by its own members. It provides perhaps the only specific local office response to the newly unemployed professional/managerial occupations. It is, arguably, one of the most innovative and effective programs initiated by the California EDD. At this point, one personnel equivalent acts as coordinator to Experience Unlimited in San Francisco. Though the membership at times reached nearly 300, it is now reduced to about 160 active members. Many members attribute this downturn to a loss of allocated space and a reduction in staff time and interest. However, a file purge and a limit on how long people could stay also reduced the number.

Youth Program

Responsive to the special problems of unemployed, out-of-school youth, one-and one-half permanent staff interview young people and develop job openings for them. This staff is enlarged during the summer months to administer the Summer Youth Program. During July, August, and September of 1995, as many as ten individuals, many of them part-time youth workers, registered 543 young people and placed 143 in jobs. EDD also maintains a Youth Office for "at-risk" young people often referred by schools. Three in-school young people, who were themselves at-risk youth and are excluded from the staff count, administer the program on a part-time basis.

California Department of Corrections

Working with adult parolees, two permanent staff provide employment services to this target population. Much of their work is off-site, at the offices of the California Department of Corrections. In September, this staff registered 18 new applicants and placed an astonishing 53 on jobs.

The Laid-Off Worker Programs

There have been a number of legislative mandates designed to deal with workers displaced by plant closures, military base closures, mass layoffs and the more recent buzz word, "downsizing." Working closely with the Private Industry Council, the San Francisco EDD office provides a total of three to four permanent staff to these programs, and more often than not their services are off-site. Though these staff people registered six new applicants and placed two on jobs during 1995 third quarter, their work is not primarily dealing with individual job seekers but providing orientation and job search workshops for threatened or laid-off employees.

Most of the programs that have been discussed thus far are designed for targeted population groups. Altogether, they absorb the equivalent of about 26 out of 38 front-line personnel equivalents, not counting supervision and management. There are, shockingly, only twelve professional, nonsupervisory personnel equivalents left to perform the basic front-line functions of the agency, most of whom are Permanent Intermittents. What do these people do?

Unemployment Insurance

The administration of unemployment insurance has and will continue to change its delivery system through phased-in technological development, consolidation, and centralization. Eventually, plans call for filing new and continued claims by telephone throughout the state. However, at this point in San Francisco, there are two offices that handle the claims load though much of the more complex aspects such as appeals, overpayments, and eligibility determinations have been shifted to the other office. Both offices handle new, continued, and interstate claims. In the office under discussion, there continues to be a UI work load, though smaller. One increasingly important function is administering the California Training Benefits Act that allows California UI claimants to receive their UI benefits while attending an approved training program. Five personnel equivalents carry the UI workload, not counting supervision. This involves approximately eight people, most of whom are PIs.

Job Service

At best, there are now only approximately eight personnel equivalents left to handle the basic work of the Job Service. At the reception counter, the flow of traffic must be given information, receive appropriate forms, get answers to endless questions and be directed to the various services. Some staff sit at phone banks, take job orders from employers and enter them directly into the Job Match system, while at another counter staff register applicants into the Job Match terminals as well. At other terminals, one or more individuals conducts a computerized search of the applicant file for every job opening that comes into the office. The most qualified applicants produced by the search must be notified and directed to apply for the job as indicated, or to come into the office. At Window C still another person must reexamine the job and the applicant and, if indicated, provide instructions and a referral card. Staff must regularly call all the employers listed to verify whether the job is still open, whether the referred individuals were hired or not, and thus keep the job order file purged and viable. In the first half of 1995, efforts were made to develop a telemarketing program to solicit job openings from employers. At least 70 openings were listed as a result of the effort, but staff to perform this necessary function is hard to come by. Nevertheless, despite the ridiculously pared down staff resources, the placement staff registered 1,168 individuals and made 480 placements in the third quarter of 1995. With a few exceptions, all of the individuals conducting all of these activities are, at this point in time, PIs, unsure of their jobs and facing the likelihood of additional cuts in hours. Predictably, these individuals on whom EDD has lavished endless hours of training, have been seeking other jobs, and a few have left.

The maxim, "program follows money" rather than the reverse is blatantly evident. Examining the use of staff, one gets a feeling of a time warp. Many of these programs have been funded and in existence, in one form or another, for many years. When, in 1990-91, unemployment rose precipitously and the offices were besieged by newly laid-off workers, the staff allocation remained essentially the same, frozen to the tasks designated by the contracts, and management didn't have the flexibility to respond immediately to the onslaught. As a result, I watched the newly unemployed flock into the office, file their claims and leave without the opportunity to talk to anyone, since nearly all of the experienced staff were busy with their case loads. Though Permanent Intermittents were hired to handle the flood of traffic, it takes time to set up and run examinations, hire, and train. Three weeks of training in the use of the computers alone is required before any useful activity can be conducted. The only service available to the newly unemployed at the local office level, outside of the omniscient computer Job Match, was Experience Unlimited. That, too, was stretched thin with over 300 members. To catch up with the backlog, staff worked evenings and Saturdays. At time-and-a-half, this further exacerbated the budget.

The shortage of placement staff has inevitable consequences. The work suffers, verification is left to an occasional volunteer, tensions mount, supervisors are mostly found filling in at the counters, and long-range planning for management is next to impossible. It's a "helluva way to run a railroad." The amazing thing is that they do, indeed, open the door at eight every morning, close it at five, and handle all of the people who come through the door with a remarkable degree of cheerful helpfulness to each other and to the job seeking public. It is true that the distancing counters are back. Fatal attacks and physical onslaughts on EDD staff in different parts of the state have made management and staff extremely security-conscious. Increasing rather than decreasing the distance between public and staff is now the goal. Whether it is because staff members seek to protect themselves by not appearing antagonistic, or because of a general change in the consciousness of bureaucracies serving a far less intimidated public, the atmosphere in the office at the counter and in the lobby is considerably less formidable than I recall. The quality of the exchange would not today have prompted a book entitled *Counterpoint*. On the other hand, it is far more impersonal, perfunctory and businesslike, though cordial. Some gain, some loss.

However, statistics are unrelenting. They tell the fuller story of the consequences of budget cuts, of inadequate staffing, and of what it means to reduce the agency to a skeletal level. Active applicants declined from 25,022 in 1990-91 to 24,790 in 1991-92, then rose to 28,529 in the recession period of 1992-93 before continuing the decline to 17, 179 in 1994-95. Openings received declined steadily from 5,057 in 1990-91 to 3,456 in 1994-95 while placements fell from 11,195 in the former year to 7,135 in the latter. (Active Applicants represents numbers of people whereas Placements and Openings Received represent transactions. One person may be placed more than once.)

The dismal picture heretofore painted of the applicant supply must be laid beside the startling changes in the demands of the labor market. One fact alone—the 1994 report of the Current Population Survey estimated that an astonishing 43.2 percent of the workforce was regularly using computers on the job. This includes not only white-collar, but also blue-collar and service jobs. Those numbers are unquestionably going up rapidly. One can imagine what the future holds for those who are computer-illiterate. The active application file of the Job Service is palpable proof of the urgent need for an increase, rather than a decrease, in job training and educational resources.

Without a doubt, the market is not the same, the population is not the same, job structures and job-getting are changing, and the Job Service must anticipate and reflect those changes. One thing is dead certain: The local office of the 1950s will never return. The funding will not be there and will, in fact, decrease. The old roles must be abandoned. If the Job Service is to survive, different and better ways to serve the people must be found, despite persistently declining resources.

Visions of the Future

EDD, along with dozens of other public service institutions, is reinventing itself. At the state level, at the area level, and down to the local office, every entity is engaged in serious planning for the future. Planning documents abound: "Strategic Directions," "California's One-Stop Career Center Vision," "Strategic Business Plan, Greater Bay Area." Concepts such as workforce preparation and School-To-Work have entered the lexicon. Task forces and work committees are busy exploring all possible avenues. It would be literally impossible to synthesize the current discussions. It might also be foolhardy, since so much is still unknown—what the congressional and even state legislative mandates will finally be, what entities will remain, what new ones will be formed, and how much less money there will be in the block grants to the states. Underlying all of the planning is a recognition that the present arrangements in the entire employment and training field are not responsive to the times, to the changes in the world, or to the local marketplace and must be tackled head-on.

Depending heavily on technology and self-help, the vision challenges most of the basic premises that have informed the agency in the past. The concepts being discussed now are much more than window dressing or tinkering. They could, if carried out, profoundly change the entire playing field.

Central to the current planning is the one-stop service center initiated by California EDD after obtaining a planning grant from the Department of Labor in November 1994. Currently, the state's large collection of diverse programs and services operate independently from each other. The plan calls for integrating all of them into a comprehensive service. The guiding principles of the planning process are: The system must offer as many employment, training, and education services as possible in a unified customer service. Its customers are conceived as employers, on the one hand, and seekers of jobs, education, and training on the other hand. The information must be comprehensive and be widely and easily accessible. The system must be customer-focused, providing users with the ability to make informed choices. Last, the system must be performance-based with clear methods for measuring agreed-upon outcomes. Depending upon technology, the network will link data bases and share client data. The system will permit and encourage electronic self-service through direct on-line access by its customers.

The one-stop service may either co-locate agencies or link them electronically. Information technology can provide customers with comprehensive information at multiple locations. The system design elements are still in the planning stage. Responsibility and authority must await federal legislation, which will likely prescribe the collaborative process and governance structure. State legislative actions may also affect the final landscape.

Without burdening this paper with more details of the vision which is still too fuzzy to be fully grasped, certain underlying and sometimes unstated themes emerge: If we conceive of jobs and job seekers as constituting a three-tiered level of both job and job seeking skills, then this change is surely aimed at attracting and increasing services to the highest tier, those that are comfortable with the computer, whether from home, a kiosk, or the office of a participating agency. These are the individuals who can conduct an effective job search on their own and whose main need is for usable information. Accompanying this perception is that, with funding scarce, there would be an inevitable decrease in services to the second and third tier of job seekers who require more costly, one-to-one staff intervention. The computer would open employer job orders to any job seeker for self-selection and referral. It is even conceived that the computer may, from the application data, develop a key-word resume and print it out for the job seeker's use. In other words, the employment service would turn itself inside out by providing the public with all of the information and knowledge that it has heretofore kept guarded unto itself. The plans appear to contemplate reducing and perhaps, eventually, discarding the broker role inherent in selection and referral.

The agency is still committed to the confidentiality rule governing employers' job orders, but most employers appear to be far less concerned with confidentiality and employment service selection than they are with broadcasting their needs more widely. As one very large employer told the area manager, "The best thing the employment service can do is to run job search workshops and at the same time advertise the availability of the jobs."

Both research and the statistical decline of employment service use support movement in the direction of an open, self-service, unrestrained mechanism, in many ways comparable to help-wanted ads. A twenty-year-old Labor Department national survey of 65,000 households is still the most comprehensive study ever made of job-seeking methods. Three times as many workers (15 percent) obtained their jobs from the want ads as did through the public employment service (5 percent). A 1978 study compared the stock and flow of jobs between the employment service and the want ads in twelve labor market areas. Despite the costs, three times as many employers used the want ads as used the free public employment service, with one-third of employers using both. All of this may have changed with the subsequent rising use of temporary help agencies. Nevertheless, it does indicate an employer preference for an unrestricted no-broker approach to recruiting, which must be considered in any plans for reinvigorating the public service.

What employers do not appear concerned about, but what society must not abandon, is concern for that second and third tier of job seekers. But how, with persistently declining resources, to serve the full range of applying employers and job seekers is the impossible current challenge of the public employment service. Yet the lessons of its sixty-two-year history leave little other choice. The alternative is increasing irrelevance in the labor exchange function that may have already occurred. The dichotomous pull in opposite directions that has bedeviled the public employment service since the 1960s must be resolved if the agency is to be revitalized or even survive. But if the agency didn't exist, its functions are still so vital that it would have to be reestablished. Reinventing the aging agency is an intimidating task confronted with innumerable potential pitfalls. It takes courage to attempt it, but it must be done. I applaud the effort and wish the planners and administrators well.

CHAPTER **8**

Contingent Work and the Role of Labor Market Intermediaries

Audrey Freedman

This chapter describes the rising incidence of contingent working arrangements, business incentives to adopt such practices, and the labor market intermediary function of temporary help firms. Workers who lose a secure job perch, as well as those who are new to employment, must fend for themselves. Under such circumstances, contingent work is preferable to unemployment because it provides income, experience, and training; enhances occupational and industrial mobility; and increases future employability. The least-cost way of finding such work is through labor market intermediaries such as temporary help firms.

What Does "Contingent Work" Mean?

The term "contingent" was first applied to employment relationships in 1985.[1] It was intended to describe ways in which firms could staff their activities to fit the current needs of the business. Intense competitive pressure during the early 'eighties was forcing large U.S. corporations to cut payroll cost, which had become more fixed than variable during the post World War era of comfort and economic hegemony. At the beginning of this drive, in 1982, imitative wage patterns were the first tradition to be broken. Next, greater scrutiny of bureaucratic overhead cut away some of the rungs in corporate hierarchies. Then personnel departments began to be pushed into thinking and performing in a more enterprise-oriented way.

Step-by-step, companies came closer to realizing that conventional management practices also contributed to the cost problem by maintaining a stable, fixed workforce within an inertial administrative pyramid. Large firms were anchored to a costly operational base that was not able to respond nimbly to new opportunity or to withdraw quickly from failed strategies. Under pressure to regain flexibility, companies began to shift their labor strategy toward contingent employment.

The term described a working relationship that was to exist only when needed by an employer. It was not a description of the qualities of individual workers, but only a relationship arising in the duration and strength of the company's needs. The contingent arrangement could include temporary employees, self-employed freelancers, and part-time workers. Contracting-out might also be arranged to supply services on a contingent basis: much of the business services sector (such as advertising, data processing, or security services) is included in the concept.

In the late 1980s, labor market analysts suggested terms such as "peripheral workers," "just-in-time employees" in Europe, or "irregular workers." (These adjectives implied some characteristics of the workers, yet less about the reason for their use.) Another term, "managed services," began to define many business service companies that provide complete facilities staffing, or outsourcing. More recently the term "staffing industry" has been applied to those firms that create a labor market for such assignments.

In the foreseeable future, we will probably continue struggling to find stable terminology for an unstable concept. It might be possible to ignore the question, except for one major problem: in order to count the number of people working in this fashion, one must have a highly specific definition. Everyone, both employers and workers, must have a clear-cut idea of what that definition contains. Most important, all "observations" of workers and employers must remain stable for a long enough period of time for counting, categorizing, and comparing. There is little chance of this for an activity so fluid and inchoate as contingent work.

This chapter will concentrate on temporary workers as the most easily identifiable example of contingent employment. It discusses the reasons for the growing trend toward using temporary help suppliers, as well as some social needs that must be met in new ways.[2] It includes critical evaluations of the trend. Using the temporary help industry as an example, the chapter suggests long-term effects on job markets, employer-employee relationships, training, and careers in the next century.

Why Have Employers Changed Their Personnel Practices?

Cost Escalation and Loss of Market Dominance

The decade of the 1970s produced two shock waves for U.S. business that pounded comfortable companies into new shapes during the next fifteen years, and continue to affect the survivors today. The Arab oil embargo of 1973 and the price increases of the oil cartel in 1973-4 and 1979 had profound effects on the world economy. In the United States, energy price inflation affected commodities; next it caused a wage spiral through the intensifying mechanism of escalation clauses in union contracts and imitative wage setting in nonunion industries. Unit labor costs rose because there were less than compensating increases in productivity. Cost-push inflation stayed with us for an entire decade, and U.S. business became less competitive in world markets.

The second major development was increased competition from foreign producers of both consumer and producer goods. This broke the market power of U.S. companies in such basic industries as steel, autos, rubber, machinery, and electrical and electronic equipment. Beginning in 1979, a series of deregulations added competitive pressure in airlines, telecommunications, trucking, railroads (and later banking). Most of these industries had been characterized by secure jobs, regularly rising wages, and (with the exception of banking) a high degree of unionization. Their slow-moving personnel policies had been based on market power, with unions able to capture some of the oligopoly premiums for their members.

The pressure to use workers in a more flexible way had already begun, but was not yet fully recognized. Layoffs began with the recessions of 1981-82, but recalls were expected with recovery, as had usually been the case. Unions tried to stave off permanent workforce cuts and management promised to trade some amount of job security in exchange for wage moderation. Political response brought a plant-closing law that required advance notice of major layoffs. Government contracts and a defense build-up were also used to prop up job security in industries such as aerospace and electronics.

Ultimately, companies were forced to devise ways of using labor on a contingent basis (Golden and Applebaum 1992). Intensified competition also brought mergers, buyouts, and other forms of restructuring that undermined employee expectations of a long-term career with one stable corporation. This was particularly shocking to white-collar employees, both support staff and managerial ranks, because of its novelty to them.

Unpredictability

As U.S. corporate giants lost market power during the 1970s and 1980s, they were less able to tolerate unpredictable change. At the least, they became painfully sensitized to their lack of control over sudden market changes. Cyclical business upswings and recessions continue to require fast business adjustment. The more uncertainty there is, the more employers would like to avoid becoming caught in a difficult position. For example, if demand suddenly spurts, a company can call upon temporary help companies to provide additional labor quickly. The temporary help firm has capability to recruit, screen, and place qualified workers on the job almost instantaneously, or "on demand." Particularly when a company is not sure how long the good times are going to last, it is unwilling to make commitments to hire its own regular workforce.

If the strong demand continues, a company may begin to add to its own payroll, perhaps by hiring those who worked in temporary positions. By then, the use of outside contractors for supplying supplemental workforces may have become a permanent part of the company's personnel strategy. On the other hand, if the added business opportunity quickly disappears, the company is not obliged to lay off its own workers, pay severance and other downsizing penalties, and undergo the difficult decisions involved in selecting which of its own workers will be retained.

Business cycles are not the only cause for uncertainty. Within a firm or an industry segment, unpredictable developments can require immediate adjustment of the workforce. Major new contracts may suddenly change the strategy of a division or an entire corporation; a merger can open new technology and market paths. Shifts in government policies suddenly remove some opportunities while creating others.

Two decades ago the term "manpower planning" was fashionable. It reflected a corporate sense that their business was a relatively closed system, in which they could manage smoothly if they got the planning right. So, companies devised elaborate five- or seven-year plans for the entire business and its divisions. This was turned over to personnel departments for their parallel manpower plan. Workers were to be purposefully steered through a series of assignments and redeployments, career ladders, transfers, and training. During slack periods companies tended to hoard personnel, or at least to keep excess levels on the payroll. The cost of such a slow-moving strategy is greater today, and business is less smug about its ability to control every situation. The term "manpower planning" has fallen into disuse. Contemporary language is more like: "it depends on what we need right now."

Loss of Union Power

Unions would, in nearly every situation, try to restrict the employment of contingent workers. The only exceptions to this general union policy might be in cases of a union-run hiring hall system or in the entertainment industry. However, during the past fifteen years, while temporary help has had its strongest growth, union power has been waning. Golden and Applebaum (1992, pp. 483, 485) conclude that "a shift in relative bargaining power has increased the ability of employers to implement core-periphery strategies that involve expanding stocks of temporary workers."

In reality, there is a more circular process at work. Unions have lost power for the *same* reasons that pushed employers toward more contingent employment practices: intensified competition and loss of market dominance (as described above). A second set of reasons why unions have lost power has to do with the rising cost differential that priced unionized employers out of the competitive market: spiral-causing wage formulas, accumulation of seniority rules, restraints on work-force redeployment, and high-cost benefits. Ultimately, this led to new scrutiny of the cost of employing.

The pressure described in the sections above drove large and mid-dle-sized U.S. corporations into a much more careful examination of their payroll costs and long-term obligations. Business survival required change.

New Scrutiny of the Cost of Employing

Comparison of Internal Wage Scales with Current Labor Market Rates

As larger companies experience the disruption of their market power and are jostled by competition, they start to discover how much higher their wage and benefit levels are, in comparison with the local labor market. In many cases, this discrepancy has developed inadvertently. Through inattention, their wage scales might be double or triple the local custom due to slow accretion: long-standing tradition of wage leadership, lifetimes on the seniority ladder, bloated hierarchies, auto-matic maintenance of historical wage differentials, union contract pre-miums—all of the standard conventions of compensation administration.

The biggest gaps between market wages and corporate salaries have often been found in numerically large groups: support staff and pro-duction workers. For example, a major corporation may be paying its senior executive secretaries around $60,000, and giving them benefits that (with high tenure) are about 40 percent more, for a total package that costs the company $84,000. Comparably generous pay-and-bene-fits packages for lower-level support staff will have been pegged to this scale.

Then a new chief executive arrives who is charged with cutting costs, bringing new competitive life to the company, and starting up new ventures in several potential markets. What are his choices? Hiring the "next" office worker at the current local rate of $25,000 with typi-cal local benefit packages would be quite disruptive to corporate per-sonnel policies, to say nothing of morale among the existing workforce. Probably illegal, too, in the case of some benefits. So what does his human resources manager begin to consider? One of the options might be to staff at least one of the new ventures with a temporary workforce, using a supplier firm that will train the temporaries exactly as required. As the new operation gains its footing, it may put some of those temporaries on its own payroll, selecting those who best fit the company's need. In the meantime, temporary office staff is being supplied as needed, at a cost that is close to the local going rate. If any are put on the company's payroll, it will also be at the market rate.

Fixed-Cost Payrolls Inconsistent with Uneven Labor Needs

There are many more occasions for labor demand to be variable, yet predictable, in today's economy. For example, when a software company is introducing its newest product it may need a large quality assurance staff for a short period of time; a mammoth shipping department for two weeks; and then specially trained help-line staff for the next six months. For a nonprofit example: a membership organization may set up a three-month fundraising drive or membership enrollment that will require major short-term supplements to their tiny core staff. As an example from political campaigns: the election season may require everything from canvassers to mailroom workers, with staff growing rapidly until election day, after which none are needed. Consumer product industries often face fickle buyers, or operate in markets that are highly seasonal, with peak demands of relatively short duration. Service industries such as entertainment and tourism have idiosyncratic peaks and deep valleys.

Organizations will not be able to carry the burden of a fixed payroll when their needs are so variable. They will move generally to a core-plus-contingent workforce as their only effective labor strategy.

Make-or-Buy Decisions

Corporate human resource departments are being held accountable for costs in this more stringent atmosphere. Recruitment expenses, search time, applicant pools, even screening costs are being closely watched. Training expense is weighed against its benefits in the short term. All of the in-house activities that devote resources to acquiring, developing, and maintaining a workforce are under scrutiny.

After considering the cost of managing various parts of its workforce, a large company may contract for the workers, handing over the whole job to a few selected suppliers or to just one firm. A temporary help company that has been designated sole supplier will supervise some or all of these functions on the customer's site. Such a contract may mean dozens of on-site temporary help managers in many plants and offices of a large customer company. This kind of large-scale contracting (sometimes currently called "staffing services") is a growing trend in the mid-1990s.

On a much smaller scale, new enterprises and smaller companies may decide to focus their business in highly specialized ways. They will deliberately choose to offload the administrative burden of recruiting and maintaining a workforce beyond the core entrepreneurial and technical group. The strategy seems to be particularly attractive to advanced technology ventures. As a result, the fastest growing part of the temporary help industry is supplying technical staff such as computer specialists, engineers, designers, and scientists, as well as other highly trained workers such as systems analysts, medical technicians, and lawyers.

From the Worker's Point of View

The trend toward contingent employment shifts responsibility to the individual. Working in an explicitly short-term relationship puts greater burdens on individuals for their own training, career development, and general morale. The psychic benefit of identifying with a corporation is unavailable. Also missing is the reward of promotion (and status) within a company's administrative hierarchy.

On the other hand, a contingent employee is more likely to be judged in terms of what he or she can do. This is because a company that wants to contract for contingent workers will define the job precisely, seek bids from outside firms to fill it, and price it according to expected performance. Often the temporary help firm will itself evaluate the job content and skill requirements before it gives a price. As a result of this objective, spot market process, each temporary worker knows what is expected. He or she will be less exposed to vague selection and assignment, "office politics," subjective judgements, and interpersonal power plays. (Obviously, a temporary help firm that characteristically relied on personal favoritism in issuing assignments would not long retain its clientele) Contingent workers are thus able to operate in a more businesslike atmosphere of arm's length, contractual relationships.

Workers Will Need a Better-Functioning Labor Clearinghouse

In today's massively fluid labor market, workers are going to need new forms of "hiring halls," employment agencies, temporary help firms, and other labor market intermediaries.

Comprehensive Job Information

With relatively frequent job changes, workers will have to choose more often and will need immediate information about jobs that are open. This means computerization that is sufficiently user-friendly to tell workers of all capacities about the available jobs. The job posting must be interactive to the extent of permitting a certain amount of maneuvering to take place in order to produce a good fit between a potential worker and the listed job. The number and variety of listings should be comprehensive in all skill categories and levels. Of course this means that potential employers must be strongly attracted by the chief benefit of their participation—the possibility of locating good workers, quickly.

Worker Credentials

Experience, references, background characteristics, training and other applicant information will have to be available and standardized so that they are usable by employers. Most of this cannot be produced by a potential employee alone. Moreover, the growing trend toward outsourcing also implies that corporate personnel offices are doing less of their own recruitment, verification of applicants' credentials, and hiring. This leaves an opportunity for outside suppliers to fill the role of making a match.

Employment Continuity and Security

Temporary help firms are able to offer a certain amount of security to workers in a labor market where short-term employment relationships are an increasing proportion of all hiring. They provide access to job assignments and the potential for steady employment, although the wages for assignments are likely to be more variable than those in a permanent job. Using a temporary help firm gives an employee maximum choice among possible jobs within his or her skill capabilities. Moreover, that choice will include the option to change assignments at will, or to take time off for short or extended periods. The temporary will often be entitled to holiday pay, perhaps also to vacation pay. Many large temporary firms also provide health benefits, usually with employee contributions.

Workers may also use the temporary route to look for more permanent jobs. Short-term assignments give an individual increasing knowledge of labor market realities, including pay rates and conditions of employment; greater exposure to many different job situations; and frequently, offers of permanent employment. Temporary help firms estimate that about a third of their employees move into permanent positions—that is, they are hired onto the payroll of one of the firms where they were assigned.

Workers Will Need to be Responsible for Their Own Training

In the fabled days of lifelong career employment, the company provided training and development opportunities according to its needs and philosophy. Formal training was more of a reality for managerial, executive, and some professional employees. But informal apprenticeships and short job-specific training was available to the ranks of production, materials handling, and maintenance workers. A firm's willingness to make such investments was greater if it planned to keep that employee in the same job, or "develop" that employee for promotions, over many years.

As this stable outlook fades, employees are beginning to sense that their training and career progression must become their own responsibility. It is not safe to expect the firm to guide and subsidize one's career development. However, there do not seem to be any new institutional trends in education, training, or the job market that can be identified as possible solutions. The best advice has been: keep busy, keep moving, always look for opportunity on your own. New pressure for self-development has resulted in rising levels of self-employment, small-firm start ups, and other forms of individual self-determination.

Workers Will Need Portable Benefits, or Self-Financed Benefits

Many of the benefits associated with long tenure are unavailable to temporary and other contingent workers. Estimates suggest that only a quarter of temporaries have access to health plans, two out of five have paid holidays, three quarters get paid vacations, but nearly none have pensions.[3] One of the solutions proposed in the early 1990s would have required employers to provide pro-rata contributions for various benefits to part-time, temporary, and other contingent workers. This would have been almost impossible to administer because of the fluid nature of their employment relationships and the difficulty of identifying the responsible employer over any period of time. Perhaps for this reason the proposals have faded from the liberal agenda.

The most serious problem for workers involves benefits that provide security against risk: health and pension plans. It seems clear that these worker needs will not be met for years to come, while contingent employment affects a higher proportion of the population. A national policy designed to accomplish universal health coverage failed in 1993 with so painful a crash that another attempt may not take place before the end of the century. Without some form of universal health care, the fragmenting of employment relationships will continue to cut access, because "private" plans will seek every opportunity to cut off potentially high-cost risks. Temporary employees must continue to cope by obtaining dependent coverage from a spouse's employer when it is possible.

Pension and savings plans are the kind of benefit that is easy to forget until mid-life; they are also most likely to be neglected when it is up to the individual to provide for retirement. Tax-favored retirement accounts might be given even more favorable terms and instituted for self-enrollment by lower-paid temporary workers.

The Temporary Help Industry

The temporary help industry has been growing rapidly, especially during the 1990s.[4] Even more remarkable, however, has been its protean ability to shift and change its service "product" according to demand and market conditions. That adaptive behavior is making the industry a leading indicator of business cycles, and possibly other new developments in human resource use and practice. A description of some trends in the service product of the industry follows.

Expansion of Types of Service Provided by the Industry

Screening, Testing, and Evaluating

Customers of the industry have pressed for continual improvements in the screening process, to ensure that an assigned worker is fully qualified for the job. A temporary firm would not last long if it regularly sent inappropriate workers to its customers. In fact, firms may seek competitive advantage over the other suppliers by doing a superior job of testing and screening; that is, sending better workers to fill assignments. Moreover, as a result of equal opportunity pressure starting in the 1970s, there are requirements for professional validation of various tests and other screening instruments. Both developments have moved the temporary help industry to high standards in evaluating employee skills and experience. It has a broader concern than any individual corporate personnel office, and a particularly acute need for cost-effective "intake" tools.

During the last decade and a half, the industry has replaced many subjective rules of thumb with innovative tools for measuring worker characteristics. It sponsors test development for skills both manual and intellectual; and it can identify personal preferences for style of supervision, work content, and workplace atmosphere. One company has determined that a critical factor in assignment success is finding out what an individual "likes to do," as well as his or her skills—and assigning that individual appropriately.

Training

As a means of increasing the value of their service, many temporary help companies are offering training of several types.

Technical Skills. Large firms have developed computer-based courses in computer programs, primarily to gain competitive advantage. Manpower, the largest temporary help company in the world, began in the late 1970s to build alliances with various computer and software companies. The object was to have training programs ready to administer the moment a new program or new computer system was introduced. Customers switching to the new system could use Manpower's temporaries to run their system from the first day and also use Manpower to teach their regular employees. In the past decade most of the larger temporary help firms have provided training in computer use, and the idea has now spread to many of the smaller local companies.

It is possible to imagine that the more vocationally oriented schools, such as community colleges, will expand their training by developing similar partnerships with technology firms, and then add enough job-placement capability that they also will be in the temporary help assignment business.

Company-Specific Skills. A second type of training might focus on the procedures and standard practices of a large customer (e.g., a bank). The temporary help firm would work with the bank to develop standards so that an assigned temporary would be job-ready and productive anywhere in the first hour. Training might involve everything that is particular and peculiar to that bank: formats used for letters, memos, background papers; accounting or other record-keeping methods; forms of address and other language usage; the organization structure and perhaps the geographic aspects of a far-flung business; even the office dress code. With this knowledge a temporary might fit into the bank seamlessly, without wasting time and resources learning how "things are done here" at a level of minor and annoying detail.

Personal-Relations Skills. For their regular employees, companies sometimes provide this type of training, but it is most often learned by observing others or as one of the lessons of life—in other words, informally. Those who do not develop the required behavior are winnowed out of regular employment. This informal training may grow weaker as the proportion of permanent long-tenure employees shrinks. People who are always on the move may, in fact, develop poor habits of dealing with others because they do not expect to be around to deal with the consequences.

Add to this problem the growing recognition that mechanical and technical skills are insufficient for productive performance in nearly every job today. Consequently, there is a growing need for systematic training in interpersonal relations. It seems likely that temporary help firms will move first to fill this gap.

Manpower has begun a quality training program that focuses on customer service, personal relationships and communication in the workplace, and work attitudes. When temporaries arrive at an assignment with positive skills in dealing with supervisors and other employees, they become an influence for higher productivity in their work group. Similarly, temporaries who have been trained to deal effectively with external and internal customers are ready to provide high-quality service. This represents a competitive advantage for the temporary help firm, possibly even in comparison to the in-house training of a customer company.

Occupational Specialization

There have been specialized temporary help firms for many decades providing engineers to aerospace industries or running nurse registries. Recently companies that focus on niche occupational groups have expanded rapidly and their specializations now include many scientific fields, legal services, finance and managerial functions, and health care. Another trend is the movement of the biggest general temporary help companies into the specialty fields. A general temporary help supplier might purchase a niche company, making it a separate technical division; or it might form a working alliance with several specialized technical suppliers (e.g., of paralegals, or of home health aides). In some cases, a large general temporary help company may add technical worker specialties to its marketing in order to provide full service to its corporate customers.

In the highly specialized and technical occupations, temporary firms operate quite differently. First of all, their best competitive advantage lies in the perfection of the "fit" between the customer's requirements and the individual assigned. The match may be accomplished solely on credentials and resumes. Assignments are likely to be for half a year or longer; few or none are short-term substitute or fill-in arrangements. For a staffing firm providing scientific, technical, or professional workers, there is very little competition based solely on price of the service.

Ancillary Personnel Services

Companies seem to be finding that temporaries are the best source for new permanent hires. A firm can "work-test" people and select the most productive. About a third of temporary workers are hired into permanent positions (and they have discovered, in fact, that temporary work is the best way to get such exposure). Temporary suppliers often charge their customers for such a transfer because it diminishes their inventory of skilled employees and cuts the number of positions being filled by the temporary agency. Recently a few customer companies have explicitly contracted with a temporary supplier to include the service of referring temporaries for regular placement. There is also a form of service identified as temporary-to-permanent.

Large-scale customers are usually provided with on-site temporary managers, generally where there is a sole source contract. They will be placed in every location where the company is using substantial numbers of the temporary help firm's employees. Their major responsibility will be to keep every position filled at all times with fully qualified and trained people.

Large user companies increasingly ask for customized reports on temporary performance and other aspects of the service, as well as cost breakdowns and usage reports covering their entire organization, sometimes by division and department. Productivity measures, where possible, may be added. This kind of full operating report is being provided already by large temporary help firms.

Temporary help firms may begin to offer complete project teams. For example, a team might work within the customer company to evaluate and help design a completely new information system. Computer cutovers might be staffed by a project manager and several groups of specialists. These teams might prepare the customer's existing system for transfer, make the transition, and begin operations under the new system—while also training the customer's regular employees in the new software. Or, a company might ask a temporary help firm to provide the designers, engineers, and project leader for the development of a new product. One-time events like marketing drives, product introductions, or geographic relocations are all possible activities that might be outsourced. In fact, many of them are already outsourced, but to one or more specialized business services firms. Thus the temporary help firms are starting to blend and penetrate other types of business services.

Among the technical staffing firms, it is possible to foresee the possibility that subcontracting, combined with narrow specialization, might create a hybrid kind of service firm. For example, a pharmaceutical company might contract for the entire clinical trials of a new drug. A transportation company might contract for the design of a new operating grid, or a completely reworked computerized package-tracking system.

Some temporary help firms have recently begun to market their training programs independently. Skills assessment tools and computer-based training are used to make temporaries more valuable, but they can be sold to other companies as well. In many cases, a trainer can go into the package, as well as customized training modules.

Some employers have begun to search for technical and professional workers by posting job openings on the Internet. Individuals can list their resumes on the Internet, and employer searches can be carried out through keyword matching and other instantaneous search techniques. As this capability becomes well-refined in the next two years, it will begin to shrink the business opportunities of temporary help firms that specialize in resume-using occupational groups: technical, professional, and managerial workers.

Consequently, the technical temporary firms are going to feel rising pressure to develop new services, rather than see their business disappear. One possibility has been mentioned above: the provision of already-assembled project teams, rather than individuals, and teams that have long experience working together. Another possible new service that the technical firms can offer, in the Internet-mediated labor market, might be a necessary credential: checked references and experience, verified educational qualifications, and guarantees that the electronic match is a "real" person with the called-for background. The new service might be a sort of national bureau of standards credential, a Good Housekeeping Seal of authenticity.

Possible Public Role of the Temporary Help Industry

Operating as a Parallel Employment Service

The federal-state public employment service has been burdened by greater social service responsibilities over the past three decades. It must authorize individuals for income supplement checks and for entry to many kinds of support services, inventory the available openings in training and social programs, and interact with various other agencies and joint programs administered by private and public "partnerships."

In short, the employment service, or Job Service as it is starting to be called, is a social welfare agency that considers its clientele to be unemployed persons.

Thus there is no public labor market intermediary that views *employers* as the true clients who need service. Employers are the ones who identify the job titles and skill mixes that they need. An employer-oriented intermediary would search on their behalf, develop valid assessments for screening job seekers, and make on-the-spot referrals. Traffic at such a recruitment center would be very heavy. Therefore, an intermediary can accrue vast information about wage offers, market-clearing wage rates, unfilled vacancies where labor demand is strong, and opportunities that require relocation. It can steer training for high-demand situations, anticipating the skills needed under changing economic and technology environments.

An employer-serving intermediary would provide substantially improved assistance to job seekers. It would likely attract large numbers of job orders from potential employers. The biggest job listings, organized in the most easily-used way for job seekers, is a needed and important public service.

If there were such a client-directed intermediary there would be an overall reduction in job search time. Employers have an incentive to list jobs quickly, and referrals would be accurately aimed. Daily referrals would be heavy and fast-moving. Such an improvement in job search effectiveness cuts the public loss in two ways: it lowers unemployment compensation and reduces search time. The unemployment rate, a function of search time, would be marginally lower. Time lost in nonproductive activity would be reduced, a gain for the entire economy.

There may have been an era when the public employment service was imagined to function in this way, but it never did. The social service demands of the past few decades have steered it farther afield. At a time of receptiveness toward privatization, the Labor Department might consider whether temporary help agencies could be enlisted to help operate the public employment service.

Assisting Welfare and School-to-Work Transitions

Temporary help companies are experts at job counselling. Their technique is informal and realistically tailored to individual behaviors.

This kind of customized attention might be effective in putting welfare recipients to work—and also in helping with school-to-work interning and apprenticeship.

A temporary help agency might alter its normal procedures only slightly. Individuals can be guided toward appropriate dress, manners, and speech. Jobs can be found in which their characteristic behavior is an asset rather than a misfit. The company may already be using sophisticated tools to discern personal preferences: whether an individual likes to work alone or in groups, with close supervision or independently, with customers or with "things," in an orderly and paced fashion or under some stress.

Critiques of Contingent Work Arrangements

The critics have focused on differences between "regular" payroll employees and contingent workers, often implying that any arrangement other than a long-term payroll attachment to a single employer is a blot on the American economy. Some have said that employers have been trying to escape government regulation of labor standards, or are trying to block union organizing drives. Others merely note that traditional employer-funded benefits are seldom available to contingent workers.[5] Legislation has been proposed, over the years, to meet these criticisms. It probably will not move to enactment because of the difficulty of regulating such a fast-changing practice.

More general (and rhetorical) criticisms have speculated that loyalty will decline, insecurity will rise, and the overall morale of American workers will deteriorate. These comments usually imply an ideal past time in which employee loyalty and employer paternalism assured American economic hegemony. There is no answer to such romanticism, nor a remedy to the loss which it laments.

Benefits

A February 1995 survey by the Bureau of Labor Statistics (U.S. Department of Labor 1995) showed that contingent workers have a much lower rate of health insurance coverage, and that "contingent

Yocheved Rappaport Levitan,
mother of Sar Levitan

Left: Rabbi Osher Nissan Halevi
Levitan, father of Sar Levitan
Right: Rabbi Shmuel Kuselewitz,
uncle to Sar Levitan and
father of Bluma (Blossom)
Kuselewitz Neushatz

Levitan borthers.
Left: Abraham (Sar)
Right: Nathan
Middle: Meyer

Sar Levitan as student at
City College of New York, 1937

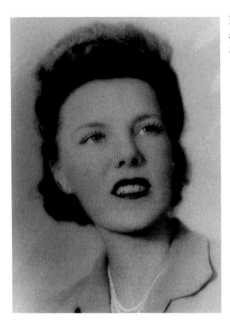

Brita Ann Buchard Kohle Levitan
about the time of her 1946 marriage to
Sar Levitan

Captain Sar A. Levitan,
1944 or 1945

Sar Levitan during Wage
Stabilization Board period,
1951-52

Sar Levitan as Assistant Director
of Presidential Railroad Commission,
1960-61

Presidential Railroad Commission staff, from left to right, Sar Levitan, Charles Rhemus, Beatrice Burgoon, unidentified, Robert Ables, Philip Arnow, unidentified

Levitan at Leopoldskron, headquarters of the Harvard-connected American Seminar at Salzburg, Austria, 1975

Levitan lecturing at Leopoldskron, 1975. From right to left, Levitan, Philip Randolph, unidentified, unidentified, Marion Mangum, unidentified, Garth Mangum in customary repose.

Sar Levitan at Berchtesgaden, 1975

Sar and Brita Levitan at home of Seymour and Ethel Brandwein in 1980s

Sar Levitan and Seymour Brandwein at latter's 1985 retirement from DOL

Brita Levitan in 1970s
or 1980s

Professor Levitan in Center
for Social Policy Studies office, late
1980s

workers with insurance were much less likely to receive it from their employers." For those employed by temporary agencies, 44.9 percent had health insurance, but only 5.7 percent received it through their agency. In contrast, 82.2 percent of noncontingent workers had health insurance, 53.9 percent of them through their employers. Although some temporary employees probably were covered by the health plans of working spouses, a major difference in coverage is apparent.

Job loss in the United States means loss of health insurance coverage, and job insecurity is probably most frightening for this reason. Rising political attention to health care reform might ultimately result in dissociating health benefits from the individual's employment (an absolute linkage unique to the United States). In the meantime, more job mobility—of any kind—will mean less health care access. Employers will continue to find ways to reduce their benefit burden even though health care cost inflation has been remarkably low in the mid-1990s.

Pension benefits are nearly nonexistent for contingent workers. There is limited tax relief for establishing one's own retirement fund for those who are self-employed. However, no contingent worker is protected in old age by a company-paid, defined contribution or defined benefit plan.

Employment Security

Job security has seemed to be self-evident for permanent employees and nonexistent for temporary and other contingent workers. In its recent survey, in fact, the Bureau of Labor Statistics defined contingent workers as those "who do not expect their job to last." But then the clarity begins to dissolve: a third of people who work for temporary help agencies *do* expect their jobs to last, and so do about 62 percent of "on-call workers and day laborers." One might imagine that thousands of employees at Chemical Banking and Chase Manhattan Bank, merged in 1995, did expect their jobs "to last" on the day before the merger announcement. That expectation can be dashed in a moment.

These sudden reversals have characterized the past decade. Corporate reorganizations and other drastic responses to heavy competition have affected the security of nearly all employees. Even government workers are less protected. There is no longer a bright dividing line between having a berth in a corporate bureaucracy and having to piece together a career of one's own.

Individuals must rely more upon their own skills and on their savings. Job search is a major personal investment, and more so when it occurs several times during a working life. Temporary help firms acting as labor market intermediaries probably increase, rather than reduce, the amount of security an individual can achieve. They can recycle people into other assignments providing income, increased "exposure," and additional skills and experience.

Training, Experience, and Development of the Workforce

Companies have little incentive to train workers who will not be with them for very long. Even when they do train permanent employees, it is usually job-specific and narrow; only high-level managers get developmental training. *The Economist* cites an OECD study that found "in America only 10 percent of young recruits had any formal training from their company, compared with about 70 percent in Japan and Germany."[6] The difference was attributed mainly to the fact that U.S. companies did not expect their employees to stay with the firm.

Therefore, whatever training American employers have provided in the past is going to be diminished by rising employment flexibility. Contingent workers will have to be their own career developers and seek their own training and experience. In the case of temporary employees, the agencies have increasingly provided training (particularly for computerized office operations) as a form of investment in their own inventory.

Loyalty to the Company

Loyalty is said to be a valuable aspect of corporate culture. It is popularly assumed that an employee's long-time identification with a company will enhance his or her performance, energy, and willingness. This has never been proved.

Just the opposite might occur, in fact. Long-time identification with a company may simply be passive, generating nothing more than inertia. If an employee at any level has the idea that "the company will take care of things in its own way," that employee will not be creative or self-directed. Individual initiative may have been squelched by years of handing over decisions and actions to a superior. In fact, he or she may also have learned not to question the traditional ways of the hierarchy. Exploratory thinking is rarely found in loyal ranks.

Current management literature has been calling for more team self-management, more independent thinking all around. In fact, corporate command-and-control systems are being criticized by nearly all business school experts. By implication, they also disapprove of the blanket of loyalty that covers the inertial corporate bureaucracies.

Contingent workers would have no reason to develop emotions of identification or loyalty toward those for whom they are working. Instead, a contingent worker is likely to think in terms of a customer relationship: the employer is his or her client. Expectations have been made concrete; the work to be done is carefully defined and has been priced on the open market. The relationship is an arm's length, businesslike one, neither emotional nor comfort-seeking. Both parties have directed their minds toward a finite product of the work, often within a finite time period.

If it were possible to compare the real productivity of loyalty-attached employees with workers whose services are explicitly purchased in a business transaction, the latter would be the more efficient.

Benefits to the Labor Market and the American Economy

The flexibility of our labor force must be included in any list of potential competitive advantages that are available to America. We have a relatively unregulated labor market compared with other industrialized nations, and one that is not much burdened by tradition. The geographic and occupational mobility of our workers has been the highest in the world. As a result, labor moves to activities where it is most productive. This fluidity is mostly the result of individual responses to incentives in a fairly free labor market.

Now, in response to greater competition, American companies have found new ways to make their labor costs more flexible. This pressure will not recede and will lead to an even greater variety of work practices. We will need various intermediaries to help workers and employers make the best adjustments at the least cost to individuals, the general public, and business. The temporary help industry is already equipped to offer some help with day-to-day adjustments in labor market opportunities, training and development, and melioration of unemployment. It continues to help business enterprise be more adaptive.

Individuals' responsibility for their own working careers will probably increase, while social policy should address the problems of rising wage inequality and a predictable growth in old-age dependency during the next decade. As the idea of corporate community fades, the society is less likely to expect business to provide social welfare. Nor is the public likely, if present trends continue, to expect much of large government. The best source of security may, in the end, be small communal organizations.

NOTES

1. Speech by Audrey Freedman to the American Productivity Center, published in the *Daily Labor Report*, July 18, 1985, pages A-4 through A-6.

2. As early as 1981-82, there was an employer survey identifying reasons for using temporary workers. Its conclusions remain true today (Mangum, Mayall, and Nelson 1985).

3. 1987 data from U.S. Bureau of Labor Statistics.

4. For a careful analysis of this growth, see Segal and Sullivan (1995).

5. See, for example, the transmittal letter at pp. 1-11, of "Workers at Risk" GAO Report HRD-91-56 on Contingent Workers, March 1991.

6. "Musical Chairs," *The Economist,* July 7, 1993, p. 67.

References

Golden, L., and E. Applebaum. 1992. "What Was Driving the 1982-88 Boom in Temporary Employment?" *American Journal of Economics and Sociology* (October): 472-493.

Mangum, Garth, Donald Mayall, and Kristin Nelson. 1985. "The Temporary Help Industry: A Response to the Dual Internal Labor Market," *Industrial and Labor Relations Review* 38, 4 (July): 599-611.

"Musical Chairs," *The Economist* (July7, 1993): 67.

Segal, Lewis M., and Daniel G. Sullivan. 1995. "The Temporary Labor Force," *Economic Perspectives* 19, 2 (March-April): 2-19.

U.S. Department of Labor. 1995. "Contingent and Alternative Employment Arrangements." Report 900, Bureau of Labor Statistics, August.

CHAPTER 9

Minimum Wage Policy and Research
What's a Person to Believe?

Stephen E. Baldwin
Robert S. Goldfarb

There has been a recent renewal of interest in minimum wage effects on the part of both policy makers and researchers. The former group includes President Clinton, who, in his January 1995 State of the Union address, called upon Congress to raise the federal minimum. Debate among researchers has been stimulated by several new studies with allegedly different findings about the impact of minimum wage changes from what the prior research literature displayed. Sar Levitan was not a believer in the earlier consensus on minimum wage effects and would have been pleased by the emergence of these new, conflicting results (Levitan and Belous 1979). Moreover, the political debate over raising the minimum that has been intensified by the new research would have appealed to his policy analyst instincts.

We view ourselves as economists interested in the research issues involved and as policy analysts concerned with the effect of additional evidence on the likelihood that the federal minimum wage will be raised any time soon. Each role presents challenges. As economists, the challenge is how to draw sensible inferences from the various contributions to this literature, especially with recent results seemingly contradicting long-held views. As policy analysts, the challenge is how to assess the advantages and disadvantages of increasing the minimum wage, since the new research emphasizes only one of several dimensions in which conflicts and trade-offs exist.

This paper is intended to extend a mostly congenial exchange of views between two economists with different orientations toward minimum wage issues, a discussion between us that has been going on for

over twenty years. Goldfarb has the typical neoclassical economics fel-
low- traveller's skeptical attitude about minimum wage legislation,
based on a healthy respect for the price system. Baldwin is much more
favorably inclined toward minimum wages, based on a healthy respect
for the institutional complexities of the labor market and the importance of forces typically excluded from the neoclassical framework.
Our aims are to discover if we can both agree on some inferences from
current and past research and policy debates, to try to identify where
and why we continue to disagree, and to specify what information
would help resolve these areas of continuing disagreement.

We believe that this topic is quite appropriate to a volume in honor
of Sar Levitan. Sar always viewed minimum wage effects and the possible policy efficacy of changing the minimum as important issues. He
was always ready to debate these issues with those less sympathetic
than he was to the use of minimum wages as a policy instrument. We
hope that this article will carry forward that on-going debate in which
Sar recurrently engaged. Paying careful attention to empirical evidence
is very much in the Levitan tradition, since concern for the integrity
and applicability of economic data was a major component of Sar's
career.

What the Recent Political Debate has been About

In the twenty-five years from 1960 to 1985, the real value of the federal minimum wage was never less than $4.50 in 1993 dollars. In the
last decade, it has remained below that level (Mishel and Bernstein
1995, table 8.42 and figure 30). The minimum was raised and/or coverage was extended in seventeen of the twenty years starting with 1961.[1]
There followed nine years during which the nominal value of the minimum was kept at $3.35 per hour, ending with the April 1990 increase
to $3.80 and the April 1991 increase to the current level of $4.25.

The Clinton administration has proposed raising the minimum to
$5.15 per hour as of July 3, 1996, which would restore much of the
purchasing power eroded since the last increase.[2] The President and
Labor Secretary Reich have both drawn attention to recent research,
especially that of David Card and Alan Krueger, which does not find

the negative relation between minimum wage increases and employ-ment losses that is a central feature of the prior research literature. Alan Krueger's recent service as Chief Economist in the Labor Department brought further attention to these results.

The Republican majorities in the House and Senate for the 1995-96 congressional term have constituted a roadblock to the administration's proposal. The only hearings in the current session were held before the Joint Economic Committee. Although Secretary Reich and Chief Economist Krueger appeared at the first hearing, most witnesses were critical of raising the minimum and of the research that purports to show there would be little cost to doing so.[3]

The Recent Research: Is There Less Here than Meets the Eye?

Minimum wage legislation can at least potentially affect workers and employers in a number of ways, including the number and quality of jobs, the extent of fringe benefits and on- the-job training, and the distribution of earnings and income. The largest body of economic research on minimum wages has had to do with employment effects. These studies typically use either time series or cross-section approaches. The former approach looks for alterations in level or trend of employment that follow on changes in minimum wages. The latter approach compares employment growth in two or more areas, states or regions that differ in terms of minimum wage regime at particular times. The employment impact of a minimum wage increase is expected to be greatest on the low-wage segment of the workforce, consisting largely of teenagers and young adults, so that both these approaches tend to concentrate on such subgroups.

Charles Brown (1988) summarized some two dozen time series studies of teenage employment. The consensus of this research is that a 10 percent increase in the minimum wage will reduce teenage employ-ment (net) by 1 to 3 percent. The employment reduction is split between increased unemployment and decreased participation in the labor force. As the increase in the real minimum is eroded over time by inflation, employment approaches its previous level. This modest net reduction conceals possibly larger changes for subgroups of the teen-age labor force and other workers.

Another issue is the extent to which minimum wage increases affect the incentives of teenagers to stay in school. Models allowing for skill differences among workers tend to find that already out-of-school youth may be displaced by enrolled teenagers who expand their labor supply in response to the higher wage (Neumark and Wascher 1995).

Another recent study, by William E. Spriggs and Bruce W. Klein, (1994) concurs in the finding of little aggregate employment effects, but makes a different distributional point. Spriggs and Klein focus on the role of the minimum wage in setting low-wage contours, especially affecting the earnings prospects of rural workers and workers with high school educations or less. They find that these workers are likely to be concentrated in jobs whose wages are linked to minimum wage adjust-ments more strongly than to movements in average wages.

The Consensus on Employment Effects is Challenged

The October 1992 *Industrial and Labor Relations Review* contained a symposium of papers on minimum wage research, edited by Ronald Ehrenberg.[4] The editor summarized one dimension of the findings by writing:

> *It is significant that none of the studies suggest that at current rel-ative values of the minimum wage, large disemployment effects would result from modest future increases in the minimum wage— increases up to, say, 10%* (p.5, italics in original).

The article by Katz and Krueger and the two articles by Card repre-sent three of the four empirical studies underlying Card and Krueger's 1995 book, *Myth and Measurement,* which has attracted unusually wide attention for anything written by economists.[5] In generating find-ings that call into question the conventional wisdom of a (small) nega-tive effect on employment from a minimum wage increase, Card and Krueger employ a method that differs from the standard time series and cross section approaches. The Card and Krueger approach uses data that are less aggregated and more focused on a particular minimum wage "episode." This strategy, which they refer to as embodying "natu-ral experiments," involves surveying employment in individual estab-lishments before and after a particular minimum wage event.[6] They argue that if the minimum wage increase is the only or the most important change that has taken place in the relevant labor market, a host of unobservable variables that didn't change can be netted out.

The most startling findings in *Myth and Measurement* have to do with Card and Krueger's contention that a minimum wage increase can be associated with an *increase* in employment. The studies reporting this finding have used surveys of fast-food establishments, a major source of low-wage jobs, especially for young workers. As the authors themselves put it:

> Our empirical findings can be summarized as follows. First, a study of employment in the fast food industry after the recent 1992 increase in the New Jersey minimum wage law shows that employment was *not* adversely affected by the law. Our results are derived from a specially designed survey of more than 400 restaurants throughout New Jersey and eastern Pennsylvania, conducted before and after the increase in the New Jersey minimum wage. Relative to restaurants in Pennsylvania, where the minimum wage remained unchanged, we find that employment in New Jersey actually *expanded* with the increase in the minimum wage. Furthermore, when we examine restaurants within New Jersey, we find that employment growth was *higher* at restaurants that were forced to increase their wages to comply with the law than at those stores that already were paying more than the new minimum. We find similar results in studies of fast-food restaurants in Texas after the 1991 increase in the federal minimum wage (Card and Krueger 1995, pp. 1-2).[7]

Card and Krueger also carry out a number of more aggregate level (time series and cross-state) analyses, which they interpret as showing much less evidence of any statistically significant disemployment effects than the previous literature displayed. It is fair to say, however, that the fast-food industry studies using new data they themselves collected have had by far the most impact.

In the July 1995 issue of the *Industrial and Labor Relations Review*, five eminent labor economists provide comments on Card and Krueger's work. In alphabetical and page order they are Charles Brown (Michigan), Richard Freeman (Harvard), Daniel Hamermesh (Texas-Austin), Paul Osterman (MIT), and Finis Welch (Texas A & M). Brown, Freeman, and Osterman can be classified as generally supportive of the Card and Krueger results and strategy. All three authors praise what Brown calls "the 'collage' strategy that the authors employ" (p. 829). This refers to Card and Krueger's attempt to bring to bear a variety of data, including newly collected survey data employing "natural experiments," that seem to shed light on the question at hand in a number of different ways and from different vantage points. This use of "many such experiments" to judge the employment effects of minimum wages provokes Freeman to the statement that "their analysis is a model of how to do empirical economics" (p. 831). In contrast, Hamermesh and Welch focus on the shortcomings of the Card and Krueger theoretical and empirical approach, with Hamermesh terming the evidence "fatally flawed" (p. 838), while Welch calls the study of New Jersey and Pennsylvania fast food stores "a monument to poor survey methodology" (p. 848).

Several specific points made by the five commentators are worth noting. First, both Brown and Freeman, while largely supportive of the Card and Krueger results and strategy, note that their estimates are of short-run employment effects; longer-run effects may well turn out to be both negative and larger. Second, Freeman makes a general point consistent with our (the Baldwin/Goldfarb) mindset: public discussion of the minimum wage issue needs to be reoriented away from focusing so narrowly and exclusively on employment effects. Freeman notes in passing that Card and Krueger themselves argue for a reorientation toward broader income-distributional issues. Freeman then goes on to cite "five issues in assessing the policy of using the minimum wage to help low-paid workers" (p. 833). These include, "Does the minimum wage redistribute income to low-wage workers? Does the minimum create outsiders who suffer long term joblessness because of it? Are low-wage workers low-income workers? How do minimum wage policies fit with other economic policies such as Earned Income Tax Credits? Third, Finis Welch carries out a detailed examination of the actual data that Card and Krueger collected in the New Jersey and Pennsylvania fast food establishment study, and on which some of their most striking results depend. He finds patterns in the data that are so anomalous as to call the reliability of the data into serious question.

The variation in the views of the five cited expert commentators, and the reasons their views vary, provide a striking testimonial to the difficulty the economist/policy analyst audience of this literature (and possibly, therefore, of other large empirical literatures in economics) has in drawing warranted inferences from it. One set of distinguished reviewers tells us the Card and Krueger work represents a "model of how to do empirical economics," while another equally distinguished set tells us their evidence is "fatally flawed," and the study is "a monument to poor survey methodology." Moreover, this last allegation about the research stems from Welch obtaining the raw data and independently evaluating them, something the other commentators (understandably) did not do. But most of us, when confronting a sizable empirical literature and trying to distill from it the weight of the evidence, are not in a position to recheck the original data and the results flowing from them. We are left with the worry that inferences from empirical literatures may in fact sometimes be built on sand.[8]

Where Does this Leave Us? What is Needed to Make More Informed Decisions about Minimum Wages?

The two of us are in agreement about the following fundamental conclusion: while employment effects are one element in a thorough evaluation of the costs and benefits of a minimum wage policy, there are other significant elements involved in such an evaluation, and these other elements may be more important than employment effects alone.

We are not alone in holding this view. It is quite consistent with Freeman's argument, cited above, that public discussion of the minimum wage issue needs to be reoriented away from focusing so narrowly and exclusively on employment effects. Much more surprising, given the almost exclusive focus in the public debate on the employment effect results in their book, is the fact that Card and Krueger hold a similar view! As they put it, even if one relies on the literature prior to their research, employment effects are small, so that "the minimum wage is mainly a distributional issue—at least in the range of the current U.S. minimum wage" (Card and Krueger 1995, p. 276).[9] Card and Krueger also cite other research by DiNardo, Fortin and Lemieux, "that the increase in the minimum wage from $3.35 to 4.25 per hour rolled back a significant fraction of the cumulative rise in wage dispersion from 1979 to 1989."[10]

Developing a Strategy for Further Research

Our agreement that more is involved than employment effects leads to differences between us concerning which additional considerations might be most crucial. This in turn leads to questions about the sorts of information that might help us to resolve these differences of opinion.

Which considerations do each of us expect to be crucial? It seems best at this point to speak individually.

Goldfarb: My long-held view, espoused since the early 1970s (see note 9) goes as follows. The most plausible case for a minimum wage (and for its periodic upward adjustment) involves the effect it is likely to have on the distribution of income. Disinterested supporters of minimum wages have over the decades tended to view it as an antipoverty device. Card and Krueger also say things consistent with the importance of the income distribution aspects of the minimum wage. Unfortunately, their research and other contributions over the past twenty years (Gramlich 1976; Kelly 1976; Horrigan and Mincy 1993) indicate that any effect of the minimum wage in the direction of reduced inequality and fighting poverty is likely to be minor. Some of the reasons for this are simple: many of those working at the minimum wage are not members of poor families, and many of those who are poor are not working.

One might argue as follows in the face of this very attenuated effect of the minimum wage on the income distribution. "Why not use the policy anyway? It will help some of the working poor, and its disemployment effects are relatively minor." In my view, one large disadvantage of this argument is that there are people in the policy arena who actually seem to believe that raising the minimum wage is a serious antipoverty device. Having succeeded in raising the minimum wage, the need to do other things to combat poverty may seem less pressing to these underinformed individuals. So, to someone like me who is sympathetic to public policies to combat poverty and aware of the possibility of placeboesque features of minimum wage increases, the cost of pressing for minimum wage increases is that it will dilute the possibility of getting much more effective antipoverty policies adopted. Those interested in really effective antipoverty policies should "keep their powder dry": that is, they should stop wasting their limited political resources on pressing for what is essentially a placebo antipoverty policy, increasing the minimum wage.

Baldwin: While the income distribution has become demonstrably less equal over the past twenty years, I would agree that minimum wage increases are not a very effective policy to reverse those trends. Rather, I base my support for periodic, moderate adjustment to the minimum wage on three other considerations. First, and most important, a statutory minimum is needed as a constraint on the behavior of employers, forming one dimension of the set of labor standards consistent with an advanced society. Sar Levitan, writing with Peter Carlson and Isaac Shapiro (1986), put this point as follows:

> The minimum wage law is a statement by society that certain work conditions are unacceptable. The (Fair Labor Standards) Act was necessary when sweatshops were commonplace and remains necessary today. Most Americans work in labor markets that offer protection against undesirable work conditions, but millions work in secondary labor markets characterized by unstable, low- wage employment. These workers need the protection of government to bring their work conditions up to socially acceptable minimal standards (p. 83).

That is, the main justification for labor standards legislation is the existence of a power imbalance at the lower end of the labor market. Persons vulnerable to exploitation tend to have certain characteristics. They are disproportionately female, poorly educated, members of minority groups, and recent immigrants—legal or illegal. Employers who take advantage of this vulnerability also share some characteristics. They are typically smaller firms, not unionized, in rural/southern locations, and in technologically lagging sectors of the economy such as apparel or food processing.

Other dimensions in which protection is needed are child labor laws, health and safety regulations, and prohibitions against employing illegal aliens. The crackdown on garment sweatshops in Los Angeles this summer is just the most recent reminder that some employers are willing to impose virtual peonage on workers whose bargaining power is nil.

Second, the level and distribution of earnings at the low end of the wage scale are affected by movements of the minimum (Spriggs and Klein 1994). It seems particularly relevant when welfare reform is being sold as a way to get more people into jobs that "making work pay" needs to be considered. A minimum wage is such a policy.

Third, wages have labor supply effects. If we as a society want to encourage low income individuals to work, wage floors may in fact encourage increased labor supply. Alterations in the income disregards and offsets of welfare payments for any earnings often impose effective marginal tax rates close to or exceeding 100 percent. A minimally skilled segment of the population that is required to offer its labor for whatever it might fetch has a depressing effect on a much wider band of the income distribution.

Goldfarb response to Baldwin's arguments: Baldwin's first argument concerns a general rationale for labor-protective legislation applied to the "bottom" of the labor market, and the additional consideration of how attractive a minimum wage is as a weapon in that labor protective legislation arsenal. I know of no serious and comprehensive discussion of the pros and cons of minimum wages as labor protective legislation in the minimum wage literature, nor am I aware of serious and continuing debate in the labor economics literature about desirability or lack thereof of labor protective legislation aimed at the "bottom" of the labor market (where "power imbalances" are presumably more likely to appear). While my neoclassical instincts make me skeptical about the general desirability of such legislation, and the minimum wage does not strike me as an obviously efficacious weapon in the labor protective legislation arsenal, Baldwin does raise a line of argument here about labor protective legislation aimed specifically at the "bottom of the market" that existing research does not seem to help us evaluate. Baldwin's second argument focuses on earnings levels (especially their variance at the low end) as having important labor market effects apart from their direct effects on income distribution. Such effects certainly deserve more attention than they appear to have gotten so far, but in my view we are currently very far from being able to confidently base a minimum wage policy on them.

Baldwin response to Goldfarb's arguments: Studies of the effect of minimum wages on the distribution of income have in recent years found little or no impact, while finding a minor positive effect on the distribution of earnings. The fact is that only about a third of minimum wage workers are in families where they are the primary breadwinner. However, the absolute well-being of low-income families is improved.

With the development of the Earned Income Tax Credit (EITC) it has become fashionable to disparage the usefulness of the minimum wage. However, the minimum helps unrelated individuals who are not targeted by the EITC but who are an important proportion of the working poor (Horrigan and Mincy 1993).

Horrigan and Mincy emphasize the interaction of differently targeted policies (minimum wage, EITC, welfare) on the behavior of the working poor. They conclude that there are insufficient data available to assess the relative effectiveness of policies aimed at reducing income inequality. However, minimum wage changes do fill in a gap left by the effects of other policies and have a potential to improve labor market equity.

Another student of low-wage labor markets, David Griffith, places even greater weight on the institutional factors. Griffith contends that the neoclassical approach is inadequate for understanding low-wage labor markets for three reasons: such workers are not atomistic free agents, but are constrained by various social relationships; their decisions and employers' actions are only partly driven by market forces; and, especially in rural areas, the extent of choice facing such workers with respect to jobs and mobility is much less than that assumed by the neoclassical model (1993, pp. 219-221).

Goldfarb's characterization of minimum wage changes as having a "placebo effect" has some merit, and I agree that excessive importance may have been assigned to minimum wages as an antipoverty tool. However, I don't agree that there is a zero-sum nature to social policy formation. The 1960s saw the greatest extent of increases in level and coverage of the minimum wage, along with the initiation of the War on Poverty. The 1990s seem to be seeing, unfortunately in my view, a rollback of antipoverty measures along with a diminution of the real value of the minimum. Political alignments have shifted and different agendas are being pursued across the whole spectrum of social policy.

What Evidence Would We Like to Have to Support/Refute These Two Views?

Given the noisiness of labor market data generally and the small magnitude of minimum wage effects in particular, it seems unlikely that any aggregate study would provide conclusive evidence on (dis)employment effects. Neither of us, for different reasons, is particularly bothered by this, since we agree that researchers and policy analysts need to shift to other, bigger questions. Neither of us would object, however, to seeing more before/after studies of establishment responses that met the criticisms of Hamermesh and Welch, i.e., that focused on hours worked rather than bodies, that identified the same persons to answer the same questions at the two (or more) points in time covered by the studies, and that looked at the establishment's overall wage structure. Such studies could provide estimates that might speak more eloquently to the disemployment question. It is possible, but not highly likely, that they would also cast light on the position in the income distribution of those affected by minimum wage changes. Continuing monitoring of the effects of minimum wage changes on earnings levels and income distributions is also highly desirable.

The discussion in the previous section also suggests the importance of addressing the dimensions of minimum wage policy that Baldwin stressed, i.e., the social constraints on what employers are able to do. A broader literature would have to be considered or, indeed, created— one that takes an institutional view of how jobs are altered by law and regulation and how firms and workers operate in such a constrained environment. Such an approach would, implicitly or explicitly, involve the value judgements of citizens, policy makers and analysts. Again, this is very much in the Levitan spirit. As Sar wrote two decades ago: "We should not kid ourselves into believing that policy choices and decisions to continue or terminate programs can be made on purely objective "scientific" grounds. In the final analysis, the policy maker will have to depend on value judgment" (1976, p. 10).

NOTES

1. Coverage has been increased over the years along with changes in the level. While about 85 percent of jobs are now covered by the Fair Labor Standards Act (FLSA), employers with annual

sales below a minimum cutoff level (currently $500,000) are exempted. The initial coverage in 1938 of the minimum wage provisions of the FLSA was restricted to employees engaged in or producing goods for interstate commerce.Subsequent amendments extended coverage: for example, the 1961 amendments took in workers in large retail and service enterprises, local transit, construction and gasoline service stations, while the 1966 amendments covered state and local government employees in hospitals, nursing homes and schools, and workers in laundries, dry cleaners, large hotels, motels, restaurants, and farms. Other government employees, some previously noncovered retail and service workers, and certain private household workers have been brought under FLSA coverage more recently (Employment Standards Administration, U.S. Department of Labor, undated Fact Sheet. History of Federal Minimum Wage Rates Under the Fair Labor Standards Act 1938-1991).

2. The administration proposal was introduced on February 14, 1995 by the Senate and House minority leaders, as S. 413 (Daschle) and H.R. 940 (Gephardt). For a summary of other congressional proposals and additional background on minimum wage issues, see Whitaker (1995).

3. Two of the economists who appeared in opposition, Daniel Hamermesh and Finis Welch, also contributed to the July 1995 symposium in the *Industrial and Labor Relations Review* on the Card/Krueger findings, discussed in the next section.

4. The authors and paper titles were: L. Katz and A. Krueger, "The Effect of the Minimum Wage on the Fast-Food Industry"; D. Card, "Using Regional Variation in Wages to Measure the Effects of the Federal Minimum Wage"; D. Card, "Do Minimum Wages Reduce Employment? A Case Study of California, 1987-1989"; D. Neumark and W. Wascher, "Employment Effects of Minimum and Subminimum Wages: Panel Data on State Minimum Wage Laws"; and R. Smith and B. Vavrichek, "The Wage Mobility of Minimum Wage workers."

5. The fourth study underlying this book is Card and Krueger (1994). An example of the unusual attention is a favorable review of *Myth and Measurement* in the Washington *Post* Book World section, Sunday, July 23, 1995.

6. In some of these "natural experiment" studies, a control group geographical area is also used. In this control group area, no increase in the minimum wage (or other minimum wage "event") has taken place.

7. Some indication of the size of the effects Card and Krueger find for the New Jersey-Pennsylvania comparisons may be useful. The federal minimum was raised to $4.25 per hour on April 1, 1991. New Jersey raised its state minimum to $5.05 per hour on April 1, 1992. If one compares full-time equivalent (FTE) employment before April 1, 1992 with FTE employment after the increase, New Jersey restaurants increased their FTE employment relative to Pennsylvania restaurants by 2.76 employees, or about 13 percent, a statistically significant difference. Adding control variables reduces the size of this effect, but it remains significant in some specifications (Card and Krueger 1995, pp. 33-40).

8. One might react that many studies are based on widely used sample surveys such as the Current Population Survey, whose properties are widely studied and well known. Even when studies use the same data set, however, it is often virtually impossible to replicate published results. For a well-known demonstration of severe replication difficulties using a different empirical literature, see De Wald, Thursby, and Anderson (1986).

9. While we share these views with Freeman and Card and Krueger, we came to them decades ago. See, for example, Goldfarb (1974). A major theme of this discussion was the central importance for policy choice of assessing the income distribution effects of minimum wage policies.

10. Card and Krueger 1995, p. 279. The paper they cite by DiNardo, Fortin, and Lemieux is "Labor Market Institutions and the Distribution of Wages, 1973-92: A Semi-Parametric Approach," unpublished paper, University of Montreal Department of Economics.

References

Brown, Charles. 1988. "Minimum Wage Laws: Are They Overrated?" *Journal of Economic Perspectives* (Summer): 133-146.

Card, David, and Alan B. Krueger: 1994. "Minimum Wages and Employment: A Case Study of the Fast Food Industry in New Jersey and Pennsylvania," *American Economic Review* (September): 772-793.

_____. 1995. *Myth and Measurement: The New Economics of the Minimum Wage.* Princeton NJ: Princeton University Press.

De Wald, William, Jerry Thursby, and Richard Anderson. 1986. "Replication in Empirical Economics: The Journal of Money, Credit and Banking Project," *American Economic Review* (September): 587–603.

Goldfarb, Robert. 1974. "The Policy Content of Quantitative Minimum Wage Research," *Industrial Relations Research Association Proceedings*, December.

Gramlich, Edward. 1976. "The Impact of Minimum Wages on Other Wages, Employment and Family Income," *Brookings papers on Economic Activity* 2: 430–451.

Griffith, David. 1993. *Jones's Minimal: Low-Wage Labor in the United States.* Albany NY: State University of New York Press.

Horrigan, Michael W., and Ronald B. Mincy. 1993. "The Minimum Wage and Earnings and Income Inequality." In *Uneven Tides: Rising Inequality in America*, Sheldon Danziger and Peter Gottschalk, eds. New York: Russell Sage Foundation.

Kelly, Terence. 1976. "Two Policy Questions Regarding the Minimum Wage." Working paper, Urban Institute, February.

Levitan, Sar A. 1976. "Can You Trust an Evaluator?" Unpublished manuscript.

Levitan, Sar A., and Richard Belous. 1979. *More than Subsistence: Minimum Wages for the Working Poor.* Baltimore, MD: Johns Hopkins University Press.

Levitan, Sar A., Peter Carlson, and Isaac Shapiro. 1986. *Protecting American Workers.* Washington DC: Bureau of National Affairs.

Mishel, Lawrence, and Jared Bernstein. 1995. *The State of Working America: 1994-55.* Economic Policy Institute.

Neumark, David, and William Wascher. 1995. "The Effects of Minimum Wages on Teenage Employment and Enrollment: Evidence from Matched CPS Surveys." Working Paper 5092, National Bureau of Economic Research.

Spriggs, William E., and Bruce W. Klein. 1994. *Raising the Floor: The Effects of the Minimum Wage on Low-Wage Workers*. Washington, DC: Economic Policy Institute.

Whitaker, William G. 1995. "The Minimum Wage: An Overview of Issues before the 104th Congress." Issue brief IB95091, Congressional Research Service, August 29.

CHAPTER 10

Public Sector Job Creation

A Review of Past Experience
and Its Relevance to the Future

William Grinker

The notion of using the public sector for job creation is, to put it mildly, not a popular idea these days. When President Clinton introduced his economic stimulus and deficit reduction package in early 1993, the modest public sector job creation effort called for in the public works portion of the package was unceremoniously shot down as a needless government pork barrel. The potential for major welfare reform under the Clinton plan of "two years and out" was thwarted by the specter of a large-scale government public job creation effort to get people off welfare. More recent plans for restricting welfare under the Republicans' "Contract With America" have avoided the jobs problems entirely by simply dictating that the states will be free to take care of the problem within a five-year time limitation. While both friends and foes of the North American Free Trade Agreement and other free trade initiatives recognized the serious potential for worker displacement, very few took seriously the idea of government-created jobs as part of an alternative, concentrating instead on support for retraining and relocation schemes.

There are exceptions, of course, such as Senator Paul Simon of Illinois who advocated a large-scale public jobs creation program to deal with both structural and cyclical employment issues as part of his abortive presidential bid in 1988. (See, *Let's Put America Back to Work*, Paul Simon, 1988; see also Remarks of Senator David Boren, *Congressional Record*, January 27, 1993.) But to this point, their views have not entered the mainstream of public debate about the future of the American workforce.

In part, this lack of serious consideration for public sector job creation either as a tool for redressing long-term structural unemployment or as a shorter-term response to cyclical economic problems, no doubt reflects a general distrust of government's ability to solve problems. And the fact that, unlike many other employment and training or social interventions, very little analytic attention has been paid to public sector job creation, leaves the public and policy makers alike prey to the perception—often encouraged by political leadership—that government work is essentially nonproductive. Finally, compounding this distrust and lack of information is the strong residue of the concerted effort by neo-conservatives in the 1970s to paint public sector job creation specifically as a gigantic boondoggle. Thus, by the election of Ronald Reagan in 1980, to paraphrase an oft-repeated *Fortune Magazine* article of the late 1970s, Public Service Job Creation (sic CETA) had become a "dirty word." The perception of incompetence and ineffectiveness, despite strong evidence to the contrary, enabled the Reagan administration quickly to dismantle the existing public sector employment program. And the idea of resurrecting it in some form to deal with today's exacerbated worker displacement and increasingly difficult structural employment issues, where the prospects of going down below a 5.5 percent unemployment rate creates great trepidation in the financial markets, is not seriously considered.

The purpose of this paper is to reexamine the primary experiences that have led to this state of affairs, and to ascertain whether there are lessons that can be applied to the future. The two most prominent government initiatives aimed at curbing unemployment through federally subsidized job creation programs were the Works Progress Administration (WPA) introduced during the Great Depression and the Public Service Employment program (PSE), the major job creation program inaugurated under the Comprehensive Employment and Training Act (CETA) in the 1970s.

The WPA

The WPA was the biggest and best known of Franklin Roosevelt's New Deal programs. Begun with funds appropriated under the Emergency Relief Appropriation Act of 1935, the WPA went on to employ over eight million people in its six-year history. The WPA, however, was not the first job creation project launched under the New Deal. It grew primarily out of two previous job creation efforts, the Federal Emergency Relief Act (FERA) and the Civil Works Administration (CWA). An examination of how FERA and CWA merged to form the WPA provides some interesting insights into many of the problems and policy issues facing any federally subsidized employment program.

Chronicled in Irving Bernstein's 1985 book, *A Caring Society: The New Deal, the Worker, and the Great Depression*, the forging of the WPA was a political battle in which powerful opposing ideologies were pitted against one another. On the one hand, Harold Ickes, head of the CWA, focused on improving the nation's infrastructure through physical projects that could be constructed through federally subsidized employment. Ickes believed that bridges, roads, dams, and other projects should be the backbone of any federally designed public employment policy. This approach stressed the need for a long-term federally subsidized effort that would stimulate the economy by increasing government spending on goods and materials needed for large-scale infrastructure building projects. On the opposing side, Harry Hopkins, at the time the head of FERA, was concerned primarily with creating jobs quickly. He considered large-scale public works projects as unnecessarily costly and not well suited to a comprehensive employment mobilization effort. He stressed stimulating the economy by boosting consumer purchasing power and an overall strengthening of the demand side of the economy. Hopkins prevailed, and went on to run the WPA. Of the $61 per worker the WPA spent each month, 76 percent went to wages, while only about 18 percent went to materials. Furthermore, of that $61, only $2 (or about 3 percent) went to a relatively small administrative staff of 30,000. (See Briscoe 1972).

At its zenith, the WPA employed 31 percent of the unemployed, a figure unprecedented to date. Approximately two million families were provided with $1.4 billion per year for six years, or approximately $10 billion per year in today's dollars. And while it was obviously of psychological benefit to a country reeling under the weight of massive unemployment, the longer-term impact of the WPA as an economic stimulus is harder to discern. For, of course, it was *not* the WPA, or any other New Deal social program, that brought the country out of recession; it was a war economy that finally spurred production and brought the nation back to full employment. Therefore, while the WPA undeniably provided temporary relief for many, its longer-term impacts are difficult to assess.

One way to measure its impact is to return to the Hopkins-Ickes debate. Ironically, what the WPA is most recognized for today is the lasting contribution made through WPA-sponsored projects: 651,000 miles of roads, 24,000 bridges and viaducts, 120,000 buildings, and countless aesthetic and artistic projects. Some would argue, therefore that it was precisely the WPA's contribution to the nation's infrastructure that laid the groundwork for the postwar economic boom. (See Noah 1982; Simon 1988). Bringing back WPA-type projects, they suggest, would not only put significant numbers back to work, but would also put the economy in a position to keep workers employed in the future. A highway built today, for example, has a multiplying job creation effect in the future, not only employing maintenance crews and toll operators, but also attracting various service industries such as gas stations and fast food restaurants.

Several factors, however, make the WPA experience less than apposite for today's economy. Obviously, the Great Depression was a unique time, with unemployment rates reaching 25 percent. The bulk of the WPA workforce were white male family heads who had worked before and came to their jobs with basic skills. Labor unions were only just achieving respectability under the protection of the Wagner Act, and the idea of large numbers of government workers being organized in public employee unions was not even on the horizon. So concerns about public worker displacement were muted. Finally, since the WPA was aimed at putting large numbers back to work fast, the majority of projects were low-skill construction projects with minimal training value or skills requirements.

In sum, the WPA experience surely belies the conventional wisdom that government, and especially the federal government, is unable to undertake large programs quickly and efficiently (but then again so does the Gulf War). While its short-term effects are difficult to measure, its long-term value for improving the nation's infrastructure cannot be gainsaid. Yet, so much has changed in the economy and the nature of the workforce in the last three score years that, attempting to recreate a federally run WPA type of undertaking seems a far fetched dream, or nightmare, depending on one's political perspective. Much closer to home is the post-World War II experience with public sector job creation, PSE under CETA, the largest back-to-work strategy since the WPA.

Public Service Employment and CETA

An extension of President Nixon's experimental Public Employment Program (PEP) of the early 1970s, PSE grew from a modest program within CETA with $370 million in 1973, to CETA's main component designed to combat both structural and cyclical unemployment with an annual budget of $4.1 billion in fiscal year 1979, again about $10 billion in today's dollars. Only two years later, in 1981, CETA was gutted by the Reagan administration, with little opposition. (See Cook, Adams, and Rawlins 1985)

PEP, inaugurated under the Emergency Employment Act of 1971, after initial rejection, was endorsed by Nixon as an answer to recession and a growing unemployment rate of 6 percent. CETA, on the other hand, enacted once recession had ebbed, was originally concerned with structural unemployment. It was created amid fears of workers being displaced by automation and technology, a fear that had proved unfounded in the 1960s and would be again in the 1970s, but which appeared again threatening in the early 1990s. Almost immediately, however, an economic downturn and a steadily ascending unemployment rate changed the original plans, and another federal emergency was declared. This time, the Emergency Jobs and Unemployment Assistance Act of 1974 (EJUAA) established Title VI under CETA, which was explicitly countercyclical. Whereas eligibility under the original jobs program (Title II) was restricted to those underemployed or unemployed for at least 30 days, Title VI loosened eligibility to fifteen days in areas of high unemployment—then characterized as being 7 percent or more.

In 1976, as the economy began to recover, and reacting to criticism that PSE was not counterstructural enough—those being helped were those least in need of help, and the jobs being appropriated were merely displacing regular government jobs—Congress passed the Emergency Jobs Program Extension Act. Under this legislation, funding for PSE was increased, but the program reverted back to a counterstructural focus by increasing eligibility standards to target the long-term unemployed. This time the structural issue was less about job loss due to automation and more directed toward those segments of the labor force without any skills and with limited work histories. This was a much more disadvantaged population and had a much larger minority cast, as large numbers of unskilled blacks, forced off the land by the civil rights struggle and the agricultural revolution, were again migrating from the rural South in search of economic security in the nation's urban centers.

To discourage displacement, these new workers were to participate in new projects set up by administrators outside of regular government. President Carter's first years revealed a heightened financial commitment to PSE, and by 1977, enrollment reached a peak of 750,000. But this flood of money had negative repercussions for CETA's image, which was irreparably tarnished by accusations in the popular press and media of widespread abuse and fraud. These accusations, coupled with the fear of many economists and labor union leaders, that CETA was still displacing workers and was little more than an inefficient revenue-sharing program, prompted the federal government to act once again. In 1978, Congress beefed up restrictions for the last time, severely tightening eligibility criteria, placing limits on how long PSE workers could remain on the payroll, and placing ceilings on how much workers could earn. But from a public and political perspective, these changes were too little too late. Ronald Reagan campaigned mightily against this great "boondoggle," and by 1981, PSE and CETA were totally dismantled.

Lessons from Public Service Job Creation Under CETA

The thumbnail history of public sector job creation set forth above contains several closely related questions that are at the heart of any analysis of public sector job creation: Should a program help the structurally unemployed or those who are more "employable" but experiencing hard times? If the focus of such a program is designed to alleviate the burdens of recession, and is therefore a countercyclical program, can the displacement of local government workers be avoided? Should displacement be avoided, or because of its revenue-sharing effects, should it somehow be factored in as an economic benefit for locally strapped governments facing their own budget crises? Similarly, if the focus of public sector job creation should be on combating structural unemployment, can the low-wage, low-skill jobs that are inevitably provided to the structurally unemployed prove viable training grounds for workers hoping to someday make the transition to unsubsidized employment? The debate as to whether PSE was to be a countercyclical or counterstructural program is seen by many to be at the crux of any discussion of the viability of public jobs programs. For it is precisely the lack of a focused vision on this issue that eventually made PSE under CETA a political impossibility. (See Nathan, Cook, and Rawlins 1981; Baumer and Van Horn 1985.)

There were three distinct periods in the life of PSE under CETA that provide a framework to view its success and failure. (Cook, Adams, and Rawlins 1985, pp 46-49). The first, beginning with PEP and extending through the first three years of CETA, is defined by lax eligibility requirements, decentralized state and local administrations, and service-oriented employment programs.

The second period, from 1976 to 1978, was characterized by increasing demands from the federal government that PSE participants be disadvantaged, and that more emphasis be placed on training. Most commentators agree that during this period, enough of a balance was created between the service objectives of local governments and the federal emphasis on combating structural unemployment, that this was a relatively successful period for PSE. While the federal government was intent on targeting the most severely disadvantaged populations in order to combat structural unemployment, local administrators were primarily interested in implementing PSE programs in ways that were beneficial to their communities, in terms of relieving fiscal pressures, creating needed community service jobs, and relieving the social ills associated with unemployment. State and local officials implementing PSE programs, guided both by federal guidelines and their own interests, hired workers who had enough skill to be placed in community service jobs with minimal training, and at the same time avoided hiring higher-skilled and educated workers in an effort to remain faithful to federal objectives of employing the disadvantaged.

The third period, characterized by heightened federal restrictions on eligibility, upset this precarious policy balance. State and local governments were unable and unwilling to employ the uneducated and unskilled in service jobs, and large numbers of workers were either passed on to nonprofit agencies or given token jobs of little service to the community.

The work of Nathan, Cook, and Rawlins makes a convincing argument that, as a countercyclical program, PSE was relatively effective, but as a structural program, it was doomed to failure. As Nathan said in a subsequent *New York Times* article,

> The program was set up to be counter-cyclical...[but] when the 1976-77 recession ended, supporters of the program....hit on helping the disadvantaged....But state and local governments resisted the new requirements for selection and training. Because the CETA workers were hard to place and supervise and often lacked job experience, most were farmed out to nonprofit organizations that provided social and community services. Some organizations did work of marginal value. Such jobs—for sex therapy clinics, experimental art and drama groups, yoga centers—fed the critics. The result: the CETA program bit the dust. (Op. Ed. in *New York Times,* January 31, 1994)

Most others who have reviewed the PSE experience under CETA agree. Baumer and Van Horn (1985) point out that efforts to target the structurally unemployed through criteria such as lower wages and tougher eligibility requirements *did* change the composition of the PSE workforce, but program administrators lost sight of the programs themselves. "While everyone made sure that the right people were enrolled in programs, that no one was paid too much for a public service job, and that proper forms were completed...local program design and performance goals were often swept aside, and local political support for employment and training initiatives eroded" (p.12).

Thus, the crucial component of PSE was the value of community service that employees were able to provide. As long as state and local administrators could focus on employing the cyclically unemployed, or those with some work experience, they were able and willing to put employees to good use. Why then, if PSE seemed to be an effective way to ease the burdens of recessionary unemployment, did the federal government revamp it to target the structurally unemployed? One answer lies in understanding some of the inherent organizational difficulties in designing and implementing a countercyclical program.

In designing a countercyclical approach to jobs programs, one must take into account the time lag between actual program implementation and stimulation to the economy. Because employment trends generally trail behind other economic indicators in a recessionary economy, by the time the government and Congress are sparked into action by high unemployment levels, the economy may actually be on the rebound. Further delays inevitably result from political debate, authorization, and implementation. Under these circumstances, the countercyclical objective of targeting and hiring those temporarily out of work until the economy can support them is undermined. As Clifford Johnson has pointed out, this is precisely what happened under CETA as the federal government responded to the 1974-76 recession.

> Although the national unemployment rate remained high in 1976 and 1977, federal outlays for local public works projects and expanded public service employment did not add significant stimulus to the national economy until more than 2.5 years after the trough of the business cycle. (Johnson 1985)

The obvious political repercussions resulted in heightened public pressure to restrict targeting to more disadvantaged segments of the population.

Another issue deserving of more attention than it has received is the issue of scale. PSE's problems under CETA did not become really apparent until its volume expanded suddenly during the Carter administration and the Labor Department began to put local governments under pressure to fill the emerging slots. When many recipients turned out to be of doubtful eligibility, the program's enemies had a field day.

Would lessened ambition or slower expansion have achieved more acceptable results?

The other key problem associated with implementing a successful countercyclical employment program is the substitution of federal funds for state and local funds. Substitution can take place in a myriad of ways, but the most common and most obvious is the displacement of regular government workers, normally paid by state and local taxes, with federally funded public service employees. State and local governments, many argue, are especially vulnerable to substitution in a recession as budgets become increasingly difficult to balance. A study conducted by William Mirengoff and Lester Rindler found that net job creation under CETA had a direct relationship to fiscal pressures faced by state and local governments. The governments facing the severest fiscal pressures were the least likely to see employment increases through PSE, while governments with few fiscal concerns had the highest rates of net job creation. These findings would seem to support critics of public sector job creation who claim that because of displacement, such programs are little more than an inefficient kind of revenue-sharing. (See Mirengoff and Rindler 1978; see also, for example, "Why CETA is in Trouble" 1978; "How CETA Came to be a Four Letter Word" 1978; and "Lotsa Buck, Little Bang" 1977).

But the displacement issue, which caused CETA much political grief among program opponents, is extremely difficult to analyze, and some who have examined it closely, such as Nathan, Cook, and Rawlins, believe that it is, upon close scrutiny, "relatively insignificant." They found, for example that, "roughly one PSE worker in five was doing a job that would have been filled even if the local government had not received PSE money." Rather than displace local jobs with CETA workers, they found state and local governments either creating new projects or subcontracting jobs to outside agencies. Furthermore, it is important in assessing substitution not to confuse displacement with "program maintenance"—the attempt by fiscally strapped state and local governments to save government services that without CETA funds would necessarily be eliminated.

Perhaps the most serious issue relating to countercyclical public service employment programs is how much net job creation is possible over the long run through the use of short- term public job creation programs set up during a contracting economy. For even if new jobs are being created temporarily, are these jobs merely training workers for jobs that in the best-case scenario are already filled and, in the worst-case scenario, will not otherwise exist? Optimistic studies found up to 94 percent of PSE dollars had a stimulating effect on the economy, through the paying of salaries and the stabilizing of taxes. However, neither the CETA nor the WPA experience cast much light on the real economic stimulus effect of such efforts (Johnson 1985, p. 32)

These issues, especially displacement, discussed above in the context of countercyclical programs, also have implications for counterstructural job creation efforts. And CETA contains other lessons about public sector counterstructural job creation programs as well. These are especially important in light of the only serious discussion about public sector job creation currently extant—that related to employing large numbers of welfare recipients in public sector jobs after two years on the welfare roles.

Perhaps the most obvious lesson to be learned from CETA is that local government can target the severely disadvantaged without great difficulty and create work for them. By 1980, as a result of tightened eligibility requirements for PSE participants (such as raising the required length of unemployment from ten days to fifteen weeks), increased restrictions on the length of time PSE participants could stay on the job, and lower ceilings on the amount of money workers could earn, 92 percent of PSE enrollees were found to be from low-income households with very limited work histories.

What is more problematic, however, is how well PSE was able to help the structurally unemployed beyond providing a small, temporary paycheck. While it can validly be argued that *any* job, regardless of its skill level, is valuable training for someone who has never held a job, research on the impact of CETA jobs programs on wage earning power finds no appreciable gains being made as a result of PSE participation. As Clifford Johnson (1985) concluded,

> earnings data [regarding CETA] indicate that work experience alone is perceived by future employers as being of relatively little value and that marked improvements in the future employability of disadvantaged adults can be achieved only when work opportunities are combined with meaningful education and training initiatives.

Furthermore, the more eligibility criteria were tightened to reach the more disadvantaged, the more program managers perceived the workers they were getting as being of extremely low productivity, and the more they tended to create jobs that had little substantive content, and to provide little supervision for its performance. For the participants, this tended to undercut the inherent value of the work experience itself. It also, of course, fed the public criticisms of make-work jobs and shiftless workers which eventually doomed PSE. Thus, while only giving large numbers of the structurally unemployed with little work history or skills a job might hold a whole host of societal benefits; in terms of getting people permanently off welfare and back into the employment sector, it was clearly not the answer.

The Western European Experience

Since World War II, Western Europe has not ventured into a massive public sector job creation effort like PSE. Of course, until the most recent recession, the growing economies of most of these countries were characterized by labor shortages and the importation of "guest workers" to meet labor demands. Many of these countries, such as Denmark, the Netherlands, and the United Kingdom, have set up some relatively modest efforts directed at a specific subset of the population, such as youth, the disabled, or the aged. These programs usually incorporate a significant training element designed to upgrade worker skills. (See Balkenbol 1981; Karsten 1981). Others, such as Belgium and West Germany, have more broad-based job creation programs as an integral part of government fiscal policy, with triggers built into legislation to spur increased public sector hiring when downturns in the economy raise unemployment rates. Programs in European countries also differ significantly from one country to another on issues such as private sector involvement, requirements for community benefits, and the duration of participation.

The Netherlands represents a fairly typical example of the variety of public sector job creation activities in a Western European country. Since 1977, the government has sponsored a temporary public sector jobs program for difficult-to-place unemployed. Temporary employment for those unemployed for at least six months is provided for up to six months for those under age 45, and for up to a year for those over age 45. In 1979, the program was expanded to include nonprofit organizations as sponsors of worksites. In 1980, the government created a special temporary work agency to provide jobs for certain workers, primarily youth, classified as having poor employment prospects. The government also has set up a Corporation for Industrial Projects to promote employment through the creation of industrial enterprises subsidized by the government. Other countries, such as the United Kingdom, Italy, and France have also focused their job creation efforts on economic development and community enterprise in order to create and subsidize businesses that will employ the unemployed.

In the 1980s, as recession created seriously higher unemployment rates in Western Europe for the first time in decades, some of the countries with targeted public sector employment programs began to expand their efforts. These expansions also were highly targeted towards specific structural employment problems. Thus Denmark, for example, began a public job creation program for handicapped workers. By 1982, this effort had been considerably broadened with a special emphasis on youth employment. Ireland, Greece, and the United Kingdom, are other countries that created public sector jobs programs primarily for unemployed young workers in the early 1980s. Other countries expanded existing programs targeted to youth. These programs generally were characterized as being relatively short-term—up to six months on the job allowed—with wages fixed at a fairly low rate to encourage transition. Often these programs try to link the job to economic development, entrepreneurial, or other more permanent job creation activities. This is done, either directly through the program itself or indirectly through mandating linkages to other economic development/job creation initiatives.

Generally, discussions in Western Europe about strategies for dealing with structural and countercyclical employment problems mirror those in the United States. Issues about targeting, appropriate wage levels, program duration, and competition with the private sector appear to be the focus of most debates on public sector job creation. (See Bekemans 1983; Faulkner 1977). And in fact, most of these countries cite the United States experience with CETA's PSE program when denigrating the notion that public sector job creation can be a major part of a strategy to increase employment and retrain the workforce. (See Beharrell 1992).

Typically, Sweden appears to have the most comprehensive and successful full-employment policy. Swedish labor exchanges, set up by the government to fill job vacancies, tightly regulate private industry by requiring all firms to notify them of job openings that are filled with apparent efficiency. Workers whose lack of skills prevent them from getting jobs through the labor exchanges are provided with intensive government-managed training or retraining, and 70 percent find jobs within six months of completion. For those who do not immediately find jobs through the training system or who may not qualify for such training, the government provides short-term work in "socially useful" types of jobs. These jobs pay prevailing wage, but are strictly time-limited, usually to ten months, and workers are encouraged to find private employment during this period. If a worker has not found an employment alternative by the conclusion of the time limit, support ceases.

These labor market policies are combined with other macroeconomic strategies designed to increase productivity, protect Swedish goods, and steady currency values. Critics claim that Sweden has traded off its policy to require a tight labor market with an unnecessarily high inflation rate. But the country has been willing to make this trade-off to protect full employment, and preserve wage levels.

It is clear that the highly integrated and occasionally draconian measures Sweden has adopted would not be practical either politically or economically in a larger and more diverse economy such as the United States. And that nation's current economic and political problems reduce its motivational value. Nevertheless, the Swedish example does support those who would argue that governments can encourage fuller and more productive employment, and that public sector job creation has a legitimate role in this process.

Current Activities and Future Prospects

There is no likelihood of an effort to reintroduce public service job creation as a major instrument of public policy on the horizon, with one significant exception. That exception is for welfare recipients who, under various proposals for reform, will be subject to stringent time limitations for staying on welfare. For example, President Clinton's original two-year limitation with a job guarantee at the end is being tested on a demonstration basis in a number of states. Other states are struggling with various strategies to limit welfare and encourage or require some kind of job creation strategy to employ welfare recipients who are unable to find jobs on their own. And the federal intent is apparently to make welfare reform a state responsibility, with lessened federal dollars but without total hands off from federal restrictions.

Most commentators would agree that the reasons for a basic lack of policy interest are more political than substantive. The perception that this policy strategy was ineffective under CETA is firmly embedded in the public mind, regardless of the reality of what actually happened and why.

Liberal supporters of public job creation, such as the late Sar Levitan, are a voice in the wilderness when they argue that,

> Jobs programs have made and can make a tangible difference in alleviating hardship, supplying valued services (including labor intensive public works), and promoting the work ethic. Past mistakes justify improving—not abjuring—future efforts. (Levitan and Gallo 1991)

As the above quotation indicates, even most supporters recognize that there are legitimate concerns with how public service employment has operated in the past. Their argument is that these problems can be corrected to make such a program more efficacious, and that the nation's most massive effort, WPA, was, in fact, highly efficient and effective.

Theoretically, there could be an opportunity to resurrect the good name of public job creation in current welfare reform efforts. Unfortunately, the essentially punitive rationale imbedded in the various initiatives to restructure welfare almost certainly doom them to failure as a public service employment strategy. Even at its most stringent, PSE and more targeted European initiatives make six months the minimum that a person must be out of work before qualifying. Yet, most proposed welfare reform strategies make such jobs available only to those who are unable or unwilling to find regular employment within a minimum two-year or five-year period while they are on welfare. This makes it likely that the population that will eventually come to public service jobs will be the least prepared to function effectively in the labor market. As the CETA experience illustrates, public sector job creation began to fall apart when it became a structural strategy designed to target the most difficult to employ. This made the creation of legitimate jobs most difficult and led program managers to search for ways to put people in jobs with little supervision and little substantive content so as not to detract from the primary missions.

The lessons from WPA and CETA should show that unemployment is not a single problem with a single solution. Individual strategies targeting specific populations have succeeded over the years, and in fact, a substantive body of knowledge exists that can provide guidance to policy makers on how to design an effective program. Cyclical unemployment can be responsive to publicly created jobs that either fill a service void that can be tailored to meet local needs or can be targeted to large- scale public works projects such as those most remembered from the WPA. These jobs can work because the population targeted for this type of program have a demonstrated work history and they understand the rigors of the working routine. They may need some retraining or orientation to a new job, but they are accustomed to work. However, these are not the people for whom jobs would be created under current proposals.

Lessons have also taught that the hardest nut to crack, the long-term welfare recipient, the most unemployable segment of society—including those who lack work experience, education, or work skills—cannot be helped by just providing a job. Many can, however, be helped by training, remedial education, or a job that has been restructured to manageable size, in which essential close supervision is provided. Unfortunately, therefore, the very populations that are likely to be targeted for public service employment under current welfare reform initiatives are those who will continue to give public service job creation a bad name because of the lack of thought being given to overcoming their job disabilities in conjunction with the job creation effort.

Exacerbating this problem are provisions in some proposals for welfare reform that require prevailing wages to be paid when jobs are created that parallel the job content of existing positions. This requirement, made in response to labor union pressures and concerns about possible displacement effects, will further likely reduce job content and supervision for most of those who would be required to participate.

Finally, because the population will be almost entirely female, the types of jobs will be limited. Efforts to create opportunities for women in nontraditional employment such as construction have been mostly unsuccessful, in large part because most women are not interested in performing such work. Thus low-skill, labor-intensive infrastructure building projects, which characterized WPA at its best, would not be a significant part of such public sector job creation efforts. To add content to welfare reform plans would require significant expenditures in areas of training, supervision, and management—expenditures that are highly unlikely, given current budget stringencies.

In sum, unless significant changes are made in current proposals under the welfare reform rubric, public sector job creation, in and of itself, is unlikely to be a successful strategy to secure longer-term, non-subsidized employment for those who are forced to participate. And, to the extent it is used as a strategy, it is likely to be viewed by the public primarily as a make-work effort designed as a less obnoxious, more equitable alternative to long-term welfare dependency.

In addition to welfare reform, there are a few relatively modest demonstration projects recently launched by the federal government that encompass principles of public sector job creation, although not advertised as such. These projects are directed at youth, with the most notable being YouthBuild, sponsored by the U. S. Department of Housing and Urban Development, and Youth Fair Chance, sponsored by the U. S. Department of Labor. Each is being operated in twenty to thirty competitively selected communities across the country. As of the fall of 1995, YouthBuild has survived federal budget cutting, but Youth Fair Chance has been zeroed out in FY 1996.

YouthBuild is designed to give poor youth training and work experience in the construction trades, primarily through the rehabilitation of housing stock in poor neighborhoods (where there is little labor union interest). The program is carried out by nonprofit sponsors who are allowed to pay the youths at the minimum wage as part of the work experience phase of the demonstration. It appears similar in many respects to a number of programs of community rebuilding and short-term job creation that are being carried out in Western European countries. Youth Fair Chance, a more comprehensive youth training and

employment demonstration, also includes a work experience component where youth are allowed to receive a weekly "stipend" of up to
$100 while carrying out any of a variety of locally selected work activ-
ities (the normal allowable Labor Department training stipend is $30).
These examples indicate that the concept of public sector employment,
when dealing with structural employment problems, if packaged and
marketed creatively, can still garner support, although certainly not, at
present, on a large scale.

Thus, building up experience with effective employment strategies
that focus on both structural and countercyclical problems and include
a public sector job creation component would certainly seem feasible
and useful as long as the public sector component is targeted at the
population that can benefit from it and structured in a way to be useful
to the community at large. The components of such a strategy should
focus on building understanding and effectiveness around a number of
issues that would need to be resolved, if such programs are to regain
the confidence of the public. In his work on public sector job creation,
Sar Levitan pointed out many of the areas that would be critical to success. Included are:

1. Defining each segment of the population to be targeted and developing an appropriate strategy for each, including eligibility standards and wage levels

2. Structuring the jobs that are created to maximize content and
   minimize the likelihood of substitution

3. Adjusting the level of supervision and other support services
   required to maximize the value of the job for participants and
   sponsoring agencies

4. Establishing the right sequence and mix of work experience and
   training or re- training and the duration of program participation
   necessary to provide real long-term opportunities for participants

Without attempting to be definitive, as examples of how the above
requirements could be implemented, a two-tier system might be created. For persons with little or no work history, emphasis would be
placed on learning how to function in the workplace. Duration would
be limited to one year. Jobs would be low-skill and entry-level, with

close supervision. Wages would be at or near the minimum wage. Opportunities for remedial education and skills training through class-room instruction would be included for the first six months, so that actual time on the job might be limited to twenty hours per week. Opportunities for advancement to higher skill levels and higher wages would be afforded after six months of successful participation.

For persons with significant prior work experience and/or higher education levels who had been out of work for at least six months, the emphasis would be on training or retraining through on- the-job work experience. Jobs would be of a higher skill content, wages would be set at 80 percent of the prevailing wage for similar occupational categories up to $10 per hour, and duration would be limited to six months. Job creation would focus on occupations where there were significant opportunities for achieving permanent placement in either the private or public sector.

Experiments in public sector job creation to refine program tech-niques and develop a stronger knowledge base need not be large-scale efforts. Given the current willingness of numerous state and local juris-dictions to develop new strategies for dealing with issues of unemploy-ment, it is likely that support could be found for a series of modest efforts to enhance learning about what works and what doesn't in tar-geting the structurally unemployed. Perhaps building on the experience of several European community development/job creation strategies and the opportunities afforded by recent federal enterprise and empow-erment zone legislation, projects could be developed which would more directly link economic development efforts to short-term public sector job creation strategies involving both government and not-for-profit organizations as program sponsors. Such projects could be tar-geted at population groups with specific needs, such as youth and wel-fare recipients, or geographically, as in depressed areas with histories of long-term and continuous levels of high unemployment.

If the federal government could be persuaded to reenter the field, programs could also focus on cyclical issues by tying short-term public service to unemployment insurance, and by focusing initiatives in areas of high worker displacement brought about by government poli-cies such as the downsizing of defense industries, base closings, or fed-eral regulations such as those related to environmental protection.

To recapture public and political support, it would be advisable to assure that any experiments that were developed would include a mix of populations that included both workers with basic skills such as those employed through the WPA, and workers with more serious employment disabilities such as those targeted in the last days of CETA and PSE.

Public sector job creation has proved to be a valuable tool in the past in providing work experience, training, and retraining. It has helped to build and rebuild the country's infrastructure, and provided useful government services. At least among state and local governments searching for new strategies under the impetus of federal block grant plans, it would appear to be an opportune time to once again take a page from past experiences and begin the process of developing new strategies for using public sector job creation as a technique for dealing with the serious dislocations that are going to continue to confront so many trying to make it in the workforce

Sar Levitan frequently reiterated the view that a PSE program of some size should be a permanent component of the portfolio of employment and training programs. Obviously we need to experiment and know much more before adopting that as general policy. But for now the issue is obviously politically moot.

This paper is an updated version of a report originally prepared for the Pew Charitable Trusts. The author wishes to acknowledge the assistance of Joshua Grinker, who carried out a substantial amount of the historical research and analysis of the WPA, CETA, and European experiences; and Suzanne Trazoff, who provided a valuable critique and edited the earlier version. The Paper itself and its findings and conclusions are solely the responsibility of the author.

References

Balkenbol, B. 1981. "Direct Job Creation in Industrial Countries," *International Labour Review* 120,4.

Baumer, Donald C., and Carl E. Van Horn. 1985, *The Politics of Unemployment,*. Washington DC: Congressional Quarterly Press.

Beharrell, Andy. 1992. "Unemployment and Job Creation." In *Economics Today.* London: Macmillan.

Bekemans, Leonce. ed. 1983. *Employment Generation in Europe.* Maastricht: European Centre for Work and Society.

Bernstein, Irving. 1985. *A Caring Society: The New Deal, the Worker, and the Great Depression.* Boston: Houghton Mifflin.

"Blitzed Again," *The Nation,* Jan 23, 1982.

Bloxom, Marguerite D. 1982. *Pickaxe and Pencil; References for the Study of the WPA.* Washington DC: Library of Congress.

Briscoe, Alden F. 1972. "Public Service Employment in the 1930's: The WPA." In *The Political Economy of Public Service Employment,* Harold L. Sheppard, Bennet Harrison, and William J. Spring, eds. Boston: Lexington Books.

"CETA— Did It Work?" *Policy Studies Journal,* Spring 1983.

"CETA: $11 Billion Boondoggle," *Readers Digest,* August 1978.

"CETAmania," *Fortune,* June 18, 1979.

"Controversy over the CETA program," *Congressional Digest,* April 1981.

Cook, Robert F., Charles F. Adams, Jr., V. Lane Rawlins, and Associates. 1985. *Public Service Employment; The Experience of a Decade.* Kalamazoo MI: W.E. Upjohn Institute for Employment Research.

Dryden, Laurel. 1987. *Employment Creation Policies & Strategies; An Annotated Bibliography1980-1986.* Geneva: International Labour Office.

"The Effect of CETA on the Post-Program Earnings of Participants," *Journal of the Humanities,* 1983.

Faulkner, M.J. 1977. "Direct Job Creation Schemes in the Member States of the European Community." EEC Study No. 77d115.

Franklin, Grace A., and Randall B. Ripley. 1984. *CETA: Politics and Policy, 1973-1982,.* Knoxville TN: University of Tennessee Press.

"How CETA Came to be a Four Letter Word," *Fortune,* April 9, 1978.

Howard, Donald S. 1943. *WPA and Federal Policy.* New York: Russell Sage Foundation.

"Impact of Government Jobs Program," *Business Week,* September 8, 1980.

Johnson, Clifford M. 1985. *Direct Federal Job Creation: Key Issues.* Washington DC: Government Printing Office.

Karsten, D. 1981. "Job Creation in the European Community." EEC study.

Levitan, Sar A. and Frank Gallo. 1991. "Spending to Save: Expanding Employment Opportunities." Social Policy Studies, George Washington University.

"Lotsa Buck, Little Bang," *Time*, Jan 24, 1977.

Mirengoff, William, and Lester Rindler. 1978. *CETA: Manpower Programs Under Local Control*. Washington DC: National Academy of Sciences.

Mirengoff, William, Lester Rindler, Harry Greenspan, and Scott Seablom. 1980. *CETA: Assessment of Public Service Programs*. Washington DC: National Academy of Sciences.

Nathan, Richard P., Robert F. Cook, V. Lane Rawlins, and Associates. 1981. *Public Service Employment: A Field Evaluation*. Washington DC: The Brookings Institution.

Noah, Timothy. 1982. "Bring Back the WPA: How We Can Pay for it and Why We Can't Afford Not To," *Washington Monthly* (September).

Raffa, Frederick A., Clyde A. Haulman, and Djehane A. Hosni. 1983. *United States Employment & Training Programs; A Selected Annotated Bibliography*. Westport CT: Greenwood Press.

Riemer, David. 1988, *The Prisoners of Welfare: Liberating America's Poor From Unemployment & Low Wages*. New York: Praeger.

Rose, Nancy E. 1988. "Production-for-Use or Production-for-Profit?: The Contradictions of Consumer Goods Production in 1930's Work Relief," *Review of Radical Political Economics* 20 (Spring).

Simon, Paul. 1988. *Let's Put America Back to Work*. Chicago: Borus Books.

U.S. General Accounting Office. 1982. *CETA Programs for Disadvantaged Adults; What Do We Know About Their Enrollees, Services, and Effectiveness?*, Washington DC: Government Printing Office.

"Using the Longitudinal Structure of Earnings to Estimate the Effects of Training Programs," *Review of Economics and Statistics*, 1985.

Weir, Margaret. 1992. *Politics and Jobs: The Boundaries of Employment Policy in the U.S.*, Princeton NJ: Princeton University Press.

"What's Wrong with Policy Analysis; Evaluation of CETA Programs," *Washington Monthly*, Spring, 1979.

"Why CETA Is In Trouble," *Business Week*, Oct 2, 1978.

CHAPTER **11**

Achieving National Economic and Social Goals

The Counterproductive Role of Post-1965 Immigration Policy

Vernon M. Briggs, Jr.

Despite the fact that the United States is in the midst of the largest immigration experience in its history, there is little recognition of the effects that immigration policy exerts on parallel policies to achieve national economic and social objectives. In its present state, immigration policy is largely designed to accommodate political goals. Its economic effects are, essentially, incidental to its designed intentions. If the resulting inflow of immigrants were small and widely dispersed, the nation probably could afford the luxury of allowing immigration to continue on its independent course. But, the magnitude of immigration is at historic highs; the human capital attributes of the vast majority of the immigrant inflow are conflicting with emerging economic trends; and the urban settlement patterns are undermining the effectiveness of policies in human resource development and equal employment opportunity that are of vital social concern. Indeed, the groups that are most adversely affected by the post-1965 revival of mass immigration are predominately the same target groups—youth, minorities, and the working poor—whom the human resource policies of this same era have sought to serve. To this degree, immigration policy is functioning in a manner that is contrary to the national interest. Significant reforms are essential.

Immigration is a discretionary policy of every nation state. No citizen of any foreign nation has a right to enter any other country for the purpose of permanent settlement or for employment just because he or she wishes to do so. The opportunities and the conditions under which they may enter are legally prescribed. Hence, in the contemporary case of the United States, it is the nation's immigration policy that is the source of the conflict with the national interest, not the actions of those who, as individuals, are merely availing themselves of its terms and opportunities.

Likewise, it is certainly not the case that all of the immigrant flow has been harmful in the post-1965 era. A significant segment of the immigrant flow has consisted of skilled and educated workers during years when there were legitimate shortages of such talent. Yet, as will be shown, the entry of such workers has often occurred despite the strictures of the nation's immigration policy, not because of its intention to actually do so.

U.S. Immigration Policy in Brief Perspective

As is well known, immigration played a major role in the pre-industrialization era of the emergence of the United States as an economic superpower.[1] Following the end of its colonial era in 1776, the new nation expanded geographically to embrace a vast land area that had an enormous amount of natural resources and a temperate climate, but relatively few people. Throughout its first century, the country had neither ceilings nor screening restrictions on the number and type of people permitted to enter for permanent settlement. The economy was dominated by agricultural production and farm employment. Most jobs required little training or educational preparation. An unregulated immigration policy was consistent with the nation's basic labor market needs during this period of nation building.

When the industrialization process began in earnest during the latter decades of the nineteenth century, the newly introduced technology of mechanization (i.e., the substitution of machines for animal and human muscle power) required mainly unskilled workers to fill manufacturing jobs in the nation's rapidly expanding urban labor markets as well as in the other related-employment sectors of mining, construction, and transportation. As Stanley Lebergott has observed in his epic study of the development of the U.S. labor force, "somewhat surprisingly, the greatest beneficiary of the flow of immigrant labor [in the 19th Century] was never agriculture, though farming was our primary industry" (1964, p. 28). Rather, it was the urban economy and its need for a vast number of unskilled workers to fill the jobs created by the industrialization process whose labor force was expanded by the arrival of immigrants.

Surplus pools of native-born workers, who were poorly skilled and barely educated who remained marginalized throughout the 1880 to 1914 era, could have filled many of these new jobs. They were mostly native-born workers who were underemployed in the rural sectors of the economy of this same era. The most notable were the freed blacks of the former slave economy of the rural South. The noted black educator, Booker T. Washington, in his famous Atlanta Exposition speech in 1895, pleaded with white industrialists of that era to draw upon the available black labor force instead of seeking immigrants to fill the new jobs that industrialization was creating (Washington 1965, p. 147). His advice was ignored. Mass immigration from Asia and Europe became the alternative of choice. Before long, immigration from China and Japan was banned in response to nativist reactions, so various ethnic groups from eastern and southern Europe became the primary sources of unskilled workers of that era.

From purely an efficiency standpoint, the mass immigration of the late nineteenth century and the first part of the twentieth century was entirely consistent with the labor market needs of the nation. The jobs created during this expansive era typically required little in the way of skill, education, literacy, numeracy, or fluency in English from the workforce. The enormous supply of immigrants generally lacked these human capital attributes. As one immigration scholar at that time wrote: "we may yearn for a more intelligent and better trained worker from the countries of Europe but it is questionable whether or not that type of man would have been so well fitted for the work America had to offer" (Roberts 1913, p. 61).

When the land frontiers of the country were overcome in the 1890s, it was not long before immigration was sharply restricted—beginning in 1914 with the events associated with World War I and followed by newly adopted immigration laws in the early 1920s. In part the imposition of legal restrictions reflected legitimate economic concerns that the mass immigration of the preceding three decades had depressed wages, hampered unionization, and caused unemployment; in part they also reflected nativist social reactions to the ethnic, racial, and religious diversity that the mass immigration of that era also brought (Briggs 1984, pp. 31-54). The Immigration Act of 1924 (also known as the National Origins Act) not only imposed the first permanent legislative ceiling on immigration (at a low annual level of about 154,000 immigrants), but it also included a screening system that was highly discriminatory as to who could enter and who could not (favoring immigrants from northern and western European countries and disfavoring or prohibiting immigration from all other Eastern Hemisphere nations). Its provisions, however, did not apply to countries of the Western Hemisphere.

For the next sixty years, the quantitative significance of immigration rapidly receded and the expansion of the economy turned to the utilization of domestic labor reserves. Originally, it was those people in the nation's vast rural areas, where workers were being displaced by the rapid mechanization of agriculture that had begun in earnest in the 1880s, who were finally given the opportunity to compete for jobs in urban America. Among the major beneficiaries of the cessation of mass immigration was the nation's black population. It was not until mass immigration ended in 1914 that "the Great Migration" of blacks to the North and the West could commence. And it did. Later during war years of the 1940s, women, youth, disabled, and older workers as well as minorities were recruited and employed in the economic mainstream for the first time.

Indicative of the declining significance of immigration on American life over this timespan is the fact that the percentage of the U.S. population that was foreign-born consistently fell from 13.2 percent in 1920 to 4.7 percent in 1970 (the lowest percentage since before the Civil War). During this period of receding influence of immigration, the U.S. economy sustained the greatest increases in real wages, employment levels, and production output in its entire economic history. It was also the time when the nation adopted an extensive array of progressive social policies pertaining to labor standards, collective bargaining, and civil rights. It was also a period when income inequality within the population was significantly reduced for the first time.

It was not until the mid-1960s that the mass immigration phenomenon was accidentally revived as a result of domestic political pressures and immigration once again became a significant feature of the U.S. economy. The primary concern of immigration reformers was to end the discriminatory "national origins" admission system. Having just enacted the Civil Rights Act of 1964, which was designed to end overt racial and ethnic discrimination in the nation's internal relationships, the logical next step in the civil rights struggle was to end overt discrimination in the nation's external relationships with the international community. There was no intention, however, to raise the level of immigration by any appreciable amount or to open the admission door to large numbers of unskilled and poorly educated persons. Indeed, the floor manager in the Senate for the Immigration Act of 1965, Edward Kennedy (D-Mass.), stated during the final debate on the legislation that "this bill is not concerned with increasing immigration to this country, nor will it lower any of the high standards we apply in selection of immigrants" (*Congressional Record*, September 17, 1965, pp. 24, 225). Subsequent events have shown that he was wrong on both counts.

The Immigration Act of 1965 was a turning point in the history of U.S. immigration policy. The level of immigrants to be admitted each year was raised to 290,000 immigrants a year plus their immediate relations (spouses, children under 21 years of age, and a new category—parents of citizens—was added). All remnants of overt discrimination on the basis of race and ethnicity were eliminated from the admission process. The new admission system specified that 74 percent of the annually available admission visas would be reserved for adult family and extended family members of persons who were already U.S. citizens or resident aliens. The percentage was increased to 80 percent in 1980. Thus, family reunification became the primary criterion for the admission of legal immigrants. Twenty percent of the available visas were reserved for the admission of workers who had skills that were needed by employers and which citizens supposedly did not possess. Thus, Congress "created a policy aimed primarily at fulfilling the private interests of its legal residents and their alien relatives and it simultaneously delegated to these individuals (and to a limited number of its employers) much of the power to select future citizens and workers in the nation" (North and Houstoun 1976, p. 8). The opportunity to redesign the nation's immigration system to serve the public interest was lost. In the place of the former system that was premised largely on racial and ethnic discrimination, a new form of discrimination—nepotism—became the overriding characteristic of the legal admission system. Whatever human capital characteristics the vast majority of legal immigrants possess at the time of their entry is purely incidental to the reason they are admitted. Only minimal concern was manifested about any possible broad economic effects that might be the product of the new law's provisions. If the scale of immigration had remained small, as its supporters had promised, the consequences of such an ill-designed law would have been of little consequence. But, such was not to be the case.

The Immigration Act of 1965 also provided a formal route for certain refugees to be admitted on the basis of humanitarian concerns. Six percent of the available visas each year were set aside for this purpose. This was the first time since immigration had become a subject of regulation that provisions were made for the continuous admission of refugees as a permanent feature of U.S. immigration policy.

This legislation was also important for what it did not do. It failed to specify any effective measures to enforce its new provisions. Its supporters did not foresee the imminent explosion of illegal immigration that quickly ensued in the years after its passage.

Within a decade of the passage of the Immigration Act of 1965, it was clear that immigration policy had gone awry. Illegal immigration had soared; refugee flows greatly exceeded the number of visas set aside for this purpose; and the number of immediate relatives arriving was far higher than anticipated. Hence, immigration reform was once more placed on the national agenda. In 1978, Congress established the Select Commission on Immigration and Refugee Policy (SCIRP). It was created to study the effects of what had transpired over the preceding thirteen years and to make recommendations for changes. Appointed by President Jimmy Carter, this sixteen-member commission, chaired by the Rev. Theodore Hesburgh, issued its comprehensive report in 1981. It stated that immigration was "out of control"; that the nation must accept "the reality of limitations"; and that "a cautious approach" should be taken in the design of any reform measures. It stated unequivocally that: "the Commission has rejected the arguments of many economists, ethnic groups, and religious leaders for a great expansion in the number of immigrants and refugees" (Select Commission on Immigration and Refugee Policy 1981, p. 7). It went on to say that "this is not the time for a large-scale expansion in legal immigration—for resident aliens or temporary workers" (p. 8).

In the wake of the SCIRP report, Congress enacted three major immigration statutes. They were the Refugee Act of 1980, the Immigration Reform and Control Act of 1986, and the Immigration Act of 1990. In part, each of these laws embraces some of the specific recommendations put forth by SCIRP. But each statute also went well beyond SCIRP's recommendations. The result has been to dramatically raise the already high levels of immigration to even higher plateaus. Indeed, a 1991 study by the Urban Institute concluded that these statutory changes "have reaffirmed the United States' role as the principal immigrant-receiving nation in the world" (Fix and Passel 1991, p. 1). The same report found it "remarkable" that policy makers enacted the Immigration Act of 1990 "with the nation poised on the brink of a recession and a war in the Persian Gulf" and at a time "when other industrialized countries are making theirs [i.e., their immigration policies] more restrictive" (p. 9).

The reason that Congress could take such "remarkable" expansionary actions is that immigration policy has been allowed to develop without any regard as to its economic or social consequences. Just as the Hesburgh Commission had warned, immigration policy had been captured by special interest groups with private agendas that simply ignore any concern for the national interest.[2]

The Revival of Mass Immigration and Its Characteristics

Starting slowly in the latter 1960s, accelerating in the 1970s and 1980s, and institutionalized in the 1990s, mass immigration—this sleeping giant from out of the country's distant past—has once more become a vital characteristic of contemporary American life. Since 1995, the legal immigration system guarantees that at least 675,000 legal immigrants will enter the country every year (it was 700,000 from 1991 through 1994). In addition, the separate refugee and asylee system now admits about 130,000 people a year (and it is subject to intermittent binges of even greater numbers). Nonimmigrant policy, in turn, permits about 400,000 foreign nationals to legally work in the United

States on a temporary basis that ranges from eleven months a year up to five years, depending on specific admission conditions. Furthermore, the U.S. Bureau of the Census estimates that about 300,000 illegal immigrants now enter the country each year and join a shadow labor force and population estimated in 1994 to total about 4 million people. To gauge the momentum of the process, it is only necessary to note that it is estimated that over 10 million immigrants entered the United States in the 1980s (not counting nonimmigrant foreign workers but allowing for an estimate of the uncounted illegal immigrants and those refugees who have been admitted but have not yet adjusted their status to be counted as immigrants). This means it was the decade of the largest infusion of immigrants in the country's history. As a consequence immigrants accounted for 37 percent of the growth of the U.S. population during the 1980s. The 1990 Census revealed that the foreign-born population (which totalled 19.7 million persons as officially measured but which undoubtedly missed many more who had illegally entered) had more than doubled the number reported only twenty years earlier in the 1970 Census. The foreign-born population in 1990 officially accounted for 7.9 percent of the population (with the real rate undoubtedly higher due to uncounted illegal immigrants). Moreover, in 1991, over 1.8 million persons entered the country or adjusted their status to become permanent resident aliens—the highest number of immigrants to do so in any single year in the country's history. Hence, the decade of the 1990s should set yet a new record, and the percentage of the population that is foreign-born should be in double digits again by the time of the census for the year 2000.

Under these circumstances, it is not surprising that an international social science research team stated in its comprehensive study of contemporary American life that "America's biggest import is people" (Oxford Analytica 1986, p. 20). But perhaps most significant of all in regards to this phenomenon is the observation by the demographer Leon Bouvier (1991, p. 18) that, unlike the nation's earlier experiences with mass immigration, the post 1965 wave of immigrants shows "no evidence of imminent decline."

Of even greater significance than the cumulative effects of the soaring level of immigration to the United States, however, has been the effect on the size and composition of the post-1965 immigrant inflow on the labor force. The U.S. Department of Labor revealed that 10.8

percent of the U.S. labor force was foreign-born in 1994. This means that roughly one of every nine workers is foreign-born. Moreover, the 1990 Census revealed that the human capital attributes of the foreign-born fall into two distinct categories. On the one hand, about one-fifth of the foreign-born adult population (i.e., persons 25 years old and over) had a bachelor's degree or higher (20.4 percent), which is about the same as the native-born adult population (20.3 percent). On the other hand, only 58.8 percent of the foreign-born adult population had a high school diploma compared to 77.0 percent of the native-born adult population and, more telling, 25 percent of the foreign-born adult population had *less than* a 9th grade education while only 10 percent of the adult native-born population had such a low level of educational attainment (U.S. Department of Commerce 1993, p. 7 of news release). The 1990 Census also disclosed that 79.1 percent of the foreign-born (5 years old and over) spoke a language other than English (compared to 7.8 percent of the native-born). Moreover, 47.0 percent of the foreign born (5 years old and over) reported that they do not speak English "very well" (p. 5). The ability to speak English in a service-oriented economy has been definitively linked to the ability to advance in the labor market of the post-1965 era (Chiswick 1992, p. 15). Billions of dollars in social spending have been directed to address the language deficiency issue, with mixed results. For these reasons and others, it should come as no surprise that incidence of poverty among families of the foreign-born population in 1990 was 50 percent higher than that of native-born families or that 25 percent of the families with a foreign born householder who entered the country since 1980 were living in poverty in 1990. (U.S. Department of Commerce 1993, p. 8 of news release).

There is also a strong pattern of geographic concentration associated with the post-1965 immigration experience. The 1990 Census revealed that 66 percent of the foreign-born population resided in only six states (California, New York, Florida, Texas, New Jersey, and Illinois). Furthermore, within all states, the foreign-born population tends to be concentrated in urban centers and especially in their respective central cities. The post-1965 immigration phenomenon is "overwhelmingly an urban experience" (Bogen 1987, p. 60). Indicative of this urban concentration is the fact that 24 percent of the foreign born population of the nation in 1990 lived in only seven cities. These cities and the percentage of their respective populations who were foreign born is as follows: New York (28 percent); Los Angeles (38 percent); Chicago (17 percent); Houston (18 percent); San Francisco (34 percent); San Diego (21 percent); and Miami (60 percent). The real percentages are certainly higher if allowances are made for uncounted illegal immigrants.

The Conflict With Economic and Social Goals

The accidental revival of mass immigration in the 1960s could not have occurred at a worse time with respect to the efforts of the nation to achieve its economic goals of full employment with rising real wages for workers and real incomes for families. It was in the 1960s that the U.S. labor market began to be transformed from the past occupational and industrial patterns that existed at the beginning of the twentieth century (Killingsworth 1978, pp. 1-13; Briggs 1992, ch. 7).

On the labor demand side of the labor market, there are new forces at work associated with the nature and pace of technological change; the expansion of international competition; shifts in consumer spending preferences; and, since 1991, substantial reductions in national defense expenditures. Collectively, these forces are reshaping the nation's occupational, industrial, and geographic employment patterns. Employment in most goods-producing industries and in many blue-collar occupations is declining, while it is increasing in most service industries and many white-collar occupations. Regional employment trends are extremely unbalanced, with growth generally more pronounced in urban (but not in central cities) than in rural areas and particularly strong in the Southeast and Southwest and weak in the Midwest and Prairie regions.

Future demand for labor lies primarily in service industries located in metropolitan areas and in occupations that stress cognitive abilities rather than physical strength and stamina. As Lester Thurow has poignantly written, "the skills of the labor force are going to be the key competitive weapon in the twenty-first century . . . [for] skilled labor will be the arms and the legs that allow one to employ—to be the masters of—the new product and process technologies that are being generated" (Thurow 1992, p. 51). Conversely, the escalation in skill requirements has led to diminishing demand for unskilled labor. William Brock, who served as Secretary of Labor during the Reagan administration, has warned that "the days of disguising functional illiteracy with a high paying assembly line job that simply requires a manual skill are soon to be over. The world of work is changing right under our feet."

On the labor supply side of the labor market, the nation's labor force has been growing in size at a pace far greater than all of its major industrial competitors combined and without precedent in its own history. The demographic positioning of the "baby boom" generation has, since the 1980s, been located in the prime working-age years (e.g., in 1995, it is located between the ages of 33 and 49 years old). As a consequence, the nation's labor force participation rate (about 65 percent) is at the highest levels in U.S. history.

Of even greater significance has been the rapid changes in labor force composition. The fastest growing segments of the labor force are women, minorities, and immigrants. Women in general and minorities in particular (with the possible exception of some Asian-American groups) have had fewer opportunities to be trained, educated, or prepared for the occupations that are predicted to increase most in the coming decade. They are disproportionately concentrated in occupations and industries already in decline or most vulnerable to decline in the near future. They now find themselves often in competition with the new immigrant inflow for jobs in these declining sectors.

Since the 1960s, there has been a marked upward trend in the nation's unemployment rate. The unemployment rates of the mid-1960s were in the mid-3 percent range. In every succeeding period of prosperity since that decade, the unemployment rate has tended to be higher than in the preceding prosperity period. The annual unemployment rate has not been below 5 percent since 1970. As of late-1995, the national unemployment rate has been hovering in the mid-5 percent range even though the economy is not considered to be in a recession. The worst affected by this secular trend of gradually rising unemployment have been the less-skilled workers whose ranks are disproportionately composed of minorities and youth. The unemployment rate for adults without a high school diploma in 1994 was 13 percent.

But even worse have been the effects of what Wallace Peterson (1991) has called "the silent depression" of declining real family incomes. This downward trend began in 1973 and has continued to this day. Studies that have focused on trends of real earnings also show that they too have been falling since 1973, but the losses have been the greatest for those with the least education (Bound and Johnson 1992). The U.S. Bureau of the Census, for example, reported in 1991 that white males aged 25-34 with less than a high school diploma experienced a 42 percent decrease in real earnings from levels that existed in 1973; high school graduates sustained a 31 percent decrease in their earnings; those with some college have had a 21 percent decline in earnings; and even college graduates have experienced a 14 percent decrease in real earnings (U.S. Department of Commerce 1991). For women and minorities, the declines have been even worse. In 1994, *The Economic Report of the President* (1994, pp. 120-121) confirmed a worsening in the distribution of income within the nation and its specifically identified immigration as one of the causative factors.

When Congress embarked on the course of adopting a politically driven immigration policy that essentially neglects economic considerations, few people recognized that the country was entering a phase of fundamental economic change. Even after the new employment trends became evident in the 1980s, the congressional committees responsible for designing immigration policy ignored them.

By definition, immigration policy can influence the size of the labor force as well as the human capital characteristics of those it admits. Currently, there is little synchronization of immigrant flows with demonstrated needs of the labor market. With widespread uncertainty as to the number of immigrant workers who will enter in any given year, it is impossible to know in advance of their actual entry how many foreign-born people will annually join the U.S. labor force. Moreover, whatever skills, education, linguistic abilities, talents, or locational settlement preferences most immigrants and refugees possess are largely accidental to the reason they are legally admitted or illegally enter.

In fact, the skills and educational attainment level of those immigrants entering since 1970 have been found to be considerably below those of earlier immigrants at similar stages of assimilation; their incidence of poverty and unemployment are also higher than was true of earlier immigrant experiences; and their labor force participation rate is lower than earlier waves (Borjas 1990, pp. 20-21; Meisenheimer 1992). As for their use of welfare programs, they did not exist when earlier waves of immigrants arrived prior to 1914 but, in comparison to native-born persons in current times, the incidence of welfare usage by immigrants has been found to be higher (Borjas and Trejo 1991, 1994, p. 2).

If immigration were insignificant in its size and if the human capital characteristics of those entering were consistent with post-1965 labor market needs, there would be little reason to worry about the consequences of such a politically driven policy. But neither condition is present. The scale of immigration, in all of its diverse forms, is without precedent. Moreover, the immigration is disproportionately supplying large numbers of unskilled, poorly educated, non-English-speaking job seekers into urban centers of the nation's largest labor markets, adding to the competition for jobs and social services with native-born job seekers who too often share the same paucity of human capital attributes. Conditions in many of these urban centers—as indicated by growing welfare rolls, high unemployment, rampant crime, and high dropout rates from schools, and growing poverty—are rapidly deteriorating to the degree that they are threatening the well-being of the entire nation.

The Imperative of Policy Changes

As indicated, there are factors other than immigration involved in causing the aforementioned conditions. But this is precisely the point. The labor market is in a state of rapid transformation (Briggs 1992, ch. 7). Many of the causative influences are beyond the capability of public policies to control—they can only try to respond in effective and compassionate manners. Likewise, social issues have also come to the forefront in these same years. The Civil Rights Act of 1964 with its historic equal employment opportunity provisions was enacted the same year that mass immigration was revived. It dramatically raised the expectations of minorities and women about their economic futures. In this period of rapid economic and social change, immigration policy should not be allowed to do harm to the nation's quest to achieve equal employment opportunity.

The number one domestic economic problem facing the United States in the 1990s is what to do with the rapidly increasing surplus of unskilled and poorly educated job seekers in an era when low-skilled jobs are rapidly disappearing. With over 30 million functionally illiterate adults and with reports by the U.S. Department of Education in 1992 indicating that 90 million adults are not proficient in reading or mathematical skills, there is no way that this nation can have any foreseeable shortage of unskilled workers in its future.

An immigration policy that is flexible in the number of persons it allows to enter the United States legally each year and that admits persons primarily on the basis of the human capital endowments they have and that the U.S. labor market needs is what is required. In other words, the nation's immigration policy ought to be accountable for its economic consequences (Briggs 1994). The present system is not. It also must be a policy that is firm in the certainty that its terms will be enforced against illegal entry and refugee abuse. It must also contain provisions that allow U.S. employers to hire nonimmigrant workers in only the most extreme labor shortage situations and that employers who rely on immigration labor be required to provide or support training endeavors for citizens and resident aliens to prevent themselves from becoming dependent on foreign nationals.

Presently, U.S. immigration policy cannot be said to meet the standard of being designed to raise the real living standards of American workers; to achieve full employment; and to avoid undermining the effectiveness of efforts to overcome the legacy of past denial of equal opportunity. Indeed, it is counterproductive to efforts to attain these goals. It is past time to place immigration reform at the top the nation's domestic policy agenda.

NOTES

1. For an elaboration of this process, see Briggs (1984, ch. 2 and 3); and Briggs (1992, ch. 3-6).

2. For a discussion of how the level of immigration accelerated when it was not intended to do so, see Briggs (1992, ch. 6).

References

Bogen, Elizabeth. 1987. *Immigration in New York.* New York: Praeger.

Borjas, George. 1990. *Friends of Strangers: The Impact of Immigrants on the U.S. Economy.* New York: Basic Books.

Borjas, George, and Stephen J. Trejo. 1991. "Immigrant Participation in the Welfare System," *Industrial and Labor Relations Review* (January): 195-211.

_____. 1994. "Eliminating SSI for Immigrants," *Migration News* (April 1).

Bound, John, and George Johnson. 1992. "Changes in the Structure of Wages in the 1980s: An Evaluation of Alternative Explanations," *American Economic Review* (June): 371-392.

Bouvier, Leon F. 1991. *Peaceful Invasions: Immigration and Changing America.* Washington DC: Center for Immigration Studies.

Briggs, Vernon M. Jr. 1984. *Immigration Policy and the American Labor Force.* Baltimore: Johns Hopkins University Press.

_____. 1992. *Mass Immigration and the National Interest.* Armonk, NY: M.E. Sharpe.

_____. 1994. "The Imperative of Immigration Reform: The Case for an Employment-based Immigration Policy." In *Still an Open Door? U.S. Immigration Policy and the American Economy,* Vernon M. Briggs, Jr. and Stephen Moore, eds. Washington, DC: American University Press.

Chiswick, Barry R., ed. 1992. *Immigration, Language and Ethnicity: Canada and the United States.* Washington, DC: American Enterprise Institute.

Economic Report of the President 1994. 1994. Washington, DC: Government Printing Office.

Fix, Michael, and Jeffrey S. Passel. 1991. *The Door Remains Open: Recent Immigration to the United States and a Preliminary Analysis of the Immigration Act of 1990.* Washington, DC: Urban Institute.

Killingsworth, Charles C. 1978. "The Fall and Rise of the Idea of Structural Unemployment." Presidential address, *Proceedings of the 31st Annual Meeting, Industrial Relations Research Association,* Madison.

Lebergott, Stanley. 1964. *Manpower in Economic Growth.* New York: McGraw-Hill.

Meisenheimer, J.R. 1992. "How Do Immigrants Fare in the U.S. Labor Market?" *Monthly Labor Review* (December): 3-19.

North, David, and Marion Houstoun. 1976. *The Characteristics and Role of Illegal Aliens in the U.S. Labor Market: An Exploratory Study.* Washington, DC: Linton.

Oxford Analytica. 1986. *America in Perspective.* Boston: Houghton-Mifflin.

Peterson, Wallace. 1991. "The Silent Depression," *Challenge: The Magazine of Economic Affairs* (August): 29-34.

Roberts, Peter. 1913. *The New Immigration*. New York: Macmillan.

Select Commission on Immigration and Refugee Policy. 1981. *U.S. Immigration Policy and the National Interest*. Washington, DC: Government Printing Office.

Thurow, Lester. 1992. *Head to Head: The Coming Economic Battle among Japan, Europe, and America*. New York: William Morrow.

U.S. Department of Commerce. 1993. "Census Bureau Finds Significant Demographic Differences among Immigrant Groups," *Commerce News* (September 23).

U.S. Department of Commerce, Bureau of the Census. 1991. *Current Population Survey* (March).

Washington, Booker T. 1965. "The Atlanta Exposition Address." In *Up from Slavery*, reprinted in *Three Negro Classics*. New York: Avon Books.

CHAPTER 12

The Baby and the Bath Water

Lessons for the Next Employment and Training Program

Burt S. Barnow
Christopher T. King

Although the nation's employment and training system has never been particularly stable, the summer and fall of 1995 were particularly noteworthy for the number and variety of approaches suggested to fix the employment and training system (Barnow 1993). We use the term "fix" with some misgivings, at least for adults, because the national impact evaluation of the Job Training Partnership Act (JTPA) Title II programs for economically disadvantaged adults and youth showed gains of about $900 (in 1993 dollars) annually for adults and no impact for out-of- school youth (Office of Chief Economist 1995; Bloom et al. 1993). Moreover, the evaluation precedes the Department of Labor's emphasis on long-term training and the enactment of the 1992 JTPA amendments.

Nonetheless, there has been considerable interest both in Congress and within the Executive Branch in replacing JTPA with an "improved" system. In this paper we consider three of the significant changes that have been suggested by various parties. We first consider the use of vouchers, where instead of having the program and the participant jointly select the training to be undertaken, the participant makes the selection. We then consider the strategy proposed by Congress of making the programs less categorical and more block grants where the states are given significantly more latitude in determining who is served and how they are served. Finally, we discuss the utility of one feature of the current JTPA system that is unlikely to survive a switch to a purer block grant system—performance management.

The Use of Vouchers

In the JTPA programs, as well as in the Comprehensive Employment and Training Act (CETA) and Manpower Development and Training Act (MDTA) programs that preceded JTPA, the type of training (e.g., classroom training or on-the-job training) and the specific vendor and course are selected jointly by the local program and the participant, with the program having primary responsibility. The Department of Labor has recently proposed that responsibility for activity selection be given exclusively to participants by providing them with vouchers redeemable at local vendors, with the local employment and training programs' responsibilities restricted to providing information about potential service providers and their track records and providing counseling and other support services when asked. Vouchers are a prominent feature of the bill currently being considered by the House of Representatives, H.R. 1617 or the CAREERS Act; the Senate bill authorizes but does not mandate the use of vouchers.

Although the Department of Labor has not worked out all the details of how such a program might operate, it is worth considering what the evidence shows about the track record of previous voucher programs for training unemployed individuals. The initial appeal of vouchers is quite strong. After all, the higher education system in the United States functions reasonably well without local programs assigning people to specific colleges and fields of study. The use of the GI Bill after World War II by large numbers of veterans is always cited as a model system of how well vouchers can accommodate the training needs of individuals. Finally, with the government stressing the importance of customer satisfaction, it is simply more appealing to let people make their own decisions on what to study and where to study it than to have program officials or locally selected contractors dictate the choices.

As noted above, none of the principal national employment and training programs have relied upon vouchers to match participants and programs. Two employment and training programs, one a special program carried out as part of a larger income maintenance experiment and the other a training program for certain dislocated workers, made use of an approach equivalent to vouchers. By examining the evidence from the evaluations of these programs, we can get some idea on how well vouchers might work for a broader-based program.

The SIME-DIME Counseling and Education Subsidy Program

The first voucher-like training program of interest is the Counseling and Education Subsidy Program (CESP) that was implemented along with the Seattle-Denver Income Maintenance Experiments (often referred to as SIME/DIME). SIME/DIME was the largest and last of a series of experiments conducted in the 1960s and 1970s to learn about the feasibility and behavioral implications of a "negative income tax" program where members of the treatment group were provided a guaranteed income, and any income earned by the participants was taxed at a specified rate. The SIME-DIME program was carried out between 1970 and 1978 in selected sections of Seattle and Denver. To be eligible for the program, a person had to meet the following requirements:

- Family income: below $9,000 (in current dollars) for a family of four (adjusted for other family sizes)

- Family structure: restricted to married couples and single parents with minor dependent children

- Race/ethnicity: family head had to be black or white in Seattle, and black, white, or Chicano in Denver

- Characteristics of family head: between the ages of 18 and 58, capable of employment, and not in military service (Christopherson 1983)

For the Counseling and Education Subsidy component of the experiment, treatment and control group members were randomly assigned to one of three counseling and training options:

- Counseling only

- Counseling plus a 50 percent subsidy for any education or training in which the person enrolled

- Counseling plus a 100 percent subsidy for any education or training in which the person enrolled (Dickinson and West 1983)

Participants were enrolled in the experiment for up to six years. Education was interpreted very broadly so that most occupational training and general education courses were approved; most of the training was occupational classroom training, and the community college was the most common provider. Participation in subsidized training was moderate. For the group with a 100 percent subsidy, about 36 percent of the married men and women participated, and 47 percent of the single female heads of household took some education or training. Participation rates were lower for those granted a 50 percent subsidy— 21 percent for the married men and women and 35 percent for the single female heads.

The hypothesis underlying the CESP was that the subsidies for training would lead to increased participation in education and training programs, which would, in turn, increase earnings. The first part of the hypothesis was confirmed, with participants in the 100 percent subsidy group taking approximately one year of additional training compared to those with no subsidy. The surprising result was that in virtually all the analyses undertaken, the training led to either no change in subsequent earnings or an actual reduction in earnings, although the negative impacts were often not statistically significant. Dickinson and West conclude:

> Up to this point we have found that, as expected, the SIME/DIME counseling and training programs increased the amount of job counseling and the amount of additional schooling received. However, we have determined they also, quite unexpectedly, reduced the earnings of those eligible to participate, with the exception of the counseling-only program for single women. Further, we have found that these negative impacts are widespread and that the programs, on the whole, were not beneficial even for select subgroups of the population (again, with the exception of counseling only for single women). Since these results are based on a comparison of randomly assigned experiments and controls and thus are not a result of the self-selection and noncomparability problems that plague most other evaluations of employment and training programs, considerable reliance can be placed on these basic findings (p. 233).

Dickinson and West undertook a number of analyses to determine if their findings somehow resulted from some type of statistical problem or nonrandom selection. In the end, they concluded that the problem was in the treatment itself:

The SIME/DIME programs were designed to maximize freedom of choice for participants. They offered nondirective counseling and a wide range of educational opportunities. Evaluation indicates that such programs in general are inappropriate for low-income individuals, causing at least some of them to form unrealistic expectations about their labor market prospects and to pursue overly ambitious goals (p. 253).

The voucher systems proposed in the current legislation may be even less promising: participants will receive counseling only if they request it.

The Trade Adjustment Assistance Program

The Trade Adjustment Assistance (TAA) program was established in 1962 to provide financial assistance and training to workers who lose their jobs as a result of imports. The program provides cash assistance through Trade Readjustment Allowances (TRA), and workers are permitted to identify and select their own training program. The program has been amended significantly several times in its history (Corson et al. 1993). The qualifying criteria were liberalized in 1974. In 1981, TRA benefits were reduced to be the same as the worker's unemployment insurance (UI) benefits, and workers could only collect TRA after they had exhausted their unemployment insurance. Training was made an entitlement and a requirement for workers on TAA beginning in 1988. Although dislocated workers covered by TAA must have their training approved by the employment service, the workers may choose their own training, and the employment service generally concurs with the workers' plans. Thus, the training component of TAA is essentially a voucher-based training program for dislocated workers who lose their job because of imports.

Mathematica Policy Research (MPR) completed an impact evaluation of TAA training in 1992. The evaluation included four groups of TAA recipients: participants who began receiving TRA benefits prior to the 1988 changes, participants who received TAA training prior to the 1988 changes, participants who began receiving TRA payments after the 1988 changes, and participants who enrolled in TAA training after the 1988 changes. The original design called for fifteen states to be included in the study, but six states refused to participate and only one was replaced, yielding a final sample of ten states. For comparison groups, the MPR researchers selected samples of UI recipients matched to the TAA samples on several criteria. The UI samples were drawn from the same states and roughly the same time periods as the TAA and TRA samples. The UI samples were drawn from manufacturing because the TAA population had been displaced largely from manufacturing jobs (85 percent in the TAA sample selected). Finally, because workers had to exhaust their UI payments to collect TRA, the analysis was restricted to UI exhaustees. The final analysis sample included 4,776 individuals, of whom 1,174 were UI exhaustees and the remainder were TRA recipients and TAA trainees. Data were gathered primarily through telephone interviews and covered approximately four years of experience.

The MPR study found that a substantial minority of TAA participants received training—37 percent in the pre-1988 sample (when training was neither an entitlement nor a requirement) and 47 percent in the post-1988 period when training was generally required but could be waived. About 70 percent of the TAA trainees completed their training, with a slightly higher proportion of the pre- 1988 group (72 percent) completing training than in the post-1988 group (67 percent). As in most studies of dislocated workers, the MPR study found that participants in TAA generally suffered substantial reductions in wage rates and earnings following their job loss.

The MPR researchers used regression analysis of the TAA samples and the UI exhaustee comparison group to estimate the impact of TAA training on the employment and earnings of participants. The researchers found that when differences in characteristics between trainees and others are controlled for, "our findings imply that, if training has a substantial positive effect on employment or earnings among all trainees, it is realized not earlier than three years after the initial UI claim" (Corson et al. 1993, p. 155). The study also found that individuals who received training had slightly lower wage rates than those who did not take training, but the differences were generally not statistically significant.

Although the TAA evaluation is another example of a voucher-like program that failed to produce significant positive impacts on the employment and earnings of trainees, the evidence here must be interpreted with caution for several reasons. First, the evaluation used a nonexperimental design, and the design may not have adequately controlled for differences between the treatment and comparison groups. Second, the evaluation may not have followed up the participants long enough to measure any gains. Finally, the failure of the program to produce significant impacts may not have been due to the voucher aspect of the program but to other features of the intervention. For example, in the post-1988 period, training was a requirement, so the results may not apply to a nonmandatory program. On the other hand, several other evaluations of training programs for dislocated workers failed to find significant positive impacts, so the problem may not result from the use of vouchers (Office of Chief Economist 1995, p. 55).

Conclusions on Vouchers

We do not interpret the evidence presented here to indicate that vouchers should never be used in training programs. For programs focused on the general population and toward higher education rather than occupational training, vouchers may be satisfactory. It is when we consider the populations that have been of greatest interest for the Department of Labor, the economically disadvantaged and dislocated workers, that one has trouble finding any evidence that vouchers will work. Based on recent experience in JTPA, one might speculate that a move toward vouchers would be counterproductive. The 1992 JTPA amendments required local service delivery areas (SDAs) to increase the assessment provided to participants, and an ongoing evaluation of the amendments indicates that most SDAs and states believe that the increased assessment has been beneficial to the program. While causality cannot be established at this time, a reasonable case can be made that for the economically disadvantaged population and perhaps dislocated workers as well, we should stay with the current system of enhanced assessment and training programs mutually agreed upon by the program and the participant, rather than switching to a voucher system where participants assume the major role in selecting their field of study and service provider. If the Department of Labor is able to implement its proposals to establish one-stop career centers and provide detailed performance ratings of all service providers, vouchers are more likely to be useful, but there appears to be no rationale for haste.

Block Grants to States

The major employment and training bills being considered by the House and Senate at the time this paper was prepared, H.R. 1617 and S. 143, reduce the federal role in overseeing and proscribing these programs, and they enhance the role of the states. The term "block grant" is generally used to describe situations where federal funds for several narrowly focused programs (often referred to as categorical programs) are combined in a single grant with much of the responsibility for design, focus, operation, and oversight transferred to the states or, less frequently, to local levels of government. There are obviously degrees to which a program is a block grant rather than categorical, with a program being more of a block grant when the state or local governments have more control over services to be provided, the target population, accountability, and the way funds are allocated to lower levels of government. Thus, JTPA and its predecessor CETA are often classified as block grants because they replaced a number of highly categorical programs (Hayes 1995). On the other hand, JTPA, and CETA before it, has a number of separate titles and funding streams, strict targeting requirements, a number of restrictions on the activities that can be carried out with the federal funds, and a performance management system with strong incentives. Thus, the General Accounting Office (1995, p. 22) quite correctly questions whether CETA—and by implication JTPA as well—was truly a block grant program. Current proposals for employment and training would replace JTPA with one or more programs giving increased responsibility to the states and fewer requirements for targeting, services, and accountability. In the remainder of this section, we review the evidence on the likely effects of moving toward a pure block grant system for employment and training.

Although block grants were first proposed as early as 1949, the first three block grant programs were established in the 1970s under President Nixon: CETA, the Community Development Block Grants (CDBG), and the Social Service Block Grants (established under Title XX of the Social Security Act). The next round of block grants was instituted under President Reagan. Nine block grant programs were created in 1981, and there are currently fifteen block grant programs in effect (General Accounting Office 1995, pp. 22-24).

In this section several of the effects of block grants are considered. We first examine what happens to funding levels for activities under block grants. We then consider the savings that some analysts have speculated will result from the use of block grants and program consolidation. Finally, we discuss how the potential benefits of block grants may erode over time as Congress changes the program. A fourth issue of importance—accountability—is considered in the next section because it is discussed in more depth.

Federal and State Funding Levels

As Peterson and Nightingale (1995) have noted, there is nothing inherent in block grants that requires any change in the level of federal support. During the Nixon era, funding was increased when block grants were implemented, but the Reagan block grants were accompanied by program cuts. In the current environment, any movement more toward the block grant end of the funding spectrum for employment and training programs is likely to be accompanied by a reduction in funding. However, given pressure on the federal budget and criticisms by GAO and others, it is possible that these reductions in spending would occur in any event.

The Reagan round of block grants did not fare particularly well over the decade after they were established. The General Accounting Office (1995) notes that the block grants established in 1981 were funded 12 percent less in 1982 than the categorical programs they replaced. Peterson and Nightingale (1995) find that for the decade following their establishment, funding generally declined for these programs, while Nathan (1995) characterizes the programs as growing "slowly, if at all." Peterson and Nightingale also note that during this period total federal grants to state and local governments increased by over 100 percent, providing additional evidence that programs replaced by block grants do not fare well in terms of federal funding.

Although some observers feared that the states would not make up for much of the reductions that resulted when block grants replaced categorical programs in the 1980s, both the General Accounting Office (1995) and Peterson and Nightingale (1995) found that states made up for a significant share of lost federal funds. State willingness to replace lost federal funds was not universal, however, and the programs that fared best were those that state governments had traditionally administered, while those that fared worst were ones where there had been little state involvement or where the funds had largely been passed through to the local level. Employment and training programs fit more into the latter category, so it is reasonable to expect declines in state support.

Administrative Cost Savings

Claims have sometimes been made that the block grant approach can lead to significant savings in operating programs. The General Accounting Office (1994) has encouraged such thinking by noting in the title of one of its reports that "overlapping programs can add unnecessary administrative costs"; if one reads the report, however, one discovers that GAO did not conduct any study of administrative savings from program consolidation but simply assumed that savings would result. A recent analysis of this issue by Pindus and Nightingale (1994) indicates that, for several reasons, the savings might not be as great as many analysts have supposed. First, administrative costs are generally a small fraction of total expenditures, often around 10 to 15 percent, so the base for potential savings is limited. Second, to the extent that programs are already coordinated in terms of paperwork and service delivery, there are limited benefits to be realized. Pindus and Nightingale conclude:

> Even under scenarios where there could be some administrative cost savings, though, the amount of savings is not likely to be great. Much of the expected savings would occur at the state level, but total state level administrative costs represent a very small percentage of total program costs to begin with (generally one to two percent of all costs). Even if half of all administrative costs at the state level were saved as a result of consolidation, that would still represent only about one percent of total federal program expenditures for all programs consolidated. Under the best-case scenario, there might also be some small savings at the local level. If, hypothetically, 20 percent of the local administrative costs could be saved, this might translate into a savings of 2-4 percent of total federal program expenditures for all programs consolidated (1995, p. 29).

Moreover, to the extent that state and local governments must learn new tasks and assume responsibilities formerly held by the federal government, cost might be expected to increase, at least in the short run.

Eroding Program Flexibility

While there is not a great deal of evidence regarding how well the states have performed in implementing block grant programs, Peterson et al. (1986, p. 28) concluded that "states have done at least as good a job in administration as the federal government had done formerly." In spite of this, there has been a tendency for recategorization of programs shortly after the establishment of block grants. Hayes (1995, pp. 15-16) refers to this phenomenon as "categorical creep," and she notes that between 1980 (prior to the Reagan block grants) and 1994, the number of categorical programs serving children and families increased from about 300 to nearly 500 in 1994. The General Accounting Office (1995, p. 40) notes that between 1983 and 1991 block grant programs were amended 58 times, adding or modifying cost ceilings, eligibility requirements, or imposing other categorical restrictions on the states.

The reason for the recategorization is not hard to identify. As GAO points out, block grants provide the states with increased flexibility and, generally, less accountability. This combination invariably leads to some instances of "bad judgment" by the states where for better or for worse they make changes that Congress does not approve of, resulting in recategorization of programs by Congress. Illustrations in the employment and training area are easy to find. The major restrictions in CETA beginning with the 1978 amendments and the 1992 amendments to JTPA resulted from state and local governments using their flexibility to run programs contrary to the wishes of Congress (and in some instances contrary to good judgment). Thus, even though the National JTPA Study found JTPA to be most effective for adults assigned to on-the-job training (OJT) or job search assistance, these programs were strongly discouraged by the 1992 amendments because the Office of the Inspector General and GAO discovered some abuses of OJT, e.g., three-month dishwasher OJT contracts, and participants receiving only job search assistance were not receiving actual training, contrary to the desires of Congress.

Conclusions on Block Grants

It is not clear how much of the current interest in making the nation's employment and training system more of a block grant stems from a desire to improve the program and how much is simply an excuse to reduce the budget. The evidence suggests that increasing state responsibility and flexibility has some advantages in terms of administrative efficiency, but there is little evidence that cost savings will result, and, based on past experience, there is a good likelihood that recategorization will occur. In addition, if states are given increased flexibility on targeting, services, and sub-state distribution, the federal government should be prepared to live with the results. Thus, we believe that decisions on budget levels should be made independently of block grant features. In addition, as is addressed in more detail below, increasing the state role without maintaining or enhancing accountability has been shown to be a recipe for program disaster.

Employment and Training Performance Management

Legislative proposals now circulating in Congress have the potential for substantially altering, and possibly all but eliminating, the performance management system which has been developed over the past decade for JTPA and more recently for a number of related employment and training (E&T) programs. Whether these pending actions represent a serious threat to the performance of E&T programs depends both on whether the performance management systems have been appropriately designed and on whether these designs have had the intended effects in promoting improved performance.

This section provides a review of recent experience with performance management in E&T programs. First, we review the essential components of these systems. Second, we examine the performance system established for JTPA. Third, we document what is known about the effects the JTPA system has had on participants served, services provided, and key program outcomes. Then, we highlight several national and state-based initiatives underway that are enhancing and changing the focus of E&T performance management. Many of these appear to be heading very much in the direction suggested by the rhetoric, if not the reality, of E&T reform bills in this Congress. Finally, we review the congressionally proposed changes to E&T performance management and offer observations concerning their possible impacts.

Essential Components of E&T Performance Management

Barnow (1992) suggested that three essential components characterize E&T performance management systems, as follows:

- Performance measures, one or more measures related closely to the actual performance expected of the programs:

- Methods for setting performance standards based on each of the selected measures, specific standards of acceptable performance, set rationally and developed so as to be understood by the (state and substate) programs being judged; and

- Rewards and sanctions tied to actual performance against standards.

A fourth component, implicit in the three listed, is that a performance management system should also be firmly grounded in a *performance management philosophy.* This philosophy should clearly articulate to all of the actors involved exactly what is expected of each at all levels; the particular measures, standards, and adjustment mechanisms; the consequences of performance, whether good or bad; how the performance management system is intended to lead to just what type of performance over time; and the rationale for all of these elements. There are any number of alternative philosophies of and approaches to performance management, tailored to varying operating contexts (e.g., centralized/decentralized decision making, funding mix, service constraints).

Three rationales have been offered for establishing performance management systems, suggesting some of the steps towards the requisite philosophy, including: identifying poor performers and taking corrective action; identifying and rewarding good performers; and modifying the objective function of the programs, in laymen's terms, bringing state and local program goals and objectives in line with national program aims.

Typically (and appropriately), the skeleton of a performance management philosophy is only partially outlined in legislation; the system's meat is added through regulations, associated technical assistance guides, training sessions, and ongoing dialogues engaging all major national, state, and substate policy makers, administrators, and service providers. Workable, effective systems are rarely top-down affairs; rather, they can be characterized as top-down/bottom-up. As such, they enjoy substantial "buy-in" from all of the affected parties.

The Current JTPA Performance Management System

Throughout the 1980s and early 1990s, JTPA had the only comprehensive performance management system of any E&T program in the country (King 1988). Now, however, a number of other E&T programs—adult and vocational education, the Job Opportunities and Basic Skills (JOBS) training program for Aid to Families with Dependent Children recipients, and the Food Stamp E&T program—have at least begun to construct their own systems. The JTPA system is examined here; none of the others can yet match it for completeness or for responsiveness to changing conditions (Baj, Sheets, and Trott 1994).

Building on the pilot experience under CETA, JTPA's performance management system was ushered in July 1983 and has been modified in response to research findings, reviews by national blue ribbon commissions, and extensive feedback from state and local programs. The latest changes resulted from the passage of the 1992 JTPA Reform Amendments. JTPA's performance management system at present is comprised of the following key components:

- Clearly articulated *goals and objectives*, i.e., increased employment and earnings and reductions in welfare dependency

- *Performance measures and associated standards*, developed through a highly participatory, top-down/bottom-up policy process with considerable input from the research community; JTPA's measures and standards now encompass both process (e.g., access/ equity of service) and outcome (e.g., youth employability enhancement, rates of employment and earnings levels, since 1988 captured at follow-up for adults and adult welfare recipients) measures for adults and youth

- A *performance standards adjustment model* with which governors may adjust performance standards for their local programs to account for economic conditions (e.g., high unemployment, low wages) and population constraints that lie beyond their control

- *Performance incentives and sanctions* tied to local performance against standards, typically as adjusted by the Secretary's performance standards model

- *Clearly sorted performance management roles and responsibilities* among the program's key players, including the federal government, governors, local private industry councils, and program administrators and service providers

- *Ongoing technical assistance and training (TAT)* on performance standards and their use, led by USDOL/ETA and assisted by states, national associations, consultants, and researchers

JTPA's approach is based on several key principles. First, to the extent feasible, measures and standards should proxy for the desired net impact on employment and earnings. Second, unintended negative effects should be avoided. For example, despite the fact that cost and change (in employment, earnings, and welfare dependency) measures were specifically called for in legislation, the former were tried but subsequently dropped when field research found their use was prompting the pursuit of low-intensity service strategies (SRI and Berkeley Planning Associates 1988); the latter were considered but never implemented because research suggested that change measures would lead to participant "creaming" and serving those who would have done well absent services. Third, underlying JTPA's system is the private sector notion that, given clear goals, objectives, and standards of performance and guidance on operating parameters, local officials should be allowed the flexibility to decide how to operate, as well as to enjoy the fruits of their success or suffer the consequences of their failure. Responses to program failure include both technical assistance, a relatively positive approach geared towards improvement, as well as program reorganization, the negative option, for continued nonperformance.

Effects of E&T Performance Management

JTPA is the only E&T program with sufficient experience in performance management to support an assessment of its effects. Barnow (1992) and Dickinson et al. (SRI and Berkeley Planning Associates 1988) provide evidence on this issue. Technical issues (e.g., estimation biases, measurement error, omitted variables) aside, several key findings emerge from this research.

First, for all its faults, JTPA's performance management system—including its principal measures—-enjoys widespread acceptance among those who must work within and around its confines. This suggests that JTPA's system has met an important test: it has been widely accepted as valid by those who are an integral part of it.

Second, when Dickinson and her colleagues conducted the legislatively mandated evaluation of the effects of JTPA standards on clients, services, and costs for the National Commission for Employment Policy, they found that standards were not the culprit they had sometimes been made out to be. Local JTPA programs (known as service delivery areas or SDAs) balanced at least three different sets of objectives, the first centered around clients' needs and serving particular client groups; the second around employer needs and interests; and the last more narrowly focused on achieving specific JTPA performance levels. Given that national performance standards for JTPA have been pegged at relatively low ("minimally acceptable") levels, their major conclusions were not surprising. Their findings suggest that local JTPA programs that have a strong sense of their goals and objectives, understand their target populations and local labor markets, and pay attention to providing appropriate E&T services will not have their programs distorted (in terms of clients, services, or costs) by the application of performance standards.

Third, on one of the more important issues—whether program termination and immediate postprogram performance indicators are sufficiently good "proxies" of the desired longer-term net impacts on participant employment, earnings, and welfare dependency—the jury is still out. Considerable research has been conducted around this issue, beginning with the pioneering study by Borus (1978). (See also Gay and Borus 1980; Geraci 1984; and Friedlander 1988). These studies have used varying methodologies applied to different programs and had access to differing gross/net impact estimates, with understandably different results. We do not yet know definitively that managing towards the current set of immediate and near-term measures and standards yields the desired net impacts; however, as the Secretary of Labor's JTPA Advisory Committee strongly recommended in 1989, a combination of tightening up eligibility at the front end (e.g., ensuring that participants are truly in need) and tightening up program performance measurement at the back end (e.g., stricter, more tightly defined outcome measures) will minimize problems associated with "creaming," serving those most likely to succeed, usually in order to produce better gross results in the short term.

Finally, it is helpful to close by listing the five major lessons USDOL (1994d) says it has learned over the course of implementing JTPA performance standards:

• performance standards drive program behavior

• performance standards should clearly reflect policy goals

• performance management incentives get results

• keep it simple

• performance standards are part of systemwide management

Promising Recent Initiatives

This appears to be a period of actively "groping along" towards a new performance management paradigm for E&T programs. The emerging paradigm is both more encompassing and complete than the current ones, and is more closely aligned with leading private sector practices. The passage of the Government Performance and Results Act of 1993 indicates that this is unlikely to diminish in the foreseeable future. Under this act, federal agencies must develop outcome-based goals, systematically measure their performance, and report on their progress. A number of promising recent initiatives are highlighted here.

Cross-Program Performance Management Initiatives. Even before USDOL began promoting the one-stop career center approach to service delivery, a number of states (notably New Jersey, Pennsylvania, and Texas) had launched their own efforts to rationalize their E&T

operations and to deliver services in a more "seamless" fashion. They also began grappling with ways to manage these programs better, whether or not they had placed them under a common roof. Some states (Oregon, for instance) established so-called human resource investment councils, overarching councils which oversaw planning for and conducted oversight across major E&T programs. Subsequent passage of the 1992 JTPA Reform Amendments encouraged other states to follow suit, and approximately fifteen states, beginning with Texas, have done so.

Second, the 1992 amendments also mandated the identification of a "core set of consistently defined data elements" for the major federal E&T programs. The Secretaries of Agriculture, Education, Health and Human Services, and Labor, joined by other partner agencies and organizations, launched this effort and produced a report identifying these core elements and setting forth recommended definitions for them (USDOL 1994a). The National Governors' Association, one of the partner organizations, engaged several states (notably Texas, Iowa, North Carolina, and Indiana) in an intensive eighteen-month project to implement core data elements and performance measures. For example, Texas has adopted five common outcome measures for gauging the performance of its JTPA, JOBS, Food Stamp, E&T, Adult and Vocational Education, and other programs.

Third, the National Commission on Employment Policy, joined by a group of policy researchers and several key states, pushed to maximize the use of unemployment insurance (UI) wage records—data already collected in support of UI benefits administration in each state—as a cost-effective, objective, and easily accessible mechanism for tracking longer-term employment and earnings outcomes for participants terminating from the various E&T programs (NCEP 1991, 1992). The availability of quarterly UI wage records in nearly all states is a recent phenomenon, a product of the 1988 amendments to JTPA; the 1992 JTPA Amendments bolstered institutional support for their use. This effort has emphasized tracking and evaluation options for JTPA, but its applicability extends *across* many of the other E&T programs as well. UI wage records have the potential to serve as a form of "common currency" for gauging E&T program performance.

Skills Standards. One of the missing pieces in E&T program performance management systems to date has been that, despite a private sector role in their application (especially in JTPA), standards were largely independent of performance expectations for jobs in the labor market. That is, while local E&T programs could be judged successful in terms of programmatically based standards (i.e., having exceeded the established employment rates or earnings levels), many participants might well be unable to meet the on-the-job requirements of private (or even public) sector employers. The Secretary's Commission on Achieving Necessary Skills report (U.S. Department of Labor 1991) recognized this issue.

A joint effort to develop industry-based occupational skills standards and certification was begun by the U.S. Departments of Education and Labor in 1992. Industry-led projects were funded in numerous industries (e.g., electronics) "to establish model frameworks that define recognized occupations, establish world-class occupational skill standards, and provide the basis for program accreditation and individual certification" (Baj, Sheets, and Trott 1994, p. 41). Subsequently, The Goals 2000: Educate America Act of 1994 encouraged the creation of a national system of voluntary skill standards, to be led by industry, and also called for the creation of a National Skills Standards Board. The School-to-Work Opportunities Act of 1994 then encouraged states to develop their own skill standards and to link them to the standards emanating from the national Goals 2000 efforts. Whether Congress will continue to support these initiatives is doubtful.

Convergence with Private Sector Performance Management. Another initiative worth noting is the convergence of private and public sector (especially E&T program) thinking regarding how best to manage performance. Both the language and practice of E&T performance management are now much closer to those of leading private sector enterprises. The publication of such popular works as *In Search of Excellence* by Peters and Waterman (1982) and *Reinventing Government* by Osborne and Gaebler (1992) has certainly helped. Elements of this convergence can be seen in the growing emphasis on *continuous improvement* over time (as distinct from simply meeting a given year's performance standard); *quality assurance* and quality generally (as compared to focusing on USDOL/ETA's "minimally-acceptable performance"); and *customer satisfaction* and related management feedback systems (in contrast to passive participant follow-up surveys). USDOL has actively pursued these new elements of performance management in ways readily apparent in its One-Stop Career Center Projects around the country; the National Governors' Association and other organizations have been key proponents as well.

Possible "Reform" Impacts

Both the House and Senate bills proposing to reform the nation's workforce education and training programs are short on details, particularly in terms of performance management, making an assessment of the possible impacts of reform difficult. The two leading bills are H.R. 1617, the Consolidated and Reformed Education, Employment, and Rehabilitation Systems (or CAREERS) Act in the House (the McKeon-Goodling bill); and S. 143, the Workforce Development Act in the Senate (the Kassebaum bill). H.R. 1617 would consolidate E&T programs into four state block grants (by target group); require that services be delivered via one-stop centers operating under required local boards; and place heavy emphasis on vouchers for adult training. S. 143 would create a federal-level governing board; consolidate somewhat fewer programs into a single state block grant (with two funding streams), organized around core activities; and allow the establishment of local boards and the use of vouchers.

Key points concerning the relevant performance-related provisions in these bills include the following:

- At the federal level, the Secretaries of Education and Labor would work to set "world-class" performance levels to ensure a national performance system in H.R. 1617, while S. 143 would give the major performance management role—including "negotiating" state performance benchmarks—to a newly constituted public/private, executive/congressional governing board.

- States have a very active role in S. 143, setting appropriate performance benchmarks, among other functions; in H.R. 1617, states set core indicators, but local boards develop the performance measures.

- H.R. 1617, which requires the use of vouchers, also mandates a system of provider certification.

• Both versions have provisions for performance incentives or bonuses and would reduce an area's basic resources a substantial amount for continued nonperformance.

There are major shortcomings in these bills from a performance management perspective. First, both are disturbingly vague on purpose, goals, and objectives, as well as the approach that would be put in place to measure them. As Sum and Harrington (1995) point out, these bills not only appear to give a much larger performance management role to states (and localities in the House bill), but they retreat noticeably from the important federal role which has been asserted over the years, i.e., establishing E&T program goals and objectives, and ensuring that data systems were in place throughout the system to measure performance reliably and consistently. The system envisioned in the Senate bill has many of the trappings of that now in place in vocational education. Not only did it take several attempts over several decades to get clear performance management provisions in federal law, but once enacted (1990), the weak federal role it embodies has allowed states such wide leeway that it is difficult for potential students to know what the system is producing from state to state or community to community. This might be understandable in vocational education where federal funds comprise a very small fraction of the total, but in federal block grants with few matching requirements, it makes very little sense.

Second, the private sector role in performance management, which has been a centerpiece of the USDOL approach since the early 1980s, is lacking altogether in these bills. This sends the wrong signal to the nation's E&T programs.

Third, while it is encouraging that H.R. 1617 would mandate a mechanism for provider certification to accompany its voucher approach, this only goes part of the way. As indicated above, the effectiveness of vouchers remains largely untested with poor target populations with low literacy and other barriers. The experiences many states and the federal government have had with proprietary schools and school loans are suggestive of some of the problems that can occur. Performance information alone is not sufficient. Given the complexity of the investment decisions individuals are being asked to make for their careers, greater emphasis will be needed on counseling them concerning choices and their consequences, interpreting the available information on provider performance.

Fourth, both bills would effect cuts in an area's basic resource allocation for continued nonperformance, an action which penalizes those in need of services as much as it does local program staff and, by association, local elected officials. Positive approaches (incentives) are far more productive than negative ones at eliciting the desired program response. Further, cutting into base area funding allocations is ill-advised. These are lessons with strong private sector parallels as well.

Finally, neither bill addresses what USDOL and the JTPA system have begun to acknowledge as crucial to achieving desired performance levels over time, constructing mechanisms to assure quality and foster continuous improvement. These principles come out of leading-edge practices in the private sector, e.g., Total Quality Management (or TQM) or the international ISO 9000 effort. In all fairness, none of the nation's E&T programs, including JTPA, has done well in these areas. A crucial missing ingredient in continuous improvement is a network of technology diffusion centers which can help to interpret and communicate new findings (research and development)—about effective program interventions and innovative service delivery practices—to state and local E&T programs, as well as provide technical assistance and training when needed to assist in implementing them. Parallels can be found in the nation's networks of Agricultural Experiment Stations and Education Service Centers, as well as in the system of Manpower Institutional Grantees (or MIGs) that existed under CETA.

In summary, these E&T "reform" proposals represent considerable regression from the system now in place for JTPA and would amount to disregarding years of progress built upon hard-learned lessons and the emulation of leading-edge national and international practices. It would be a terrible irony to choose to revert to a fragmented, state-based E&T system, featuring inconsistently measured performance against incompletely defined goals and objectives, when, in the face of increasing economic globalization, many of our trading partners are going the other way.

Concluding Observations

We have examined several topics now featured prominently in the national debate over the future of E&T programs, namely vouchers, block grants, and performance management. The evidence on the efficacy of vouchers for providing services to low-income populations is limited, and the evidence that is available is not encouraging. Relying on vouchers as the principal mechanism for providing E&T services for key E&T target populations might well prove counterproductive. In addition, past experience with using block grants for E&T and related programs also suggests little room for optimism. The current move to legislate E&T block grants may be largely a product of the desire to cut federal expenditures in this policy area. We should not expect turning to block grants to yield measurable savings in administrative costs or to produce substantially better decision making on the part of state and local governments who would inherit the newly devolved responsibility for E&T program decisions.

The JTPA program in particular has established a reputation for program accountability. It did so early in its implementation and has continued to do so over the years, learning from its mistakes, building on its successes, and emulating some of the best private sector performance management practices. JTPA's performance management approach is not without its faults (or its critics), but is by far the best such system yet implemented in the E&T realm. Leading congressional proposals to reform E&T programs are remarkably vague and ill-defined in terms of performance management, leaving much to be desired. In addition, JTPA's record for adults has shown continuous improvement in recent years. The table below shows how wages at placement and length of stay have steadily increased for adults between 1989 and 1993

Year	1989	1990	1991	1992	1993
Average length of stay for adults (in weeks)	12	24	27	28	33[a]
Average wage at placement for adults	$5.64	$5.85	$6.08	$6.40	$6.87

a. Length of stay for 1993 may not be strictly comparable to data from earlier years.

There is a disturbing incongruity between the visions being pursued by the new leadership in Congress and the perspectives of researchers, policy analysts, and practitioners. Even with E&T vouchers and block grants, we would still need ways to demonstrate to taxpayers and the Congress that services are being effectively delivered both in the present and over time. It is unclear how this can be accomplished absent tightly defined standards and consistently measured performance across states. We sincerely hope that cutting federal expenditures on E&T programs is not a hidden aim of the current fervor for E&T program and other block grants. We should stop to ask whether it makes sense to throw out the baby with the bath water.

References

Ashenfelter, Orley. 1978. "Estimating the Effects of Training Programs on Earnings," *Review of Economics and Statistics* (February).

Baj, John, Robert G. Sheets, and Charles E. Trott. 1994. *Building State Workforce Development Systems Based on Policy Coordination and Quality Assurance.* Washington, DC: National Governors' Association, Employment and Social Services, Center for Policy Research.

Barnow, Burt S. 1987. "The Impact of CETA Programs on Earnings: A Review of the Literature," *Journal of Human Resources* 22 (Spring).

_____. 1992. "The Effects of Performance Standards on State and Local Programs." In *Evaluating Welfare and Training Programs, Charles F.* Manski and Irwin Garfinkel, eds. Cambridge, MA: Harvard University Press.

_____. 1993. "Thirty Years of Changing Federal, State, and Local Relationships in Employment and Training Programs," *Publius: The Journal of Federalism* (Summer).

Bassi, Laurie J. 1984. "The Effect of CETA on the Postprogram Earnings of Participants," *Journal of Human Resources* (November).

Bloom, Howard S. et al. 1993. *The National JTPA Study: Title II-A Impacts on Earnings and Employment at 18 Months.* Bethesda, MD: Abt Associates, January.

Borus, Michael E. 1978. "Indicators of CETA Performance," *Industrial and Labor Relations Review* 32, 1 (October).

Christopherson, Gary. 1983. "Locating, Enrolling, and Maintaining the Sample." In *Final Report of the Seattle-Denver Income Maintenance Experiment, Vol.1: Design and Results.* Menlo Park, CA: SRI International.

Commission on the Skills of the American Workforce. 1990. *America's Choice: High Skills or Low Wages!* Rochester, NY: National Center for Education and the Economy.

Corson, Walter, Paul Decker, Philip Gleason, and Walter Nicholson. 1993. *International Trade and Worker Dislocation: Evaluation of the Trade adjustment Assistance Program.* Princeton, NJ: Mathematica Policy Research, April.

Dickinson, Katherine P., and Richard W. West. 1983. "Impacts of Counseling and Education Subsidy Programs." In *Final Report of the Seattle-Denver Income Maintenance Experiment, Vol.1: Design and Results.* Menlo Park, CA: SRI International.

Friedlander, Daniel. 1988. *Subgroup Impacts and Performance Indicators for Selected Welfare Employment Programs.* New York: Manpower Demonstration Research Corporation, August.

Gay, Robert, and Michael E. Borus. 1980. "Validating Performance Indicators for Employment and Training Programs," *Journal of Human Resources* 15, 1 (Winter).

Geraci, Vincent J. 1984. "Short-Term Indicators of Job Training Program Effects on Long-Term Participant Earnings." Project Working Paper No. 2, Center for Economic Research, The University of Texas, August.

Hagen, Jan L., and Irene Lurie. 1994. *Implementing JOBS: Progress and Promise.* Albany, NY: Rockefeller Institute of Government, State University of New York-Albany, JOBS Implementation Study.

Hansen, Janet S., ed. 1994. "Preparing for the Workplace: Charting a Course for Federal Postsecondary Training Policy." Report of the Committee on Postsecondary Education and Training for the Workplace, National Research Council.

Hayes, Cheryl D. 1995. *Rethinking Block Grants: Toward Improved Intergovernmental Financing for Education and Other Children's Services.* Washington, DC: The Finance Project, April.

King, Christopher T. 1988. "Cross-Cutting Performance Management Issues in Human Resource Programs." Research Report 88-12, National Commission for Employment Policy Research, August.

Levitan, Sar A., and Frank Gallo. 1988. *A Second Chance: Training for Jobs.* Kalamazoo, MI: W.E. Upjohn Institute for Employment Research.

Marshall, Ray; and Marc Tucker. 1992. *Thinking for a Living: Education and the Wealth of Nations.* New York: Basic Books.

Nathan, Richard P. 1995. "Block Grants—Key to the 'New(t) Federalism,'" Presentation to "The Harassed Staffer's Reality Check" sponsored by the Sar Levitan Center for Social Policy Studies at the Institute for Policy Studies, Johns Hopkins University, June.

Nathan, Richard P. and Fred C. Doolittle. 1987. *Reagan and the States.* Princeton, NJ: Princeton University Press

National Commission for Employment Policy (NCEP). 1991. "A Feasibility Study of the Use of Unemployment Insurance Wage-Record Data as an Evaluation Tool for JTPA: Report on Project's Phase I Activities." Research report 90-02, January.

_____. 1992. "Using Unemployment Insurance Wage-Record Data for JTPA Performance Management." Research report 91-07, June.

Office of the Chief Economist. 1995. *What's Working (and What's not).* Washington, DC: U.S. Department of Labor, January.

Orr, Larry, et al. 1995. *Longer-term JTPA Net Impacts and Costs.* Bethesda, MD: Abt Associates.

Osborne, David, and Ted Gaebler. 1992. *Reinventing Government: How the Entrepreneurial Spirit is Transforming the Public Sector.* New York: Plume Books.

Peters, Thomas J., and Robert H. Waterman. 1982. *In Search of Excellence.* New York: Warner Books.

Peterson, George E. 1995. "A Block Grant Approach to Welfare Reform." In *Welfare Reform: An Analysis of the Issues*, Isabel V. Sawhill, ed. Washington, DC: Urban Institute.

Peterson, George E., Randall R. Bovbjerg, Barbara A. Davis, Eugene C. Durman, and Theresa A. Gallo. 1986. *The Reagan Block Grants: What Have We Learned.* Washington, DC: Urban Institute Press.

Peterson, George E., and Demetra Smith Nightingale. 1995. "What Do We Know about Block Grants?" Washington, DC: Urban Institute, July.

Pindus, Nancy, and Demetra Smith Nightingale. 1994. *Administrative Savings Resulting from Federal Program Consolidation.* Washington, DC: Urban Institute, December.

Puma, Michael J., and Nancy R. Burstein. 1994. "The National Evaluation of the Food Stamp Employment and Training Program," *Journal of Policy Analysis and Management* 13, 2 (Spring).

SRI; and Berkeley Planning Associates. 1988. "JTPA Performance Standards: Effects on Clients, Services and Costs." Research Report 88-16, National Commission for Employment Policy, September.

Sum, Andrew, and Paul Harrington. 1995. "Guiding Principles for National Employment and Training Reform." In *The Harassed Staffer's Reality Check,* Pines et al., eds. Baltimore, MD: Sar Levitan Center for Social Policy Studies, Institute for Policy Studies, Johns Hopkins University.

U. S. Department of Labor. 1994a. "Core Data Elements and Common Definitions for Employment and Training Programs: Final Report." Office of Strategic Planning and Policy Development, Employment and Training Administration. July 14. Prepared by Nancy Bross and Terri Thompson, KRA Corporation.

_____. 1994b. *Guide to JTPA Performance Standards for Program Years 1994 and 1995.* Washington, DC: Employment and Training Administration, July 29.

_____. 1994c. "Improving the Performance Management System for Employment and Training Programs." Background Paper for the [Chief Economist's] Roundtable Discussion, September 23.

_____. 1994d. "Lessons Learned." Brief paper prepared for the [Chief Economist's] Roundtable Discussion, September 23.

_____. Job Training 2000 Performance Standards Subgroup (n.d.). *Performance Measurement in Federal Job Training and Education Programs.*

Employment and Training Administration, Office of Strategic Planning and Policy Development, Division of Performance Management and Evaluation.

_____. 1989. *Working Capital: JTPA Investments for the 90s.* JTPA Advisory Committee, March.

_____. 1991. *What Work Requires of Schools: A SCANS Report for America 2000.* Secretary's Commission on Achieving Necessary Skills.

U.S. General Accounting Office. 1994. *Multiple Employment Training Programs: Overlapping Programs Can Add Unnecessary Administrative Costs.* GAO/HEHS-94-80, January.

_____. 1995. *Block Grants: Issues in Designing Accountability Provisions.* GAO/AIMD-95-226, September.

_____. 1995. *Block Grants: Characteristics, Experience, and Lessons Learned.* GAO/HEHS-95-74, February.

CHAPTER 13

Toward Quality Programs for At-Risk Youth

Susan P. Curnan
Alan Melchior
Alan Zuckerman

Despite over thirty years of public investment in remedial programs on their behalf, the diminished outlook for at-risk youth remains a national concern. Nearly four million of the nation's 67 million children and youth under 18 are growing up in severely distressed neighborhoods in which there are high levels of poverty, female-headed families, high school dropout rates, unemployment, and heavy reliance on welfare. Minorities are disproportionately among those at risk. While they are only 25 percent of all children in the country, African-American and Latino children comprise over 80 percent of the children living in those severely distressed neighborhoods. These communities have few resources and lack institutions that can offer young people developmental services, opportunities, or support. Lacking role models, adequate education, workforce preparation, and economic opportunities, these youth foresee little likelihood of self-sufficient productive futures.

In addition to these youth burdened by residence, teen parents, the physically or mentally challenged, juvenile offenders, and others are vulnerable by virtue of their status and people's attitudes, fears, stereotypes or prejudices. They, too, are at risk. Other young people are at substantial risk at particular times in the course of their development. Often young people need help making certain transitions, from school to school, from school to work, or youth to adulthood. Many in-school youth are at times at risk of dropping out or of tuning out. In 1992 the school dropout rate was 11 percent nationally, but in some urban school districts it approached 50 percent. While the dropout rate is generally dropping, the costs of dropping out are rising, with lower earnings and tax revenues and higher welfare and social support burdens among those costs.

One youth program after another has come on line since the early sixties but, with the exception of the expensive Job Corps, their evaluations have been consistently negative. What else could be expected when they generally tried to provide remedies in about the same number of weeks as the number of years these youths had been immersed in their destructive environments. Nevertheless, in response to both the persistent problems and the discouraging results, the last few years have been marked by a steady stream of new legislation and experimental programs in search for better answers. An ongoing stream of research and national commission reports has documented the mismatch between the increasing labor market requirements and the inadequate basic skills of American young people. As a result there began in the late 1980s and early 1990s a significant shift in national policy towards strategies that promote the establishment of ambitious national standards, the targeting of services to those with the poorest skills, and the development of more comprehensive service strategies, particularly those that provide a stronger link between work and education. These changes are evident in a number of key pieces of legislation, including the 1992 JTPA Amendments, the School-to-Work Opportunities Act, the Goals 2000: Educate America Act, and the National and Community Services Trust Act. Included also were changes in JTPA's performance standards system as well as the development of a number of major national youth initiatives such as Youth Fair Chance, Youthbuild, and Americorps.

At the core of this change in national policy was the recognition that there needs to be a fundamental shift in the way we prepare young people, particularly economically disadvantaged youth, for productive citizenship and employment. Implicit in that policy change was also a shift from an overwhelming emphasis on *employment* as the primary goal of youth-oriented programs to an emphasis on *employability development* and a corresponding shift towards longer-term, more comprehensive strategies and towards the targeting of services to those most in need of assistance.

While there has been substantial progress on the legislative and policy front, most practitioners and policy makers would agree that the
translation of policy into working, high-quality programs in the field
remains a major challenge. Under JTPA, the investment in staff development has been minimal, and much of that has focused on compliance rather than program redesign or improved services. Guidance for
local policy makers and program managers has also been limited.
Changes in performance standards have provided general goals, but
offer little in the way of clear standards of quality for program design
and development. The timing for all of that has been especially unfor-
tunate in that youth programs have a difficult time defending themselves in a time of budgetary pressures. The progress of the past few
years is currently at risk, in part because of lack of time to produce
results and prove effectiveness.

But the experience has not all been negative, and it is possible to
describe from that experience what works for whom and what the characteristics of an effective program for at-risk youth would be. To that
purpose, this paper seeks to answer from experience—our own and
that of other youth program practitioners—as well as the literature on
adolescent psychology, evaluation research on alternative schools, cognitive development research, and the like, the questions:

5. What are the elements of an effective program for at-risk youth?

6. What do we know about "what works" for at-risk youth?

7. How can we begin to translate that knowledge into standards for
high quality youth programs?

In the discussion that follows, we argue that the answers to these
questions can be framed in terms of four broad themes:

1. The need to focus on youth as youth, and to address the developmental needs of youth within our program strategies

2. Connecting work and learning, by creating learning-rich work
experiences and transforming the way in which learning takes
place in classrooms

3. Providing opportunities for longer-term sequences of services
that recognize employability development as a long-term invest-

ment for some youth, and that provide the support that many at-risk youth need to develop the higher-level skills needed for long- term employment

4. Promoting quality in a decentralized system, through significant investments in staff development and in gathering the data (through assessment and evaluation) needed for effective management and improvement

Finally, our goal in this paper is to present the basis for a much more extended discussion. While we believe that research and experience do point towards criteria for effective practices, we make no claim that the criteria presented here represent the *only* way of defining those standards or a complete list. Rather, they are conceived as a starting point and a framework that can inform and advance the discussion to come.

The Context: Youth Need Clear Standards and Local Variations

The starting point for any discussion of the effectiveness of programs for youth is the recognition that there is no single program model that works for all youth. The young people we serve differ widely in terms of their age, skills levels, knowledge and experience, and life circumstances. While one young person may benefit from (and be ready for) a highly structured occupational training program, another may need a more basic introduction to work and workplace skills.

When we talk about the criteria for effective programs, then, we need to do so in a context that recognizes the need for flexibility in the application of those criteria to individual programs. We *know*, based on research in such areas as adolescent development and education, that younger adolescents are different from older youth (and different from adults) and generally respond to different types of instructional strategies. We *know* that skill levels, in terms of basic academic and work-related skills, vary substantially among young people, ranging from youth who can read and write at only the most basic levels and who have never worked to those who are essentially ready to move into a demanding training or employment environment. We *know* that young mothers require a mix of services, including child care, medical services, flexible scheduling and the like, that may be different from other young adults and that their program participation depends, in large part, on the degree to which those service are offered. We also know that programs need to build on local resources and circumstances. The history of replication efforts in employment and training and elsewhere highlights the dual need for clear standards and local variations.

The first point, then, is that effective program design begins with an awareness and understanding of the needs and characteristics of young people and the need to target program design (that is, to apply the elements of effective practice) in ways that address the needs of the particular population being served.

The second, related point is that program design also needs to recognize the skill demands of employers and the labor market. The goal of every effective employment and training program for youth is to prepare young people for long-term employability. To meet that goal, practitioners and policy makers need to have a clear understanding of the skills, knowledge, and behaviors that are required for success in the labor market and to integrate those skills as the goals of their programs. It is within these two parameters—the needs and characteristics of program participants and the needs and requirements of employers—that program design takes place, and it is within that context that we can begin to define a more general set of criteria for quality programs.

A Framework for Program Quality

Our combined experience suggests a set of four broad research and policy themes as ways of organizing the major lessons from program experience and research and defining the critical building blocks for effective youth programs. While by no means the only framework, they represent an effort to present a growing body of research in a clear and understandable way.

Youth Development

The first of these themes is the need to integrate the ideas of youth
and adolescent development into youth program design and to provide
developmentally appropriate experiences (including work experience)
for young people as part of every employment and training initiative.
Most employment and training programs today have been designed for
adults and older youth, with relatively little attention paid to the developmental needs of younger adolescents. But the research on adolescent
development is clear that young people bring a different set of characteristics and developmental tasks to education and training than do
adults. In the words of two knowledgeable practitioners, "youth coming to second-chance programs are undergoing the psychological,
emotional, and social development that is an inherent part of the passage through adolescence." They are trying to establish an independent
identity, learning to think in new ways, testing out new roles and relationships, learning about different behaviors and strategies. For young
people to make the successful transition to adulthood and employability, they need an opportunity to practice those new skills and to master
these developmental tasks. (See Smith and Gambone 1992; see also
Gambone 1993.)

There are three related sets of implications and basic criteria that
flow from this theme:

1. Program designs need to be age and stage appropriate. In broad
   terms, programs for younger participants need to be more exploratory in nature, have more variety in their activities, and include
   more group than individual work. Materials and activities for
   younger participants (particularly middle school programs)
   should not simply be "dumbed-down" versions of those used
   with older youth or adults.

2. All youth employment programs need to be developmentally oriented and include a range of opportunities for young people to
   engage in developmentally appropriate activities. Perhaps the
   most critical of these is an opportunity to participate in a task-
   based relationship with an adult. It is through the development of
   ongoing relationships with adults—workplace supervisors, men-
   tors, case managers, or others—that young people have a chance

to test out new roles, practice relating to adults in work-related settings, learn about adult responsibilities and expectations, and test out their skills. But other elements of program design are developmentally important as well. Young people also need opportunities to develop positive peer relationships, to demonstrate competency (and hence build self-esteem, and to gain experience in dealing with a variety of work and social situations. Finally, young people also need an opportunity to review and reflect on what they are experiencing and learning so that the lessons of their own experience have a chance to be integrated into daily thinking and behavior.

Not surprisingly, well-structured work experiences offer many of these opportunities: task- based relationships with adults, peer relationships, and opportunities to learn and exercise skills and achievement and to function in a variety of settings and situations. This is a critical point, because *in this context,* work experience becomes a tool for youth in employability development and an integral part of the adolescent development process rather than a final outcome. One implication of this is the need to build work experience back into youth program design as a basic element. A second is a new emphasis on the *quality* of work experience (in terms of the quality of the supervision and the skills required) as a key program effectiveness criterion.

It is also important to recognize, however, that other experiences can supplement work in providing developmental opportunities. Much of the emphasis of the youth development movement is on the importance of providing positive, structured experiences for young people, including community service and recreation. Again, the point here is to create opportunities for young people to develop the broader social, emotional, and cognitive experiences that they need and will draw on in the workplace.

3. A youth-centered approach also requires an assessment process that can identify the needs and developmental stages of young participants and link them to appropriate services. As will become evident later in this paper, a high-quality assessment system is one of the program effectiveness criteria that relates to all aspects of program design and management.

Connecting Work and Learning

The second major theme is the importance of strengthening the link between work and learning and of providing opportunities to develop basic and cognitive skills in a "real world" context. This theme lies at the heart of much of the transformation of employment and training policy during the last decade, dating back to the 1986 JTPA Amendments which required, for the first time, the integration of basic skills instruction in the Summer Youth Employment and Training Program. The benefits of combining basic skills education and occupational training has also been one of the long-term lessons from the Job Corps and the YEDPA demonstrations and directly informed projects such as the Jobstart demonstration.[1]

More recently, educational research on cognitive development and the myriad reports on the growing demand for applied basic and higher order thinking skills in the "high performance workplace" have led to a new sophistication and understanding of the work and learning connection. Whereas the lesson from YEDPA and the Job Corps was "combine work and learning," the lessons from SCANS, America's Choice, and similar studies is "integrate work and learning by teaching basic skills in work-related settings." In effect we have learned that simply combining basic skills education and work in the same program is not enough. If young people are to learn to use their skills in the workplace of the future, they need to learn and practice those skills in a work-related setting.[2]

There are a number of implications of an integrated work and learning strategy for program design and management:

1. Both worksites and classrooms need to provide opportunities for active, hands-on learning using work-related materials and situations. In the Summer Beginnings program, practitioners spoke of the need to create "learning-rich work" by making the worksite a learning laboratory through the use of work-based curriculum and instruction. In the same vein, project participants also spoke of "transforming classrooms" by organizing the classroom into high performance, task-based work organizations and by using real work situations and projects as the basis for in-school learning.

Integral to this transformation are a number of fundamental changes in the way in which learning, teaching, and supervision are organized. At the core of the transformed classroom and worksite is the idea of active learning, where youth are actively engaged in individual and team-oriented projects where *they* research, plan, implement, and evaluate the work. In that context, teachers become guides, coaches and facilitators rather than lecturers, and need to bring an understanding of workplace skills and how to create situations where young people can learn and use those skills. Worksite supervisors also take on a somewhat different role, with a commitment to learning and an understanding of how to create learning opportunities on the job. Finally, worksite supervisors and teachers need to be able to work together so that classroom-based and worksite-based learning reinforce each other.

2. Programs also need to develop a broad set of workplace-related basic skills that meet the needs and expectations of employers. One of the major elements of the work and learning connection is the need to interpret "basic skills" in the broadest possible context (the SCANS term is "workplace know-how") and to teach not only the foundation skills (reading, writing, calculation), but the social and interpersonal skills needed to function in a flexible, interactive workplace. To accomplish that goal, once again, programs need to provide opportunities for participants to practice a wide variety of skills—teamwork, communication, problem solving, and others—in a practical setting. Here, too, one might note, a well-structured and supervised workplace provides at least one setting in which skills can be learned and practiced in context.

3. Ongoing assessment needs to be an integral part of program design, and the assessment approach needs to match the skills being measured. Few of the skills and competencies included in "workplace know-how" can be measured through traditional paper and pencil, multiple choice tests. In order to assess workplace-related skills effectively, programs need to adopt a mix of performance-based assessment strategies.

4. Finally, the research and practice associated with school-to-work transition also makes clear that programs need a clear connection from the educational process into the broader labor market—a career plan and path to education or employment that reduces the "milling around" common to young people in the labor market and that helps young people ensure that they are gaining the skills they need. In the language of the School-to-Work Opportunities Act, these "connecting services," which include career counseling, job search assistance, and the like represent the link between an integrated work and learning strategy and its ultimate outcome of a job.

Extending Services Over Time

The third basic theme is the need to develop a *sequence* of services that extends over time as well as a comprehensive *mix* of services. Experience, common sense, and research point in the same direction: the more at risk the population, the more extensive services must be to achieve substantial employment and income impacts. In the same vein, to the extent that we view employability development as a *developmental process* rather than a one-time *intervention*, we need to provide the capacity for young people to move through a series of programs and learning experiences over an often extended period of time.

Accomplishing these goals, however, requires a serious rethinking about both program design and our expectations about how young people gain the skills and experience needed to be employable. In many ways, our existing employment and training system is constructed on the assumption that young people (and adults) enter a program and stay there until they are job-ready. Within that paradigm, employability development is viewed as a one-time intervention, and longer-term services simply means staying within a single program for a longer period of time.

But research and personal experiences in the labor market point to the fact that for many youth, education and the acquisition of career-related skills and experience take place in stages, and often in fits and starts. Research on both high school dropouts and college students tells us that many young people drop out and back into the educational process over a period of time. Reports from the Jobstart demonstration, New Chance, and other programs for youth also tell us that young people are regularly forced by external factors to interrupt their education and training—to care for children, earn a living, or deal with a family crisis—even when a full set of "comprehensive" supports are available. Research on the entry of young people into the labor market also argues that initially youth often move from job to job (and possibly program to program) until they find a "match" that fits their needs and lets them move forward.

The point here is a simple one: as we think about longer-term, comprehensive services for young people, we need to recognize that long-term employability development is often made up of a series of short-term commitments. At the program and "system" level, we need to design strategies that allow for this "in and out" process and that provide opportunities to sequence education and training in a flexible manner over a period of time. Some of the implications for program design include:

1. Individual programs and community-level "systems" need to provide for flexible entry and exit through a developmental sequence of programs and services. The idea of open entry/open exit within programs is a familiar one, and has long provided a means for youth and adults to match program participation with the other demands on their time. What is needed in addition is a mechanism for open entry and exit within a *system* of programs, so that young people can complete a set of services, leave to work, and return to upgrade to the next skill level over a period of time, without having to terminate and re-enroll or lose eligibility for services. An essential part of the process is the provision of postprogram follow-up services that provide an ongoing point of contact for participants as they move back and forth between programs or between training and work.

2. Programs and communities also need the capacity to match youth to appropriate services and to track progress over time. The basic element here is a communitywide assessment and case management system that has the capacity to identify interests and needs on an ongoing basis, develop clearly defined goals and

plans, help young people move between programs, provide longer-term follow-up services and track progress over time. To accomplish this, youth-serving programs and institutions need to establish mechanisms for sharing assessment data, common protocols for accessing services, and a shared referral process.

3. Programs and communities need to establish communitywide interagency partnerships to provide for both long-term and comprehensive services. Long-term and comprehensive services require a communitywide strategy to ensure the availability of services, to provide for easy transition from program to program (or from summer to school year, for example), and to provide a broad mix of funding to support a flexible mix of services.

4. Finally, the ideal system will also provide a variety of program strategies for participants to choose from. One of the clear lessons from experience is that no single program strategy works for all youth. Not only do programs need to address different age and skill levels among participants, but ideally participants should have an opportunity to select a program that matches their learning style. We know, for example, that 25 percent of the youth in Conservation and Service Corps programs drop out within the first month, presumably because they realize that the corps approach does not work for them (Branch, Liederman, and Smith 1987). A "youth-centered" or "customer-driven" approach suggests that the more options a community can offer young people for acquiring employability skills, the more likely a young person will find a good "match" and gain the skills needed for employment.

Promoting Quality in a Decentralized System

As a largely decentralized system both locally (through networks of service providers) and nationally, the employment and training system faces a constant challenge in promoting the quality and effectiveness of its programs. As the emphasis on providing services to more "at-risk" youth grows, and as the employment and training system moves towards the provision of more complex, comprehensive, and longer-term services, the issues of program quality and effectiveness are becoming more critical. One of the implications of these developments is the need for significant and strategic investment in capacity building among employment and training professionals. We need to recognize that in the same way that American competitiveness depends on the development of a highly skilled workforce, the quality of employment and training services also ultimately depends on building the skills of the professionals responsible for implementing them.

While capacity building is key, the implementation of effective strategies for defining and measuring program quality is also vital. For the employment and training system, this means an investment in ongoing assessment and evaluation and a system for performance management based on clearly defined goals and outcomes. In that context, three key elements stand out in promoting quality and effectiveness at the local level include:

1. *Active investment in capacity building and professional development.* Professional development needs to move beyond occasional conference attendance and training on compliance issues. Effective capacity building needs to take place on a regular basis and to address such service-related issues as adolescent development, workplace skills and the changing labor market, curriculum and instruction for work-based learning, and performance-based assessment to ensure that all staff have the skills and knowledge needed to put effective programs into operation.

2. *An assessment system that can provide accurate information for matching youth to services, assessing gains, and tracking progress through a sequence of services.* As suggested in earlier sections, an effective assessment system is individualized and ongoing, performance-based, and functionally oriented. Assessment information on the skills of participants, skill gains, the degree to which program services match the needs of participants, and relative program performance provide a powerful tool for program management and continuous improvement.

3. *A clearly defined, meaningful set of program outcomes that form the basis for an ongoing performance management system.* An effective performance management system might include a clearly defined set of goals and participant outcomes, developed

with employers and the community (perhaps beginning with the SCANS skills as a framework); strategies for evaluating both program performance (through assessment) and "customer" satisfaction; a means for establishing accountability for performance, and a process for reporting results to the broader community.

Summary

We conclude then that quick fixes are ineffective and that long-term coherent youth development services are essential; that current quality assurance mechanisms are inadequate and must be replaced by higher standards, outcome measures and professional development capabilities; that youth program governance is fragmented and must be replaced by a national system of youth program planning and accountability; that there are islands of excellence in a sea of mediocrity which require bridges to connect best practices; that "administrivia" gets in the way and needs to be replaced by a seamless, simplified management information system. The elements outlined here are by no means comprehensive. But they represent a broad framework that, we believe, can stand as a starting point for a more substantial discussion of program quality and effectiveness. As national policy continues to move towards a more youth- and development-focused vision of employability development, we need to find new ways of translating that vision into the day-to-day operations of local programs and practitioners. Clearly, one step in that process is the translation of research and experience into principles and criteria that can be used by local policy makers and professionals to guide program design and to establish standards that promote high-quality services for young people.

For those reasons and more, the National Youth Employment Coalition, a composite of more than seventy youth-serving organizations, recommended to the Secretary of Labor in 1994 that a White House Youth Development Summit be convened to launch a process to develop national youth development goals, that the process lead to the creation of a national professional development capacity, including the establishment of accrediting mechanisms for organizations seeking to serve at-risk youth, and that the Department of Labor conduct national demonstrations to learn better how to help out-of-school youth successfully join the workforce. In a year in which just defending the current limited youth program funding was an overwhelming challenge, none of that has happened. But responsibility resides not only at the national level. States need to be experimenting and federal agencies need to supply cross-program waiver authority to facilitate that experimentation. Local agencies, such as school districts and Private Industry Councils, need to be involved in local demonstrations for collaborative program funding, services, and management information systems. It is our conviction that from such collaborative effort can come:

For Youth—Hope

Too many young people have no hope because they are surrounded by the despair of their families, friends, and neighbors. As one young program participant told program operators, "If it wasn't for the support and promise this program provides to me, my mother would be going to another funeral—mine. Instead, this young man is fulfilling his hopes, working full time, and even writing a play. In a recent city by city NYEC dialogue, young people asked for the respect of their elders. They demonstrated why they should be included in the development of plans and programs to help them. Though the services and supports current youth programs can provide are less comprehensive and developmental than what youth need, they are, until something better comes along, the last, best hope for many of our nation's youth.

For Youth Programs—Positive Youth Development

We have an opportunity to build on what works. Youth programs will need to refine or redefine their vision and purpose. Some programs will need to become more coherent, intensive, flexible, and responsive. Others need improved accountability mechanisms or more rigorous oversight. Some need to build capacity through concerted staff development and training. A few may need to be eliminated. All programs need to insure that they treat youth individually, taking into account age-related and gender-related needs, and holistically viewing the youth as a whole person. In short, programs and services must be coherent, client-centered, and readily accessible—these are the key elements in positive youth development. But the last thing needed is abandonment.

For Current Programs—Change

The current emphasis on short-term services, quick job placement, and little or no follow-through, and lack of coherent government leadership in encouraging collaborations across programs provides a flawed framework for a youth development system. However, we must not allow our own ability to "get it right" to serve as a convenient excuse to abandon our neediest youth. Young people who are out of school, out of work, disaffected, and disconnected, or in school with little motivation to learn or acquire skills, still need to become productive and contributing adults. And they won't get there from here without help. We need to connect all of our youth-serving efforts—across and among federal, state, and local, public and private—to weave a youth development web from childhood to early adolescence to adulthood. Within this framework, a job would not be considered an "end," but merely one of many developmental benchmarks along the way.

For the Federal Government—Investment and Leadership

Though its role is currently being called into question, it is essential that the federal government continue to invest in the future of all youth, especially at-risk and out-of-school youth. Further, it is incumbent upon the federal government to provide the coherent leadership needed to develop policies and devise incentives to integrate youth development initiatives across agencies, among sectors, and throughout the nation. This investment and leadership will shape the state of America's workforce and could significantly determine our place in the world in the next century.

For Communities—Collaboration

Community resources must be combined and leveraged in ways that support the development of all young people. Customer surveys or community town hall-type meetings can help ensure that programs are designed to meet identified needs of both youth and employers. We need to make special efforts to provide youth with meaningful jobs and work experience in their own neighborhoods and within their larger communities. We need a public commitment on all levels to building a youth development system that embodies the best education, training, guidance, and supports in the world for all youth in our communities where they live, learn, play, and work. If by the time these words are published and read the Congress of the United States has fulfilled its threats to devolve all such responsibilities upon states and communities, providing reduced resources in the process, there may be no other choice.

NOTES

1. The initial goal of adding academic enrichment to the summer jobs program was to reduce summer learning loss. One of the major positive findings of the Summer Training and Education (STEP) program was that summer learning loss *did* take place in the absence of any intervention and that programs like STEP, which combined a half-day of education with a half-day of work, could effectively reduce learning loss among disadvantaged teens. See Grossman and Sipe (1992) and Walker and Vilella-Velez (1992). For the Job Corps and YEDPA findings, see Hahn and Lerman (1985). Also see Auspos (1987).

2. See U.S. Department of Labor (1991) and Commission on the Skills of the American Workforce (1990). One of the more influential of the educational researchers on this issue is Lauren Resnick (1987). See her paper for her argument on the need to teach in "real world" settings.

References

Auspos, Patricia. 1987. *Launching JOBSTART: A Demonstration for Dropouts in the JTPA System.* New York: MDRC.

Branch, Alvia, Sally Liederman, and Thomas J. Smith. 1987. *Youth Conservation and Service Corps: Findings from a National Evaluation.* Philadelphia: Public/Private Ventures.

Commission on the Skills of the American Workforce. 1990. *America's Choice: High Skills or Low Wages!* Rochester, NY: National Center on Education and the Economy.

Gambone, Michelle Alberti. 1993. *Strengthening Programs for Youth: Promoting Adolescent Development in the JTPA System.* Philadelphia: Public/Private Ventures.

Grossman, Jean Baldwin, and Cynthia Sipe. 1992. *Summer Training and Education Program: Report on Long-Term Impacts.* Philadelphia: Public/Private Ventures.

Hahn, Andrew, and Robert Lerman. 1985. *What Works in Youth Employment Policy?* Washington, DC: National Planning Association.

Resnick, Lauren. 1987. "Learning In School and Out," *Educational Researcher* 16: 13-20.

Smith, Thomas J., and Michelle Alberti Gambone. 1992. "Effectiveness of Federally Funded Employment Training Strategies for Youth." In *Dilemmas in Youth Employment Programming: Findings from the Youth Research Technical Assistance Project.* Washington, DC: U.S. Department of Labor.

U.S. Department of Labor. 1991. *Wlhat Work Requires of Schools. A SCANS Report for America 2000.* Washington, DC: Secretary's Commission on Achieving Necessary Skills.

Walker, Gary, and Frances Vilella-Velez. 1992. *Anatomy of a Demonstration: The Summer Training and Education Program (STEP) from Pilot Through Replication and Post-program Impacts.* Philadelphisa: Public/Private Ventures.

CHAPTER 14

Welfare Reform

Lessons from the JOBS Program

Irene Lurie
Colletta Moser

For three decades, Sar Levitan chronicled and analyzed efforts to reduce poverty and reform the welfare system, particularly through employment and training programs. From one of his earlier publications on the topic, *Work and Welfare Go Together* (with Martha Rein and David Marwick 1972 and 1976) through one more recent, *Jobs for JOBS: Toward a Work Based Welfare System* (with Frank Gallo 1993), Sar Levitan emphasized the symbiotic relationship between poverty reduction, welfare reform, and employment.

The Current Context

Today, the federal government is once again considering a major reform of the Aid to Families with Dependent Children (AFDC) program, one that would make more fundamental changes than any reforms enacted since passage of the Social Security Act of 1935. After campaigning on a promise to "end welfare as we know it," President Clinton proposed legislation that would move toward imposing a two-year time limit on a family's eligibility for AFDC payments. After the Republicans captured control of the 104th Congress, leaders in both houses sought not only to impose time limits but to transform the open-ended federal matching grants that help finance state AFDC payments into block grants that would cap federal payments to the states and give them wider discretion in designing their AFDC programs. Meanwhile, at least half of the states have seized the initiative to reform their welfare programs by requesting waivers from federal law, and the Clinton administration has approved many of these waivers and signaled its openness to new approaches.

What has brought us to the brink of scrapping the arrangement of sixty years and moving toward time limits, block grants and, thereby, an end to welfare as a statutory entitlement for many poor families? Why is the nation considering reforms that Sar Levitan, as both scholar and humanitarian, would have undoubtedly deplored? Certainly, pledges by both the President and Congress to rein in the federal budget deficit have motivated their proposals to reform the welfare system, while governors argue that welfare costs are a heavy burden on state finances. But in actuality, federal expenditures for AFDC accounted for only 1 percent of all federal outlays in 1993 and state expenditures for the program comprised an average of only 3.2 percent of total state expenditures in 1994 (National Association of State Budget Officers 1995, p. 87). Additional factors beyond the financial burden of welfare expenditures must explain the draconian changes being considered by Congress and implemented by some of the states.

From our observations of recent events, we see three sets of additional explanations for the current focus on welfare reform. One set of explanations can be detected in the changing values about the role of women in the labor force and about the responsibility of parents for the support of themselves and their children. A second set can be found in the apparent inability of government to implement programs that significantly increase the work effort and earning capacity of welfare recipients and decrease welfare dependency and costs. The newest welfare employment program, enacted with great fanfare in 1988, is in many respects an improvement over previous programs, but was not given the chance to fulfil its promise. Finally, it is clear that political actors stand to gain by taking a tough, visible stance toward welfare reform and that even largely symbolic actions serve a useful political function, perhaps more useful than the financially costly and administratively difficult tasks involved in program implementation.

Methodology

The primary basis for these conclusions is a study of the implementation of the Job Opportunities and Basic Skills Training (JOBS) program created by the Family Support Act of 1988. The implementation study followed the progress of ten states as they moved through successive stages of developing their programs. It focused on the design and structure of the JOBS program, on the processing of individuals through the program, and on the resulting changes in the opportunities for recipients and in the demands placed upon them. No attempt was made to measure the effects of the JOBS program in reducing welfare dependency and costs or in increasing participants' earnings.[1] The study's primary question was not "Is the JOBS program effective?" but "What is the JOBS program?" The ten states, chosen to be broadly representative of the nation and illustrative of a range of state experience in implementing JOBS, include Maryland, Michigan, Minnesota, Mississippi, New York, Oklahoma, Oregon, Pennsylvania, Tennessee, and Texas.[2] To examine the implementation of JOBS at the front lines, three local sites were selected in each of the ten states: a large urban area, a mid-sized city, and a small or rural community.

The methodology for the study was field network research, an approach used by Richard Nathan (1982) and others to examine the responses of states and localities to other federal initiatives. The essential feature of this approach is a network of policy analysts in each state who collect and analyze information using a common instrument and then report their jurisdictions' responses in a uniform format. The first round of field research was conducted soon after the mandatory implementation date of October 1990, the second round during the summer of 1991, and the third round during the summer of 1992; the field associates updated their findings during 1994 or 1995.[3]

This paper begins with a review of the changing values underlying the progression of employment programs for AFDC recipients that began in 1967. It then briefly highlights some of the major lessons about implementing welfare employment programs reached by the ten-state study. After taking this broad view, we focus on Michigan, which served as a leader in rousing the wave of sentiment that encouraged the Clinton administration to recommend time- limited welfare benefits and approve the states' requests for waivers from federal law, and that served as a model for Republicans in the 104th Congress as they pressed for welfare block grants and an end to the welfare entitlement.

Changing Values

The Social Security Act of 1935, which created the ADC program, was written with the expectation that mothers would stay home with their children, and it consequently did nothing to encourage mothers to work. Few mothers with young children were in the workforce and "a mother's place is in the home" was the dominant value. Anticipating that the typical ADC mother would be a widow and that the ADC program would wither away as coverage for survivors expanded with the maturation of the Social Security system, the Act's framers gave relatively little thought to the ADC program's design, much less to the issue of mothers' employment. In addition, the high jobless rate during the Great Depression years did not make employment appear to be a promising source of income for people with little work experience, particularly mothers burdened with the care of young children.

By the 1960s, when the nation next focused attention on the plight of the poor, several important changes had occurred. While most widows were covered by Social Security, as had been expected, the caseload continued to grow as the number of divorced, separated, or never-married mothers increased and the number of poor, female-headed families rose. The expectation that mothers would stay home to care for their children faded as the labor force participation of women rose, increasing from 27 percent in 1940 to 58.8 percent in 1994, with a much more dramatic increase among married women with children, especially those with children under the age of six. With middle-class mothers going off to work and a strong economy generating new jobs, employment became a more feasible alternative to welfare than it had been during the 1930s. As a result of these developments, in 1967 Congress required that all states operate an employment and training program for AFDC recipients, the Work Incentive (WIN) program. In 1971, as AFDC caseloads continued to mushroom, Congress mandated states to impose a work test that required recipients to register with the WIN program and accept offers of suitable employment.

Despite the WIN program and the work test, the number of families headed by single mothers and the AFDC caseload continued to rise. When Reagan became president, his determination to halt this trend led to the enactment of federal legislation that gave states several new options for encouraging welfare recipients to work. The Reagan years were also notable for a shift in attitudes among both conservatives and liberals concerning the role of government in assisting the poor. In the wake of harsh criticism of welfare programs, many political leaders, policy analysts, and scholars argued that government should place greater demands on single parents (Murray 1984; Mead 1986). Government has an obligation to give financial assistance to poor parents, they argued, but parents have an obligation to help themselves become economically self-sufficient (National Governors' Association 1987). The idea that welfare involves a set of *mutual* obligations gained popularity both in statehouses and Congress. With the support of the National Governors' Association and its chairman, Governor Bill Clinton, Congress sought to put this idea into place with the Family Support Act of 1988.

The Family Support Act was hailed as landmark legislation that represented a new consensus on the nature of the "social contract" between government and welfare recipients. As Senator Moynihan, a chief architect of the legislation, described the contract: "Congress laid down a set of mutual obligations. Society owed single mothers support while they acquired the means of self-sufficiency; mothers owed society the effort to become self- sufficient" (1990, p. C1). To enable parents to become self-sufficient, the Act eliminated the WIN program and created the JOBS program in its place.

The JOBS program is like the WIN program in many respects, but it is stronger (1) by providing more federal funding for services and child care, (2) by requiring states to offer more types of services, and (3) by setting clear goals that states must meet in order to receive their full share of federal matching funds. States can provide a wide range of services under the JOBS umbrella, including virtually any type of education, training, or employment activity available to the general public and several work programs designed around the welfare grant. The Act emphasizes education by requiring states to offer any educational

activity below the postsecondary level that is appropriate to a participant's employment goal. The Act also strengthens the financial incentive for recipients to take a job by continuing to finance their child care
and Medicaid coverage for a year after they earn enough to become
ineligible for welfare. But like the AFDC program, the JOBS program
is a state responsibility, so whether it would lead to significant change
would depend on its implementation by the states and the agencies
operating the program at the local level.

Implementing the Jobs Program

Not surprisingly, the field research found that states implemented
the JOBS program in very diverse ways. Some of these differences
reflect the criteria for selecting the ten states, while others stem from
differences in the leadership and philosophy of elected and appointed
officials, the infrastructure of organizations with capacity to provide
JOBS services and child care, the organizational "culture" in the welfare agency, the strength of labor markets, and other factors. But the
field associates also found considerable similarity in certain aspects of
the states' implementation efforts, patterns that offer explanations for
the states' waiver initiatives, Clinton's proposal to reform welfare, and
the congressional Republican's efforts to dismantle the system.

The Mix and Supply of JOBS Services

JOBS implementation was generally incremental, with states building their programs upon the foundations laid by the WIN program and
the options introduced in the early 1980s, so that the states' prior experience in operating these programs set them moving on different paths.
Six of the study states—Maryland, Michigan, Minnesota, New York,
Oklahoma, and Pennsylvania—had fairly well-developed welfare
employment programs prior to passage of the Family Support Act.
These states had already charted a course consistent with the federal
legislation, and they expanded their programs to serve more people and
to bring a broader range of services into additional areas of the state.
With the exception of Michigan, which began with incremental

changes but then dramatically altered the design and organization of its program, the federal legislation supported and reinforced the initiatives these states had chosen earlier.

Another group of states—Mississippi, Tennessee, and Texas—had not taken advantage of the previous federal options to introduce major welfare-to-work initiatives. They did not have programs in place that could, with minor modifications, meet the requirements of the JOBS legislation. Their earlier approach to limiting welfare dependency and costs was to maintain low AFDC benefits rather than to operate strong employment and training programs. To increase the number of JOBS participants, the primary strategy of these states was to draw upon existing services that were free of charge to the welfare agency, particularly the activities financed by the Job Training Partnership Act and programs offered by public school systems and community colleges. In Texas, the welfare agency used its funding for child care to bargain for resources from other organizations.

Despite differences in the magnitude of their efforts, both groups of states placed a large share of JOBS participants into educational activities: adult literacy and other basic education, preparation for the GED examination, and both two- and four-year college programs. The focus on education reflects the intent of the federal legislation which, for the first time, mandated educational services as a major strategy to reduce welfare dependency. But the focus on education also indicates the educational deficits of many AFDC recipients and a recognition of the importance of education as an avenue of escape from poverty. Finally, educational services were frequently available at no cost to the JOBS program, and funding from the education system of some states was made available to match federal JOBS funds, compensating for inadequate funding from the welfare system.

Job skills training was emphasized in several states, particularly in Pennsylvania and Maryland, where JTPA was the contractor for JOBS services, and in the early days of Michigan's program, where skills training was available from both contractors and the adult education system. But the JOBS program was generally not training people for jobs that were likely to lift them well out of poverty. Many participants were being trained for clerical jobs, health-care related jobs, and other service-sector jobs that pay relatively low wages and offer few ladders to more lucrative employment.

In the absence of adequate job opportunities, requiring that welfare recipients work has remained an elusive goal of the JOBS program. Yet the field research did document some success in placing participants in jobs.

Both Oregon and Michigan began their JOBS program with an emphasis on education, although even Oregon initially assigned people with basic and vocational skills directly to training in job search techniques. After several years of this approach, however, state officials changed their program's strategy to emphasize job search as an "up front" activity. One rationale for up-front job search is that some recipients already possess the ability and skill to work in available jobs, so that job search serves as a screening device to separate people who are capable of working from those who need some sort of preparation for employment. Using job search in this way to identify "job ready" recipients enables the welfare agency to focus its education and training resources on people who are more disadvantaged. As discussed later, Michigan's switch to emphasize job search was one part of an ambitious plan by the governor to transform the "culture" of welfare— not by tinkering with the program design but by altering the gestalt of the entire system.

Not only was JOBS implementation incremental in most states, but administrators had limited resources for implementing a predetermined program model so that the design of the program was somewhat haphazard. Until the Family Support Act, federal legislation gave the states no goals regarding the participation of recipients in their WIN program, with the result that many people found the program to be little more than a paper process of registering for services that were never delivered. But the Family Support Act requires states to serve a minimum percent of the people who are required to participate in JOBS: 7 percent in 1990 and 1991, 11 percent in 1992 and 1993, 15 percent in 1994, and 20 percent by 1995.[4] These federally mandated participation rates drove the implementation effort. State funding for JOBS was limited, so that few states spent enough to draw down their full share of federal JOBS funds, and in Oregon, which did obtain its full share, the field associate argued that "under-funding of the entire program is a persistent and chronic problem." Because funds for the JOBS program were scarce, welfare agencies could not purchase enough education and training services to meet the participation rate. To get enough education and training slots, welfare agencies relied upon the programs of other organizations, such as public schools, the JTPA, and community colleges, for a supply of services. This meant that, in many areas, the JOBS program lacked control over the availability of services. The people served and the types of services offered were based not just on an assessment of each individual's need for services, but on the existing infrastructure of organizations and programs. So rather than implementing a clear program model, the programs of many states were "service-driven," placing recipients in the services that were available.

Expanding the types and quantity of education, training, and job search activities was generally easy when funds were available to purchase these services. Many organizations are willing and even eager to serve JOBS participants if they are paid in exchange, including local school districts, community colleges, and public, nonprofit, and proprietary training organizations. To say it another way, the supply of education, training, and employment services is elastic in response to increased funding, so that the capacity to deliver services is generally not a constraint in operating welfare employment programs. Other favorable news from the field research is that the willingness of organizations such as JTPA and the public school systems to supply services to JOBS participants free of charge, without payment of JOBS funds, was generally good. Interagency coordination of this type is often considered to be difficult, hindered by turf battles, conflicting agency goals, differences in eligibility rules and definitions of terms, and other incompatibilities. In the states and sites included in the study, the degree of interagency cooperation emerges as one of the success stories of JOBS implementation. Coordination was not good everywhere, but there was progress. The combination of a lack of funds for JOBS and the federally mandated participation rate was a powerful motivation for welfare agencies to develop formal and informal linkages with other agencies. Strong state and local leadership was most in evidence around issues of interagency coordination. But whether a lot more services can be obtained through coordination is an open question.

Administrative Challenges

Other aspects of operating the JOBS program proved more troublesome and help explain the impatience and dissatisfaction with the approach taken by both WIN and the JOBS program. In particular, the prosaic tasks involved in processing recipients through the program are difficult for administrators to monitor and control, especially when they involve the personal interaction between the caseworker and the client. Do caseworkers inform clients about the availability of JOBS services with enthusiasm? Do caseworkers have sufficient time to do an in-depth assessment of a client's abilities and needs? Do they make an effort to learn about the client's real interests and concerns? How much effort do they exert to find an appropriate school or training program or to locate child care that meets the client's needs? Thinking about these tasks are eye-glazing to policy makers and scholars who are uninterested in the internal workings of organizations, but whether the tasks are performed with energy and commitment or with a paper-pushing mentality can make the difference between a successful and unsuccessful program.[5]

A related challenging task was insuring that individuals conform to the federal mandate that they participate in the JOBS program. Some recipients were highly motivated to participate, but mandating the participation of recipients who were not motivated was far from a trivial matter. In order to impose a participation requirement, a program needs a supply of education, training, and employment services, as well as funding for child care. A welfare agency also needs to devote staff to monitoring participation and to operating the conciliation and sanctioning process for people who refuse to participate. A fair hearing is also a right for people whose benefits are being cut or terminated. The field associates found that some caseworkers thought the conciliation and sanctioning process was too time-consuming, too much of a hassle. They also learned that participation in the JOBS program was in practice voluntary in certain states. The high cost in terms of staff time connected with mandating participation in welfare employment programs and requiring that recipients accept suitable employment goes a long way in explaining the current popularity of time-limits on welfare eligibility.

More generally, the field work indicated an imbalance between our expectations for welfare offices and the resources and respect that we give caseworkers in welfare agencies. Some framers of the Family Support Act argued that JOBS would change the "culture" of welfare agencies by shifting the focus of their attention from administering welfare benefits to providing employment and training. But the field associates found that state and local governments were reluctant to budget more money for the staff of their welfare agencies. Even when a lack of welfare agency staff was perceived to be the major bottleneck in implementing JOBS, governments failed to hire more caseworkers. In Michigan, the state welfare agency hired more staff only when the state received the Child Care and Development Block Grant and caseworkers could be hired entirely on federal money.

The high cost of child care may be one of the major constraints to expanding the JOBS program. Participants could tap into the services of other agencies for education, training, and job search, but few other funding streams were available for funding child care. The total cost of JOBS services was about $1.1 billion in 1992 and 1993. The total cost of child care in 1992 was at least $755 million, or almost three-quarters as large as the cost of JOBS services.

Finding and creating appropriate job opportunities for participants has often proven to be difficult. One JOBS component—work supplementation, or grant diversion, where a recipient's benefit is paid to an employer as a wage subsidy—is a potentially powerful tool for encouraging private sector employers to hire welfare recipients. But few sites made use of this option: 0.1 percent of participants were in work supplementation. The Family Support Act required that these be "new jobs"; employers were reluctant to hire welfare recipients when they could hire unemployed people with more recent work experience; they did not want to deal with the paperwork of hiring welfare recipients; and there may also be stigma attached to people on welfare. The poor track record of work supplementation suggests that creating jobs is not a simple task.[6]

State Welfare Politics: The Case of Michigan

Michigan represented an unusual departure in the study primarily because of its dramatic shifts in program emphasis from the human capital investment model to the job search/immediate employment model. But the real implementation of the change, a program called "Work First," did not take place until October 1994--four years after we began our study of the JOBS program. Along the way, however, the Michigan experience illustrated the power of gubernatorial leadership in changing the focus of state welfare programs and setting an example for Congress.

Michigan had been one of the states selected for the ten-state study as one with considerable experience in operating employment-based welfare programs. The welfare/employment program in Michigan at the time of the implementation of the federal JOBS program was called the MOST program, and it continued to be called the MOST program. In fact, in Michigan as in some of the other states, keeping local titles for the new JOBS program often meant that even many of the Department of Social Services employees didn't realize that a new federal program was in place.

In order to put the programmatic changes in perspective, we need to examine changes in political leadership and in the economy that occurred during this period. With respect to political changes, the most significant change was, of course, the election of Governor John Engler, a state senator from the central area of Michigan. Although Engler, a conservative Republican with a farm background, had considerable experience in state government, his election was unexpected. Many attributed his victory to the enthusiasm of his conservative supporters and a "poor voter turnout" of Democrats in the Wayne County (Detroit) area, by far the largest concentration of voters in the state.

Among other things, Engler campaigned on a platform of welfare reform. With this goal in mind, one of the first controversial moves with respect to welfare changes was the elimination of the state-funded General Assistance (GA) program and it's employment program "Job Start." One of the justifications for the elimination of the GA program was that it was necessary in order to minimize cuts in the AFDC program. The GA program focused on single welfare recipients, whereas AFDC was a "family-oriented" program. The welfare philosophy of the Engler administration was articulated in the document, "To Strengthen Michigan Families." This document became the cohesive philosophic element in the evolution of the Michigan JOBS program.

But the story of the changes in the implementation of the federal JOBS program does not result from these political changes alone. Michigan was, after all, in the midst of a serious recession at the time of these political changes. The opportunity for a dramatic shift in demands on welfare recipients with respect to JOBS programmatic options was limited by the high unemployment rate and the limitations of the state fiscal ability to meet the federal JOBS match. Thus, it appeared to us that the major changes in the AFDC employment program focused on such things as getting waivers for greater earned employment limits and restructuring the daycare program that had serious administrative problems. So in the second year of this review of the implementation of the JOBS program, the emphasis of the Michigan MOST program was still on (1) education as the primary activity of the participants; and (2) priority in serving participants being given to volunteers, the self-initiated, and those without high school completion. It should be noted that while the educational activities included both adult education through the k-12 program and postsecondary education, the latter activity was classified as "self-initiated," since postsecondary education was not a component in the MOST plan. Tuition was not paid. Moreover, although clear patterns in terms of treatment of the participants emerged among the individualized sites in the study, there was no real dictated state policy for client flow except for those participants who fell under the federal policy with respect to age and lack of high school completion.

Then during the second year or so of this study, the Michigan MOST program developed a program to utilize the state's existing educational institutional structure, including its highly developed system of publicly paid adult education; this program became eligible for compensation under the federal JOBS program. Moreover, the state was willing to appropriate additional education funds for this program called EDGE.

EDGE projects represented a holistic approach to the education and employment barriers faced by MOST participants who did not have a high school diploma, providing an array of services, such as assessment, job readiness, customized basic education, customized skills training, job placement, and often transportation to classes and on-site child care. While the results of the EDGE program were somewhat mixed, in some counties it was clearly a success in meeting the needs of many hard-to-serve MOST participants, such as those in Port Huron, a rural county in the "Thumb" area of Michigan. The results of a small study indicated considerable success with the program as exceeding its goals in some cases in terms of education and employment outcomes.

It was even successful in recruiting women for the nontraditional Building Trades Technician program, which placed its participants at the highest wage rate.

The EDGE program was said to be too costly and was eliminated in order to use funds for the most significant programmatic change in Michigan's welfare/employment program: Work First, a program as its name implies, that focuses on immediate employment as opposed to education and training.

Another important development in the evolution of Michigan's current welfare/employment program was the implementation of a concept called the "Social Contract." The Social Contract stipulated that if welfare recipients were to receive benefits from the government they had a contractual obligation to do something for those benefits. Thus recipients were to sign a contract that they would do at least 20 hours a week of some meaningful activity of betterment, including such things as volunteering, going to school, working, or engaging in certain health or nutritional activities for their family.

The Social Contract is now a mandatory part of the Michigan program. It represents a significant departure from the JOBS implementation program as we first viewed it. In fact, it was at first voluntary and, in a sense, it seemed more of a substitute for the federal program. Moreover, unlike the EDGE program, which was extremely costly, the Social Contract did not involve contracting with outside agencies and was relatively cheap to administer.

Another important undertone about the MOST program developing in mid-1993 was that it was taking on more of a mandatory tone (even though technically participation had always been mandatory). When we first began reviewing the program, the "20-hour rule," the federally mandated requirement that JOBS participants be involved in program activities for at least 20 hours per week, was understood by administrators and caseworkers in only one of the Michigan sites. Even at the state level, administrators seemed to be looking the other way. Later, however, along with the notion of 20-hours in an activity under the Social Contract, the 20 hours rule for regular MOST/JOBS participants was being emphasized and noted in agreements with subcontractors. EDGE participants frequently exceeded those hours.

Beyond the 20 hour rule, the MOST program took on a more punitive tone as it became the "punishment" for those who did not fulfill their Social Contract. In other words, those recipients not complying with the Social Contract became a priority group for the MOST program. So the notion of self-initiating into MOST began to diminish. Also, in interviews conducted at the state and local sites, we found the sanction process being taken more seriously than during the first phase of our study.

Why then if Michigan's implementation of the JOBS programs was as good, if not better than, that of the majority of the other states in our study and already had a higher than average percentage of AFDC recipients employed, did Michigan change its modus operandi? Governor Engler, in a February 1994 address to the National Press Club on "Welfare Reform," focused on the Michigan Model, which emphasizes employment for welfare recipients, noting that over 25 percent of Michigan's AFDC recipients were employed compared with about 10 percent nationally. In part the answer seems to lie in the political philosophy of the Governor's office, especially with his second election looming. The "get tough on welfare" stance and the elimination of General Assistance had brought considerable national recognition to Governor Engler. Now there were further political criticisms by conservatives in Michigan of the length of time welfare people were spending in education—particularly higher education. The Governor preached the philosophy that people could go to school at night, i.e., work and go to school on their own. This notion too had considerable public appeal. So the program philosophy began to move from one of education support to early employment advocation.

But often overlooked in the analysis of the programmatic change in Michigan is the change in the Michigan economy. The condition of the Michigan economy, with its above-average degree of cyclicality, changed dramatically over the period of this study. In November 1994, Michigan's unemployment rate was 4.6 percent, the lowest in over twenty years. In contrast, at one point in the early 1990s, with its unemployment rate slightly over 10 percent, Michigan was one of the greatest labor surplus states in the United States. For a number of months in the late 1994-95 period, the unemployment rate had been at or below the national average, with employers complaining of worker shortages.

So a strategic development in late 1994 was that a new program, Work First, would become a part of the state's solution to the labor shortage situation. Welfare recipients would be turned over to the JTPA offices to be given job readiness classes, job search, and employment as quickly as possible (a minimum of a 30-day test of the job market). The welfare program was to be a part of the state's economic development strategy. This strategy highlights the change that occurred—from a program that focused on the needs and wants of the welfare recipient, (e.g., self-initiated programs) to one that focuses on the employer's labor needs for economic development. In traditional welfare and employment/training programs, the recipient is viewed as the "client" or "customer"; in economic development programs, the employer, i.e., the firm, is typically viewed as the client. One hopes that there is a synergistic relationship between the two goals and client groups.

Finally, it should be noted that one of the administrative actions of Governor Engler, which took place early in 1994 and which contributed to the economic development thrust of the welfare program, was the institution of the "Michigan Jobs Commission." It was at first a temporary agency, but has recently become a formal agency, the last one allowed by Michigan's constitution.

From eight different units of state government, the Michigan Jobs Commission consolidated staff and 35 programs related to job generation and worker preparation. One effect of the consolidation was that the Michigan Jobs Commission, which now also included JTPA, assumed much of the JOBS responsibility for employment and training services, taking this role out of the welfare agencies. While the action was indicative of the Engler administration's taste for consolidation and block grants in the employment and training area, it may also have been an attempt to change the culture of the program, as in Massachusetts. Robert D. Behn, in *Leadership Counts: Lessons for Public Managers* (1991) gives a vivid account of how Governor Dukakis of Massachusetts and his appointees in the welfare agency changed the attitudes and behaviors of caseworkers so they strongly motivated recipients to prepare for work and seek employment.

However, it should be noted that even without block grants, Governor Engler and Department of Social Services Director Miller were able to make a series of changes to focus more attention on the employment-based nature of the welfare program. A strong and coherent document early on presented a strategic vision for welfare reform.

Besides, Engler was able to gain national visibility with his welfare policy; there were political rewards to taking a tough stance on welfare.

The state of the economy has a considerable impact on the effectiveness of not only work-based welfare programs in general, but also on the choice of program model: human capital investment or job search/ job placement. Early findings from the JOBS evaluation being performed by MDRC in the early 1990s show that Grand Rapids, Michigan was successful in increasing average earnings and reducing welfare expenditures by using a job search model. But the welfare agency in Grand Rapids is atypical. First, administrators were proud enough of their program to volunteer to participate in the MDRC evaluation. Second, sites for the evaluation were limited to agencies with mature programs. Third, Grand Rapids operates a mandatory program, as indicated by its sanctioning rate, which is the highest in the state. The strength of conservative Republicans in the area permits and may even explain this. Finally, the economy of Grand Rapids is unusually robust for Michigan, even in periods of high unemployment, so that job search is likely to be a more effective strategy than in some other parts of the state.

Lessons from the Implementation Study

Ample evidence has accumulated that welfare agencies are capable of operating programs that increase employment and reduce welfare expenditures by an amount exceeding program costs. The benefits of these programs are not uniformly greater than their costs, however, with the net benefits varying considerably according to the particular program and the characteristics of recipients. Also, programs appear to be more effective in reducing welfare costs than in increasing total family income and reducing poverty. Finally, the evidence of positive net benefits comes primarily from evaluations of job search and work experience programs rather than education programs, where benefits accrue over a longer time period and are not yet apparent from ongoing evaluations (Gueron and Pauly 1991; LaLonde 1995). For these reasons, the payoffs to the individual components of the JOBS program remain uncertain.

Even if the technology for designing effective programs were understood with greater certainty, the challenge of *implementing* successful programs would remain. The ten-state study contains some good news in this regard: the supply of education, training, and employment services expands readily with increased funding. But there are challenging financial, political, and interorganizational tasks that must occur in order for implementation to take place as planned. In addition, welfare administrators must be willing and able to make changes internal to the welfare agency, such as creating an environment in which caseworkers effectively motivate recipients to get off welfare. Although some state officials, such as those in Michigan, have implemented JOBS with gusto, directives and financial incentives from Washington have been insufficient to guarantee that all states renegotiate the Social Contract to demand an obligation by welfare recipients.

The efforts of the 104th Congress to impose time limits and block grants can be viewed as a brute force way to motivate state leaders and welfare agencies to implement successful programs and to motivate recipients to take advantage of them and join the workforce. Will such a tough approach achieve its purpose? The answer depends on several factors. First, a time limit on welfare presumes that sufficient jobs are available to absorb people who loose their eligibility for welfare. Recent research indicates that the economy is generating jobs for low-skilled workers, particularly women, so that the availability of jobs per se is strong. The more serious problem will be the low wages paid by these jobs and the poor prospects for advancement into middle-income employment (Blank 1995). Substantial government spending on child care, health care, and wage supplements like the Earned Income Tax Credit will continue to be necessary if many of these families are to remain at their current level of well-being. So while more people may work, the cost to government may not fall in states concerned with poverty among families with children.

Second, the implementation study illustrates the political dynamic around welfare reform. Strong leadership has been visible in the states recently, but the direction of leadership has been less toward aggressively implementing the JOBS program and more toward reforms that limit welfare eligibility and benefits and condition benefits on certain behavior. This suggests that governors and welfare commissioners prefer to take the initiative in seeking welfare reform rather than respond to mandates imposed by the federal government. When federal legislation of the early 1980s gave states the option to operate new welfare employment programs, many state leaders were enthusiastic in designing a new program and taking ownership of their creation. But when federal legislation required states to implement the JOBS program, consisting of services that many states were already providing, JOBS became just another federal mandate requiring program changes and additional expenditures. Rather than *devoting* political capital to increasing expenditures for the JOBS program, some state leaders chose to restrict welfare eligibility and benefits as a way of *generating* political capital. One state welfare commissioner explained that officials stand to benefit from this tough approach because "the public blames the welfare system for problems in their own life." At low cost to the majority of voters, a hard-line stance on welfare policy offers state leaders and Congress an easy opportunity for political gain.

Yet if state leaders are actually faced with time limits and block grants, their political calculus may change. They may no longer be able to attribute their welfare problems to federal mandates and will instead be responsible for devising and implementing ways to spread limited funds to feed, house, and clothe poor children. Unless they are willing to be accountable for an increase in the number of destitute and homeless children, which we optimistically believe is unlikely, their opportunities for creating political capital at the expense of poor mothers and children will be exhausted or at least reduced. Instead, they may once again turn to the federal government for financial help and accept the accompanying strings. As shown by the implementation study, they will also be creative in complying with the federal mandates that remain. So although time limits and block grants will increase the pressure on states to prepare welfare recipients for work and move them into the labor force—and to discourage women and girls from bearing children they cannot support—we do not view them as stable policies that will persist over time. Welfare has been reformed about every five years, in 1967, 1971, 1976, 1981, and 1988. If the 104th Congress makes sweeping changes, they may well be reversed when the next recession raises welfare rolls and reduces state revenues.

NOTES

1. The Manpower Demonstration Research Corporation is evaluating the JOBS program in seven sites using random assignment to a control group to measure the effectiveness of alternative

programmatic approaches. Preliminary findings from this evaluation are presented in Frudman and Friedlander 1995.

2. The sample of states was selected to provide diversity in several characteristics: per capita personal income, poverty rate, the level of fiscal stress expected in 1990, the structure of public assistance administration (i.e., administration by the state government or by local government under state supervision), prior experience in operating a welfare employment program, and geographic region.

3. Hagen and Lurie (1992); Lurie and Hagen (1993), and Hagen and Lurie (1994). Funding for the study was provided by The Pew Charitable Trusts, the U.S. Departments of Labor and Health and Human Services, the New York State Department of Social Services, and the Foundation for Child Development. Irene Lurie served as the project's co-principal investigator, Colletta Moser as the field associate for Michigan.

4. The federally mandated participation rate for AFDC-UP families, two-parent families whose principal wage-earner is unemployed, is 40 percent in 1994 and rises to 75 percent by 1997. In 1994, only nine states achieved a 40 percent rate of participation.

5. The success of the JOBS program in Riverside, California is frequently cited as an example where "organizational culture" positively affects program effectiveness. MDRC GAIN Evalua- . tion.

6. We also found that implementing work experience programs was costly and infrequently used. The time needed for site development and monitoring of these positions was more than most welfare agencies could afford.

References

Behn, Robert D. 1991. *Leadership Counts: Lessons for Public Managers.* Cambridge, MA: Harvard University Press.

Blank, Rebecca M. 1995. "Outlook for the U.S. Labor Market and Prospects for Low–Wage Entry Jobs." In *The Work Alternative: Welfare Reform and the Realities of the Job Market*, Demetra S. Nightingale and Robert H. Haveman, eds. Washington, DC: Urban Institute Press.

Frudman, Stephen, and Daniel Friedlander. 1995. *The JOBS Evaluation Early Findings on Program Impacts in Three States.* U.S. Department of Health and Human Services/U.S. Department of Labor, July.

Gueron, Judith, and Edward Pauly. 1991. *From Welfare to Work.* New York: Russell Sage Foundation.

Hagen, Jan L., and Irene Lurie. 1992. *Implementing JOBS: Initial State Choices.* Albany, NY: Rockefeller Institute of Government.

_____. 1994. *Implementing JOBS: Progress and Promise.* Albany, NY: Rockefeller Institute of Government.

LaLonde, Robert J. 1995. "The Promise of Public Sector–Sponsored Training Programs," *Journal of Economic Perspectives* 9,2 (Spring): 149–168.

Levitan, Sar A., and Frank Gallo. 1993. "Jobs for JOBS: Toward a Work-Based Welfare System." Washington, DC: George Washington University Center for Policy Studies.

Levitan, Sar A., Martha Rein, and David Marwick. 1972 and 1976. *Work and Welfare Go Together.* Baltimore: Johns Hopkins University.

Lurie, Irene, and Jan L. Hagen. 1993. *Implementing JOBS: The Initial Design and Structure of Local Programs.* Albany, NY: Rockefeller Institute of Government

Mead, Lawrence M. 1986. *Beyond Entitlement.* New York: Free Press.

Moynihan, Daniel Patrick. 1990. "The Children of the State," *Washington Post*, November 25.

Murray, Charles. 1984. *Losing Ground.* New York: Basic Books.

Nathan, Richard P. 1982. "The Methodology of Field Network Evaluation Studies." In *Studying Implementation: Methodological and Administrative Issues*, Walter Williams, ed. Chatham, NJ: Chatham House.

National Association of State Budget Officers. 1995. *1994 State Expenditure Report.* Washington, D.C., April.

National Governors' Association. 1987. *Making America Work: Productive People, Productive Policies.* Washington, DC: American Enterprise Institute for Public Policy Research.

CHAPTER 15

What Should Be Our Human Capital Investment Policy?

James J. Heckman

While we did not always or even often agree on matters of economic policy, Sar Levitan and I exchanged views on both economic policy and econometric methodology. On several occasions, we discussed the changing labor market for unskilled labor and what the proper role was for government policy. This paper records my side of our conversations. I make six points.

First, I discuss the magnitude of the human resource problem confronting the American economy and the size of investments required to solve the problem. Second, I comment on the general ineffectiveness of current government training policies. Third, I comment on the general effectiveness of private sector training. Fourth, I discuss the conflict between economic efficiency and pursuit of the work ethic. Fifth, I consider a broader array of policy options including extensions of the tax code and revisions of educational subsidies. Finally, I distinguish between the long view and the short view in approaching human resource problems.

Presently, the economy has a large group of unskilled workers, many of whom can be trained to be skilled labor only at a prohibitively expensive cost. In an era of tight budgets, it is far from obvious that investments in such workers are justified on any but political grounds. The real cost of such investment is the diversion of investment away from the young and the more trainable for whom a human capital strategy is likely to be more effective and for whom it is likely to produce favorable outcomes in the long run. Missing from most discussions of job training is any discussion of the rather convincing evidence that investment is most profitable when it is made in the young.

Also, missing from current discussions is any consideration of priorities or the need to prioritize. In an era of tight government budgets, it is impractical to consider active investment programs for all persons. The real question is how to use available funds wisely. Government investments have not been shown to be effective in any meaningful cost/benefit sense for severely disadvantaged adults or older workers. For these groups, wage subsidies may be more effective tools for keeping persons employed than skill investment programs. The available evidence supports the policy proscription: Invest in the young; subsidize the old and the severely disadvantaged.

There is also a strong presumption in current discussions that investment in persons should be supplied by the government sector. This leads scholars of human resource problems to ignore a potentially important role for tax incentives in encouraging training by private firms to raise the demand and wages of labor. The evidence suggests that the returns to firm-supplied investment in human capital are larger than the returns to government training. This alone would justify greater reliance on the public sector. However, the better performance of private firms may be due to the lower skill level of trainees in the government programs. Evidence of their lower skills does not vindicate continued investment in such persons. No investment may be the best short-run strategy for low-skill adults, contrary to a central implicit premise of current job training strategies.

The New American Labor Market

There is much evidence to support the view that wage gaps have widened across the skill levels. In purchasing-power-constant or deflated dollars, male high school graduates earned 4 percent less per week in 1989 than in 1979. Male high school dropouts earned 13 percent less per week than in 1979. In contrast, male college graduates earned 11 percent more per week (Blank 1994). These comparisons widen further if we consider annual earnings. By any measure, labor incomes for men have become more unequally distributed. For women, the story is somewhat different. The real weekly earnings of female high school graduates have risen but the rise has been even greater for female college graduates.

For both men and women, inequality of labor incomes has risen. The returns to schooling and skill have increased. The relative earnings of workers at the bottom of the skill distribution (less than high school graduate) have definitely declined for persons of either gender. Youth have been hit hardest in the shifting market for skills.

A corollary phenomenon is the decline in labor market activity, especially among the unskilled. Labor force measures show increasing joblessness and longer unemployment spells for workers at all skill levels. Particularly problematic are less-skilled youth (those with high school education or less) who appear to flounder in the market for years before they find stable jobs. These youth are a source of major social problems. Teenage pregnancy, crime, and idleness are on the increase in most areas. It is very likely that diminished labor market opportunities for youth help to create these problems.

The problem of a deteriorating market for unskilled or semiskilled workers is not solely a problem of youth. Displaced adults, primarily factory workers, are a major concern. Middle-age workers displaced from high-wage jobs are at a major disadvantage in the new market for labor that has emerged since many of these workers first took their jobs. Displaced workers constitute 10-20 percent of the unemployed, or roughly 1 to 2 million workers. Recent evidence on the patterns of earnings losses experienced by workers displaced by mass layoffs suggests that the losses are significant and long-lasting, especially for those previously employed in unionized industries or occupations (Jacobson, LaLonde, and Sullivan 1993).

The Level of Investment Needed to Reduce the Current Levels of Wage Inequality

There have been many proposals for investments in human capital designed to increase the wage levels of the less-skilled. An investment generally yields returns over many years after initial costs are incurred. For human capital, a round, and roughly correct, average rate of return is 10 percent. Thus, for each $10 invested in a person, the expected annual return is $1. Some claim that this number is lower and some claim that it is higher, but most economists would accept a 10 percent return as a good starting point for estimating the aggregate investment needed to upgrade the skills of the low-skilled segment of the workforce.

At this rate of return, to add $1,000 in earnings per year to the average person it is necessary to make a one-time investment of $10,000 in that person. Using a 10 percent rate, the investment needed to reduce any wage gap is ten times the amount of the gap.

To put the magnitude of recent developments in the labor market in perspective, consider the following two questions:

1. How much would we have to invest in our workforce in 1989 dollars to restore real earnings of male high school dropouts and graduates to their real 1979 levels?

This question is meaningful only for men because real weekly earnings for women have risen or remained roughly constant over the period 1979-1989. A second question is:

2. How much would we have to invest in our workforce in 1989 dollars to restore 1979 earnings ratios between lower-education groups and college graduates, without reducing the 1989 earnings of college graduates?

Using a 10 percent rate of return, it would require an investment of $25,000 in each high school dropout or a staggering $214 billion in 1989 dollars to restore male high school dropouts participating in the workforce to their 1979 real earnings level. To restore all high school graduates to their real 1979 *levels* would take an investment of $10,000 per high school graduate, or more than $212 billion 1989 dollars, for a total of $426 billion in 1989 dollars.

The answer to question 2 is even larger. Table 1 shows the amount needed to restore the 1979 earnings ratio between high school graduates or high school dropouts and college-educated full-time workers over age 25. To restore real earnings for both male and female workers over age 25 who are high school-educated or less to their 1979 *relative* positions with respect to college graduates (holding the latter at 1989 real wage levels) would require an investment of more than 1.66 trillion dollars. These cost estimates are optimistic because they do not consider persons below age 25 or persons who do not participate in the workforce at the current wage levels. They are also optimistic for another reason: few, if any, government training programs have returns anywhere near 10 percent. Zero percent is a much closer approximation to the true return.

One might wish to qualify these calculations in many ways. One might want to adjust down the rate of return as more difficult-to-train persons receive training. Or, one might wish to account for the fact that as persons have their skills upgraded, the real wages of the lower-skill workers are likely to increase as they become more scarce and the real wages of those with higher skills are likely to decrease as their supply increases. Still, under most plausible scenarios, the costs of restoring skill parities to their 1979 levels are huge.

Investment in human capital may still not reduce income inequality. Raising the skills of a few need not reduce overall inequality. By moving some workers from low-skill to high-skill status, some standard measures of earnings inequality might actually increase. Many programs train only the high end among the low-skill workers. Such training efforts could polarize the labor market. In addition, *it takes skilled labor to produce skilled labor.* A large-scale increase in training activity might therefore *increase* earnings inequality in the short run since it would further expand the demand for skilled labor to train the unskilled labor.

Finally, the most efficient training policy may not be to train the unskilled. As first noted by Jacob Mincer (1962), there is strong evidence that those who complete more school invest more in postschool training. It may be economically efficient to invest in higher-skilled workers and to alleviate concerns about income and earnings inequality through income transfers or through wage subsidies. However, to the extent that working fosters socially desirable values among those who work, it may still be desirable to invest inefficiently or subsidize the employment of low-skill workers in order to promote those values.

Table 1. Investment in Human Capital Required to Restore Earnings to 1979 Levels and to Restore 1979 Relative Wage Ratios Using a 10 Percent Rate of Return
(in billions of dollars)

To Restore Earnings to 1979 Levels

Males	
Investment needed to restore average male high school dropout earnings in 1989 to average real earnings of male high school dropouts in 1979	$214
Investment needed to restore average male high school graduate earnings in 1989 to average real earnings levels of male high school graduates in 1979	$212
TOTAL	$426

To Restore 1979 Earnings Ratios

Males	
Investment needed to restore average male high school dropout earnings in 1989 to the level needed to achieve the 1979 high school dropout/college earnings ratio (holding 1989 college graduate wages fixed)	$382
Investment needed to restore average male high school graduate earnings in 1989 to the level needed to achieve the 1979 high school graduate/college earnings ratio (holding 1989 college graduate wages fixed)	$770
Females	
Investment needed to restore average female high school dropout earnings in 1989 to the level needed to achieve the 1979 high school dropout/college earnings ratio (holding 1989 college graduate wages fixed)	$136
Investment needed to restore average female high school graduate earnings in 1989 to the level needed to achieve the 1979 high school graduate/college earnings ratio (holding 1989 college graduate wages fixed)	$378
TOTAL	$1.66 Trillion

SOURCE: Wages are from Blank (1994).
NOTE: We assume workers work 50 weeks a year. The figures on the educational breakdown for the labor force are from Table #616, *Statistical Abstract of the United States, 1992.* We delete all persons out of the labor force and those less than age 25. On these criteria, our estimated investment costs are downward-biased.

The Ineffectiveness of Public Training Programs

In this section, I examine the evidence concerning the rate of return to government training. The evidence suggests that the 10 percent rate of return assumed in the above calculations is wildly optimistic. Few programs earn anywhere near this return.

The Summer Youth Employment and Training Program

It has been proposed that the Summer Youth Employment and Training program under the Job Training Partnership Act be increased. The stated purpose of this program is to preserve and upgrade the skills of low-income youth during the summers between school terms. The new twist on this program is that an "investment" argument has been given to support it. Barbara Heyns and her associates have argued that knowledge acquired in schools deteriorates through disuse during the summer (Heyns 1987). The new proposals recognize this possibility and suggest that summer youth programs should be enhanced by learning enrichment activities. What are the prospects for success of this program? A recent evaluation of a similar effort, the Summer Training and Education Program (STEP), has been presented by Public/Private Ventures, a Philadelphia-based nonprofit corporation that evaluates and manages social policy initiatives aimed at helping disadvantaged youth. STEP offered two summers of employment, academic remediation, and a life skills program to low-achieving youth ages 14 and 15 from poor families. The objective of the program was to reach youth at the crucial ages at which they are deciding whether or not to drop out of school or become pregnant. Part-time summer work at the minimum wage was supplemented with remedial reading and math classes and courses on the long-term consequences of drug use, unprotected sex, and dropping out of school.

Using randomized trials, 4,800 youth in five cities were enrolled into or randomized out of the program. Both treatments and controls were followed for eight years. A high quality evaluation was conducted using state-of-the-art demonstration methods for three cohorts of participants. The findings from this evaluation are disappointing. STEP participants experienced measured short-run gains including increases of half a grade level in their math and reading competency test scores.

These gains held up even after 15 months, though gains in the second summer were less than those in the first. Especially large was short-run growth in knowledge of contraceptive methods.

This short-term promise did not translate into longer-term gains. Three-and-a-half years after their STEP experience, at the ages of 17 and 18, work rates and school completion rates were identical and low for treatments and controls. Some 22 percent of young women had children and 64 percent of these were receiving public assistance in some form (Walker and Viella-Velez 1992).

Since STEP is, if anything, more intensive than the proposed summer youth programs, this evidence suggests that summer youth programs are *not* efficient investments. There is no evidence that they have lasting effects on participants. They may protect the peace, prevent riots, and lower the summer crime rate, but there is no firm evidence of such effects.

Evidence About Conventional Workforce Training and Work-Welfare Programs

How effective are current programs in moving people from welfare to work and in increasing their employment and earnings? Robert LaLonde recently addressed this question (LaLonde 1992). His evidence is summarized below along with my own evidence on the Job Training Partnership Act (JTPA).

Adult Women

Employment and training programs increase the earnings of adult female AFDC recipients. Earnings gains (a) are modest, (b) persist over several years, (c) arise from several different treatments, and (d) are sometimes quite cost effective. Table 2 displays evaluation results for a variety of programs. For example, participation in an Arkansas job search program was required for AFDC recipients with children over age three. Participants attended a group job search club for two weeks and then were asked to search as individuals for an additional two months. A program in San Diego required all AFDC participants to take job search assistance and mandated work experience. The gains were high for participants in both programs. The National Supported Work program provided intensive training and job search assistance at

Table 2. Experimental Estimates of the Impact of Employment and Training Programs on the Earnings of Female Welfare Applicants and Recipients

Services tested/demonstration	Net cost per participant	Annual earnings gain (loss) after:	
		1 Year	3 Years
Job Search Assistance:			
Arkansas	140	220**	410**
Louisville (WIN-1)	170	350**	530**
Cook County, IL	190	10	NA
Louisville (WIN-2)	280	560**	NA
Job Search Assistance and Training Services:			
West Virginia	320	20	NA
Virginia Employment Services	520	90	330*
San Diego I (EPP/EWEP)	770	600**	NA
San Diego II (SWIM)	1,120	430**	NA
Baltimore	1,160	190	630**
New Jersey	960	720*	
Maine	2,450	140	1,140
Work Experience and Retraining:			
AFDC Homemaker-Health Care	11,550	460**	NA
National Supported Work	16,550	460**	810**

SOURCES. Gueron and Pauly (1991, pp. 15-20); Bell et al. (1987, tables 3 and 4); Couch (1992, table 1).
NOTE: All figures in the table are expressed in 1990 dollars.
*Statistically significant at a 10 percent level.
**Statistically significant at a 5 percent level.

a cost of about $16,550 per recipient. The estimated rate of return to this program was only 3.5 percent.

The results from the recent experiment evaluating the Job Training Partnership Act (shown in table 3) corroborate these findings. The largest impacts are for adult women, many of whom were collecting AFDC during their participation in JTPA. The impacts are not sufficiently large to move more than a tiny fraction of women out of poverty. As a general rule, conventional employment and training programs are often cost effective for adult women (especially if the opportunity cost of trainee time is ignored or is sufficiently low), but do not produce dramatic changes in participant earnings.

Table 3. Impacts on Total 18-Month Earnings and Employment: JTPA Assignees and Enrollees, by Target Group

	Adults		Out-of school youths	
Impact on:	**Women**	**Men**	**Female**	**Male**
Per assignee				
Earnings				
In $	$ 539**	$ 550	$ -182	$ -854**
As a %	7.2%	4.5%	-2.9%	-7.9%
Percentage employed	2.1%**	2.8**	2.8	1.5
Sample size (assignees and control group combined)	6,474	4,419	2,300	1,748
Per enrollee				
Earnings				
In $	$ 873[b]	$ 935[b]	$ -295[b]	$-1,355[b]
As a %	12.2%	6.8%	-4.6%	-11.6%
Percentage employed[a]	3.5[b]	4.8[b]	4.5[b]	2.4[b]

SOURCE: Bloom et al. (1993). Enrollee estimates obtained using the procedure in Bloom (1984).
a. At any time during the follow-up period.
b. Tests of statistical significance were not performed for impacts per enrollee.
*Statistically significant at the .10 level, **at the .05 level, ***at the .01 level (two-tailed test).

Adult Men

The evidence for this group is consistent across programs. Returns are low but usually positive. Job search assistance is an effective strategy but produces only modest increases in mean earnings levels. This program is worth keeping but I do not think that it will make much of a difference in closing the emerging wage gap.

Youth

Evidence from the JTPA experiment indicates that this program produces only low or negative impacts on earnings. For male youth, the estimated negative effect is unbelievably low. If taken seriously, participation in JTPA has a more negative impact on the earnings of male youth than participation in the Army, loss of work experience, or the cost of incarceration as measured by many studies.

Only the Job Corps has a demonstrated positive impact on earnings. It is an expensive program, costing around $20,000 per participant, with an estimated return of roughly 8-9 percent. There is some basis for supporting expansion of this program, but even for this program the evidence is weak. The evaluation of Job Corps program is not experimental. Part of the high return comes from the very large value imputed to human life and the slightly smaller rate of committing murders found among persons who participate in the Job Corps. With lower values placed on lives saved, the gains from Job Crops tend to weaken greatly. (See Donohue and Siegelman 1995).

Workfare and Learnfare

How effective are the recent learnfare and workfare programs? An evaluation of two programs conducted in Wisconsin is of interest (see Pawasarat and Quinn 1993). One program, the Community Work Experience Program (CWEP), required mandatory participation in unpaid community service jobs for nonexempt AFDC participants. A second program, Work Experience and Job Training, provided AFDC clients with assessment, job search activities, subsidized employment, job training, and community work experience. Participants who failed to find employment after completing their education and training were also required to participate in CWEP jobs.

Using randomized trials for one county and nonexperimental methods for the rest, researchers found *no effect* of these programs compared to existing program alternatives. The reduction in AFDC participation that is widely cited as a consequence of these programs is essentially due to the improvement in the Wisconsin economy during the time the programs were in place. These results are disappointing but consistent with previous studies of the efficacy of such programs by the Manpower Demonstration Research Corporation (Gueron and Pauly 1991). Mandatory work experience programs produce little long-term gain. No cheap training solution has yet been found that can end the welfare problem. Lifting a welfare woman out of poverty by increasing her earnings by $5,000 per year ($100 per week) will cost *at least* $50,000. This is the scale of required investment. No "quick fix," low-cost solution is in sight.

Training Programs for Displaced Workers

As noted above, displacement of older workers with substantial experience in the labor market has become an increasingly important phenomenon in recent years. In response to this trend, Congress passed Title III of the Job Training Partnership Act in 1982 and the Economic Dislocation and Worker Adjustment Assistance Act in 1988.

Although studies evaluating these programs directly are not available as yet, evaluations of state-funded programs providing a similar mix of services have been conducted. Leigh (1990) summarizes the evidence on a variety of these programs. Results from some of these evaluations suggest small to moderate wage gains lasting only about a year. A more recent evaluation by Mathematica (see Corson et al. 1993) of training provided under the Trade Adjustment Assistance Act to workers displaced as a result of foreign trade finds no evidence of any effect of this long-term training program on the earnings and employment of recipients. Consistent with the other studies of government employment and training programs already discussed, the overall pattern for programs aimed at displaced workers is one of weak impacts for most groups.

Private Sector Training

Due to a lack of data and a bias in favor of funding studies of government training, the returns to private sector training are less well understood. Studies by Lynch (1992) and Lillard and Tan (1986), find sizable effects of private sector training. In comparison with studies of public sector training, most of these studies do not attempt to control for the likely case that more able persons are more likely to take training, so the estimated rates of return would overstate the true returns to training by combining them with the return to ability. Thus, part of the measured return may be due to more motivated and able persons taking training. Estimated initial returns range from 10 to 20 percent (Mincer 1993), but they tend to decline after a few years as technical progress renders the training essentially obsolete. To the extent that rapid technical progress in many fields causes the knowledge obtained through training to lose its value after only a few years, fears about the detrimental effects of turnover in the labor market on the volume of human capital investment may be exaggerated.

An important feature of private sector training is that the more skilled do more investing even after they attain high skill levels. Different types of training and learning have strong complementarities with respect to each other.

Even though the evidence is weak, the direction of the evidence is clear. To the extent that effective training can be produced on the job, it is produced in the private sector and not in the public sector. The best hope of getting reasonable returns from job training is to encourage private sector investment.

It is important to note, however, that private sector training typically excludes low-skilled persons. Firms can be exclusive in a way that government training programs for disadvantaged workers are designed not to be. The lack of interest of private firms in training disadvantaged workers indicates the difficulty of the task and the likely low return to this activity. Training programs are an inefficient transfer mechanism and an inefficient investment policy for low-skill adult workers.

The Conflict Between Economic Efficiency and the Work Ethic

To the extent that there are strong complementarities between different types of skill investments, there is a conflict between policies that seek to alleviate poverty by investing in low-skill workers and policies that raise the wealth of society at large. Taking the available evidence at face value, the most economically justified strategy for improving the incomes of the poor is to invest more in the highly skilled, tax them, and then redistribute the tax revenues to the poor. However, many people view the work ethic as a basic value and would argue that cultivating a large class of transfer recipients would breed a culture of poverty and helplessness.

If value is placed on work as an act of individual dignity, because of general benefits to families, communities, and society as a whole, then all individuals in society may be prepared to subsidize inefficient jobs. Job subsidies are not, however, the same as investment subsidies. The evidence points strongly to the inefficiency of subsidizing the investment of low-skill, disadvantaged workers. Investment may have some additional nonpecuniary returns. In this case, a purely economic evaluation of investment policies may be inappropriate. If, however, economically inefficient investments are to be made, the cost of reducing the skill gap grows beyond the already enormous sums presented in table 1.

The Quality of the Evidence on Credit Constraints and Participation in Schooling and Training Programs

The evidence cited by advocates of training programs that persons from low-income families have high rates of return to schooling leads them to conclude that credit market restrictions are important factors in generating schooling and training outcomes. Another interpretation is possible, however. Family income as measured in those studies is a proxy for a whole range of background factors—not just short-term liquidity constraints that might be eased by more generous fellowship policies. Persons from poor family backgrounds may attain fewer years of schooling because of diminished family motivation for child learning and because family background may affect the child's learning ability. Given diminishing returns to schooling, it is not surprising that marginal rates of return are higher for persons who have fewer years of school. At issue is what family income really represents. It is significant in this regard that Murray and Herrnstein (1994) find that after they control for the effects of a score on a combined achievement and ability test, measured family income plays only a small role in explaining schooling attainment. It appears that longer-term factors such as family background that produce the test score are more important.

Alternative Policy Recommendations: Choice in Schools, Tax Policy Wage Subsidies and Antitrust Policy

In the long run, significant improvements in the skill levels of American workers, especially workers not attending college, are unlikely without substantial change and improvement in primary and secondary education. Mincer's evidence that learning begets learning demonstrates the value of early training in making subsequent training effective. Much of the recent discussion about improving postsecondary education is misplaced when the value of early schooling is put in context.

Methods for improving primary and secondary education receive much attention in current policy discussions but are treated as completely separate issues in discussions of traditional training programs. Increasing the extent of consumer choice in the educational system would help to realign incentives in the right way to produce more effective schools. Choice among secondary training vendors is an important aspect of the German apprenticeship system. (See Heckman, Roselius and Smith 1994). Advocates of strong government activity in the training area do not consider the failure of governments to provide adequate skills to students.

Current tax rules tend to promote human capital formation (see Quigley and Smolensky 1990). However, there is much evidence that they discriminate against low-skill and disadvantaged workers. Firms can immediately write off all of their training expenditures. They do not have to be amortized like investments in physical capital. This favors investment in human capital over physical capital. In addition, training expenditures can include tuition paid by employers for each employee up to $5,250 per year, though tuition support is restricted to undergraduate level education (U.S. House of Representatives, Joint Committee on Taxation 1992). Since many community colleges qualify as undergraduate institutions, there is an incentive for firms to sponsor vocational training. The bias in the tax code favors vocational training over academic education.

Because tuition paid by employers is exempt from federal personal income tax, individuals have an incentive to seek training on the job. Additionally, portable vocational or employer-based training can be sold to employees by firms and paid for by lower wages. The forgone higher earnings are *de facto* written off on personal income taxes. To the extent that direct costs of books and educational materials are paid for by lower wages, current tax laws favor on-the-job training activities over off-the-job training activities. Thus, they act to shift human capital investment activity away from formal schools and toward workplace environments.

Conversely, individuals cannot write off direct tuition costs for formal schooling if it is not expressly job-related. Write-offs are not given for training in skills useful in other jobs. Thus workers training to switch occupations cannot write off their educational expenses for this activity. Moreover, there is a floor level of training and education expenditures that must be met before persons can write off such self-investment activity. To be eligible for this tax break, it is necessary to itemize deductions and to incur training costs that exceed 2 percent of adjusted gross income. This tax policy likely biases human capital accumulation toward vocational over academic training, because vocational training is typically more narrowly defined and justifiable.

Since 1986, persons have been unable to deduct interest on educational loans from their taxable income. This removes an important incentive that promotes investment in human capital of all forms (Heckman 1976). However, since mortgage interest is still deductible, it is possible for persons with home equity to take out mortgages to finance their education or that of their children or to rearrange their portfolios toward mortgage debt in order to finance educational loans.

The tax code for individuals favors human capital accumulation for higher income persons (and their children) who itemize their taxes and have equity in their homes. Low-income persons who pay no taxes receive little encouragement to invest in human capital from the current personal tax code. However, firms that employ them may write off training expenditures devoted to them. The personal tax code thus encourages low-skill workers to make training investments on the job. It does not encourage investment in general skills or academic education except for company tuition programs. Unfortunately, these programs (defined under section 127 of the 1988 Tax Code) have not received consistent treatment by the tax authorities. In recent years, companies have operated under uncertainty whether or not section 127 would apply to them in a given tax year. Tax policy is an attractive option that should receive more discussions in future policy discussion about stimulating skill formation.

The evidence on government training programs previously summarized suggests that they can make at best only a modest contribution to aggregate human capital formation. Given the strong evidence of complementarity between schooling and training, it may be more efficient to focus training on high-skill workers, and then use the tax system to transfer resources to the less-skilled through wage subsidies or inefficient investment. If the goal is to raise their incomes, the extra surplus generated through more efficient investment can more than compensate low-skilled workers for the training they forgo.

Support of cooperative activity among employers could allow firms within an industry to overcome free rider problems in the provision of general training by contracting to provide similar levels of industry-specific training or general training to their employees. This suggests a role for antitrust policy that is rarely mentioned in discussions of training strategy.

A Life-Cycle Perspective

Economic theory demonstrates that the returns to human capital investments are greatest for the young. This is so for two reasons: (1) younger persons have a longer horizon over which to recoup the fruits of their investments, and (2) skill begets skill. Early learning facilitates later learning. At the same level of ability, it pays to invest in the young.

Surprisingly little empirical evidence is available on the returns to early childhood investments. Early childhood interventions of high quality appear to have lasting effects. Despite very small samples, disadvantaged subnormal children randomly assigned to the Perry Preschool program have higher earnings and lower levels of pathological behavior in their late twenties than do comparable children randomized out of the program. (See Schweinhart, Barnes and Weikart 1993). Reported cost-benefit ratios are substantial. Evidence on Head Start is less clear but the program is quite heterogeneous. These programs do not boost IQ but they do appear to foster valuable social skills that enhance performance in society at large and in the workplace.

At the same time, skill remediation programs for young adults with severe educational disadvantages seem to have negligible effects as do training programs for more mature displaced workers. The available evidence clearly suggests that adults past a certain age, and below a certain skill level make poor investments. Transfers or wage subsidies to employers make more sense than investments for such persons.

NOTE

Some of the research reported here was supported by the National Science Foundation and the Russell Sage Foundation.

References

Blank, R. 1994. "Employment Strategies: Public Policy to Increase the Work Force and Earnings."In *Poverty and Public Policy: What Do We Know? What Should We Do?*, S. Danziger, G. Sandfur, and D. Weinberg, eds. Cambridge, MA: Harvard University Press.

Bloom, H., L. Orr, G. Cave, S. Bell, and F. Doolittle. 1993. "The National JTPA Study: Title II-A Impacts on Earnings and Employment at 18 Months," Abt Associates, January.

Corson, W. et al. 1993. *International Trade and Worker Dislocation: Evaluation of the Trade Adjustment Assistance Program*, Princeton, NJ: Mathematica.

Couch, K. 1992. "New Evidence on the Long-Term Effects of Employment Training Programs," *Journal of Labor Economics* 10, 4.

Donohue, John, and Peter Siegelman. 1995. "Is The United States at the Optimal Rate of Crime?" American Bar Foundation.

Gueron, Judith, and Edward Pauly. 1991. *From Welfare to Work*. New York: Russell Sage Foundation.

Heckman, J. 1976. "A Life Cycle model of Earnings, Learning and Consumption," *Journal of Political Economy,* August.

_____. 1981. "Heterogeneity and State Dependence", in S. Rosen (ed.), *Studies in Labor Markets*. University of Chicago Press.

_____. R. Roselius, and J. Smith. 1994. "U.S. Education and Training Policy: A Reevaluation of The Underlying Assumptions Behind The New Consensus." In *Labor Markets, Employment Policy and Job Creation*, A. Levenson and L. C. Solmon, eds. Santa Monica, CA: Milken Institute for Job and Capital Formation, October.

Heyns, B.1987. "Schooling and Cognitive Development: Is There A Season For Learning?" *Child Development* 58: 1150-1160.

Jacobson, L., R. LaLonde, and D. Sullivan. 1993. "Earnings Losses of Displaced Workers," *American Economic Review* 83, 4 (September): 685-709.

LaLonde, R. 1992. "The Earnings Impact of U.S. Employment and Training Programs." Unpublished manuscript, University of Chicago, January 29.

Leigh, D. 1990. *Does Training Work for Displaced Workers?* Kalamazoo, MI: W. E. Upjohn Institute for Employment Research.

Lillard, L., and H. Tan. 1986. *Private Sector Training: Who Gets It and What Are Its Effects?* Santa Monica, CA: Rand.

Lynch, L. 1992. "Private-Sector Training and the Earnings of Young Workers," *American Economic Review* 82, 1.

Mincer, J. 1962. "On the Job Training: Costs, Returns, and Some Implications," *Journal of Political Economy* 70, Supp. (October): 50-79.

_____. 1993. "Investment in U.S. Education and Training." Discussion Paper 671, Columbia University, November.

Murray, C., and R. Herrnstein. 1994. *The Bell Curve*. New York: Free Press.

Pawasarat, J., and L. Quinn. 1993. "Evaluation of The Wisconsin WEJT/CWEP Welfare Employment Programs." Employment and Training Institute, University of Wisconsin, April.

Phelps, E. 1994. "A Program of Low-Wage-Employment Tax Credits." Working Paper No. 55, Russell Sage Foundation, May.

Quigley, J., and E. Smolensky. 1990. "Improving Efficiency in the Tax Treatment of Training and Educational Expenditures," *Research in Labor Economics* 11: 77-95.

Reich, R. 1991. *Work of Nations: Preparing Ourselves for 21st-Century Capitalism.* New York: A. A. Knopf.

Schweinhart, L., H. Barnes, and D. Weikart. 1993. *Significant Benefits: The High/Score Perry Preschool Study Through Age 27.* Ypsilanti, MI: High Scope Press.

U.S. House of Representatives, Joint Committee on Taxation. 1992. *Description and Analysis of Tax Provisions Expiring in 1992.* Washington, DC: Government Printing Office.

Walker, G., and F. Viella-Velez. 1992. *Anatomy of A Demonstration.* Philadelphia: Public and Private Ventures.

CHAPTER 16

Employment and Unemployment Statistics Revisited

Markley Roberts

You too can be a quick expert on labor statistics if you have handy the *BLS Handbook of Methods* with its summary description of twenty labor statistics programs.[1] It also helps to have a nodding acquaintance with the evolution of labor statistics. Hence, this revisiting of employment and unemployment statistics.

Employment and unemployment statistics are key economic indicators and also key indicators of human welfare. I will be looking here at some related issues—the recently redesigned household survey, the census "undercount," economic hardship, establishment payroll employment, unemployment insurance data, state and local unemployment, funding for labor market information, and the danger of politicized statistics—in light of recommendations by the commission on labor statistics chaired by Sar Levitan.

The Levitan Report

On Labor Day 1979 the nine-member National Commission on Employment and Unemployment Statistics—set up under Public Law 94-444 and chaired by Sar Levitan—made its final report (hereafter the 1979 Levitan Report) with some 100 wide-ranging recommendations for changes and improvements in the nation's labor force statistics.[2] The Levitan Report dealt with concepts, definitions, data needs, collection and processing issues, state and local statistics, administration, presentation, and dissemination of labor force statistics.

The Levitan Report—like its predecessor, the 1962 report of the President's Committee to Appraise Employment and Unemployment Statistics, chaired by Robert Aaron Gordon (the Gordon Report)—was the result of concern, not only among professionals in the field of labor statistics, that concepts should be clear and data should accurately reflect changing labor force conditions. In the 1979 Levitan Report these would include increasing labor force participation of women, declining participation of older men, rising concern about structural unemployment, training needs, discrimination, poverty, hardship, and unemployment-related formula distribution of federal funds at state and local substate levels.

It's not fair to compare the Gordon Report and the Levitan Report since they reflect different times and different conditions. They cover many of the same issues, but the Levitan Report's wider coverage probably reflects seventeen additional years of experience with the nation's labor statistics. It may also reflect the unusually open process of receiving input from ninety witnesses at public hearings, thirty-three background papers, and widespread circulation of an advance draft for comments. And it has an index, which the Gordon Report does not.

In 1989 Sar Levitan and Frank Gallo, in a report written for the Joint Economic Committee of Congress, called for another successor "broadly representative, expert commission, jointly appointed by the Congress and the President" which "could help to formulate a consensus on statistical needs and priorities" and "also could help design an agenda for the years ahead." The Levitan-Gallo report declared:

> Though the precise challenges facing those who collect our labor force statistics have changed somewhat during the last decade, the basic conclusion of the National Commission on Employment and Unemployment Statistics has not. The Nation is served by a comprehensive labor force data system expertly prepared by a cadre of dedicated public servants. But if the statistics are to reflect changing economic conditions and meet policy needs, periodic revisions and improvements are necessary (p. ix).

This paper will review action and inaction on the 1979 Levitan Report, the 1989 Levitan-Gallo report, the 1994 revisions in the Current Population Survey (the CPS or household survey), 1995 changes in the Current Employment Statistics (the "790" CES establishment payroll) survey, state and local, and other labor statistics. In an ideal world I would call for additional funds to widen the range of good labor force statistics needed for good decisions in both the public sector and the private sector. Instead, I gloomily consider 1995 budget-cutting by Congress and its bad effects on labor force statistics.

Household Survey Redesign

The Current Population Survey, which involves monthly interviews of people in 60,000 households, is the prime source for employment and unemployment statistics for the nation, for eleven big states, and for the Los Angeles and New York City metropolitan areas. Census Bureau interviewers collect data which the Bureau of Labor Statistics (BLS) analyzes and publishes. The survey divides people 16 years and over into three groups—employed, unemployed, and not-in- the-labor-force.

In January 1994 a major redesign of the CPS household survey went into effect. Janet Norwood, former Commissioner of Labor Statistics, called the redesign "the most important change in labor force statistics in more than half a century" (1994, p. 1). The redesigned household survey reflects in large part 1979 Levitan Report recommendations on discouraged workers, hours of work, and a variety of other issues. The redesign also reflects joint BLS-Census Bureau planning since 1986 to use new cognitive research to improve the interview questionnaire, to add more questions, and to use computers to improve the process of interviewing.

Detailed BLS description and discussion of the redesigned household survey appear in the September 1993 *Monthly Labor Review* and the February 1994 *Employment and Earnings*.[3] Objectives of the BLS redesign included:

- Better measurement of well-defined concepts not measured precisely in the old questionnaire, such as employment/unemployment status, layoffs, hours worked, self-employment/unpaid family work, and earnings.

- Better definition of concepts not well explained in the old questionnaire, such as part-time workers, especially those working part time involuntarily, and status of persons not in the labor force.

- Revised definition of discouragement, adding job search within the past year and current availability to take a job to the present question relating to expressed desire for a job.

- Fewer wrongly reported changes relating to industry, occupation, and duration of unemployment.

- Regular reporting on such topics as multiple jobholding, usual hours worked, earnings from overtime, tips, and commissions, and child-care for part-time workers.

- More direct information on such topics as the existence of a business in the household, full-time/part-time work status, and the reason for that status.

- With computer-aided interviewing, reduced burden on interviewees, particularly those whose status is less likely to change from month to month, such as retired, disabled, and unable- to-work persons.

The new questionnaire is designed for computer-aided interviewing, using laptops in the interviewee's home or by telephone (CAPI: computer-assisted personal interview). About 20 percent of the sample is interviewed from centralized telephone centers in Hagerstown, Maryland, and Tucson, Arizona, and Jeffersonville, Indiana. (CATI: computer-assisted telephone interview).

An eighteen-month test of the new questionnaire (July 1992 to December 1993) suggested that the new national unemployment rate would be half a percentage point higher than the rate from the old questionnaire—raising women's unemployment rate more than men's and reporting more unemployment among teenagers and workers 65 years and older. Labor force participation for women was higher in the test survey by a full percentage point (to 59.5 percent), but was down for men by half a percentage point (to 76.4 percent). However, subsequent research at BLS shows no significant difference between the national total unemployment rates resulting from the questionnaire changes introduced in 1994. But there were many other changes: a decrease in those classified as discouraged workers, an increase in the number of part-time workers, a decrease in persons working part time for economic reasons, an increase in self-employed workers, an increase in managerial and professional occupations, and a decrease in operators, fabricators, and laborers, all relative to findings from the old household questionnaire.

Census Undercount

Adjusting the household survey for the census "undercount" was a 1979 Levitan Report recommendation adopted in the BLS redesign. The 1989 Levitan-Gallo report suggested that "The undercoverage of minorities in the decennial census and the CPS may underestimate the economic hardship minorities experience in the labor market." The legal status of Census Bureau adjustment of the decennial census was still in limbo in mid-1995, with a Justice Department appeal to the Supreme Court after conflicting federal court rulings on the constitutionality of adjusting the direct count.

However, bravely pushing ahead, BLS is making basic population estimates built on the 1990 census and now adjusted from a variety of data sources as described in the February 1994 *Employment and Earnings*. For 1993 the adjustment increased the civilian noninstitutional population 16 years and older by about 1.3 million or 0.7 percent. The civilian labor force was raised by about 1.1 million or 0.9 percent. Unemployment went up by 200,000 or 2.3 percent, raising the overall unemployment rate by 0.1 percentage point "primarily because of the large upward adjustment for Hispanics."

The 1989 Levitan-Gallo report to the Joint Economic Committee called for doubling the CPS sample to 120,000 households to raise reliability of data from small states, major metropolitan areas, and other groups, including particularly union members, youth, and minorities. The 1979 Levitan Report had called for doubling the sample size for minority households to get more reliable monthly data on blacks, Hispanics, Asians, and Native Americans. Unfortunately, congressional budget-cutting in mid-1995 will bring a smaller household survey sam-

ple and fewer directly measured employment and unemployment statistics.

One recommendation from the 1979 Levitan Report seems destined
for oblivion. The report called for including the nation's armed forces
in the United States in the national labor force count and specifically in
the "employed" total. The rationale was that military service was voluntary so workers were free to choose between employment in the
civilian sector and military service. BLS did, in fact, start including the
armed forces in the "total labor force" starting in 1983, but quietly
dropped this series a few years ago from the monthly BLS "Employment Situation" news release—and no one noticed. I see this as the
result of the winding-down of the Cold War with the downsizing of the
armed forces, which lowered interest in the armed services as an alternative to civilian employment. Also the change was never popular with
the media and the public, who had been confused by the two sets of
"labor force" numbers. BLS also quietly dropped its monthly news
release table on veterans' unemployment as the Vietnam War receded
further into history and veterans' unemployment problems seemed to
be the same as those of nonveterans of the same age. Veterans' labor
force status is still reported monthly in *Employment and Earnings*.

Economic Hardship

Economic hardship was an issue of continuing interest to Sar Levitan, and the 1979 report called for an annual report linking "economic
hardship" resulting from low wages, unemployment, and labor force
participation with earnings and with family and household income.

In explicit response to the Levitan Report, BLS published annual
reports on "employment problems and economic status" using published data for the years 1979 through 1982, but this series was discon-
tinued for a time, partly because the reports used data already available
and partly because BLS found little public or professional interest in
the reports. After a hiatus, in 1989 BLS resumed publishing an annual
report called "A Profile of the Working Poor," the first covering data
from 1987 and the most recent, the 1995 report, covering data from
1993 (Castillo 1995). The focus is on workers who spent more than

half the year in the labor force, either working or looking for work, but remained in poverty. In 1993 such workers numbered 8.2 million or 21 percent of the 39.3 million persons in the Census Bureau poverty count.

Establishment Payroll Survey

The "790" federal-state Current Employment Survey (CES) of some 400,000 nonfarm establishment payroll records is a basic source for employment, hours, and earnings with considerable industry detail. Big establishments have a high probability of being in the sample, and small establishments have a lower probability of being in the sample. The data are cyclically sensitive, and they are key components of statistics on production, income, output, productivity, wage trends, and labor costs. With a "shuttle form" which goes back and forth between the establishment and the state agency collecting the data (which collects the data for its own purposes as well as for BLS), the payroll survey provides relatively simple and straight-forward information.

The 1979 Levitan Report made relatively few recommendations for the payroll survey but noted: "The lack of many detailed recommendations for improvement should not be misconstrued; it is intended to alert the reader to the urgent need to upgrade the design and implementation of the BLS-790 program and to document what is being done."

The 1979 Levitan Report expressed concern about inadequate service sector coverage—then about 130 service industries, now about 300. Part of the problem then and now is the preponderance of small firms in service industries with relatively high birth and death rates, which complicate the survey sample and lead at times to employment trends difficult to explain and differing from household survey employment trends. In general, however, the household data and the establishment payroll data move in similar patterns.

An unusually large benchmark revision to the CES nationally and particularly in California for March 1991 raised questions of confidence in the establishment data. This led BLS to ask the American Statistical Association to investigate and report on the establishment survey (ASA 1993). The ASA panel, chaired by Barbara Bailar, noted that the large 1992 BLS revision of March 1991—a 640,000 downward national revision of which most was in California—was caused by "a one-time noneconomic phenomenon associated with improved reporting" as a result of new software used by employers "that eliminated some overcounting of employment totals prior to that date." In 1993 the ASA panel called for more BLS research to support the establishment survey and the ES-202 unemployment insurance administrative statistics that provide its underpinnings, more frequent (quarterly rather than annual) benchmarking and smaller revisions, more and better information on establishment births and deaths, more consistency between national and state estimates, and more documentation of methodology.

An appendix to the ASA report by Audrey Freedman offers a broad spectrum of users' reactions to the establishment survey. They like the industry and locality detail. They don't like data revisions. "Their greatest frustration is with the revisions, which require major reworking of their models and an about-face on previous analysis," Freedman reports.

A less temperate reaction to the 1991 benchmark revisions and subsequent historical revisions came from a UCLA forecaster discombobulated by revisions of California data. "Heads should surely have rolled for the damaging consequences to the agency and to data users, but it does not appear that they did. What assurance, therefore, has the data-using public that such an occurrence could not be repeated?" asks Daniel J.B. Mitchell (1995).[4]

In June 1995 BLS announced a CES 790 research and sample design program stretching from 1995 through the year 2000 —a program consistent with ASA and Levitan Report recommendations to get more accurate national, state, and metropolitan area series and to eliminate risk of large bias resulting from adjustments for new business births and other survey limitations. (USDOL, Bureau of Labor Statistics 1995).

Unemployment Insurance Statistics

Administrative statistics from the federal-state unemployment insurance (UI) system provide information for a wide variety of statistics purposes, including the "790" establishment survey, state and local employment and unemployment data, and other BLS surveys. The ES-202 Covered Employment and Wages (UI) program covers more than 98 percent of all civilian wage and salary workers, with employment and wage data by industry at national, state, and local levels. It does not cover some 10 million self-employed persons, 700,000 domestic workers, 600,000 state and local government workers (out of an 11 million total), 300,000 workers covered by the railroad UI program, and 300,000 farm workers.

State "employment security" agencies collect the UI employment data quarterly from some 6.5 million employers and send the data to BLS with a six-month lag, but the state agencies collect unemployment claims data weekly and send them to the U.S. Labor Department immediately. The number of unemployed workers newly claiming UI benefits is considered a sensitive cyclical indicator, although the weekly total contains a lot of statistical noise.The 1979 Levitan Report made recommendations for more timeliness, more quality control, and more funding at the state level for the ES-202 UI employment program. The 1989 Levitan-Gallo Report noted improvements in the program but added that "the untapped potential of UI data for labor market analysis remains considerable."

State and Local Unemployment

The biggest problems with state and local unemployment data are inadequacy and unreliability. The 1962 Gordon Report noted these problems but devoted only nine pages to them. The 1979 Levitan Report expressed considerable concern about state and local labor force statistics and devoted two chapters and 36 pages, 12 percent of the total, to these problems.

As noted earlier, the Levitan Report called for a 42,000-household expansion of the CPS household survey to raise reliability of state and local employment and unemployment estimates. (Three commission members dissented on grounds that the benefits would not justify the $15 million added cost.). The Levitan Report called on Congress to consider using quarterly, annual, and five- year data and to avoid using unreliable monthly unemployment data in formulas for allocating federal funds to state and local areas. The report also called for BLS research and improvements in the so- called "70-step" procedures for estimating state and local unemployment first set forth in 1960 and refined in subsequent years with econometric models for the nondirect (non-CPS) states and "building block" estimates for local substate areas, with both procedures relying heavily on UI employment data and UI benefit claims and payments.

There are no easy or cheap answers on improving measurement of unemployment in states and local areas. And with budget-cutting by Congress in 1995 things are going to get worse rather than better as the basic household survey is cut back. BLS has an understandable reluctance to publish unreliable data. Therefore the BLS report on "Unemployment in States and Local Areas" is difficult to get, available only by microfiche subscription.[5] This is a monthly report on labor force, employment, and unemployment in 6,500 geographic areas, including all nondirect states, labor market areas, and counties and cities with population of 25,000 or more. It is the basis for eligibility and allocation of federal funds under a variety of federal aid programs.

Labor Market Information

Where are today's jobs? Where will they be five years from now? Where are the layoffs? What skills are needed today? How are skill requirements changing? What are the structures and trends of compensation? There is always more demand than willingness or ability to supply labor market information (LMI) and a vast range of related social and economic information. Everybody wants a comprehensive, integrated labor market system that produces good national, state, and local LMI data, but nobody wants to pay for it.

The 1979 Levitan Report called for more LMI data on services of volunteers and homemakers who are not in the labor force, terms and conditions of work sought, income sources other than employment, full- and part-time school attendance, women's work experience, labor force experience of minorities, migrant workers, undocumented workers, and disabled workers, occupational mobility, and occupational projections. BLS has implemented most of these recommendations in principle, but follow-through costs more money.

In 1994 an LMI review panel (Milton Martin, project director) consisting mainly of state labor department officials issued a "Review of the Nation's Labor Market Information System."[6] Not surprisingly the panel found "The lack of support for meeting state and local needs is the most serious failure of the present system." And the panel warned:

> Since the 1980s, federal funding cuts have made it all but impossible for labor market producers in the states to meet growing demands for information. Unfunded mandates have added to this problem. The federal government's role with respect to policy and coordination has also diminished (p. viii).

The 1994 LMI review panel recommended a uniform national framework of data collection and dissemination with consistent definitions and methodologies, standardized wage data for all states and local areas, use of state wage records to evaluate employment and training programs, assured and adequate funding, investment in information technology and training, and action by Congress to recognize the limitations of state and local area labor force data when setting federal funding allocation formulas. It sounds as if the 1994 LMI panel consulted the 1979 Levitan Report. So also do the Clinton administration's 1994 ALMIS proposal (America's Labor Market Information System) and other proposals in Congress in 1995 for a more comprehensive labor market information system. In any case, it is clear that the passage of time has re-enforced the significance of the Levitan Report LMI recommendations.

We always need more and better LMI and labor force statistics. But are we willing to pay the price? The 1995 labor statistics budget cuts by Congress suggest the answer too often is "No."

Concluding Remarks

Recessions and elections greatly increase politicians' appetite for employment and unemployment statistics. But severe federal budget constraints for the foreseeable future—certainly into the first five years of the twenty-first century—will seriously delay needed progress toward more and better employment, unemployment, and other labor market information at national, state, and local levels. The fiscal 1995 BLS appropriation was almost $300 million, but it faced fiscal 1995 and 1996 cuts by Congress ranging from 15 to 25 percent.[7]

Other employment-unemployment issues deserve attention—for example, trade-related employment and unemployment, mass layoff statistics, occupational classification, occupational surveys and projections, longitudinal surveys, and gross labor force flows, to name only a few.

But I want to re-emphasize what both the Gordon Report and the Levitan Report said about the importance of maintaining nonpolitical, nonpartisan, objective, professionalism in producing and reporting the nation's employment and unemployment statistics. There was evidence in 1995 that strong "fire walls" are essential to prevent political tampering with key national statistics.[8] For this reason I oppose a Central Statistical Bureau or stronger central coordination of the existing statistical system, as proposed by Janet Norwood (1995). This nation can afford and will benefit from some relatively minor overlap, duplication, and efficiency losses in our statistical system to avoid the political dangers of excessive centralization.

Good, sound economic and social policy depend on good, sound, nonpolitical, nonpartisan labor statistics. Such statistics don't come cheap. Expansion and improvement of basic employment and unemployment statistics don't come cheap. But the cost of good, solid labor statistics and labor market information still comes at a bargain price if scholars and policy makers use them as the basis for sound, economic and social policy.

NOTES

1. U.S. Department of Labor, Bureau of Labor Statistics (1992). For a short summary of labor market trends and outlook, see U.S. Department of Labor (1994).

2. National Commission on Employment and Unemployment Statistics (1979). Other commission members were Bernard A. Anderson, Glen G. Cain, Jack Carlson, Michael Moskow, Rudy Oswald, Samuel L. Popkin, Mitchell Sviridoff, and Joan Wills.

3. U.S. Department of Labor, Bureau of Labor Statistics (1994b). See also Polivka and Miller (1995) and Bregger and Haugen (1995), which announces replacement of the old U-1 through U-7 range with a new U-1 through U-6 range.

4. I am amused by this excessive indignation, which might better be directed at economists who fail to publicize their bad forecasts based on good data as well as their bad forecasts based on bad data.

5. Starting with January 1996 data, the "Employment Situation" news release, based on the cut-back CPS household survey, no longer contains a table with "direct" measures of employment and unemployment in the 11 biggest states. For these states the data will appear with a two-month delay in the monthly release "State and Metropolitan Area Employment and Unemployment," which is produced by the indirect "70-step" method.

6. Review commissioned by the U.S. Department of Labor pursuant to a 1993 request by the House Appropriations Committee, H.R.2516, House Report 10343.

7. Major elements of the fiscal 1995 BLS appropriations: labor force statistics—$103 million; prices and cost of living including CPI revision—$100 million; compensation and working conditions $61 million; productivity and technology—$7 million; and employment projections—$4 million. In July 1995 the Labor Department gave $18 million to the states to help implement computerized labor market information systems with industry and occupation projections, more wage data, better training for LMI professionals, and better dissemination of LMI. The awards ranged in size from $164,000 to Vermont up to $836,00 to New York State and $1.4 million to California (*Employment & Training Reporter,* August 9, 1995 (26:47, 984)).

8. Republican Speaker of the House Newton Gingrich warned the Bureau of Labor Statistics on the CPI: "If they can't get it right in the next 30 days or so, we zero them out, we transfer responsibility to either the Federal Reserve on the Treasury and tell them to get it right" (John Barry, "GOP Leaders Join Challenge to Price Index," *The Washington Post,* January 16, 1995).

References

American Statistical Association (ASA). 1993. *A Research Agenda to Guide and Improve the Current Employment Statistics Survey*, Alexandria, Virginia.

Bregger, John, and Steven Haugen. 1995. "BLS Introduces New Range of Alternative Employment Measures," *Monthly Labor Review* (October): 19-26.

Castillo, Monica. 1995. "A Profile of the Working Poor, 1993." Report No. 896, Bureau of Labor Statistics.

Levitan, Sar A., and Frank Gallo. 1989. *Workforce Statistics: Do We Know What We Think We Know—and What Should We Know*. Joint Economic Committee, U.S. Congress, December 26 (cited as the 1989 Levitan-Gallo Report).

Mitchell, Daniel J.B. 1995. "Statistical Discrepancy in the Federal Data Programs," *Challenge* (July/August): 38-45.

National Commission on Unemployment Statistics. 1979. *Counting the Labor Force*. Washington, DC: Government Printing Office (cited as the 1979 Levitan Report).

Norwood, Janet. 1994. "Measuring Unemployment: A Change in the Yardstick," *Policy Bites* 21, Urban Institute, March: 1-4.

_____. 1995. *Organizing to Count: Change in the Federal Statistical System*. Washington, DC: Urban Institute.

Polivka, Anne, and Stephen M. Miller. 1995. "The CPS after the Redesign: Refocusing the Economic Lens."Paper presented at NBER/CRIW Labor Statistics Measurement Conference, December 1944; BIS Working Paper 269, March 1995; forthcoming in NBER Conference volume.

President's Committee to Appraise Employment and Unemployment Statistics. 1962. *Measuring Employment and Unemployment*. Washington, DC: Government Printing Office (cited as the 1962 Gordon Report).

U.S. Department of Labor. 1994. "Labor Market Development: Key Long-Term Trends, Likely Future," In *Report on the American Workplace*. Washington, DC: Government Printing Office.

U.S. Department of Labor, Bureau of Labor Statistics. 1992. *BLS Handbook of Methods*. Bulletin 2414, September.

_____. 1994a. "Current Population Survey: Three Reprints from the *Monthly Labor Review*," September.

_____. 1994b. "Revisions in the Current Population Survey Effective January 1994." Reprinted from *Employment and Earnings*, February.

_____. 1995. "BLS Sample Redesign for the Current Employment Statistics Survey." June 2.

CHAPTER 17

The Prospects for Arbitration in the Nonunion Sector

Trevor Bain

Rights disputes arise from the claim of an aggrieved worker that there has been a violation of a collective agreement, of the provisions of work rules, of unilateral management policies, including disciplinary rules, or of provisions of an individual contract of employment. There may also be situations in which management claims that its rights have not been respected. This is different from interest disputes, which are disagreements over the terms of a collective agreement. Collective bargaining contract negotiations are a legislative process through which the law of the workplace is jointly determined. The usual mechanism for resolving disputes over rights in the unionized setting in the United States is a joint labor-management grievance procedure with the final step of binding arbitration. Without this judicial system, every time there is a dispute over the application of the contract at the workplace a strike is necessary to resolve the issue by force. Or, every time one party chooses to ignore the contract it can be enforced only by a strike or a lockout. The grievance procedure culminating in arbitration makes contract administration viable.

Grievance procedures are not new to labor-management relations (Fleming 1965). The first recorded instance of voluntary arbitration in the United States took place in 1865 in a dispute involving the iron puddlers of Pittsburgh (Smith 1992). The best known grievance procedure during the early twentieth century was established in a 1911 agreement between Hart, Schafner and Marx clothing manufacturers and the Amalgamated Clothing Workers Union. Employee representation plans in the 1920s are characterized as a large grievance committee through which management could learn of workers' complaints (Chamberlain 1951). Employee representation plans that sought to avoid the union were declared illegal under the National Labor Relations Act (1935). But the greatest growth in grievance arbitration began during World War II. The National War Labor Board (WLB) encouraged unions and employers to include an arbitration clause in their agreements and sometimes required it. When the parties didn't agree on an arbitrator, the WLB appointed one. President Truman convened a Labor-Management Conference in 1945, and George Taylor of the University of Pennsylvania reported that one of the few agreements by the parties to that conference was that arbitration would be the final step in a grievance procedure (U.S. Department of Labor 1994). This laid the foundation for the practice of ending the grievance procedure with the final step of arbitration. That was an important change from the 1920s employee representation plans, which were internal plans without the use of an impartial neutral. Arbitration became the *quid pro quo* for ending strikes. The grievance procedure eliminated strikes over grievances and brought stability and predictability to the bargaining relationship.

Federal statutes that affect the grievance procedure and arbitration in the private sector are the Labor-Management Relations Act (LMRA) in 1947 and the Railway Labor Act (RLA) in 1926. The LMRA, Section 301, authorizes suits in federal courts for violation of collective agreements and, in 1959, the Supreme Court held that Section 301 authorized federal district courts to enforce arbitration provisions in collective bargaining agreements. In 1960, the Supreme Court, in three cases termed the "Steelworkers' Trilogy," took major steps to fashion a federal law of labor arbitration that gave legal substance to an arbitrator's award. The results of these three cases can be summarized as: the courts should send to arbitration all disputes subject to the arbitration clause; interpretation of the agreement is for the arbitrator and not the courts; courts should not reject an award unless the arbitrator exceeded the authority under the contract; courts should not reexamine the merits of a grievance; and awards need not be set aside for incompleteness. Many of the states followed the direction of the federal government, and by 1975, three-fourths of the states had enacted an arbitration statute.

The grievance procedure culminating in final and binding arbitration that developed in the unionized sector became so admired that it has been adopted as alternative dispute resolution (ADR) to resolve disputes related to divorce, the environment, construction, consumer claims, and customer claims against brokerage firms. While practitioners and scholars of labor arbitration continue to debate arbitration's future in the unionized sector, the discussion of its application to the nonunion sector has exploded.

The final report of the Commission on the Future of Worker-Management Relations (1994), usually called the Dunlop Commission, encourages the development of in-house dispute resolution procedures, while the Worker Representation and Participation Survey conducted by Freeman and Rogers (1995) reported that the majority of respondents were favorably disposed to using arbitration to resolve disputes. The question is whether what works so well in the unionized sector and appears to work well in many other ADR situations can be an effective means of employee protection in nonunion employment.

The objectives of this paper are to assess the current coverage and legal status of nonunion arbitration; evaluate what has been learned from private sector labor arbitration as a guide to the nonunion sector; examine the issues related to the use of arbitration in the nonunion sector; present some recommendations for improving its use; and assess the probability of its success in the nonunion sector.

Coverage and Legal Status

Considerably less is known about the extent and nature of alternative dispute resolution procedures for nonunion employees than for union employees. A Conference Board study (Berenbein 1980) surveyed the nonunion companies and concluded that two-thirds of them had adopted some type of grievance procedure by 1978. A survey conducted by Ichniowski and Lewin (1988) found that about one-half of nonunion business lines in each occupational group have a procedure for processing employee grievances with a low of 43.7 percent for managers and a high of 54.4 percent for production workers. They also reported that the growth in ADR procedures is more recent in the nonunion sector than the union sector, covering 5 percent of all occupational groups in 1960 and growing by four to five times between 1960 and 1980.

Arbitration is increasingly being used in statutory rights cases. The motivation for the employer to initiate ADR is less union avoidance than the fear of court suits and large settlements for the employee, particularly with regard to employment discrimination claims. The popular literature indicates that employers favor ADR to court litigation but that they initiate mechanisms which do not use third-party neutrals. A recent survey of 2,000 businesses with 100 or more employees by theU.S. General Accounting Office (1995) found that all private employers used some type of internal ADR procedure to resolve discrimination suits. Negotiation and fact finding were used most often, while arbitration was one of the least common approaches; some employers using arbitration make it mandatory for all workers.

The possibility of arbitrating employment discrimination claims arose after the passage of the Civil Rights Act of 1964. In *Alexander v. Gardner Denver Co.*, the Supreme Court held that the employees' right in a unionized setting to sue under Title VII was not precluded by the arbitrator's award.[1] However, the Supreme Court's attitude toward arbitration of statutory claims has changed. In the case of *Gilmer v. Interstate/Johnson Lane Corp.*, Gilmer, a brokerage employee, was required to sign an agreement to arbitrate any controversy arising out of employment or termination of employment.[2] Gilmer filed a complaint against his former employer under the Age Discrimination in Employment Act and the Supreme Court held that his claim was required to go to arbitration. Ever since *Gilmer*, more employers are moving toward employees signing agreements to arbitrate all disputes arising out of their employment. Advantages to the employer of such an agreement are: the avoidance of punitive damages under the 1991 amendments to Title VII, and the ability to keep arbitration decisions confidential. The Equal Employment Opportunity Commission has also announced that it will initiate a voluntary ADR program using mediation to handle some of the nearly 100,000 discrimination charges it receives each year. The program will select employees and employers to work with a neutral mediator to settle disputes.

Lessons from the Union Sector

ADR procedures vary in formality, ranging from an informal "open door policy," through a corporate ombudsman, to a grievance and arbitration procedure. Lewin and Peterson (1988) identify the four functions of the grievance procedure as compliance, adjudicative, administrative, and political. The grievance procedure also introduces the notion of fairness, or distributive and procedural justice, into the workplace. Gordon (1988) defines distributive justice as the perceived fairness of the allocation of company resources among employees and procedural justice as the perceived fairness of the process through which decisions are made to allocate company resources. The literature on union grievance procedures can be divided into three areas by following the steps of the grievance procedure: (1) determinants of grievance initiation and activity, (2) determinants of grievance resolution and settlement, and (3) determinants of grievance effectiveness. To adapt this literature to the nonunion firm we substitute the employee handbook for the contract and employee-management relations for union-management relations.

With regard to the determinants of grievance initiation and activity, grievance initiation can be viewed by employers as a benefit to the firm because it can serve as a voice for worker discontent. Workers may choose to initiate grievances rather than exit the company or stay away from work, both of which are costly to the firm. The research indicates that the process can be improved with programs that provide employees and supervisors with the skills to effectively use the grievance procedure (Bemmels, Reshef, and Stratton-Devine 1991). Changes in technology and stress in the work environment were also likely to increase grievance activity (Peach and Livernash 1974, Muchinsky and Maassaran 1980).

With regard to the determinants of grievance resolution and settlement, the clearer the contract language with regard to the rights and facts of a grievance, the more likely it is to be resolved (Meyer and Cooke 1988). A case's resolution also effects relations between employees and management (Gordon and Bowlby 1988). When a case is settled in favor of management, relations deteriorate between the employee and both lower- and higher-level management, but the relationship is unchanged when the grievant wins. Lewin and Peterson (1988) conclude that the larger the unit, the higher the steps at which grievances were settled and the slower the speed of settlements. Expedited grievance procedures were found to raise the employees' and managers' perceptions of the equity of a grievance settlement, and experience in handling a grievances also affects resolution.

With regard to the determinants of grievance effectiveness, the principal benefits to employees from the grievance procedure are that it provides a mechanism for due process and that it can be perceived as providing a procedure for fairness in dealing with the issues (Gordon 1988). For the union, it demonstrates the union's role in representing the membership. The benefits for management may include a reduction in work slowdowns and improvement in the company's economic performance. The possibility of multiple benefits leads researchers to agree that effectiveness is not a single concept (Clark and Gallagher 1988), but instead depends on which party is being discussed. Compared with a conventional contract, the union-management relationship is a continuing one. The same can be said for the employee-employer relationship, and the benefits of a grievance procedure or the settlement of a grievance may extend into the future.

Additional measures of effectiveness are related to the grievance procedure as providing a mechanism for workplace justice or procedural justice and serving as a collective voice for union members. The grievance procedure can provide procedural justice, since it lays out how decisions are made, and distributive justice, since there are consequences of the decisions. Gordon and Miller (1984) find little research that either supports or refutes the contention that grievance procedures promote workplace justice. With regard to the common law rights of workers, Knight (1986) concludes that the grievance process has not expanded rights beyond the specific contract.

It is difficult to come up with a simple conclusion or set of conclusions of the grievance process based on the literature (Peterson 1992). There are, however, several conclusions that can be drawn from the research. A labor-management contract that is clear and free of ambiguities reduces grievances and leads to early settlements. The same analogy can be used for the employee handbook. Feedback to union officials and management also assists early settlements. This analogy can be used for employees and management. Finally a good industrial relations climate, for both union and nonunion firms, reduces grievance filing, speeds settlement, and increases productivity.

Issues in Adaptation

If employers were to initiate a grievance procedure that results in final and binding arbitration, a process which currently does not exist in most organizations, what are the issues to be resolved?

First is the issue of a contract between the employer and employee. The employer has made the rules of employment and may or may not have set them down in an employee handbook. If not, there is no contract, or law of the workplace, for the employee to work with. The right to challenge management decisions and the procedure for doing it have to be clearly set out in some communication, such as a handbook, that every employee knows about and is required to read.

Second is the acceptance of arbitration by employees. Insight into how employees view arbitration as a vehicle for resolving disputes over employment issues is provided by the Freeman and Rogers survey (1995). A large fraction of employees view courts and agencies as vehicles for resolving disputes concerning employment issues. However, when asked whether they would prefer an alternative system to deal with disputes in which an elected committee of employees and management would jointly choose an outside arbitrator to resolve the dispute, approximately 55 percent of employees said they would prefer the alternative system, while 37 percent wanted to go to court or to an agency. The employees who responded to the survey were favorably disposed to using arbitration to resolve disputes, but most employees want such a system to be jointly administered by employees and management. This result addresses the issue of perceived fairness and justice.

Third is employee representation. In the union setting, the employee is represented by the union but few employees have the ability to present their own case effectively. Even the most effective employee would face experienced management representatives. Employees could be represented or accompanied by fellow employees, but they would still not possess the expertise that management has in presenting their case to the arbitrator. Therefore, effective representation involves the expense of hiring a lawyer. Without the union there should be some provision for an employee advocate or the perception of justice may be undermined. Eighty-two percent of the employees (Freeman and Rogers 1995) want a system in which "expert help" is available to the grieving employee.

Fourth is the selection of an arbitrator. The evidence indicates that the selection of a neutral outside party, especially in the formation of the procedure, is important. Employees must perceive the arbitrator as fair and competent. A controversy exists within the National Academy of Arbitrators (NAA) as to whether members should hear grievances under arbitration procedures established by nonunion employers. In a survey conducted by Nye (1994), more than 90 percent of the arbitrators indicated a conditional willingness to serve and more than 54 percent had done so.

Fifth involves compensation for the arbitrator. The employee may not be able to pay part of the arbitrator's compensation, particularly if there has been a discharge. The perception of procedural and distributive justice that both parties should accept may not be present if the issue is not resolved to the employees' satisfaction and the arbitrator has been paid by the employer. Forty-three percent of respondents to the Freeman and Rogers Survey (1995) want management and employees to pay the expenses of the system.

Sixth is enforcement of the arbitrators award. There is at present no machinery for enforcement other than the courts. If the employer ignores the arbitrator's decision, the grievant has no choice but to employ a lawyer and go to court for enforcement.

Seventh is whether employers can require employees to use ADR as a condition of employment. By almost a 4-1 margin, employees believe that such a requirement should be illegal (Freeman and Rogers 1995). There are currently some limitations to the employers' ability to force employees to arbitrate their claims of employment discrimination. No case requiring arbitration of an employee's claims, not even *Gilmer*, has expressly overruled *Alexander v. Gardner Denver Corp.*, which suggests that unionized employees claiming discrimination may still pursue judicial claims separate and distinct from their claims under the collective agreement. Whether the court would extend this right in the nonunion setting hasn't been decided. The cases requiring arbitration of discrimination claims have all involved some agreement other than an employment contract as the vehicle imposing the obligation to arbitrate. In *Gilmer* and other securities industry cases it was a stock exchange registration agreement that contained the arbitration agreement, and in *Williams v. Katten, Muchin & Zavis*, the law firm's partnership agreement imposed the obligation to arbitrate[3] Another consideration limiting the trend to force arbitration stems from a recent decision by the U.S. Court of Appeals for the 9th Circuit. In *Prudential Insurance Co. of America v. Lai*, it was held that an employee must have knowingly agreed to waive the right to a judicial forum in order to be forced to arbitrate discrimination claims.[4] The Supreme Court on October 2, 1995 let stand this ruling.

Finally, the employee's agreement to arbitrate employment disputes must also be voluntary. A federal district court in Houston recently ordered an employer to cease and desist from requiring employees to sign an arbitration agreement; employees who refused to sign were fired. The court held that forcing employees to give up their right to resort to the courts for resolution of employment discrimination claims violated Title VII.

Recommendations

Companies use ADR to reduce litigation costs, to avoid unions, or to increase employee satisfaction. Appeals procedures vary in formality, ranging from the least formal "open door policy," through a corporate ombudsman, to a grievance and arbitration procedure. The Brown and Root System described in the Dunlop Report (U.S. Department of Labor 1994b), includes an open door policy, successive steps, mediation, and arbitration. A great deal of the research on this topic is anecdotal. Some of it is reported by Peterson and Peterson (1987). If arbitration is to be the only recourse available to employees short of exiting the company, then arbitration must be seen as neutral. The values and expectations of employees may determine the acceptance of a formal grievance procedure (Gundry and Briggs 1993). Employees who identify with the organization are less likely to need a formal procedure and less likely to go as far as arbitration (Boroff 1994). The payoff to the employee is not as apparent as the payoff to the employer. With the limited judgment authority available to arbitrators, the cost to the company is significantly less than a comparable lawsuit. Therefore, employer-initiated arbitration is likely to expand in all sized firms and not just in large and medium-size firms where most human resources innovations occur. The GAO report (1995) found no statistically significant difference in use of arbitration based on business size.

The GAO report also echoes what many critics of employer-initiated grievance systems have said: employers use ADR to resolve discrimination complaints, and fairness is not always part of these systems. Quality standards that should be implemented to bring fairness to nonunion arbitration procedures are identified by the Dunlop Commission (1994) as:

- a neutral arbitrator who knows the laws in question and understands the concerns of the parties
- a fair and simple method by which the employee can secure the necessary information to present his or her claim;
- a fair method of cost-sharing between the employer and employee to ensure affordable access to the system for all employees
- the right to independent representation if the employee wants it
- a range of remedies equal to those available through litigation
- a written opinion by the arbitrator explaining the rationale for the result
- sufficient judicial review to ensure that the result is consistent with the government laws

The Future

Arbitration provides employees and employers with a great deal of flexibility to resolve employment relationship disputes without resorting to the courts. It can be quicker, less costly, and less adversarial, as long as both parties view it as providing an equitable forum. While the parties may disagree over the results of arbitration in the unionized setting, the process is viewed as being fair. However, the same cannot be said for arbitration in the nonunion setting. There is considerable inequality in economic power between employees and employers in the nonunion setting, and in order for arbitration to succeed as an alternative to the courts, equity and fairness standards have to be assured for employer-initiated procedures. This may require installing some institution or activity that gives nonunion employees some of the economic power they gain in the unionized setting, including binding arbitration.

NOTES

1. 415 U.S. 147 (1974).
2. 500 U.S. 20 (1991).
3. 837 F. Supp. 1430 (N.D. 211., E.D., 1993).
4. 66 FEP Cases 933 (9th Cir. 1994).

References

Bemmels, Brian, Yonatan Reshef, and Kay Stratton-Devine. 1991. "The Roles of Supervisors, Employees, and Stewards in Grievance Initiation," *Industrial and Labor Relations Review* 45, 1 (October): 15-30.

Berenbein, Ronald. 1980. "Nonunion Compliant Systems: A Corporate Appraisal." Report No. 770, The Conference Board.

Boroff, Karen. 1994. "The Probability of Filing a Grievance," Proceedings of the Forty-Fifth Annual Meeting, Industrial Relations Research Association Madison.

Chamberlain, Neil W. 1951. *Collective Bargaining*. New York: McGraw-Hill.

Clark, Paul F. and Daniel G. Gallagher. 1988. "Membership Perceptions of the Value and Effect of Grievance Procedures", Industrial Relations Research Association, *Proceedings of the Fortieth Annual Meeting*, Madison.

Fleming, R.W. 1965. *The Labor Arbitration Process*. Urbana, IL: University of Illinois Press.

Freeman, Richard, and Joel Rogers. 1995. *Worker Representation and Participation Survey: Second Report of Findings*. Princeton, NJ: Princeton Survey Research Association.

Gordon, Michael E. 1988. "Grievance Systems and Workplace Justice: Tests of Behavioral Propositions About Procedural and Distributive Justice," Industrial Relations Research Association, *Proceedings of the Fortieth Annual Meeting,* Madison.

Gordon, Michael E., and Roger. L. Bowlby. 1988. "Propositions About Grievance Settlements: Finally, Consultation with Grievants," *Personnel Psychology* 41: 107-123.

Gordon, Michael E., and Sandra J. Miller. 1984. "Grievances: A Review of Research and Practice," *Personnel Psychology* 37, 2 (Spring,): 117-146.

Gundry, Lisa, and Steven Briggs. 1993. "The Cultural Context of a Grievance Process; Employee Values and Expectations in Dispute Resolution," *Journal of Business and Psychology* 8: 129-140.

Ichniowski, Casey, and David Lewin. 1988. "Characteristics of Grievance Procedures: Evidence from Nonunion, Union, and Double-Breasted Businesses," Industrial Relations Research Association, *Proceedings of the Fortieth Annual Meeting*, Madison.

Knight, Thomas R. 1986. "Feedback and Grievance Resolution," *Industrial and Labor Relations Review* 39, (July): 585-548.

Lewin, David, and Richard B. Peterson. 1988. *The Modern Grievance Procedure in the United States*. New York: Quorum Books.

Meyer, David, and William Cooke. 1988. "Economic and Political Factors in Formal Grievance Resolution," *Industrial Relations* 27, 3 (Fall): 318-335.

Muchinsky, Paul M., and Mounawar A. Maassaran. 1980. "Work Environment Effects on Public Sector Grievances," *Personnel Psychology* 33 (Summer): 403-414.

Nye, David. 1994. "Issues in Alternative Labor Dispute Resolution: Views of Members of the National Academy of Arbitrators." Dissertation, Auburn University.

Peach, David A., and Robert E. Livernash. 1974. *Grievance Initiation and Resolution: A Study in Basic Steel.* Boston: Graduate School of Business Administration, Harvard University.

Peterson, Richard B. 1992. "The Union and Nonunion Grievance System." In *Research Frontiers in Industrial Relations and Human Resources*, David Lewin, Olivia S. Mitchell, and Peter D. Sherer, eds. Madison: Industrial Relations Research Association.

Peterson, Richard B., and Mark R. Peterson. 1987. "Toward a Systematic Understanding of the Labor Mediation Process." In *Advances In Industrial and Labor Relations*, D. Lewin, D.B. Lipsky, and D. Sockell eds. Greenwich, CT: JAI Press.

Smith, Clifford E. 1992. "Introduction to the NAA Survey." In *Labor Arbitration in America,* Mario F. Bognanno and Charles J. Coleman, eds. New York: Praeger.

U.S. Department of Labor and Department of Commerce, *Fact-Finding Report*, Commission on the Future of Worker-Management Relations, 1994a.

U.S. Department of Labor and Department of Commerce, *Final Report*, Commission on the Future of Worker-Management Relations, 1994b.

U.S. General Accounting Office. 1995. "Employment Discrimination: Most Employers Use Alternative Dispute Resolution." GAO/HEHS-95-150, Washington, DC, July.

Sar A. Levitan
BIBLIOGRAPHY
1950–1994

Books

Ingrade Wage-Rate Progression in War and Peace: A Problem in Wage Administration Techniques. Plattsburg, NY: Clinton Press, 1950.

Federal Aid to Depressed Areas: An Evaluation of the Area Redevelopment Administration. Baltimore: Johns Hopkins University Press, 1964.

The Design of Federal Antipoverty Strategy. Ann Arbor: Institute of Labor and Industrial Relations, March 1967.

Making Sense of Federal Manpower Policy, with Garth L. Mangum. Ann Arbor: Institute of Labor and Industrial Relations, March 1967.

Antipoverty Work and Training Efforts: Goals and Reality. Ann Arbor: Institute of Labor and Industrial Relations, August 1967.

Antipoverty Housekeeping: The Administration of the Economic Opportunity Act, with Roger H. Davidson. Ann Arbor: Institute of Labor and Industrial Relations, September 1968.

Federal Training and Work Programs in the Sixties, with Garth L. Mangum. Ann Arbor: Institute of labor and Industrial Relations, 1969.

The Great Society's Poor Law: A New Approach to Poverty. Baltimore: Johns Hopkins University Press, 1969.

Economic Opportunity in the Ghetto: The Partnership of Government and Business, with Garth L. Mangum and Robert Taggart. Baltimore: Johns Hopkins University Press, 1970.

Social Experimentation and Manpower Policy: The Rhetoric and Reality, with Robert Taggart. Baltimore: Johns Hopkins University Press, 1971.

Big Brother's Indian Programs—With Reservations, with Barbara Hetrick. New York: McGraw Hill, 1971.

Job Crisis for Black Youth: A Report for the Twentieth Century Fund, with Robert Taggart. New York: Frederick A. Praeger, 1972.

Work and Welfare Go Together, with Martha Rein and David Marwick. Baltimore: Johns Hopkins University Press, 1972 and 1976.

Old Wars Remain Unfinished: The Veterans Benefit System, with Karen Cleary. Baltimore: Johns Hopkins University Press, 1973.

Work is Here to Stay, Alas, with William F. Johnston. Salt Lake City: Olympus, 1973.

The Quest for a Federal Manpower Partnership, with Joyce K. Zickler, Cambridge, MA: Harvard University Press, 1974.

Employment and Earnings Inadequacy: A New Social Indicator, with Robert Taggart. Baltimore: Johns Hopkins University Press, 1974.

Still a Dream: The Changing Status of Blacks Since 1960, with William B. Johnston and Robert Taggart. Cambridge, MA: Harvard University Press, 1975.

Child Care and ABC's Too, with Karen Cleary Alderman. Baltimore: Johns Hopkins University Press, 1975.

Indian Giving: The Federal Government and Native Americans, with William B. Johnston. Baltimore: Johns Hopkins University Press, 1975.

The Job Corps: A Social Experiment that Works, with Benjamin H. Johnston. Baltimore: Johns Hopkins University Press, 1975.

Minorities in the United States: Problems, Progress, and Prospects, with William B. Johnston and Robert Taggart. Washington, DC: Public Affairs Press, 1975.

The Promise of Greatness, with Robert Taggart. Cambridge, MA: Harvard University Press, 1976.

Too Little But Not Too Late: Federal Aid to Lagging Areas, with Joyce K. Zickler. Lexington, MA: Lexington Books, 1976.

Human Resources and Labor Markets, with Garth L. Mangum and Ray Marshall. New York: Harper & Row, 1972, 1976 and 1981.

Jobs for the Disabled, with Robert Taggart. Baltimore: Johns Hopkins University Press, 1977.

Shorter Hours, Shorter Weeks, with Richard S. Belous. Baltimore: Johns Hopkins University Press.

Work and Welfare in the 1970s. New York: Ford Foundation, 1977.

Warriors at Work: The Volunteer Armed Force, with Karen Cleary Alderman. Beverly Hills: Sage Publications, 1977.

More than Subsistence: Minimum Wages for the Working Poor, with Richard S. Belous. Baltimore: Johns Hopkins University Press, 1979.

Evaluating Federal Social Programs: An Uncertain Art, with Gregory Wurzburg. Kalamazoo, MI: W.E. Upjohn Institute for Employment Research, 1979.

Second Thoughts on Work, with Clifford M. Johnson. Kalamazoo, MI: W.E. Upjohn Institute for Employment Research, 1982.

Working for the Sovereign: Employee Relations in the Federal Government, with Alexandra Noden. Baltimore: Johns Hopkins University Press, 1983.

Business Lobbies: The Public Good and the Bottom Line, with Martha Cooper. Baltimore: Johns Hopkins University Press, 1984.

Productivity: Problems, Prospects, and Policies, with Diane Werneke. Baltimore: Johns Hopkins University Press, 1984.

Beyond the Safety Net: Reviving the Promise of Opportunity in America, with Clifford M. Johnson. Cambridge, MA: Ballinger, 1984.

Protecting American Workers, with Peter E. Carlson and Isaac Shapiro. Washington, DC: Bureau of National Affairs, 1986.

Working but Poor: America's Contradiction, with Isaac Shapiro. Baltimore: Johns Hopkins University Press, 1987.

A Second Chance: Training for Jobs, with Frank Gallo. Kalamazoo, MI: W.E. Upjohn Institute for Employment Research, 1988.

What's Happening to the American Family? Tension, Hopes, Realities, with Richard S. Belous and Frank Gallo. Baltimore: Johns Hopkins University Press, Revised Edition, 1988.

Families in Flux: New Approaches in Meeting Workforce Challenges for Child, Elder, & Health Care in the 1990s, with Elizabeth Conway. Washington, DC: Bureau of National Affairs, 1990.

Programs in Aid of the Poor. Baltimore: Johns Hopkins University Press, Sixth Edition, 1990 (five previous editions, various dates).

Edited Volumes

Dimensions of Manpower Policy: Programs and Research, with Irving H. Siegel, eds. Baltimore: Johns Hopkins University Press, 1966.

Blue-Collar Workers: A Symposium on Middle America. New York: McGraw Hill, 1971.

The Federal Social Dollar in Its Own Back Yard. Washington, DC: Bureau of National Affairs, 1973.

Emergency Employment Act: The PEP Generation, with Robert Taggart, eds. Salt Lake City: Olympus, 1974.

CETA Training: A National Review and Eleven Case Studies, with Garth L. Mangum, eds. Kalamazoo, MI: W.E. Upjohn Institute for Employment Research, 1981.

The T in CETA: Local and National Perspectives, with Garth L. Mangum, eds. Kalamazoo, MI: W.E. Upjohn Institute for Employment Research, 1981.

The Feds in the Workplace. Conference Proceedings. Washington, DC: National Council on Employment Policy, October 3, 1985.

Contributions to Symposia & Selected Presentations

"An Appraisal of the Frontiers of Research in Industrial Relations." In *Research Frontiers in Industrial Relations Today*, proceedings from the

14th Annual Conference of the Industrial Relations Centre. Montreal: MCGill University, April 26-27, 1962.

"The Impact of Technological Change Upon Communities and Public Policy," with Harold L. Sheppard. Prepared for IRRA volume *Adjustments to Technological Change*. U.S. Department of Commerce, Area Redevelopment Administration, May 1962.

"The Program of the Area Redevelopment Administration—Its Present Scope and Effectiveness." Presented at the 49th Annual Meeting of the National Industrial Conference Board, Session L, Revitalization of Depressed Areas, New York, May 21, 1965.

"Evaluation of Occupational Data and Their Use in Education Planning." Conference on Occupational Data Requirements for Education Planning Center for Vocational and Technical education, University of Wisconsin, June 16, 1965.

"Area Redevelopment: A Tool to Combat Poverty?" In *Poverty in America,* M. Gordon, ed. San Francisco: Chandeler, 1965.

"Program Strategies Designed to Minimize Human Waste." Third Annual Commonwealth Conference on Urban Leadership and community Leadership: Continuing Problems of Poverty, Pennsylvania State University, April 5, 1966.

"Work Relief: Social Welfare System." Conference on Augmenting the labor Force: Education and Training for Employables," Institute for Research on Human Resources, Pennsylvania State University, June 15, 1966.

"Is this Poverty War 'Different'?" In *Dimensions in Manpower Policy: Programs and Research*. Baltimore: Johns Hopkins University Press, 1966.

"The War on Poverty: A Progress Report." Eighth Annual Conference, National Planning Association, Washington, D.C. April 27, 1967.

"Our Work has just Begun." Michigan State University Sesquicentennial Conference *Breaking the Poverty Cycle*, August 25, 1967.

"The Need to Invest in Education." In *Focus on Vocational Education*. New York: Publication of Education Committee, National Association of Manufacturers, December 8, 1967.

"Manpower Aspects of the Economic Opportunity Act." Proceedings of the Industrial Relations Research Association Winter meeting, 1967.

"Discussion." Proceedings of the Social Statistics Section, American Statistics Association, 1967.

"The Economic Development of the Central City: Programs and Prospects," with Robert Taggart. Conference on Ghetto Economic Development, Clark College, Atlanta, March 15, 1969.

"Are We Planning Ersatz Manpower Programs for the 1970s?" Temple University Symposium on Social Economics: *Agenda for Americans*, March 21, 1969.

"Facts, Fancies, and Freeloaders in Evaluating Antipoverty Programs." Written for *Poverty and Human Resources*, and delivered before the American Social Association, San Francisco, September 4, 1969.

"Development of a National Manpower Policy." Conference Commemorating the 10th Anniversary of the Enactment of the Manpower Development and Training Act of 1962, March 16, 1972.

"Jobs for Neglected Sectors of the Workforce." Edison Electric Institute Symposium: *Meeting the Urban Needs: Definitions and Evaluations*, December 19, 1977.

"An Economist's (Solicited and Surprisingly) Cheerful Message to Vocational Educators." In *The Future of Vocational Education*, Albert J. Paulter, Jr., ed. Columbus: Center for Vocational Education, Ohio State University, 1977, pp. 53-62.

"Reduced Worktime: An Alternative to High Unemployment," with Richard S. Belous. In *Job Creation: What Works?* Robert Taggart, ed. Salt lake City: Olympus, 1977, pp. 75-92.

"The Unemployment Number is the Message." *Forty-First Annual Proceedings of the Interstate Conference of Employment Security Agencies*. Washington: ICESA, 1977, pp. 11-18.

"Labor Force Statistics: Where Do We Go From Here?" National Commission on Employment and Unemployment Statistics, Washington Statistical Society, February 15, 1978.

"Vocational Education in the 1980s." In *Vocational Education's Role in a Changing Economy: Symposium Proceedings*, Steven L. Van Ausdle, ed. Spokane: Washington Council of Local Administrators of Vocational Education, April 1978, pp. 8-10.

"Labor Force Statistics to Measure Full Employment." Governor's Conference on Full Employment, Phoenix, May 15, 1978.

"Can the Federal Government Distribute Funds to Prime Sponsors Fairly and Squarely?, "How Good Are Our Labor Force Statistics?" and "Improving Productivity with Training." Seattle University, September 12-13, 1978.

"Labor Force Statistics: Time for a Change?" In *Labor Force Yardsticks: A Guide to Policies for Reducing Unemployment*. Information Bulletin No. 45. New York: The Conference Board, September 1978, pp. 17-19.

"Roadblocks to Improving Our Labor Force Statistics." Eleventh Annual New Researchers Conference, sponsored by the National Council on Employment Policy, Washington, D.C., September 28, 1978.

"What's the Labor Force Commission Up To?" Seventh Annual Conference, National Association of County Manpower Officials, Phoenix, October 31, 1978.

"Education and Work: Issues for the 1980s." National Center for Research in Vocational Education, Ohio State University, November 1, 1978.

"A Selective Summary." Conference on International Manpower Program Evaluation Methods, National Council on Employment Policy, December 6, 1978.

"Work and Welfare in the 1970s." In *Welfare: The Elusive Consensus*, Lester M. Salamon, ed. New York: Praeger, 1978, pp. 235-38.

"The Welfare Question." In *Revitalizing the Northeast*, George Sternlieb and James W. Huges, eds. New Brunswick, NJ: Center for Urban Policy Research, 1978, pp. 354-60.

"Productivity and the Work Ethic." In *Productivity in Today's Economic Climate,* Pace University, March 22, 1979.

"The Doubtful Link Between Productivity and Education." *1979 "Patterns" Conference Proceedings.* Rochester, NY: Rochester Institute of Technology, July 1979, pp. 1-12.

"Final Report of the National Commission on Employment and Unemployment Statistics." In *Jobs and Numbers*. Washington: National Governors' Association. Labor Market Information Project, July 17, 1979, pp. 75-80.

"Our Labor Force Statistics in the 1980s." Federal Statistical Users Conferences, Twenty-Third Annual Meeting, November 28, 1979.

"Jobs in the 1980s: Society's Work Will Be Done." Seventy-Third Vocational Meeting, American Vocational Association. Anaheim, CA, December 1, 1979.

"Congress vs. President: The Myth and the Pendulum." In *The Presidency and the Congress: A Shifting Balance of Power?*, William S. Livingston, Lawrence C. Donn, and Richard L. Schott, eds. Austin: Lyndon B. Johnson School of Public Affairs, University of Texas, 1979, pp. 182-96.

"Labor Force Statistics to Measure Full Employment." In *High Employment: Problems and Solutions*, Paul L. Burgess and Jerry L. Kingston, eds. Phoenix: Arizona State University, 1979, pp. 25-32.

"What's In a Number?" Symposium of Hispanics and CETA, University of Texas, January 30, 1980.

"Unemployment and Minimum Wages in the Welfare State: A Minority View from South of the Border." Economic Council of Canada, Ottawa, May 16, 1980.

"Doing the Impossible, Planning a Human Resource Policy." National Extension Manpower Workshop, May 19, 1980.

"Thank God, There is Work to be Done." Mid-American Conference on Voc/ Tech Education, May 22, 1980.

"The Economy—A Prognosis." State Job Service Directors, Salt Lake City, May 28, 1980.

"A Long Wait for Good Economic News." Metropolitan Human Services Commission, Columbus, June 24, 1980.

"Youth Unemployment." Briefing on Youth Unemployment, U.S. Civil Rights Commission, September 18, 1980.

"Family and Its Discontents." Conference on Women and Changing Life-styles, Washington Journalism Center, November 20, 1980.

"Let the Kids Go and They Will Come Back." Annual Meeting, American Vocational Association, New Orleans, December 8, 1980.

"Is Family Working?" University of Arizona, Tucson, January 28, 1981.

"Liberal Agenda in Orderly Retreat." Fourth Annual Social Workers in Politics Conference, sponsored by the National Association of Social Workers, April 12, 1981.

"Implications for the United States." Columbia Conference on International Income Maintenance Policies in Eight Countries, Carnegie Endowment for Peace, April 29, 1981.

"CETA Reauthorization and Lots More." Advisory Committee, National Alliance of Business and Private Industry Council, Washington, D.C., June 11, 1981.

"Reaganomics Needs a Prayer." Mid-America Conference for Voc/Tech Educators, Appleton, Wisconsin, June 16, 1981.

"Bridges to the Private Sector: Remedial Employment and Training Programs," NCEP Conference on CETA Reauthorization, June 25, 1981.

Implementing Recommendations of NCEUS." Federal Statistics Users, October 31, 1981.

"Human Resource Implications of Reaganomics." Industrial Relations Research Association, Annual Meeting. Washington, D.C., December 18, 1981.

"A Review of Youth Employment Policies in Germany." In *Youth Without Work: Three Countries Approach the Problem*, Shirley William, ed. Paris: Organization for Economic Co-operation and Development, 1981, pp. 89-170.

"Doing the Impossible—Planning a Human Resource Policy." *The Future of Vocational Education,* 1982 Yearbook of the American Vocational Association, 1981, pp. 272-80.

"Comments." *Report of the Minimum Wage Study Commission.* Volume V. Washington, DC: Government Printing Office, 1981, pp. 517-25.

"Rehabilitation, Employment, and the Disabled," with Robert Taggart. In *Alternatives in Rehabilitating the Handicapped*, Jeffrey Rubin, ed. New York: Human Sciences Press, 1981, pp. 89-150.

"The 1983 Budget and the New Federalism." National League of Cities, February 28, 1982

"Reforming Work." Ilustre Colegio Central De Titulares Mercantiles Commemorative Centennial Conference, Madrid, March 4, 1982.

"Reaganomics: A Steady Diet of Ideology." National Youth Work Alliance, Washington, D.C., July 7, 1982.

"Occupational Projections." National Center for Research in Vocational Education, 2nd Annual Policy Forum on Responsiveness to Changing labor Market Demands, September 23, 1982.

"Summing Up (based on selective hearing)." *What's Happening to American Labor Force & Productivity Measurements?* Proceedings of a June 17, 1982 Conference of the National Council on Employment Policy. Kalamazoo, MI: W.E. Upjohn Institute for Employment Research, 1983, pp. 127-34.

"Occupational Projections." In *Responsiveness to Changing Labor Market*, Robert Taylor, ed. Columbus: National Center for Research in Vocational Education, 1983, pp. 101-110.

"The Survival of Work," with Clifford M. Johnson. In *The Work Ethic: A Critical Analysis*. Industrial Relations Research Association, 1983.

"What Future for the Work Force." Twenty-Seventh Union-Management Conference on Increasing the Nation's Jobs, University of Notre Dame, June 8, 1984.

"Did the Great Society and Subsequent Initiatives Work?" with Clifford M. Johnson. Conference on The Great Society Revised, University of Colorado, Boulder, June 12, 1984.

"The Evolving Welfare System." Industrial Relations Research Association, Spring Meeting, Detroit, April 19, 1985.

"Work and Welfare Go Together." Conference on Alternatives to the "Loosing Ground" Perspective, American Public Welfare Association, Washington, D.C., May 7, 1985.

"The Evolving Welfare System." *Labor Law Journal* (August) 1985, pp. 577-586.

"Rethinking Protective Labor Legislation." Urban Institute Conference on Rethinking Employment Policy, Washington, D.C., September 5, 1985.

"Employment Policy." The Ford Foundation, Project on Social Welfare Policy and the American Future, and the Johnson Foundation, Conference on Future Welfare Policy Options, Wingspread, Racine, Wisconsin, November 3-5, 1985.

"The Shape of the Labor Market 1995." Employment and Training Policy conference, Working Smart: Using Today's Technology to Improve State Government, National Governors Association, Washington, D.C., December 18, 1985.

"Last But Not Final Word." NCEP Feds in the Workplace Conference, February 1986.

"The Unnaturally Inflated Rate of Unemployment," with Peter E. Carlson. Fortieth Annual Symposium, National Committee for Full Employment, March 6, 1986.

COMMENTARY, "A Boost of the Minimum Wage is Overdue." An Information Service of the National Job Training Partnership, April 21, 1986.

"Work and Training Go Together." Third Annual Conference, Ohio Job Training Coordinating Council, Columbus, September 10, 1986.

"A Question of Equity." Advancing Economic Productivity and Equity through Job Training, Employment Training Panel, Performance Standard Seminar, UCLA, Los Angeles, October 21, 1986.

"The Limits of Workfare." Conference on Poverty and Social Policy: The Minority Experience, Institute for Research on Poverty, Arlie House, Virginia, November 7, 1986.

"The Workplace—1996." Human Resources in the U.S. Economy, National Defense University, Washington, D.C., November 18, 1986.

"A Second Chance: Training for Jobs." Nineteenth Annual Conference, National Alliance of Business, September 15, 1987.

"The Workplace—1997." Washington Journalism Center, Conference on Employment and Unemployment: Where Will Jobs Be in the Next Decade? Washington, D.C., January 14, 1987.

"Jobs for the Hard to Employ." Chicago TRUST Urban Policy Forum, February 6, 1987.

"Innovation in Human Resources Management." National Planning Association, Washington, D.C., May 2, 1987.

"From Ozzie and Harriet to the Cosbys: Changing Family Workplace Policies." Sixth Annual National Conference on Corporate Community Involvement, Public Affairs Council, Atlanta, May 15, 1987.

"Revitalizing the Partnership: Preparing for the Future." Iowa State Department of Economic Development, Private Industry Council and Local Elected Official Conference: Holes in the Safety Nets: Poverty Programs and Policies in the States, Des Moines, Iowa, June 28, 1988.

"Labor and Employment Policy in the United States." Labor and Employment Policy in the United States: A Working Meeting, Michigan State University School of Industrial Relations, East Lansing, Michigan, September 16, 1988.

"Public Policies in the Coming Decade: The Impact on Children and Families." Annual Conference, Michigan League of Human Services 1988, Lansing, October 28, 1988.

"Contingent Workers: Numbers and Policies." Conference on the Contingent Economy, National Planning Association, Washington, D.C., June 27, 1989.

"Commitment and Cooperation: Empowering the Working Poor." The 1989 Eloise S. Cofer Family Living Seminar, Families: North Carolina's Best Investment, North Carolina State University, Raleigh, June 16, 1989.

"State of the Economy: Impact on Older Workers." Textbook Author Conference, sponsored by Business Partnerships, AARP Worker Equity, Washington, D.C., October 25, 1990.

"Flexibility and Workplace Regulation: The European and American Experience." Joint International Conference on European and American Labor Markets: Past, Present, and Future Perspectives, Freidrich-Ebert Foundation and National Planning Association, Washington, D.C., October 8, 1990, pp. 170-180.

"Uncle Sam's Helping Hand: Education, Training, and Employing the Disadvantaged," with Frank Gallo, *New Developments in Worker Training: A Legacy for the 1990s.* Madison, WI: Industrial Relations Research Association, 1990, pp. 225-256.

"Reforming Training with Good Intentions." In *Making Sense of Federal Job Training Policy,* Sar A. Levitan et al., eds. National Youth Employment Coalition, William T. Grant Foundation Commission on Work, Family, and Citizenship, July 27, 1992.

"Older Workers in Today's Economy." Textbook Authors Conference Business Partnerships, October, 21, 1992, pp. 17-22.

European and American Labor Markets: Different Models and Different Results. Sar A. Levitan, Richard S. Belous, Rebecca S. Hartley, Kelly L. McClenahan, eds. Washington: National Planning Association, 1992, pp. 51-54.

Occasional Papers & Essays

"The Businessman's Role in Organized Local Economic Growth." George Washington University, 1963.

"The Industry that Forgot Collective Bargaining," 1963.

"Youth Employment Act (S. 1, H.R. 1, and H.R. 1890, 88th Congress)." W.E. Upjohn Institute for Employment Research, February 1963.

"Second Anniversary of ARA," presented to the Washington Round Table, May 1, 1963.

"Vocational Education and Federal Policy (Administration Bills H.R. 3000 and S. 580 Congressman Carl D. Perkins H.R. 4955 Senator J. Caleb Boggs S. 1222." W.E. Upjohn Institute for Employment Research, May 1963.

"Federal Manpower Policies and Programs to Combat Unemployment." W.E. Upjohn Institute for Employment Research, February 1964.

"Reducing Work Time as a Means To Combat Unemployment." W.E. Upjohn Institute for Employment Research, September 1964.

"Economic Conditions in the United States and their Impact upon the Commonwealth," (unpublished). October 1964.

"Syracuse Faces its Youth Unemployment Problems." W.E. Upjohn Institute for Employment Research, January 28, 1965.

"Programs to Aid the Unemployed in the 1960's," with Joseph M. Becker and William Haber. W.E. Upjohn Institute for Employment Research, January 1965.

"Minimum Wages—A Tool to Fight Poverty." W.E. Upjohn Institute for Employment Research, July 10, 1965.

"Role of the Appalachian and Depressed Area Programs in Combatting Poverty." W.E. Upjohn Institute for Employment Research, July 14, 1965.

"Programs in Aid of the Poor." W.E. Upjohn Institute for Employment Research, December 1965.

"Manpower Programs for the Disadvantaged." Conference on Manpower Policy, University of California, June 21, 1966.

"What's Happening, Baby—Essential Research for the War on Poverty." American Statistical Association, August 18, 1966.

"Making Sense of Federal Manpower Policy," with Garth L. Mangum. Policy Papers in Human Resources and Industrial Relations No. 2, Ann Arbor/ Detroit, Institute of Labor and Industrial Relations, University of Michigan/Wayne State University.

"Alternative Approaches to Manpower Policies." September 7, 1967.

"Head Start: It is Never too Early to Fight Poverty." December 1967.

"A Redesign of OEO." January 6, 1969.

"Bedford—Stuyvesant Economic Development Efforts," with Robert Taggart. January 29, 1969.

"Helping the Original Americans." February 13, 1969.

"The Reluctance of Uncle Sam's Bureaucrats to Fight Poverty with the Poll," with Judith W. LaVor. August 1, 1969.

"Minority Economic Development in the United States." American Economic Association, December 29, 1969.

"Manpower Programs Under Republican Management." February 17, 1970.

"Big Brother's Last Stand," with Barbara Hetrick. May 1, 1970.

"Federal Manpower Programs in a Slack Economy." October 12, 1970.

"Data for Vocational Education Planning," for Vocational Education's Annual Long-Range Planning Institute, Little Rock, October 6, 1970.

"The Recession is a Depression for Ghetto Youth," with Robert Taggart. April 16, 1971.

"Manpower Programs as a Tool to Combat Inflation and Unemployment." October 11, 1971.

"Does Work Have A Future?" December 1973.

"The Effect of Veterans' Benefits on Reenlistment," with Joyce Zickler. December 7, 1972.

"Evaluation of Decentralized Manpower Programs," with Joyce Zickler, written for John Barry, December 12, 1973.

"The Economics of Youth Unemployment in the United States," with Robert Taggart. Joint Council on Economic Education, 1973.

"An Old Budget for New Legislation: Impact 1974," with Garth Mangum. February 21, 1974.

"Do Vietnam Veterans Get Enough?" February 1974.

"Creation of Jobs for the Unemployed." NCMP Analytical Paper No. 4, March 1975.

"Job Creation Program to Combat the Recession." April 15, 1975.

"Fighting Unemployment with Questionable Statistics." 1975.

"Social Programs Do Work." June 9, 1976.

"Coping with Teenage Unemployment." July 27, 1976.

"Labor's Demand: Reduce Work Hours for the Same Pay," with Richard Belous. October 21, 1976.

"Is There a Future in Shorter Hours?" with Richard S. Belous. December 22, 1976.

"Employment and Training Policies for Teenagers," with Robert Taggart. February 17, 1977.

"The Last Hurrah: Ford's 1978 Employment Policies and Carter's Adaptations," with Robert Taggart. March 1, 1977.

"Youth Employment Demonstration Projects for Military Rejects and Discharges." June 24, 1977.

"Is the Unemployment Rate an Outmoded Index?" with Richard S. Belous. August 19, 1977.

"Poverty." October 1977.

"Youth Employment Strategies," with Robert Taggart. 1977.

"The Unemployment Number is the Message." Occasional Paper No. 38, Center for Vocational Education, Columbus, 1977.

"Can We Afford to Employ All the Poor?" with Marilyn E. Park. April 4, 1978.

"Can You Trust an Evaluator?" Unpublished manuscript, 1976.

"Counting the Labor Force: A Multibillion Dollar Sweepstake." December 8, 1978.

"Minimum Wages: Do Gooders Can Do Good," with Richard S. Belous. March 28, 1979.

"The American Family." International Communication Agency, August 1981.

"Unemployment in the American Economy: the 1981-1982 Recession." International Communication Agency, February 1983.

"Poverty-Labor Market Connection," with Peter E. Carlson. October 15, 1983.

"The Changing Work Place: Perceptions, Reality." Trend Analysis Program (TAP) Social Research Service, American Council of Life Insurance, March 1984.

"Federal Policies Affecting American Workers," with Isaac Shapiro. U.S. Congress, Joint Economic Committee, August 1986.

"The Need for a New Applied Policy Institute." George Washington University, Center for Social Policy Studies, November 12, 1986.

"American Child Care: Problems and Solutions," with Elizabeth A. Conway. Special Report no. 12, National Report on Work and Family, Buraff Publications, Inc., a division of the Bureau of National Affairs, December 1988.

"A Proper Inheritance: Investing in the Self-Sufficiency of Poor Families," with Marion Pines and Garth Mangum. George Washington University, Center for Social Policy Studies, 1989.

"The Paradox of Homelessness in America," with Susan Schillmoeller. George Washington University, Center for Social Policy Studies, January 1991.

"Spending to Save: Expanding Employment Opportunities," with Frank Gallo. George Washington University, Center for Social Policy Studies, May 1991.

"Got to Learn to Earn: Preparing Americans for Work," with Frank Gallo. George Washington University, Center for Social Policy Studies, September 1991.

"Enterprise Zones: A Promise Based on Rhetoric," with Elizabeth I. Miller. George Washington University, Center for Social Policy Studies, March 1992.

"The Evaluation of Federal Social Programs: An Uncertain Impact." George Washington University, Center for Social Policy Studies, 1992.

"The Economics of Recitude: Necessary But Not Sufficient," with Garth L. Mangum and Stephen L. Mangum. George Washington University, Center for Social Policy Studies, July 1992.

"A Training Program for the 1990s: Reflecting on Campaign Proposals," with Garth L. Mangum and Stephen L. Mangum. George Washington University, Center for Social Policy Studies, October 1992.

"Hardship," with Andrew Sum and Robert Taggart. February 1993.

"Jobs for JOBS: Toward a Work-based Welfare System," with Frank Gallo. George Washington University, Center for Social Policy Studies, March 1993.

"The Equivocal Prospects for Indian Reservations," with Elizabeth I. Miller. George Washington University, Center for Social Policy Studies, May 1993.

"Preparing Youth for Work: Don't Run Before You Walk," with Larry Wohl. George Washington University, Center for Social Policy Studies, August 1993.

"Education Reform: Federal Initiatives and National Mandates, 1963-1993," with Frank Gallo. George Washington University, Center for Social Policy Studies, November 1993.

"Federal Human Resource Policy: From Kennedy to Clinton," with Garth L. Mangum. George Washington University, Center for Social Policy Studies, February 1994.

"The Displaced vs. the Disadvantaged: A Necessary Dichotomy?" with Stephen L. Mangum. George Washington University, Center for Social Policy Studies, May 1994.

Government Reports

"Working Capital on Government Project." Prepared for the Hoover Task Force on Water Resources and Power, april 29, 1954.

"Taxes on Public Projects." Prepared for the Hoover Task Force on Water Resources and Power, May 25, 1954.

"A Federal Program for Community Redevelopment." Library of Congress Legislative Reference Service, April 1955.

"Federal Responsibility in Community Redevelopment Program." Library of Congress Legislative Reference Service, May 4, 1955.

"Guaranteed Annual Wage." Library of Congress Legislative Reference Service, September 1, 1955.

"Selected Materials on the Economy of the South," Levitan et al. Report for the Committee on Banking and Currency of the U.S. Senate, October 5, 1956.

"Federal Assistance to Labor Surplus Areas." Report for the Committee on Banking and Currency of the U.S. House of Representatives, April 15, 1957.

"Jurisdictional Standards of the National Labor Relations Board," Levitan et al. Report for the Committee on Labor and Public Welfare of the U.S. Senate, March 19, 1957.

"Government Regulation of Internal Union Affairs Affecting the Rights of Members." Library of Congress Legislative Reference Service, 1958.

"Labor Management Reporting and Disclosure Bill of 1958 (S. 3974)." Library of Congress Legislative Reference Service, September 1, 1958.

"Welfare and Pension Plans Disclosure Act (Public Law 836, 85th Congress S. 2888 and H.R. 13507." Library of Congress Legislative Reference Service, September 17, 1958.

"Labor Unions in the United States." Library of Congress Legislative Reference Service, October 23, 1958.

"Federal Unemployment Insurance Standards: An Analysis of S. 791 and H.R. 3547," with I.M. Labovitz. Library of Congress Legislative Reference Service, April 2, 1959.

"National Policy and the Public Interest in Labor-Management Relations," Levitan et al. Report for the Committee on Education and Labor of the U.S. House of Representatives, May 1959.

"Amendments to Kennedy-Ervin Bill (S. 1555)." Library of Congress Legislative Reference Service, July 22, 1959.

"Restrictions on Organizational and Recognition Picketing (S. 1555 and H.R. 8342)." Library of Congress Legislative Reference Service, July 24, 1959.

"Hot Cargo Provisions (S. 1555, Section 707 and H.R. 8342, Section 705(a))." Library of Congress Legislative Reference Service, July 27, 1959.

"Background, Provisions, and Issues in Labor-Management Reporting and Disclosure Bill of 1959 (H.R. 8342, 86th Congress)." Library of Congress Legislative Reference Service, July 31, 1959.

"Comparison of H.R. 8342, H.R. 8400, and H.R. 8490 Labor-Management Reporting and Disclosure Bills (86th Congress, 1st Session)." Library of Congress Legislative Reference Service, August 7, 1969.

"Southern Italian Development Legislation." Library of Congress Legislative Reference Service, February 27, 1961.

"West German Area Development Legislation." Library of Congress Legislative Reference Service, February 27, 1961.

"The Poor in the Workforce." W.E. Upjohn Institute for Employment Research, Chamber of Commerce of U.S., Task Force on Economic Growth and Opportunity (Study Area No. 4), March 18, 1965.

"Work Experience and Training." Report for the Senate Subcommittee on Employment, Manpower, and Poverty, Vol. 1, No. 5, August 1967.

The Emergency Employment Act: An Interim Assessment, with Robert Taggart. Prepared for the U.S. Senate Committee on Labor and Public Welfare. Washington, DC: Government Printing Office, 1972.

Evaluation of the First 18 Months of the Public Employment Program, with Robert Taggart. Prepared for the Subcommittee on Employment, Poverty, and Migratory Labor of the Committee on Labor and Public Welfare. U.S. Congress. Washington, DC: Government Printing Office, 1973.

Congressional Testimony

Testimony before the Senate Subcommittee on Manpower, June 7, 1963.

Statement before the Senate Public Works Committee, December 10, 1963.

Testimony on the 1965 Manpower Report before the Subcommittee on Employment and Manpower, Senate Committee on Labor and Public Welfare and the Select Subcommittee on Labor, House Education and Labor Committee, April 28, 1965.

Statement before the House Committee on Education and Labor, H.R. 8311 and H.R. 10682, July 12, 1967.

Statement before the House Committee on Education and Labor, May 5, 1969.

Statement before the Select Subcommittee on Labor, House Committee of Education and labor, January 28, 1970.

Statement before the Select Subcommittee on Labor, House Committee on Education and Labor, on H.R. 11167 and H.R. 11413, October 28, 1971.

Statement before the Select Subcommittee on Labor, House Committee on Education and Labor, November 1, 1971.

Statement before the Subcommittee on Equal Opportunities, House Committee on Education and Labor, February 7, 1973.

Statement before the Subcommittee on Employment, Poverty, and Migratory Labor, Senate Committee on Labor and Public Welfare, September 16, 1974.

Statement before the House Committee on the Budget, March 4, 1975.

Statement before the Subcommittee on Economic Growth, Joint Economic Committee, June 3, 1975.

Statement before the Subcommittee on Employment, Poverty, and Migratory Labor, Senate Committee on Labor and Public Works, June 4, 1975.

Testimony before the Senate Committee on Banking, Housing, and Urban Affairs on the Humphrey-Hawkins Amendments (S. 50), May 21, 1976.

Statement before the Subcommittee on Equal Opportunities, House Committee on Education and Labor, March 16, 1976.

Testimony before the Intergovernmental Relations and Human Resources Subcommittee of the House Committee on Government Operations, July 19, 1977.

"Administration of the AFDC Program." Statement before Subcommittee on Intergovernmental Relations and Human Resources, House Committee on Government Opertions, July 19, 1977.

"The Role of the National Commission on Employment and Unemployment Statistics." Statement before Senate Committee on Human Resources, July 21, 1977.

"Minimum Wage to Protect the Working Poor." Statement before Subcommittee on Labor, Senate Human Resources Committee, August 3, 1977.

"Economic Outlook for fiscal Years 1978 and 1979." Statement before House Committee on the Budget, 1978.

"Labor Force Statistics for Full Employment." Statement before the Joint Economic Committee, February 3, 1978.

"Employment-Unemployment." Statement before the Joint Economic committee, April 6, 1979.

"The National Commission on Employment and Unemployment Statistics Comments on the Subterranean Economy." Statement before Oversight Subcommittee, House Ways and Means Committee, October 9, 1979.

"Reducing Working Hours to Combat Unemployment." Statement before Labor Standards Subcommittee, House Committee on Education and Labor, October 24, 1979.

"The Vietnam Veterans Bill." Statement before Senate Committee on Veterans' Affairs, March 4, 1980.

"Facing Up to Youth Problems." Statement before Subcommittee on Employment, Poverty, and Migratory Labor, Senate Committee on Labor and Human Resources, March 5, 1980.

Statement before House Census and Population Subcommittee, Committee on Post Office and Civil Service, November 10, 1981.

Statement before Subcommittee on Employment Opportunities, House Education and Labor Committee, March 7, 1983.

"Education and Jobs for Combatting Youth Unemployment." Statement before the Subcommittee on Employment Opportunities of the House Committee on Education and Labor, Hearing on Summer Youth Education and Employment, May 22, 1985.

"Opposition to Job Creation Under the Welfare System: A Conservative Ideology." Statement before the Democratic Caucus Task Force on Job Training, June 19, 1985.

"Fair Pay for Federal Employees." Statement before the House Budget Committee Income Security Task Force, October 9, 1985.

"The Current Labor Market Situation." Statement before the House Domestic Monetary Policy Subcommittee of the Committee on Banking, Urban Affairs, and Finance, U.S. House of Representatives, June 10, 1986.

"Raising the Minimum Wage." Statement before the House Small Business Committee, August 6, 1987.

"Job Training Partnership Act." Statement before the Committee on Education and Labor, September 29, 1988.

"Targeted Jobs Tax Credit." Statement before the Subcommittee on Select Revenue Measures, House Committee on Ways and Means, June 6, 1989.

"A Proper Inheritance: Investing in the Self-Sufficiency of Poor Families," with Marion Pines and Garth Mangum. George Washington University, Center for Social Policy Studies, 1989.

"Workforce Statistics: Do We Know What We Think We Know—And What Should We Know?" with Frank Gallo. Statement before Joint Economic Committee, December 26, 1989.

"The Quality of Federal Statistics." Statement before the Joint Economic Committee, hearing on Economic Statistics, March 29, 1991.

"Needed: A Jobs Program." Statement before the House Budget Committee Task Force on Urgent Fiscal Issues, Hearing on the Budgetary Examination of the Unemployment Insurance System, June 6, 1991.

"The Contributions of the Welfare System." Statement before the Joint Economic Committee, Hearings on the War on Poverty, September 25, 1991.

"The Budgetary Examination of the Health of the Unemployment Insurance Program." Statement before the Task Force on Urgent Fiscal Issues of the House Committee on the Budget, January 4, 1992.

"Enterprise Zones: A Promise Based on Rhetoric." Statement before the Subcommittee on Economic Stabilization of the Committee on Banking, Finance, and Urban Affairs, Hearings on Pending Enterprise Zone Legislation, February 20, 1992.

"Enterprise Zones." Testimony before the Subcommittee on Economic Stabilization of the House Committee on Banking, Finance, and Urban Affairs, February 20, 1992.

Articles, Interviews & Opinion Pieces

"Union Attitudes toward Job Evaluation and Ingrade Progression," *Industrial and Labor Relations Review* 4, 2 (January) 1951.

"Professional Organization of Teachers in Higher Education," *Journal of Higher Education* 22, 3 (March) 1951.

"Jurisdictional Disputes (Under Labort Management Relations Act)," *Labor Law Journal* (February) 1953.

"Individual Wage Adjustments Under the WSB," *Labor Law Journal* (September) 1953.

"Intraplant Inequities and Wage Controls," *Labor Law Journal* (November) 1953.

"Incentive Systems and Wage Controls," *Labor Law Journal* (February) 1954.

"Application of Fair Labor Standards Act to Retail Trade," with Geraldine Fowle, *Daily Labor Report* 75 (April 17) 1957.

"A Federal Assist to Guarantee the Rights of Union Members," *Labor Law Journal* (February) 1959.

"The Public Interest in Internal Union Affairs," *Labor Law Journal* (July) 1959.

"Labor Under the Taft-Hartley Act," *Current History* 37, 217 (September) 1959.

"Union Lobbyists' Contributions to Tough Labor Legislation," *Labor Law Journal* (October) 1959.

"Common Site Picketing in Construction," *BNA's Construction Labor Report* 246 (June 8) 1960.

"Our Creeping Unemployment," *The Reporter* (September 29) 1960.

"Union Trusteeships: The Federal Law and an Inventory," *Labor Law Journal* (December) 1960.

"An Appraisal of the Anti-trust Approach," *The Annals of American Academy of Political and Social Science* (January) 1961.

"Poverty in America: What Will Congress Do?" *The Reporter* 24, 5 (March 2) 1961.

"Structural Unemployment and Public Policy," *Labor Law Journal* (July) 1961.

"Area Redevelopment Administration Research," *IRRA Newsletter* (Spring) 1962.

"Youth Unemployment—A Problem that's Getting Worse: What's to be Done?" *Vital Issues* 8, 5 (January) 1963.

"The Politics and Provisions of the Landrum-Griffin Act," with J. Joseph Loewenberg, *IRRA Newsletter* (Spring) 1964.

"Area Redevelopment: An Analysis of the Program," *Industrial Relations: A Journal of Economy and Society* 3, 3 (May) 1964.

"A Valiant Attempt to Do too Much," *Challenge* 12, 7 (April) 1964.

"Can We Afford *Not* to Reduce Hours of Work?" *Challenge* 13, 5 (June) 1965.

"Poverty: Survey and Outlook," *Science* (May 13) 1966.

"An Evaluation of the social Security System as an Income Protection Program," *Pension and Welfare News* 2, 12 (September) 1966.

"A Note on the Coordination of Federal Manpower Programs," *Poverty and Human Resource Abstracts* (PHRA) 4 (September-October) 1966.

"Minimum Wage Legislation in the 89th Congress," *PHRA* 4 (September-October) 1966.

"Anatomy of the Poverty Program," *Economic Affairs* (Special Report) (October 31) 1966.

"Coming to Grips with Unemployment," with Garth Mangum, *The Reporter* 35, 8 (November 17) 1966.

"The Military: A New Recruit in the War on Poverty," *American Child* 48, 4 (Fall) 1966.

"An Antipoverty Experiment: The Jobs Corps," *IRRA* (December 29) 1966.

"Design for a Federal Manpower Policy," with Garth Mangum, *PHRA* 2, 1 (January-February) 1967.

"Taxation and the Relief of Poverty—Comment," *Review of Social Economy* 25, 1 (March) 1967.

"The Pitfalls of Guaranteed Income," *The Reporter* 36, 10 (May 18) 1967.

"Work and Training for Economic Independence," *PHRA* 2, 4 1967.

"What's New on the Poverty Front?" *PHRA* 2, 4, 1967.

"Meaningful Jobs for the Jobless: Programs and Priorities," with Garth Mangum, *The Reporter* 37, 3 (September 7) 1967.

"Can the War on Poverty Rise Above Partisan Politics?" *PHRA* 2, 5 (September-October) 1967.

"Will Employers be Induced to Train the Poor?" *PHRA* 2, 6 (November-December) 1967.

"What We Could Have Learned from the Anti-Poverty Efforts," *Mountain Life and Work: The Magazine of the Appalachian South* 44, 2 (March) 1968.

"Is OEO Here to Stay?" PHRA 3, 2 (March-April) 1968.

"The Poor and the Law: OEO's Legal Service Program," with Jeffrey Burt, *PHRA* 3, 3 (May-June) 1968.

"Priorities in Fighting Poverty: Cash and Services," *PHRA* 3, 4 (July-August) 1968.

"An Evaluator's Second Thoughts," *Poverty and Human Resources* (September/October) 1968.

"Community Self Determination and Entrepreneurship: Their Promises and Limitations," *Poverty and Human Resouces* (January-February) 1969.

"Entrepreneurship—Another Option Toward Equal Opportunity," with Robert Taggart, *PHRA* 4, 2 (March-April) 1969.

"Developing Business in the Ghetto," with Robert Taggart, *Conference Board Record* 6, 7 (July) 1969.

"The Welfare State, Nixon Style," *Poverty and Human Resources* (July-August) 1969.

"Ghetto Business Development—Performance and Prospects," with Robert Taggart, *Manpower* (September) 1969.

"The Community Action Program: A Strategy to Fight Poverty," *Annals of the American Academy of Political and Social Science* 385 (September) 1969.

"Manpower Programs and the 'New Federalism'," *Conference Board Record* 7, 4 (April) 1970.

"Has the Blue-Collar Worker's Position Worsened?" with Robert Taggart, *Monthly Labor Review* (September) 1971.

"Human Resources Issues for the 70s," with Garth Mangum and Ray Marshall. *Manpower* (November) 1971.

"Blue-Collar Workers and the 'Ordeal of Change'," with Robert Taggart, *Conference Board Record* 8, 10 (October) 1971.

"The Mounting Welfare Problem," with David Marwick, *Current History* 61, 363 (November) 1971.

"Creating Jobs is One Way to Fight Unemployment," *New Generation* 54, 1 (Winter) 1972.

"Our Evolving National Manpower Policy," *Conference Board Record* 9, 5 (May) 1972.

"The Emergency Unemployment Act: An Interim Assessment," with Robert Taggart, *Monthly Labor Review* (June) 1972.

"The Emergency Employment Act: A Progress Report," *Conference Board Record* 9, 9 (September) 1972.

"The Emergency Employment Act: An Assessment," *Manpower* 4, 12 (December) 1972.

"The Poor: Dimensions and Strategies," *Current History* 64, 382 (June) 1973.

"U.S. Manpower Programs: Retreat or Reform?" with Garth Mangum, *Conference Board Record* 10, 7 (July) 1973.

"Job Redesign, Reform, Enrichment—Exploring the Limitations," with William B. Johnston, *Monthly Labor Review* (July) 1973.

"Work and Training for Relief Recipients," with David Marwick, *Journal of Human Resources* 8 (August 1) 1973.

"Employment and Earnings Inadequacy: A Measure of Worker Welfare," with Robert Taggart, *Monthly Labor Review* (October) 1973.

"Changes in Work: More Evolution than Revolution," with William B. Johnston, *Manpower* (September) 1973.

"Job Satisfaction: Work Is Here to Stay, Alas," with William B. Johnston, *Journal of American Labor* (January) 1974.

"Employment and Earnings Inadequacy: A New Social Indicator," with Robert Taggart, *Challenge* (January-February) 1974.

"The 1975 Manpower Budget," with Garth Mangum, *Conference Board Record* (May) 1974.

"Manpower Programs and Black Progress," with Robert Taggart and William B. Johnston, *Manpower* (June) 1974.

"Block Grants for Manpower Programs," with Joyce Zickler, *Public Administration Review* (March-April) 1975.

"Does Public Job Creation Offer Any Hope?" *Conference Board Record* 12, 8 (August) 1975.

"Job Corps Experience with Manpower Training," *Monthly Labor Review* (October) 1975.

"The Rough and Rocky Road to Full Employment," *Baltimore Sun* June 27, 1976.

"On Reforming the Employment Act," *Conference Board Record* 13, 9 (September) 1976).

"Where We Are and How We Got Here," *Manpower* (November) 1976.

"The Hardship Index," with Robert Taggart, *Across the Board* (November) 1976.

"The Great Society Did Succeed," with Robert Taggart, *Political Science Quarterly* (Winter) 1976-1977.

"Plain Talk About the Work Force, Questions and Answers," *Worklife* (January) 1977.

"Employment Problems of Disabled Persons," with Robert Taggart, *Monthly Labor Review* (March) 1977.

"Thank God It's Thursday!" with Richard S. Belous, *Across the Board* (March) 1977.

"Work in the Welfare State," *The Humanist* (March-April) 1977.

"Evaluating Social Programs," *Society* (May-June) 1977.

"The Great Society Was Not a Great Big Failure," *Baltimore Sunday Sun,* March 13, 1977.

"Jobs for Youth," with Robert Taggart, *Challenge* (May-June) 1977.

"Work and the Welfare State," *Challenge* (July-August) 1977.

"The Poor Are Still With Us," *Newsday* August 3, 1977.

"Work-sharing Initiatives at Home and Abroad," with Richard S. Belous, *Monthly Labor Review* (September) 1977.

"The Military as an Employer: Past Performance and Future Prospects," with Karen C. Alderman, *Monthly Labor Review* (November) 1977.

"Workers Should be Counted as (a) Employed or (b) Forced into Idleness, Right? ...Wrong," with Richard S. Belous, *Across the Board* (December) 1977.

"Labor Force Statistics: Time for a Change?" *Conference Board Information Bulletin* (September) 1978.

"Reduced Worktime: Tool to Fight Unemployment," *Adherent* (December) 1978.

"Unemployment Statistics: Why We Need to Know More," *E.P.O.* (March-April) 1979.

"The Unemployment Numbers Are the Message," *Economic Impact* (April) 1979.

"The Minimum Wage Today: How Well Does It Work?" with Richard S. Belous, *Monthly Labor Review* (July) 1979.

"A Living Minimum Wage," *New York Times*, July 27, 1979.

"The Work Ethic Lives!" *Across the Board* (August) 1979.

"Rational Evolution of American Society Causes Lamented 'Slump' in Productivity," *Washington Star,* September 16, 1979.

"An Advance Briefing of the National Commission on Employment and Unemployment Statistics Findings Before Congressional Staffers," *Congressional Record* (September 19) 1979.

"Labor Force Statistics to Measure Full Employment," *Society* (September-October) 1979.

"Reaching Beyond Our Current Employment and Unemployment Statistics," with Richard S. Belous, *Thrust* (Winter) 1979.

"What's in a Number?" Symposium on Hispanics and CETA, University of Texas, San Antonio, January 30, 1980.

"Despite the Rhetoric, Hold the Obit, Says One Liberal," *County Employment Reporter* (February) 1980.

"Our Growing Welfare State," *New York Times* May 16, 1980.

"Human Resource Policy and the Welfare State," *Adherent* (September) 1980.

"The Welfare State Under the Reagan Administration," *John Herling's Labor Letter* (December 6) 1980.

"What Shall We Do For (or To) Our Youth in the 1980s?" *New Generation* (Winter) 1980.

"Has Paper-Pushing Buried the Great Society?" *AVA Journal* (January-February) 1981.

"Private Sector May Not Be Able to Respond," *Youth Alternatives* (April) 1981.

"A Liberal Agenda in Orderly Retreat," *Dallas Morning News* April 13, 1981.

"8-Hour Day Follows in Dinosaur Tracks," *BNA Daily Labor Report* (April 14) 1981.

"The U.S. Family," *New York Times,* July 27, 1981.

"The Family Unit is an Evolving Species, Not an Endangered One," *LA Herald Examiner* July 28, 1981.

"On the Road Back to Majority," *Washington Post,* September 7, 1981.

"Working Wives and Mothers: What Happens to Family Life?" with Richard S. Belous, *Monthly Labor Review* (September) 1981.

394

"Human Resource Implications of Reaganmics," Proceedings of the Industrial Relations Research Association 34th Annual Meeting, December 28, 1981.

"What's in Store for the American Family," *U.S. News and World Report,* April 26, 1982.

Trick, Trickle, or Treat. 1983: The Budget and New Federalism," *Thrust* (Winter/Spring) 1982.

"The Family Survives," *GW Times* (May-June) 1981.

"Budgeting States' Rights," *Transaction/Society* (July-August) 1982.

"A Jobs-Watcher Holds Little for Quick Improvement," with Robert Pear, *New York Times,* September 5, 1982.

"Labor: Still Alive," *New York Times,* September 12, 1982.

"After Hard Times—What Hope for Labor-Management Cooperation?" with Clifford M. Johnson. *BNA Daily Labor Report* (September 17) 1982.

"The Future of Work: Does It Belong to Us or the Robots?" with Clifford M. Johnson, *Monthly Labor Review* (September) 1982.

"A Self-Destructive Assault on the Bureaucracy," *Washington Post,* September 1, 1982.

"The Politics of Unemployment," with Clifford M. Johnson, *New Republic,* September 20-17, 1982.

"Working But Poor," with Robert Taggart, *New York Times,* October 28, 1982.

"What's Happening to the American Family," *Independent News Alliance* (syndicated) November 6, 1982.

"Things We Should Do Now To Start Getting People Back To Work," *Washington Post,* November 8 1982.

"The Survival of Work," with Clifford Johnson. *IRRA* "The Work Ethic" (November) 1983.

"On the Other Hand, Here's How Reagan Could Win Reelection," *Washington Post,* January 23, 1983.

"Congress Can Put the Nation to Work," *Los Angeles Times,* February 13, 1983.

"A Cynical, Ineffectual Jobs Bill," with Clifford M. Johnson, *New York Times,* February 25, 1983.

"The Bitter Fruits of Labor," with Robert Taggart, *Challenge* (March-April) 1983.

"The Attempt to Rationalize Federal Pay," *Federal Service Labor Relations Review* (Spring) 1983.

"Indictment of Reagan: No Brother's Keeper," with Clifford M. Johnson, *New York Times,* July 22, 1983.

"Here's How We Can Keep the U.S. Recovery Going," *Los Angeles Times,* August 16, 1983.

"Labor Day," with Clifford M. Johnson, *Los Angeles Times,* September 5, 1983.

"ERW Interview," *Employee Relations Weekly* (September 5) 1983.

"Women's Growing Strength on Job Scene Forcing Change," *Dallas Morning News,* September 5, 1983.

"Labor and Management: The Illusion of Cooperation," with Clifford M. Johnson, *Harvard Business Review* (September-October) 1983.

"The Contradictions of Industrial Policy," with Clifford M. Johnson, *Journal of the Institute for Socio-Economic Studies* (Winter) 1983-84.

"The Changing Work Place: Perceptions and Reality," with Clifford M. Johnson, *Annals* (May) 1984.

"A Quarter Century of Employment and Training Policy: Where Do We Go From Here?" with Garth L. Mangum, *Jobs for the Future: Strategies in a New Framework* (May) 1984.

"Worker Participation and Productivity Change," with Diane Werneke, *Monthly Labor Review* (September) 1984.

"The Changing Workplace," *Society* (September-October) 1984.

"Middle-Class Shrinkage?" with Peter E. Carlson, *Across the Board* (October) 1984.

"Forces Driving or Impeding Changes in Labor Force Statistics," *IRRA 37th Annual Proceedings* (December) 1984.

"Books in Review—Loosing Ground: American Social Policy 1950-1980," *Society* (May-June) 1985.

"Poverty," *Americana Annual/Encyclopedia* (July) 1985.

"Comparable Worth: In Praise of Muddling Through," with Clifford M. Johnson, *The Journal/Institute for Socioeconomic Studies* (Summer) 1985.

"A Message to Labor Secretary Brock," with Clifford M. Johnson, *National Forum* (July) 1985.

"The OSHA Test," with Isaac Shapiro, *National Forum* (July) 1985.

"Opposition to Job Creation: A Conservative Ideology," *Congressional Record—Extension of Remarks* (September 17) 1985.

"How the Welfare System Promotes Economic Security," *Political Science Quarterly* (Fall) 1985.

"The Minimum Wage: A Sinking Floor,' with Isaac Shapiro, *New York Times,* January 16, 1986.

"An Affirmation of Faith," *Society* (January-February) 1986.

"Should Congress Raise the Minimum Wage? The Working Poor Deserve a Raise," with Isaac Shapiro, *New York Times,* March 30, 1986.

"Technology and the Workplace," *Employee Relations Weekly* (April 18) 1986.

"The Workplace in 1996," *Employment Management Association* (April 24) 1986.

396

"Individual Accounts for Training: A New But Not Improved Idea," *Entrepreneurial Economy* (May) 1986.

"A Scenario for the Future," *American Politics* (June) 1986.

"The Workplace in 1996," *EMA Journal* (Summer) 1986.

"A Weaker Net Under Workers," with Isaac Shapiro, *New York Times,* September 1, 1986.

"Professor Urges Creating System That Combines Work and Welfare," *Employee Relations Weekly* (October 20) 1986.

"Working but Poor," with Isaac Shapiro (unpublished) December 15, 1986.

"Individual Accounts for Training: A New But Not Improved Idea," with Frank Gallo, *Labor Law Journal* (December) 1986.

"Unemployment Insurance: The Fundamental Employers' Service," with Isaac Shapiro. *Perspective: Essays and Reviews in Employment Security and Employment and Training Programs* 1986, pp. 3-14.

"The Editors Interview," an Interview with Sar A. Levitan. *New England Journal of Human Services* (January 22) 1987.

"The Fall of the Minimum Wage," with Isaac Shapiro, *Congressional Record* (February 10) 1987.

"Should Minimum Wage Be Raised? Many Labor in Poverty," *American Forum: Minimum Wage, Gannett News Service* (March 16) 1987.

"Helping People with Labor Market Problems: An Overview of Key Policies." In *Employment and Training Policy: Changing Federal , State, and Local Perspectives*, Allan Rosenbaum, ed. Thomas M. Bradley Center for Employment and Training Education and Research, May 1987.

"Workfare Not Enough to Escape Poverty," *Youth Policy* (February) 1987.

"What's Missing in Welfare Reform," with Isaac Shapiro, *Challenge* (July-August) 1987.

"The Little Tax Credit That Could, But Hasn't: A Federal Program Designed to Expand by Job Opportunities for the Poor Has Gotten Off Track," with Frank Gallo, *Across the Board* (July-August) 1987.

"The Targeted Jobs Tax Credit: An Uncertain and Unfinished Experiment," with Frank Gallo, *Labor Law Journal* (October) 1987.

"Beyond Trendy Forecasts: The Next 10 Years for Work," *The Futurist* (November-December) 1987.

"Shortchanged by Part-Time Work," with Elizabeth A. Conway, *New York Times,* February 27, 1988.

"To Cure Reaganism Take a Pure Liberal Agenda—Job Training Programs Can Be the Ticket Out of Poverty for the Poor," with Isaac Shapiro, *Newsday,* February 29, 1988.

"Part-timers: Living on Half-rations," with Elizabeth A. Conway, *Challenge* (May-June) 1988.

"Don't Give Up: Poverty Programs that Work—Let Them Eat Software," *Washington Monthly* (June) 1988.

"The Minimum Wage: Bread and Dignity," *Across the Board* (September) 1988.

"Labor Shortages? Don't Bet Your Job On It?" with Frank Gallo, *Newsday,* October 11, 1989

"Can Employee Associations Negotiate New Growth?" with Frank Gallo, *Monthly Labor Review* (July) 1989.

"Collective Bargaining and Private Sector Professionals," with Frank Gallo, *Monthly Labor Review* (September) 1989.

"The Shortsighted Focus on Labor Shortages," with Frank Gallo, *Challenge* (September-Octover) 1989.

"Labor Shortages in the 1990's," *Employee Relations Weekly,* February 26, 1990.

"Work and Family: the Impact of Legislation," with Frank Gallo, *Monthly Labor Review* (March) 1990.

"Mr. Bush's Perverse Optimism," *New York Times,* March 4, 1990.

"Skills Shortage Looms / We Can Handle It," *HR Magazine*, Society for Human Resource Management (April) 1990.

"Poverty," *Academic American Encyclopedia.* Danbury, Connecticut: Grolier, July 1990.

"Wanted: Federal Public Service Program," with Frank Gallo, *Challenge* (May-June) 1991.

"Preparing Americans for Work," with Frank Gallo, *Looking Ahead,* National Planning Association (July) 1991.

"Making a Case for a Fiscal Jolt," *New York Times,* July 10, 1992.

"The Limits of Random Assignments in Evaluating Social Programs," *The Partnership Advantage* (November) 1992.

"Evaluation Industry Impacts Policy," *Workforce* (Fall) 1992.

"The Missing Link: Jobs for Jobs," *The Forum on Fighting Poverty in America* (January 4) 1993.

"A Training Agenda for the 1990s," with Garth L. Mangum and Stephen L. Mangum, *Workforce* (January 6) 1993.

"Measurement of Employment, Unemployment, and Low Income," *Workforce* (February) 1994.

"Chicago's House of Hope," *Policy Review* (Winter) 1994.

NOTE: June 1994. This bibliography was prepared at the request of Dr. Garth L. Mangum by Meraiah M. Foley. While it is assumed to be mostly complete, it is possible that, due to a lack of records kept at the Center for Social Policy Studies, certain pieces or contributions may not be included in this bibliography.

Index

About the Institute

The W.E. Upjohn Institute for Employment Research is a nonprofit research organization devoted to finding and promoting solutions to employment-related problems at the national, state, and local level. It is an activity of the W.E. Upjohn Unemployment Trustee Corporation, which was established in 1932 to administer a fund set aside by the late Dr. W.E. Upjohn, founder of The Upjohn Company, to seek ways to counteract the loss of employment income during economic downturns.

The Institute is funded largely by income from the W.E. Upjohn Unemployment Trust, supplemented by outside grants, contracts, and sales of publications. Activities of the Institute are comprised of the following elements: (1) a research program conducted by a resident staff of professional social scientists; (2) a competitive grant program, which expands and complements the internal research program by providing financial support to researchers outside the Institute; (3) a publications program, which provides the major vehicle for the dissemination of research by staff and grantees, as well as other selected work in the field; and (4) an Employment Management Services division, which manages most of the publicly funded employment and training programs in the local area.

The broad objectives of the Institute's research, grant, and publication programs are to: (1) promote scholarship and experimentation on issues of public and private employment and unemployment policy; and (2) make knowledge and scholarship relevant and useful to policymakers in their pursuit of solutions to employment and unemployment problems.

Current areas of concentration for these programs include: causes, consequences, and measures to alleviate unemployment; social insurance and income maintenance programs; compensation; workforce quality; work arrangements; family labor issues; labor-management relations; and regional economic development and local labor markets.